SERVANT
LEADERSHIP

To Olga Gisela,
my wife and best friend,
a wonderful leader at home, school, church, and community;

And to our children
Joel and Jasmin,
young, strong, and intelligent–
important future leaders, each in their own way, for sure.

χαρὰν γὰρ πολλὴν ἔσχον καὶ παράκλησιν ἐπὶ τῃ ἀγαπῃ σου

SERVANT
LEADERSHIP

JESUS & PAUL

EFRAIN AGOSTO

CHALICE
P R E S S
ST. LOUIS, MISSOURI

Cover art: FotoSearch
Cover and interior design: Elizabeth Wright

Visit Chalice Press on the World Wide Web at
www.chalicepress.com

10 9 8 7 6 5 4 3 2 1   05 06 07 08 09

Library of Congress Cataloging-in-Publication Data

Agosto, Efrain.
  Servant leadership : Jesus and Paul / Efrain Agosto.
      p. cm.
  Includes bibliographical references and index.
  ISBN 13: 978–0-827234-63-5 (pbk. : alk. paper)
  ISBN 10: 0-827234-63-5
  1. Christian leadership–Biblical teaching. 2. Jesus Christ–Leadership. 3. Bible. N.T. Gospels–Social scientific criticism. 4. Paul, the Apostle, Saint. 5. Bible. N.T. Epistles of Paul–Social scientific criticism. I. Title.
  BS2555.6.L42A34 2005
  262'.1–dc22
                                                          2005003650

Printed in the United States of America

Contents

Acknowledgments

This book began as an expansion of my dissertation research on leadership and commendation in Paul. I want to thank Professor J. Paul Sampley, professor emeritus of Boston University and my advisor on the original research, for encouraging my study in this area. He also read a full manuscript of this new manifestation, providing a very kind endorsement of the project. I am also thankful to the Hispanic Theological Initiative, which, with funding from the Pew Charitable Trusts, provided the initial post-doctoral grant that allowed me to begin the project in Spring 1999. At the other end of the journey, the Association for Theological Schools, with funding from the Lilly Endowment, provided a Lilly Faculty Fellows Grant in Spring 2003, which allowed me to move closer toward completion of the project. In both instances, I could not have proceeded without the generous sabbatical policy of Hartford Seminary, the wonderful institution on whose faculty I have served for ten happy years. I am very grateful to all these and many other supporters during the preparation of this book.

Early in the process the former dean of Hartford Seminary, Professor Richard Valantasis, formed a reading group of the younger scholars at Hartford (of which I was the oldest, although not necessarily the wisest!). Later, Dean Worth Loomis asked Professor David Bartlett of Yale Divinity School to shepherd this group. Many of the early drafts of this book were read and critiqued by the colleagues who comprised this group, including Kelton Cobb, Judy Fentress-Williams, Ingrid Mattson, and Scott Thumma. I am grateful to my colleagues, including Professors Valantasis and Bartlett, for their helpful suggestions for improving the text. Several of the chapters were also shared along the way with the rest of the Hartford Seminary faculty during our monthly "Collegial Sharing" lunches. Several very important suggestions, including current-day material on leadership theory, came from those sessions. Thanks very much colleagues. Special thanks also to Dean Ian Markham and President Heidi Hadsell, who encouraged me toward completion of the project when that final push was greatly needed.

I am grateful to my editors at Chalice Press, past and present: Jon Berquist, Jane McAvoy, and Trent Butler. I was saddened when Jane passed away suddenly and could not see the project to its completion. I am thankful to Trent Butler for stepping in at a difficult time and working patiently with me to make sure I finished. To them and all the terrific staff at Chalice, thanks!

Finally, a special word of thanks to my friends and family. Good friends, Pastors Edwin Ayala and Pablo Diaz, read early drafts of the book when I needed to be sure that I was headed in the right direction in making this material accessible to informed pastors and leaders like them. *Muchas gracias, hermanos.* My family suffered long and hard during my emotional ups and downs as the project dragged on for several years. In gratitude for their patience and undying love throughout the experience, I have dedicated the book to my wife Olga and my children Joel and Jasmin.

Introduction

Modern-day pastors and church leaders often ask how they can develop the qualities of good leadership in themselves and their constituency. Many of them turn to the Bible for help in the leadership development task. However, the Bible is not exactly a book about leadership. In it we find the struggles of various faith communities to establish themselves, strengthen their relationships with God, and, indeed, find good leaders to help them do this. By studying the stories of these struggles that we find in the Bible, we come closer to some models of good (and bad) leadership.

In this book I explore two models of faithful leadership in the early church—Jesus and Paul, the two major figures of the New Testament. By studying Jesus and his movement, especially as reflected in the synoptic gospels, I explore the pictures and expectations of leadership that emerge from the earliest Christian communities, both at the level of the historical Jesus, and the later gospel writers. The apostle Paul, his churches, and his leaders will occupy a major portion of the study. Given the questions of modern congregational leadership, some very fruitful conversation can take place with the Pauline correspondence. Those concerned with the qualities of a church leader, the development of leaders, and the legitimate functions of leadership will benefit immensely from a careful review of what Paul writes and practices in these areas. Paul's letters reflect his work with actual congregations; and to the extent that we can determine his approach to various conflicts in those congregations, we can see more clearly the leadership qualities needed to address similar concerns in our own day.

Motivations for This Study

The motivations for this study are twofold. First, as a Puerto Rican raised in New York City, I know persons, especially in the storefront

1

Pentecostal churches of my youth, who lacked access to traditional opportunities for training and leadership. Nonetheless, they exercised significant leadership roles within the Latino Christian church, as well as other community institutions of the city. After seminary, I began to work on the theological education of such individuals, and I also pursued graduate studies in New Testament. I became intrigued by the question: Is there a biblical perspective relative to the issue of access to and opportunity for leadership? Thus in my graduate studies and beyond I have explored the question of who became leaders in the churches founded by Paul and what was the social status of those leaders with respect to the strict, hierarchical social structure of Greco-Roman society. I hoped to make a biblical-theological contribution to the work of urban theological education, including the preparation of Latino and Latina church leaders in our communities. I strongly believe that such a motivation and line of inquiry contributes to leadership issues in churches of all races and denominations.

Although some of this is changing, historically many U.S. Latino churches, especially in urban areas, have been led by charismatic, grassroots leaders who often lacked the academic credentials expected in North American society. For example, the history of the Hispanic Pentecostal church includes stories of many indigenous leaders who, having little in material possessions or social status, sacrificed much for the good of the gospel and grew large, vital congregations in a relatively short span of time.[1] In addition, many of these Latino churches have also produced a significant cadre of community leaders, both ministerial and lay. "Few institutions in society provide Hispanics the inter-personal and political skills that are nurtured in the minority church."[2]

We can all learn from this experience of the U.S. Latino church for the practice of leadership in many churches. In the New Testament, I have found similar models of indigenous, grassroots development of local leaders through the Christian faith communities. This book explores those models in the person of the New Testament's two prime exemplars, Jesus and Paul, and in their respective communities of faith. In the final chapter, I will return to some implications of leadership in the New Testament for faith communities today, especially in light of the need for vigorous religious leadership in the aftermath of the tragic events of September 11, 2001. At this point, I only wish to note that the issues in Latino and minority church leadership inform and motivate the pursuit of this topic in my New Testament research.

Social Scientific Analysis of the New Testament

The method of studying the New Testament that employs theories and models from the social sciences also motivates my study of New Testament leadership. Interpreters who employ social scientific analysis of the New Testament posit that the study of the New Testament must include not only the theological affirmations one finds in New Testament documents but also the social reality of the people and communities who made and read such affirmations.[3] One aspect of social reality that had a direct bearing on my own research in the leadership issue was the question of the social status of the early Christians. Earlier studies argued that the first Christians belonged to the "socially depressed groups" of Greco-Roman society.[4] More recent studies have posited a broader social class representation in the early church. For example, Paul wrote that in one of his congregations "not many…were wise…, not many were powerful, not many were of noble birth" (1 Cor. 1.26). This implies that at least "some" in that church were from the well-educated, politically powerful, and noble classes of society. Such a heterogeneous constituency was probably the case in most of Paul's congregations, although the poorer groups of the Roman Empire tended to predominate in terms of numbers, if not always in terms of influence, as we shall see in our study of Paul's letters in this book.[5]

In addition to questions of status, theories of social conflict inform many dynamics in the New Testament. The diversity of social and economic classes found in a congregation such as the one at Corinth inevitably lead to conflict among those classes. In 1 Corinthians one sees the variety of problems that emerge because of conflict between a small number of socially elite Christian leaders and the lower-class majority that constituted the rest of the church.[6] Paul addresses these conflicts in a way that is instructive for understanding his views on leadership. The social dynamics of the real people lying behind these documents provides a fruitful avenue for the study of leadership in the New Testament. Social scientific analysis of the New Testament facilitates such study.

The social theory of the late nineteenth-century German sociologist Max Weber provides another connecting point to the issue of leadership in the New Testament. Weber posited a trilogy of leadership styles or "authority types." The first, "charismatic authority," is based on "devotion to the exceptional sanctity, heroism or exemplary character of *an individual person* and of the normative patterns or order revealed or ordained by him."[7] For example, in the New Testament, charismatic authority is often ascribed to Jesus, the apostles, and the Jerusalem and Palestinian wing of the primitive church because of that community's total reliance on the person of Jesus and his immediate successors, the apostles.[8]

Weber called the second stage of his trilogy "traditional authority" and the third "legal authority." Traditional authority rests "on the established belief in the sanctity of immemorial traditions and the legitimacy of those exercising authority under them [i.e., the traditions]."[9] Legal authority goes beyond dependence on the singular individual or the remembered tradition to "a belief in the legality of enacted rules and the right of those elevated to authority under such rules to issue commands."[10] Thus in the two latter stages, leaders exercise authority by means of tradition or prescribed rules, not by the sheer force of personality as in the charismatic stage. In the New Testament, the pastoral letters (1 and 2 Timothy, and Titus), which I will explore briefly in the final chapter of this book, depict a church that has begun to institutionalize and function under "legal authority."

What about the Pauline mission? It represents a kind of hybrid between a charismatic and traditional church. Indeed, Weber himself conceded that there is no "pure" charismatic authority. As soon as a charismatic group is established, it moves toward some kind of institutionalization. Weber called this process "the routinization of charismatic authority." To stabilize and thus ensure its survival, the Pauline movement "routinized" or channeled the charismatic authority of the Jesus movement into the formation of house *ekklēsiae* ("assemblies," Paul's term for his congregations) and into the identification of a "staff," Paul's coworkers. In this situation, all believers in Paul's congregations had responsibilities for the community's development, but some began to stand out as leaders precisely because they showed the utmost concern for the well-being of the community. Thus the Pauline mission emerges from the phenomenon of routinized charisma to function with a "dialectical authority," which means that all have some responsibility, including those who are specifically charged to lead.[11]

I will expand on these matters in the Pauline church in chapters 4–6 below, but again we see that a classic social theory—Weber's authority types— helps us identify some issues of leadership in the New Testament. What kind of leadership style do our churches today have: charismatic, traditional, or legal? And how do these relate to the social status of our church leaders in the larger society? Answers to these questions will benefit from a biblical study that approaches similar questions in the New Testament, especially in the writings about Jesus and those of Paul.

However, I have another concern. It is not enough to apply a theory to a text, especially a modern theory to an ancient text. One must better understand the context from which that text emerges. If our topic is leadership, we must seek to better understand how the concepts and practices of leadership functioned in the world of the New Testament, the world of second temple Judaism, Hellenistic culture, and Roman imperialism. Thus, I turn to another important aspect of social scientific analysis of the New Testament—social-cultural description.

The Social World of the New Testament

The first followers of Jesus were Jews, but they were also part of a larger social, economic, and political matrix known as the Greco-Roman world of the first century C.E.[12] Historians describe Greco-Roman society as a highly structured, hierarchical social system. It had a few wealthy and powerful at the top, and masses of the poor and powerless at the bottom. In this steep, social pyramid, people possessed practically no social mobility.[13] Access to power depended upon several well-defined criteria:

namely, wealth, family origins, and occupation. Thus leadership and power were confined to those classes that already had such status elements as significant wealth, Roman senatorial or equestrian rank, and "bloodlines" to families with both wealth and rank. Whether Jew, Greek, or Roman, the world of the New Testament functioned in a climate with the "monopolizing of leadership by a narrow circle, generation after generation..."[14]

This narrow circle kept their leadership intact by means of an informal, but pervasive, system of social relations well known, even today, as patronage. Patronage entailed the reciprocal exchange of goods and services between persons of higher and lower social status to achieve higher status for both.[15] Clients–those with less wealth and status–sought patrons–those with wealth, property, and status. Clients could be former slaves, military personnel with little accumulated wealth, trades persons, and artists. They sought higher status and often a better means of livelihood by attachment to patrons who had access to jobs, financial support, and other patrons looking for clients. Having many clients afforded the patron a measure of increased honor and status.

Thus patronage could be found everywhere in the Greco-Roman world, especially in the cities of the Empire in which the early Christian movement grew. Ancient cities, like today, drew many people, especially former slaves and artisans in search of economic opportunity. A quote from an older study on this phenomenon illustrates how patronage maintained control over economic and political power, and thus leadership, throughout the Roman Empire of the first century C.E.:

> From the parasite do-nothing up to the great aristocrat there was no man [sic] in Rome who did not feel himself bound to someone more powerful above him by the same obligations of respect, or to use the technical term, the same *obsequium*, that bound the ex-slave to the master that manumitted him.[16]

No one escaped patronage in the Greco-Roman world. Its impact on the development of the early church and its leadership will be addressed later in this book, especially when we talk about Paul and his churches.

This, in a nutshell then, was the world of the New Testament. How the writers of the synoptic gospels, and Paul, addressed the nature of leadership within their faith communities in the midst of this world is the theme of this book. Two additional factors should be noted, however. First, I address this topic of leadership in Jesus and Paul through the lens of a U.S. Latino religious leader and scholar who recognizes that his people are also part of a society in which their access to the leadership ranks remains limited, albeit in more subtle ways than in Greco-Roman society. Indeed, the struggle for access continues and should be a concern of Latino theology and ministry. This book hopes to contribute to that debate and effort by means of a biblical study of leadership in the New Testament communities of

Jesus as presented in the gospels, and of Paul. Moreover, the questions of leadership access and opportunity are not limited to the Latino church. Most Christian churches face similar concerns: How can we be sure that everyone who wants to be a leader in the Christian church has the opportunity and develops the skills to do so? Further, how can leaders developed in the church contribute to Christian mission and presence outside the church? For example, to make sure we are responding correctly as a nation in the aftermath of September 11, 2001, we need to hear from a wide variety of voices of political *and* religious leaders, and from "just plain folks" from all walks of life. This book will hopefully contribute in some small way to those questions of wider community involvement and leadership from a New Testament perspective.

A second issue remains. What do we mean by leadership? Much has been written about it, and a review of that literature is well beyond the scope of this introduction or even this entire book. However, some guidelines are needed so that when I speak about leadership in the context of this study, the reader understands the author's perspective.

Defining Leadership

Leaders have followers, but more than that they guide those who would follow toward new and challenging paths. Indeed one of the tasks of authentic leadership is to create opportunities for others to lead. Understanding one's followers, their dreams and hopes, as well as the goals and purposes of the group one leads, is a fundamental function of leadership today, even in the corporate world.[17] "A search for capabilities and possibilities in people is gradually supplanting the search for liabilities. It is a more optimistic philosophy."[18] Similarly, although we expect Christian leadership to be confrontational and assertive at times, it must also be open to creating opportunities for others to exercise their gifts and, therefore, their leadership. Good leaders move others to respond to their own personal calls and commitments.[19] "Every leader who cares about people is taught by them how to become the leader they need."[20]

Leadership must be distinguished from authority. "A leader can only request, an authority can require…In the leadership relation, the person is basic; in an authority relation, the person is merely a symbol."[21] Thus "leadership style" can be described as "…the behavior pattern that a person exhibits when attempting to influence the activities of others."[22] Contemporary leadership has shifted from a focus on "power, position and authority to a relative situational quality and a participative involvement on the part of all."[23] Robert Greenleaf evokes biblical imagery when he writes, "the great leader is seen as servant first."[24] The "servant-leader" strives "to make sure that other people's highest priority needs are being served."[25] By meeting people's needs for growth and development, the goals of a particular organization are being met. Margaret Wheatley discusses these developments in leadership theory in conjunction with "the new science," which suggests that attention to the whole rather than mechanized parts characterizes the activity of the natural world. What seems like "chaos" is actually a natural reorganization into "a higher level of organization."[26] Similarly, the practice of leadership in organizations, businesses, and institutions ought to pay more attention to relationships and needs of the individuals in a complex whole, rather than as divided compartments or "a collection of discrete parts."[27] Thus, leadership, an amorphous phenomenon that has intrigued us since people began organizing, is being examined for its relational aspects. Few if any theorists ignore the complexity of relationships that contribute to a leader's effectiveness.[28]

Terms and issues such as "partnership, followership, empowerment, teams, networks, and the role of context" have thus become the subjects of leadership studies.[29] Indeed, one theorist wants to forego the use of the term "leadership" because it speaks of hierarchy, of someone on top deciding how those below ought to do their work. Instead, we should talk about "stewardship," in which everyone at all levels takes responsibility or accountability for making sure that all goes well in a particular enterprise, be it business, health, or education. Thus, Peter Block advocates replacing "leadership" with "stewardship," choosing partnership over patriarchy and choosing service over self-interest.[30]

I do not agree that leadership has to be defined only as a matter of hierarchy, but I am intrigued by Block's use of such terms as "stewardship," "partnership," "kingdom," and "service," all biblical terms. In typical leadership situations, argues Block, a "board" decides vision, for example, while the hired leader, even a pastor in some congregational settings, implements, and the rest of us sit around and watch. That's patriarchy, argues Block. What is needed is "partnership": Everyone gets involved in deciding what direction a company or a congregation should take, and everyone takes responsibility in their sphere of influence in making sure that the vision is implemented. I would argue that it takes leadership to make sure all parties involved at every level have the training and resources needed to make sure that the vision is in fact implemented, that we not set up people for failure and therefore return to the easier, older models of patriarchy and hierarchy, where the leader at the top decides and implements, while the rest of us either comply or "get out of the way."

What all these leadership theorists–Greenleaf, Wheatley, and Block in particular–present is that a less hierarchical approach to leadership has emerged in the discussion of both secular and religious leadership. Relationships and mutual responsibility are more important than prescribed roles and expectations.

Many of these issues parallel leadership discussions in the Bible. Perhaps the greatest leaders of the Hebrew Bible, the prophets, focus on their call as the impulse to respond to mission and leadership on behalf of their people.[31] From the prophets we also learn the importance of leaders who understand their role in the context of history, events, and crises, and who see these with spiritual, theological, and political eyes.[32]

The civil rights movement in the United States represents a significant recent example of a leadership approach very much modeled after the biblical prophets. In his book *Black Leadership,* Manning Marable studies the influence of major African American leaders in the United States during the last one hundred years, and the impact of their various styles of leadership. The study includes such divergent leadership approaches as Booker T. Washington, with his self-help but accomodationist approach to improvement, and W. E. B. Dubois, with his focus on "the politics of culture," which touted empowerment through a recognition of the beauty and power of black history and culture.[33]

Marable notes that among all the various approaches to leadership in "black America," one model has prevailed, "a tradition characterized by a charismatic or dominating political style." He writes, "A number of black personalities have possessed a powerful, magnetic presence and the ability to articulate deeply held grievances and hopes among their people." These leaders included Frederick Douglass, Booker T. Washington, Marcus Garvey, Malcolm X, and Martin Luther King Jr.[34]

Marable further argues "the political culture of black America since slavery was heavily influenced by the Bible, particularly the Old Testament saga of Moses and Joshua as 'deliverers' of an oppressed, enslaved people who found themselves in a foreign land." Because of the harsh situation and struggles for black survival, black America merged the secular and the spiritual, argues Marable: "Messianic leadership expressed itself as the ability to communicate effectively programs that in some measure represented the interests of most blacks while also constructing bonds of collective intimacy through appeals to the spirituality and religiosity among African American people."[35]

However, black leadership had another aspect, also biblical in my estimation. This aspect paralleled but received less notoriety than that of the major political/religious figures. Marable cites the example of Ella Baker, a lesser known figure of the civil rights movement, but one who did important work as field secretary of the NAACP and director of the Southern Christian Leadership Conference's national office. From her practical experience in this work, she offered "that it was preferable to promote the development of 'group-centered leaders' rather than 'leader-centered groups.'" Thus she encouraged the younger, emerging leaders in the movement, those who formed the Student Nonviolent Coordinating Committee (SNCC) to "cultivate a more egalitarian, participatory approach to politics."[36]

In many ways, Marable's study of black leadership in America parallels developing leadership theories in business, organizations, and education. This all underlines the need for a more participatory and less hierarchical approach to the leadership task, "group"- rather than "leader"-centered "leadership." How do these developments correspond to what we read on leadership in the New Testament, particularly in the lives and ministries of Jesus and Paul, and in the communities they served?

Leadership in the New Testament: An Overview

Perhaps one must also discuss leadership in terms of function and not just theory. One can define leadership by what the leader does, rather than by discussing some abstract concept of leadership. The religious leader, according to much of the Bible, responds to a call to action. He or she does so in a particular, personal style or approach to that action; flexibility is key. And the biblical leader undertakes his or her approach contextually, that is, always with the specific needs of concrete faith communities in mind.[37]

Let me identify some functions leaders in New Testament communities undertook. I will come back to these throughout this study of leadership in Jesus and Paul. These might also have some correlation to the necessary functions of leaders in our own faith communities today.

First, I think questions about the use of authority and power are fundamental to the New Testament experience of leadership. One cannot avoid these questions in studying Jesus, Paul, or the early church, especially in light of the tremendous exercise of power and control politics in the world outside the New Testament communities. How did our Christian forebears navigate through the domination system that was the Roman Empire in that first century of the movement's existence? We in the United States do not live overtly in an imperial culture, although recent developments in our government's actions after the tragedy of September 11, 2001, might speak to the contrary. The excesses of the Patriot Act and the invasion of Iraq arguably reflect imperialist tendencies, notwithstanding the need to respond to the September 11 attacks in some form. In any case, as communities and persons of faith, congregations and religious leaders still have to respond prophetically to abuses of leadership, authority, and power in our society. And, of course, we live in a global village! Communities of faith and their leaders must speak in some form to abuses of power worldwide.

Second, leadership today needs to function in a climate of crisis and change, and this was also true of New Testament leadership. Much of this was to due to the diverse and cross-cultural nature of the early Christian movement with its mixture of Jew, Greek, and Roman, of rich and poor, of slave and free, and of male and female. Paul, for example, posited an idealistic expectation for this cross-cultural reality: "There is no longer Jew or Greek, there is no longer slave or free, there is no longer male and female; for all of you are one in Christ Jesus" (Gal. 3:28). Nonetheless, his congregations had problems with this diversity, and sometimes he himself contradicted his own stated principle, especially in several statements about women. Similar inconsistencies with the challenge of diversity conflict the religious leader today. What can we learn from Jesus and Paul with regard to how Christian leaders should handle conflict and diversity?

A third function of leadership worth noting here has to do with the leader's relationships with his or her "followers," or to play on that term using a Pauline assignation, "fellow workers." All good leaders must be about the business of developing the leadership potential of others. How does this happen in the New Testament gospels and Pauline writings, and how can we appropriate a relational approach to leadership and leadership development today? Under this function I should note specifically the need to develop women leaders in ministry, as well as leaders from other underrepresented constituencies. We know the New Testament has something to say about the role of women in earliest Christian leadership and ministry. We also know that certain quarters of the church today still struggle with that issue more than others. By rereading New Testament texts through the lens of leadership issues, this book will revisit the issue of women in ministry.

Finally, we must ask how New Testament leadership functions theologically. For example, how does the theology of the cross inform the practice of leadership? Because Jesus died on the cross, does "the paradox of power through weakness, life through death" become a paradigm for the exercise of leadership in the Christian community?[38] I think it does; we will see how it plays out in the New Testament communities of Jesus, as shown by the synoptic gospel writers, and of Paul. However, the larger question remains. How does theological reflection on leadership in the New Testament challenge our own "praxis" (action and reflection) today?

These then are some initial functions of leadership that will guide my exploration of the New Testament texts in the remainder of this book. Others will emerge in particular contexts of specific texts, but the functions of authority, conflict, relationships, and theology are all instrumental in the practice of leadership across all the first Christian communities. They remain similarly instrumental in our own. So in this study we define leadership functionally, by what leaders do "on the way," as well as by what they say. Before entering fully into the journey of this book, however, let me map out how that journey will take place.

Structure of the Book

I begin by setting the context for an exploration of leadership: namely, the first century C.E. in Palestine, the region under Roman domination in which the very first Christian communities, those early charismatic congregations of the Jesus movement, emerged. I approach this study in two ways. First, I draw an overall picture of life in first-century Palestine as a domination system, with Roman conquerors and urban elites oppressing the majority population of rural peasants and urban poor. All kinds of religious and political movements arise throughout the first century, each with its own indigenous popular leaders, to resist this domination system. These various movements met with various degrees of success and failure, mostly the latter.

Second, within this milieu, Jesus and the movement he engendered rises as an intimate, radically egalitarian religious association of "wandering charismatics."[39] Thus, I describe what leadership might have been like for Jesus and the community that formed right after his departure.

In chapters 2 and 3, I explore what happened to this egalitarian community and its picture of leadership as reflected in the communities represented by the synoptic gospels. Chapter 2 in particular grounds my discussion of leadership more directly in several textual studies of synoptic gospel passages that illustrate further that Jesus did reverse accepted power and leadership relationships within his community of followers. Moreover, the later Jesus communities tried to ameliorate his call for radical gospel leadership, but did not always succeed. Thus, I argue that both Jesus and the synoptic gospel tradition support a radical departure from typical structures of leadership and power in Greco-Roman society, at least within the limits of early Christian congregational practice. By its sheer existence and practice, the earliest church served as a challenge to the larger society's approach to leadership and power. Chapter 3 approaches this aspect of Jesus' action by looking at the events surrounding his arrest and crucifixion as precipitated by a direct challenge of Jesus to the elite leadership of his day.

With the fourth chapter, I turn to the example of the Pauline mission. In chapter 4, I discuss in general several "windows" into Paul's leadership, including Paul's urban world, his own self-understanding about leadership based on statements he makes and actions he takes, and finally how his letters as a whole function as instruments of leadership. In chapter 5, I turn to a another "window" into Paul's leadership, the various leaders he mentions throughout his letters, what he writes about them, and how he "commends" their leadership. I devote chapter 6 to a major source of information about Paul's practice and theology of leadership, the "Corinthian Correspondence," especially 1 Corinthians. In all of these sections of the book, I address the fundamental question of how Paul's approach to leadership corresponds to that of Jesus and of the Jesus tradition of confronting the structures of power in their day. I ask whether or not Paul ameliorates the radicality of leadership in the Jesus tradition. Moreover, if Paul displays inconsistency in his application of the tradition, then we must ask what does lie at the heart of Pauline leadership theology.

The final chapter summarizes the findings on leadership in Jesus and Paul with a very brief exploration of what might have happened to the Jesus and Pauline tradition of leadership in what Raymond Brown called the "sub-apostolic" communities.[40] In my conclusion, I make brief reference to the post-Pauline communities of the pastoral letters (1 and 2 Timothy, and Titus), the Johannine community in the gospel and letters of John, the Petrine traditions of 1 Peter and 2 Peter and Jude and the apocalyptic tradition of the book of Revelation. I will suggest (and only suggest) that practically all New Testament communities adjusted the more radical, charismatic leadership efforts of the earliest movement founders and followers (including Jesus and Paul) to realities of the late first-century church. These realities included the delay of the "parousia" (the return of Christ), the death of the apostles, and the need for successors and long-term survival of the movement in its social and political context.

What did new generations of believers in the latter third of the first century do with the Jesus tradition of leadership and with Paul's interpretation of that? The conclusion also explores how the traditions of leadership in Jesus and Paul might impact our practice of religious leadership today, especially in the crises we face in the aftermath of the tragedies of September 11, 2001. What must we do to have faithful leaders today in the tradition of Jesus and Paul, with similar spirits of service and sacrifice in trying times?

1

The World of Jesus and Paul

The first century of the Common Era in Palestine exhibited the rise of many movements, with a variety of movement leaders. The Jesus movement, the first group of believers to organize around the person and ministry of Jesus of Nazareth almost immediately after his death, represents once such movement. A discussion of the extent that it corresponded or deviated from other organized movements of the era will occupy us in this chapter as we try to understand the nature of the social, religious, and political world from which the Jesus movement and its leaders arose.

Questions about the nature of earliest Christianity must come in three forms:

1. What happened to Jesus and his followers during his lifetime?
2. What did his immediate followers do and teach after his death?
3. How and why did the stories about Jesus and those first followers come to be written into that unique form called the "gospel?"[1]

For the most part, our sources for all three types of questions have been the New Testament gospels: Matthew, Mark, Luke, and John—especially the former three, known as the "synoptic gospels" because they share a similar outline and body of material. Although useful for understanding all three stages of earliest Christianity, both historically and especially theologically, these documents represent products of the third phase. The gospels were written by and for the Christian communities as they existed toward the latter third of the first century, with their particular, contextual set of community needs and responses to those needs. Gerd Theissen described this phenomenon well: "We can presuppose that those who handed down [traditions about Jesus] shaped the tradition in accordance with their life." At the same time, "we should assume a continuity between Jesus and the Jesus movement and in so doing open up the possibility of transferring insights into the Jesus movement to Jesus himself."[2]

In our inquiry about aspects of leadership in earlier stages of the Jesus movement, we must inquire about the world during the time of Jesus, including other social, political, and religious movements and *their* quest for effective leadership. It is also important to look beyond the years of Jesus' life and ministry to the beginning of this new movement that formed around him and around memories of him. How did this movement form and grow? What leadership was necessary for that to happen? Such will be the focus of this chapter. In the next chapter, I will explore what the gospels say, as far as we can tell, about those earlier stages, but also about their very own stage of the movement in the latter third of the first century. What qualities do the gospel writers promote for leadership in their own faith communities? How do these correspond to what Jesus himself expected?

Finally, in this chapter we must also take stock of the world of the apostle Paul, as he takes the movement beyond the immediate environment of Palestine and Palestinian Judaism into Diaspora Judaism and the Greco-Roman world of the Eastern Mediterranean. I will introduce the topic here, but come back to it when we turn to Paul in chapter 4.

The World of Jesus

The world of first-century C.E. Palestine was one of domination and oppression. Indeed, since the period of exile under the Babylonians and then the Persians, except for a brief period of about one hundred years in the second-century B.C.E., Palestine remained under the autocratic rule of outside forces. The Babylonians and the Persians controlled Palestine from 587 B.C.E. to 333 B.C.E. Then Israel came under the control of Alexander the Great and his successors, the Seleucids and the Ptolemies. Increased pressure to "Hellenize," i.e., to adopt Greek ways over Jewish ones, precipitated the famous Maccabean revolt of the 160s B.C.E., involving largely northern Judean priests and peasants led by a family of priests, the Maccabees.

This revolt ushered in that one brief period of Jewish independence from 168 to 63 B.C.E. Then the Romans, led by the general Pompey, came at the invitation of a competing faction to the descendants of the Maccabees, the Hasmonean dynasty. With Rome's invasion, a fair amount of Palestinian autonomy ended, and outside domination and control continued. Resistance to Rome's presence ultimately brought about the end of a distinctly Jewish state, with the Jewish Wars of 66–70 c.e. and the Fall of Jerusalem in 70. A brief flare-up, known as the Bar Kochba rebellion of 132 c.e., also failed to restore Jewish autonomy in Palestine. Thus the status of the Jews as a diaspora community, which began with the Babylonian exile in 587 b.c.e., became a *fait accompli*.[3]

A Peasant Society

Several factors need to be noted about this history at this point. First, we must remember that the world of first-century Palestine was a peasant society. "In any traditional society such as Jewish Palestine in the first century c.e., the peasantry comprise 90 percent or more of the population."[4] As in other societies, peasants were at the bottom of the socioeconomic totem pole in Palestine. In addition, continuous occupation by foreign powers took its toll on the economic well being of Israel's peasantry. Not only did they have to concern themselves with feeding their own families, typically as subsistence farm-workers; but increased taxation from outsiders, especially from Rome with its need to pay, for example, for occupying armies, placed unbearable burdens on the peasantry.[5]

Besides paying outside taxes, the peasant population in Palestine also helped support the religious center of the Jews, the Jerusalem temple. This they had done, gladly, from the beginning of Israel's history, as many of their neighboring nations did for their gods. Peasants everywhere worked to "produce an abundance of goods to be brought to the temple storehouses, where the priests and 'great ones' would then tend to the care and feeding of the gods."[6]

By the time of the Roman occupation of Palestine, the burden of both foreign taxation and increasing temple costs had become unbearable. Many peasant farmers had to borrow money from their landlords and other Jerusalem elites to pay the political and religious taxes and to feed their own families. In many cases, those few who owned their own plot of land ended up having to sell and enter "indebted slavery."[7] Thus a state of "permanent debt" permeated the rural areas of Palestine. The source the peasantry depended on as "highly positive symbols of the unity of the people and their link with God"–the high priesthood and temple elite– offered no relief.[8] This hoped-for relief in the form of reduced temple taxes did not come, and a climate of peasant revolt was created. Thus the nature of temple leadership must come under some scrutiny in our study, for it represents the leadership that Jesus and his followers, among others, confronted in their day.

The Jewish Aristocracy

As noted above, Israel's peasantry was loyal to the Jerusalem temple and would withstand almost any hardship to support the ongoing viability of their religious center. However, key to this loyalty was the legitimate status of temple leadership, and when that was not forthcoming at various points throughout the first century C.E. in Palestine, tensions rose. The family of the high priest, in particular, was not only from an illegitimate line of Zadokite priests, but they owed their position of wealth and power, in part, to the Romans. The "compromised position and exploitative behavior of the Jewish ruling class" during the period of Roman domination in Palestine precipitated a series of peasant revolts, culminating in the one that destroyed Jerusalem for many centuries to come in 70 C.E.[9]

In Israel's history, the establishment of a priestly aristocracy resulted from exile and return. Israel prided itself on its theocratic governance from early in its history. However, that "rule of God" was always mediated by the "rule of the priestly aristocracy."[10] By the time of Herod the Great–the powerful, but Rome-controlled king of Judea from 37 to 4 B.C.E.–the high priesthood in Jerusalem acquiesced to his rule. Herod consolidated power around himself by appointing only those priests loyal to him. The Pharisees had secured significant power during the Hasmonean period, especially among the peasantry, because they supported the Maccabean revolt and subsequent independence movement. These Pharisees lost influence during Herod's reign. They "became less a political party and more a loose association of religious brotherhoods."[11] They turned from "politics to piety."[12]

Thus, the large peasant population in Palestine had little recourse for their social and economic ills. The temple priesthood was beholden both to Herod the Great and to his sons who divided Palestine among themselves after their father's death with Roman imperial blessings. Thus the priests were also beholden to the Herodian patrons, the Roman imperial court. For the most part, Pharisaic leadership yielded little power as they increasingly paid more attention to legal-religious interpretation of Jewish life and religion rather than the social-economic well being of the Jewish masses.[13] Roman invasion meant more taxation and "a situation of imperial domination (occupying troops, intercultural misunderstandings, etc.)."[14] Things only got worse when Rome took direct control of Judea, and, therefore, the heart of Jewish life, Jerusalem, by bringing it under control of the provincial governor of Syria and assigning a Roman pro-consul, Pontius Pilate, to oversee Judean affairs directly in 26 C.E. Unlike the gospels' picture of him as a benign, distant dictator, beholden to the Jewish masses and their leaders, Pilate ruled with a particularly repressive hand.[15]

During Pilate's rule the Jewish aristocracy, which included the high priests, the elders, and the scribes, all protected their own status as elites, centering their power on the Jerusalem temple and its ruling council, the Sanhedrin. The Sanhedrin consisted of the high priest, elders, and the scribes (cf. Mk. 15: 1). The high priests represented the "aristocracy of worship," the elders, the "aristocracy of the rich," and the scribes, "the aristocracy of the educated."[16] Entry into the first two groups depended on "dynastic or economic privileges"; the third depended on education in the law and religion. Thus a "circulation of elites" predominated the political scene in Judea. Some Pharisees became scribes, but for the most part Pharisees stayed away from the political center of Judaism and concentrated on exercising "spiritual power."[17] The other groups combined their political power to ensure their survival in the face of the real power—the Roman Empire.

Resistance Movements

The collusion between the Jewish aristocracy and Rome created a vacuum of leadership at the bottom of the socioeconomic ladder. First under Hellenistic rule and then under Roman, the loss of economic well being and cultural dominance persisted for three hundred years in Palestine and so did a period of peasant revolt (approximately 200 B.C.E. to 132 C.E.). Now economic power ruled in Palestine rather than religious or cultural traditions. By aligning themselves with the building and tax programs of first Alexander's Hellenists and then the Roman imperialists—including Herod the Great and his sons—the temple elite promoted "a new kind of power based on financial influence" rather than "traditional theocratic authority" (i.e., "the rule of God"). Financial success by certain families secured entrance into Jerusalem's ruling classes, whereas previously ancestral ties and Torah observance were fundamental for such inclusion. The combination of political-economic alliances with the outsiders and decreased Jewish cultural and religious influences created further gulfs between the Judean peasantry and the temple elite.[18]

Resistance and revolt became the answers for many peasants. Popular movements led by grassroots, charismatic leaders persisted throughout the era of Hellenistic and Roman domination. Some experienced great successes like the Maccabean revolt in the 160s B.C.E., but most proved to be terrible failures like the Jewish Wars of the 60s C.E. In between sporadic peasant uprisings dotted the landscape of Jewish-Roman relations in the first century C.E. in response to increasing Roman domination.[19] These popular movements shared several common characteristics.

First, they sought to restore the notion of theocratic rule in Palestine. Such religious movements as the Essenes, especially their extreme manifestations such as the Dead Sea Scrolls community in Qumran who withdrew to the hills from their regular life in Palestine, awaited divine deliverance from their oppressed situation.[20] They lamented the shift in Judea from an "ethnos," a separate people, to a "polis," a Hellenistic citizen-body, which favored the rich and educated. This shift, in which Greek traditions replaced the Torah, galvanized peasant revolts. Moreover, grassroots leadership emerged in the countryside, rather than depending on the established leadership of the Jerusalem elite.

Second, these movements responded to increased socioeconomic pressures, including taxation and Hellenization, with a climate of protest. However, it was protest from the bottom up, with leaders from among "the common people, lower-class Jerusalemites, or peasants, or both."[21]

Third, what precipitated many of these protests was the failed leadership of the aristocracy, both Jewish and Roman: "The high priestly families, Herodians and much of the wealthy aristocracy…were engaged in mutually beneficial collaboration with the Roman imperial system in maintaining control in Jewish Palestine."[22] Thus the established leaders of the community, both religious (the temple aristocracy) and political (the Herodians), failed the peasantry. Rather than help the peasantry in the midst of increased economic woes, they sought to protect their own interests. Indeed, they often intensified violence against the peasantry. They would call upon Rome to send troops to put down any peasant rebellion. Roman governors like Pilate paid little heed to the common people's cry for help, while the people's supposed representatives "sat idly by or collaborated in their oppression."[23]

Thus a variety of movements flourished in the first century C.E. These included social banditry, much like the Robin Hood stories we read about from centuries later in England. In the mid–first century, bandits "provided leadership for Judean peasants seeking justice when the Roman governor was slow to act."[24] The peasantry supported their leadership because, as in Robin Hood, brigands righted the wrongs of "the usual enemies of the poor: wealthy landowners and overlords, church prelates and genteel clerics who live in leisurely style off the labor and tithes of the peasants, and foreign rulers and others who have upset the traditional order of life."[25] Many examples illustrate how local village leaders and elders in the Judean and Galilean countryside supported social bandits or "brigands" and protected them from the arm of the law, and even got punished for it. These peasant brigands stood against "the wealthy Galilean gentry who had joined forces with Herod in order to reassert their control over the country." Eleazar ben Dinai fashioned a twenty-year career of opposing Rome and the Jerusalem elite with forays and robberies in support of the peasant classes of regions such as Galilee.[26]

Social banditry flourished in the mid–first century C.E. because peasant appeals to established leadership for justice repeatedly fell on deaf ears. Peasants wanted restoration of the "legitimate, traditional state of affairs." However, when, for example, "Galilean families journeyed to their holy city looking to the central political-religious institutions as their court of justice" to redress grievances related to economic woes, they were continually rebuffed by the "king-high priest and the Sanhedrin."[27] Failed leadership from established authorities fueled the development of grassroots leadership from among the peasantry at the bottom of the social-economic rung.

Other more overtly religious expressions of protest and resistance also developed during this period. Harking back to the golden days of Israel's kingships of David and Solomon, certain royal pretender and messianic movements flourished, particularly at the turn of the century after the death of Herod the Great, and later during the war years of the 60s. Such figures as Judas son of Hezekiah (c. 4 B.C.E.) and Simon bar Giora (68–70 C.E.) aroused the messianic expectations of peasant populations because of Roman domination, puppet kings, and failed religious leadership.[28]

Another form of protest movement was related to yet another ancient tradition from Israel's history—prophecy. Both popular prophetic movements led by grassroots charismatic leaders in opposition to established authorities and oracular prophets who denounced the Jerusalem elite in public arenas flourished at about the time of Jesus of Nazareth. Such figures as John the Baptist (late 20s C.E.), the "Samaritan" (c. 26 to 36 C.E.), and the "Egyptian" (c. 56 C.E.) gathered followers by denouncing Roman and Jewish leadership and proclaiming a divine intervention. They tended to be eschatological and apocalyptic in their style and approach.[29]

All of these movements fed into the development of the final revolt against Rome in Jerusalem in the 60s. They all shared certain characteristics:

• They were peasant movements led by unofficial leadership.
• They protested against established leadership, both Roman and Jewish.
• They failed terribly in the final assault, the Jewish Wars of 66–70 C.E.

Practically the only surviving Jewish groups of that war were the Pharisees, who over time went on to redefine postwar Judaism into Rabbinic Judaism, and the Jesus movement, which did not remain part of Judaism, but eventually became the Christian movement. The postwar era was also the time the first gospels developed, beginning with Mark around 70 C.E. and in the following decade or so Matthew and Luke. They represent a particular picture of the Jesus movement and its leadership. How did their perspective compare to the picture of the movements and the leadership we just discussed in these other first-century Jewish peasant resistance movements? I turn to this qustion in the next section of this chapter.

The Jesus Movement

Wandering Charismatics

Jesus and the movement he fostered have been called a movement of "wandering charismatics."[30] Jesus himself has been designated as a "Spirit person," a "sage," a "movement founder" and a "prophet."[31] All of these designations, and others, agree on one fundamental factor from the context of the historical Jesus: He was a Jewish peasant of the first-century C.E. Palestine, a member of that oppressed class that I have discussed above.[32]

The notion that Jesus was the founding leader of "wandering charismatics" derives from the gospel picture of him traveling in and around Galilee and then from Galilee to Jerusalem with a group of followers. Moreover, his followers continued beyond his death preaching and proclaiming his message as a traveling movement. Jesus started a movement of "traveling apostles, prophets and disciples who moved from place to place and could rely on small groups of sympathizers in those places."[33] Scholars refer to such activity as "charismatic" because the role of its leaders involved a call to action, rather than any institutionalized position.[34] In fact, as a renewal movement within Judaism, the early Jesus movement could be characterized, like the others we have discussed above, as founded in opposition to the established leadership of the Roman and Jewish elite.

One characteristic of the Jesus movement of wanderers was their *homelessness*: "Foxes have holes, and birds of the air have nests; but the Son of Man has nowhere to lay his head" (Mt. 8:20). The discourse sending out the Twelve in Matthew 10 and parallels describes this life of wandering expected of Jesus' followers:

> Take no gold, or silver, or copper in your belts, no bag for your journey, or two tunics, or sandals, or a staff; for laborers deserve their food. Whatever town or village you enter, find out who in it is worthy, and stay there until you leave. As you enter the house, greet it. If the house is worthy, let your peace be upon it; but if it is not worthy, let your peace return to you. If anyone will not welcome you or listen to your words, shake off the dust from your feet as you leave that house or town. (Mt. 10:9–14)

The motifs of journey, hospitality, and staying and leaving signal the sense of homelessness and the need for local support in this traveling ministry.

Second, the *lack of family* characterizes these wanderers. After all, these are leaders called to "hate" their families in comparison to the traveling ministry that they must carry out if the ministry is to be successful (Lk. 14:26). Also, they exhibit a *lack of possessions*, indeed a *criticism* of possessions. The parable of the "rich young ruler" (Mk. 10:17–22) indicates the requirements of leadership in this movement. Leaders must be willing to leave behind their possessions, if need be, to serve in this movement, especially because it is an itinerant movement. Possessions could otherwise hold one down. In the book of Acts, the author cites Barnabas as one movement leader with possessions willing to give them up for the cause (Acts 4:36–37). The words of encouragement in Matthew 6:25–32 ("Do not worry") point to "the harshness of the free existence of the wandering charismatic, without homes and without protection, traveling through the country with no possessions and no occupation."[35]

Finally, the wandering charismatic leader of the early Christian community *lacked protection.* He or she could only "turn the other [cheek]" (Mt. 5.38–42). Their only protection was the Holy Spirit, who would give them words to speak when they needed them (Mt. 10:16–23). Any retaliation would be counterproductive to the message of peace and love that was their responsibility.

Thus, ethical radicalism marked Jesus and his movement of wandering charismatics. It was a movement, similar to others in first-century Palestinian Judaism, of outsiders: the sick and crippled, prostitutes, tax collectors, and prodigal sons. As with prophetic and messianic movements, *eschatological expectation* marked this movement and fueled its lifestyle. That's why they could be so disinterested in permanency, family, possessions, and protection. The end was near.[36]

This end-time expectation issued into another characteristic: *intimacy.* Any group formed in opposition to an existing order (including the established political and religious leadership of Rome and Jerusalem) and awaiting the end of that order creates a close bond around itself. Insider stories, nicknames, and even jokes tighten these bonds.[37] Many of the parables Jesus told carried special meaning that only insiders could understand: "To you has been given the secret of the kingdom of God, but for those outside, everything comes in parables" (Mk. 4:11; cf. Mt. 13:10–16; Lk. 8:9–10).

Such intimacy and sense of insider status creates a close-knit community where everyone has a voice in its ongoing development. True, these are usually centered around a singular individual, as was the case of the Jesus movement, with Jesus as the founding leader; but everyone else has a feeling of belonging to a family where voices are equal, and everyone belongs to one another rather than to an elaborate organization.[38] In fact, having Jesus as the singular founder-leader allowed the group to focus on his person as the centering experience for all of them, thereby creating a cohesion that no institutionalized group could have. Their relationship to Jesus sustained them in their ministry as wandering charismatics and made each wanderer one with the other.

Such intimacy, of course, begins to change once a movement becomes more settled. In the case of the Jesus movement that happened almost immediately because the wandering charismatics needed settled believers to sustain them while they traveled. Settled local communities of the movement became the initial ground for a more institutionalized movement within a generation or two after its initial beginnings.

The Nature of Settled Christian Communities

Wandering charismatics needed a settled group of sympathizers. In the gospels, we find examples of homes where Jesus found a welcome: in Peter's house (Mt. 8:14, when Jesus heals Peter's mother-in-law); with Mary and Martha (Lk. 10:38–42); with Simon the Leper (Mk. 14:3–9, where Jesus' feet are anointed by a women with expensive ointment); and with the women supporters of his ministry (Lk. 8:1–3). "Such sympathetic families were probably the nucleus of later local communities."[39] While these may have not been the exact names and homes of movement sympathizers, they certainly represent examples of the types of homes that became the "settled communities," especially "the communities of God in Judea."[40]

What was leadership like for such communities? First, it should be noted that the wandering charismatic leaders remained the authorities for these local communities as long as their size remained relatively small. The gospel saying, "Where two or three are gathered in my name, I [Jesus] am there among them" (Mt. 18:20) reflects this early loose structure of authority, where "hierarchy was superfluous."[41] When problems did arise, the whole community resolved them, as in Matthew 18:15–19, which may very well reflect an early tradition. In this text, the community has the authority to "bind" or "loose." Otherwise, they must wait for the wandering charismatic, as in Matthew 16:19, where the author depicts Peter as a wandering charismatic leader who has the power to "bind" or "loose" as well.[42] Moreover, this self-reliance, whether in the leadership of the local believing community or its charismatic leader, is a direct challenge to the established political and religious leadership in the world outside of the settled community, in this case, Matthew's. "Matthew claims that where the recent and current leadership has failed, his group, and their leaders as exemplified by Peter, will succeed."[43]

A text from Matthew 23 further illustrates this tension between community authority and the authority of a single leader. Jesus warns against the official authority of Jerusalem (scribes and Pharisees) and against earthly teachers such as "rabbis," "fathers," and "instructors" (Mt. 23:1, 8–10). Disciples should follow their heavenly Teacher, Father, and Messiah, who are one authority, not many. However, the text later supports the authority of Christian "prophets, sages, and scribes," sent directly from God (Mt. 23:34), i.e., the wandering charismatics. Why accept one set of multiple leaders and not the other? The answer lies with the stages of church and community development in the period of the gospels' writing:

> The less the structures of authority in local communities had come under the control of an institution, the greater was the longing for the great charismatic authorities. And, conversely, the greater the claim of these charismatics to authority, the less interest there was in setting up competing authorities within the communities. But when the local communities grew in size, they experienced a need for internal government that inevitably competed with the wandering preachers.[44]

The gospels thus reflect several stages of the Jesus movement's leadership approach. First, we can see instances of a more *egalitarian approach* locally, with equal voices by all in expectation of visits by wandering charismatic leaders who may have carried the final word on a variety of community issues.[45] Second, over time more *institutional leadership* within the local gospel communities emerged. This eventually led to a more hierarchical approach to leadership, certainly by the time we reach the second century of the movement's history.

Our efforts at a historical and sociological reconstruction of the earliest stages of the Jesus movement in the aftermath of his departure from the scene discover these discernible aspects of leadership. However, we also have indications, especially in the synoptic gospels, of what Jesus himself might have pronounced with regard to leadership, particularly in light of the political, social, and religious controversies that he and his followers faced in the volatile climate of first-century C.E. Palestine. The next chapter will take a closer look at some of these texts, as well as at how the gospel writers utilized the traditions about Jesus and his leadership for their own understandings of the leadership needed in their late first-century C.E. communities.

Summary of Jesus and His World

This chapter has established the world of Jesus as one that demanded the response of grassroots leadership to the domination system of the Roman Empire, especially given the negligence of those in power locally. A variety of renewal and resistance movements from the peasantry emerged in Palestine, especially during the first half of the century, in reaction to social and economic oppression from the Empire and its local supporters. Among these one must consider peasant movements started by John the Baptist, and a related one by one of his followers, Jesus of Nazareth. Spiritual and prophetic leadership in response to political and economic crises among the peasant poor and their sympathizers characterized these movements. Both grassroots leaders, John and Jesus, as in the case of other movement leaders of the era, paid for their activity with death at the hands of the established leadership of the Empire. However, the Jesus movement survived its martyred leader, as his followers, led by charismatic itinerant preachers, carried the movement forward.

Paul and His World

One of those who carried the message about Jesus forward, even beyond Palestine, was the apostle Paul. Although he apparently began his ministry soon after the death of Jesus, Paul practiced his gospel leadership in a world somewhat different from that of Jesus precisely because he took the movement into the broader Greco-Roman context, beyond Palestine. Moreover, Paul's ministry focused on the major cities of the Empire in the largely Greek-speaking world of the Eastern Mediterranean. Such cities as Corinth, Philippi, Thessalonica, and Ephesus represented the major urban centers of the Roman Empire's domination over Greece and Asia Minor.

Former Greek cities with local democratic assemblies (*ekklēsiae*, in Greek) were now in the process of being transformed into Roman colonies. Paul established his gospel communities in these cities because they afforded him a broad constituency from which to solicit converts. Also, he could easily find work in their bustling economies to support his ministry and that of his associates. Third, the cities, with their Roman roads protected by Roman armies, offered easy access in and out for travel to the next city once his faith communities were founded and able to function on their own (more or less, as a study of Paul's letters shows).

Paul called his newly formed communities *ekklēsiae*, "assemblies," or as they came to be known in the English translations, "churches" (from the German word for *ekklēsia*, "*Kirchen*"). Paul borrowed a word from the language of the former Greek democratic assemblies, a word the Romans had made obsolete.[46] One scholar argues that, therefore, "Paul's assemblies were political as well as religious."[47]

I will return to these matters from Paul's context in subsequent chapters. Already we see how the urbane, cosmopolitan world of the Greco-Roman city in which Paul exercised the bulk of his ministry is somewhat removed from the largely agricultural world of Jesus and his initial movement in Galilee.[48] Yet, at the same time, both Jesus and Paul seem to address the crisis of Roman domination by exercising leadership in what Richard Horsley calls "an alternative society."[49] As we shall see throughout this book, the message of Jesus, including attention to the poor and oppressed in the face of domination, lay at the heart of gospel leadership and remained consistent throughout the ministry of Jesus, his immediate followers, and the apostle Paul.

2

Leadership in the Synoptic Tradition

Discipleship, Mission, and Audience

Gospel study entails significant layers of complexity. On one level lies the study of each gospel individually to determine its own contextual message for its own contemporary readers. At another level, scholars throughout the centuries have attempted to employ the gospels to paint a wholistic picture of the life, ministry, and message of Jesus of Nazareth. In particular, the three synoptic gospels (Matthew, Mark and Luke), which share significant material and a similar outlook, often have become the heart of such efforts. The fourth gospel, John, has been viewed as a more explicit theological interpretation of the life and ministry of Jesus for a late first-century audience. One church father called it a "spiritual gospel." Today, students of the New Testament agree that each of the four gospels presents its own theological orientation in its depiction of Jesus and his teachings, and that John's gospel is a significant contributor to our knowledge, such as it is, of the historical Jesus.

In addition to the contributions of each gospel and the wholistic picture we might draw from them, the interpreter must always consider the various sources for each gospel and for the gospels as a whole, especially the synoptics. These, in particular, are known for the famous "Synoptic Problem": How do Matthew, Mark, and Luke share similar narratives, sayings, and teachings of Jesus in a similar order, yet also exhibit significant differences, including changing the wording and meaning of some of the shared material? What earlier sources in oral and written traditions do they share, and which sources contribute solely to one or another gospel? Matthew and Luke share a significant portion of material not found in Mark. We now call this shared material "Q" (for the German word, "*quelle*," which means "source"). Indeed, "Q" as a whole could very well be the product of yet another gospel community besides those that produced Matthew, Luke, and Mark.[1]

Furthermore, recent Jesus scholarship has begun to pay more attention to noncanonical gospels, such as the gospel of Thomas and the gospel of Peter. Some argue for greater legitimacy to be given to some of these documents in determining the life and ministry of the "historical Jesus," regardless of how early or late dating is determined to be in comparison to the canonical gospels. A more direct link to the historical Jesus is often seen in these "sayings" gospels, such as the gospel of Thomas, because the theological interests of the more organized and recognized communities among early Christians, as represented by the canonical gospels, are less in the forefront.[2]

In light of these complexities, I make several choices in this chapter and the one that follows. I decide to paint a broad picture of leadership in the Jesus movement as understood by the synoptic gospel writers. I analyze several key synoptic texts that I believe present a consistent picture of leadership. This picture is somewhat at the level of Jesus and his immediate followers, as best we can discern it, but closer to the needs and concepts of the communities that produced these documents in the latter third of the first century C.E. I will make some reference to noncanonical gospels and John, but the heart of my inquiry will be with the synoptic gospels. Their perspective on leadership, which I believe at its core can be traced to the historical Jesus, will be the focus of my study. In making such choices, I follow, with some variation, the approach of Walter Pilgrim when he states:

> Instead of attempting to uncover the teaching and activity of the historical Jesus, I invite the reader to hear the four canonical voices who remember, preserve, and pass on the story of Jesus in the early church.[3]

In a footnote, Pilgrim adds that when he refers to "Jesus" in his work, he means "the Gospels' presentation of Jesus and not necessarily the historical Jesus."[4] For the most part that will be the case below, except for several instances where I argue that a pericope, a teaching, or, at the very least, an attitude, should be plausibly connected to the historical Jesus.[5]

Several questions guide the selection and analysis of synoptic texts, particularly in this chapter.

First, I ask, "Who leads with Jesus?" Here I concentrate on the leadership of John the Baptist and the disciples that follow Jesus.

Second, I ask "Who is Jesus' target audience, and what is his message to them (and to those whom he allows to 'listen in' on the conversation)?" Thus, I look at Jesus' message of compassion for the poor and oppressed, and his actions of service and sacrifice on their behalf. Such a message for such an audience becomes a signpost for gospel leadership for those who would follow Jesus, both his immediate disciples and the readers of these written gospels.

In the next chapter, I discuss in more detail the confrontation Jesus had with the established leaders of his day, both Roman and Jewish. I show how his death at the hands of those leaders also becomes a sign of the servant leadership Jesus expects of his followers, and that the gospel writers expect of their readers. In particular, the final confrontation of Jesus in the Jerusalem temple with Rome and the temple leadership brings together these themes of sacrifice and leadership.

In the analysis of both chapters on leadership in the synoptic tradition, I accept the limitations of the gospel record with regard to how much actual data we can ascertain about the historical Jesus. Thus I affirm the validity of and fundamentally adhere to Pilgrim's approach. However, on the topic of leadership I argue that a fundamental correlation exists between the message of the historical Jesus and the practice of the late first-century synoptic communities. Attention to the poor and neglected in the face of a complete and oppressive Roman domination system of oppression was a key, indeed, a *sine qua non*, expectation of gospel leadership. Whether gospel communities by the end of the first century adhered to this fundamental expectation of leadership in every case becomes a question for further study, which I will explore only briefly in the concluding chapter of this book. It seems evident to me that the synoptic record retained this earlier sense of concern for the poor and therefore believed in its praxis. With these factors in mind, then, let me turn to an analysis of discipleship, mission, and audience in the synoptic traditions about Jesus and leadership.

Who Leads with Jesus?

The synoptic record is consistent, first of all, in showing that Jesus leads initially as a follower of John the Baptist and that, second, he leads by surrounding himself with disciples, whom he empowers to carry on the ministry.

The Baptist

John the Baptist remains one of the most enigmatic persons in biblical studies, but no one can deny that he was a dynamic, charismatic leadership figure. Outside the New Testament, the testimony of the Jewish historian Josephus affirms this:

> John was a good man, who demanded that the Jews be intent on virtue, and conduct themselves with justice towards one another and piety towards God, and to come together in baptism...But when others rallied behind him—for they were greatly stirred up by his speeches—Herod feared that such convincing eloquence among the people might lead to some sort of uprising, for they seemed to heed his every word.[6]

Josephus goes on to explain that as a result of this popularity Herod Antipas had John arrested and executed, an action that is described in two of the synoptic gospels (cf. Mt. 14:3-12; Mk. 6:17-29).

In these gospel accounts, Herod's second marriage—to his brother's wife—precipitates John's arrest because of the latter's loud protests about it ("For John had been telling Herod, 'It is not lawful for you to have your brother's wife'" [Mk. 6:18]). However, Richard Horsley and John Hanson argue that what concerned John was not just "old-fashioned marital morality."[7] Herod's first marriage was to a Nabatean princess. This marriage held her father, Aretas IV, at bay from invading Herod's realm on the eastern flank of the Roman Empire. When he married his brother's wife and returned the princess to her native land, Herod created his own diplomatic troubles. The popular prophet's preaching could only exacerbate these troubles by provoking inhabitants of the region to join forces with Aretas in revolt against their king.[8] Thus John the Baptist and his prophetic denunciations of established leadership, both religious and political, had serious political implications. He was a leader in the countryside against those in places of power who abused their power in detriment to the peasantry, an activity I described in the previous chapter with regard to resistance movements.[9]

According to the gospels, John had all the trappings of an ancient Hebrew prophet like Elijah or Isaiah. He "wore clothing of camel's hair" and ate "locusts and wild honey" (Mt. 3:4; cf. Mk. 1:6). He also had quite a following: "Then the people of Jerusalem and all Judea were going out to him, and all the region along the Jordan" (Mt. 3:5). Mark is more explicit about his greatest following—the peasantry, as well as the people from the city: "And people from the whole Judean countryside and all the people of Jerusalem were going out to him" (Mk. 1:5).

What was John's message? First, his message was one of preparation and renewal for the people Israel. According to Luke's account—which has significant parallels in the birth narratives of both Jesus and John—John's father, the humble priest Zechariah, predicts a prophetic role for his son:

> "And you, child, will be called the prophet of the Most High;
>   for you will go before the Lord to prepare his ways,

to give knowledge of salvation to his people
    by the forgiveness of their sins." (Lk. 1:76–77)

Thus Luke depicts part of John's leadership agenda in the song of the Baptist's father. That agenda is a prophetic one. "…John arrived at the conviction that the end was near and that, because of its nearness, he should urgently proclaim an immersion of repentance for the remission of sins."[10] He was an eschatological prophet, proclaiming God's impending judgment on an unjust society and preparing Jewish people from all walks of life for that divine action.[11]

The synoptic tradition pictures John himself understanding his preaching ministry this way. The bare-bones testimony about him in Mark's gospel claims that "John the baptizer appeared in the wilderness, proclaiming a baptism of repentance for the forgiveness of sins" (Mk. 1:4). His was a renewal movement in Israel, one in whose tradition Jesus followed, as evidenced by the fact that Jesus, too, was baptized by John, as were many others. Thus, "before the development of Jesus' own movement, he had already lived in an environment of charismatic prophecy and been shaped by the eschatological message of the Baptist."[12]

John had clearly undertaken a significant ministry of his own. His message not only included a call to repentance for all, but, according to Q–the shared traditions of Matthew and Luke–a harsh word of rebuke for the established leaders of the community:

> When he saw many Pharisees and Sadducees coming for baptism, he said to them, "You brood of vipers! Who warned you to flee from the wrath to come? Bear fruit worthy of repentance. Do not presume to say to yourselves, 'We have Abraham as our ancestor'; for I tell you, God is able from these stones raise up children to Abraham. Even now the ax is lying at the root of the trees; every tree therefore that does not bear good fruit is cut down and thrown into the fire. (Mt. 3:7–10; cf. Lk. 3:7–9)

Matthew's description of the Pharisees here and throughout his gospel as virulent opponents of John and Jesus probably reflects more his community's response to increasing conflict between the followers of Jesus and Pharisaic communities in the post-70 era after the fall of Jerusalem.[13] Given the Pharisees' concern for piety and ritual observance of the law, many of them probably would not have minded a call to repentance and renewal for the people of Israel, such as John offered in his message.

Nonetheless, reference to the Sadducees, the temple elite of Jerusalem, and to those who "presume to say to" themselves, "We have Abraham as our ancestor," points to the established leadership of John's time, including the priestly aristocracy. So now in the situation John the Baptist addresses, it is the same social strata, the priestly aristocracy and gentry (perhaps indicated by "the Sadducees") who trust in their supposedly sacred lineage and sacral position. John, by contrast (like Jeremiah), is the spokesperson for the common people, from whom comes the demand for simple justice. This demand has now turned to God's eschatological wrath for its vindication.[14]

Thus John, like other movement leaders around him, and like one of his followers, Jesus of Nazareth, directly engaged the class conflict of his day. His strong challenge to entrenched power on behalf of the common people in Israel strengthened his status as a reform movement leader.

Luke records an even stronger challenge, which adds a highly ethical note to John's message:

> And the crowds asked him, "What then should we do?" In reply he said to them, "Whoever has two coats must share with anyone who has none; and whoever has food must do likewise." Even tax collectors came to be baptized, and they asked him, "Teacher, what should we do?" He said to them, "Collect no more than the amount prescribed for you." Soldiers also asked him, "And we, what should we do?" He said to them, "Do not extort money from anyone by threats or false accusation, and be satisfied with your wages." (Lk. 3:10–14)

John's message included not only ritual cleansing and repentance as preparation for a new day in Israel's history, but a return to the just, ethical practices of Israel's ancient covenant with God. This covenant called for simple justice and equity to prevail at all levels, whether among the common people (such as "the crowds" that came to hear John), the well-to-do (such as the tax collectors in John's day), or the military (which in John's time included Roman "soldiers"). Again, as a movement leader, John posited a challenge to the status quo in first-century Jewish and Roman Palestine. For this, like the leader that followed him, he paid dearly—with his life.

The "Coming One"

According to the redaction of the gospel traditions, John's message ultimately had a connection to a "Coming One." For the early Christians that "coming one" referred to Jesus. Nonetheless, a close look at the relationship between Jesus and John helps us see how one man's leadership mantel became another's.[15]

John's message about the "Coming One" represents an important and distinctive aspect of his leadership, an aspect that the gospel tradition sought to celebrate. According to the gospels, John was willing to give up his leadership position for another, more powerful than he. Moreover, his ministry was to prepare the way for that other one to do even more than John was able to accomplish:

> "The one who is more powerful than I is coming after me; I am not worthy to stoop down and untie the thong of his sandals. I

have baptized you with water; but he will baptize you with the Holy Spirit." (Mk. 1:7–8; cf. Mt. 3:11–12; Lk. 3:15–18)

John prepared the way by acknowledging his role and pointing the people in another direction, not solely his:

> As the people were filled with expectation, and all were questioning in their hearts concerning John, whether he might be the Messiah. (Lk. 3:15)

John pointed them toward Jesus by baptizing him in preparation for his own coming ministry. Matthew justified the greater ministry of Jesus over a still popular John in Matthew's own time by recording a sampling of John's humility:

> Then Jesus came from Galilee to John at the Jordan, to be baptized by him. John would have prevented him, saying, "I need to be baptized by you, and do you come to me?" But Jesus answered him, "Let it be so now; for it is proper for us in this way to fulfill all righteousness." Then he consented. (Mt. 3:13–17)

While it is clear that Matthew wants to show Jesus' superiority over John, we can also see that the tradition points to an important leadership quality practiced by John in baptizing Jesus, that of *humility* and preparing the way for another. The baptism of Jesus by John also highlights another important leadership quality: *affirmation* of the call to leadership and ministry. With the baptismal voice recorded in all three synoptic gospels ("You are my Son, the Beloved; with you I am well pleased" [Mk. 1:11; Lk. 3:22].), the baptismal experience affirms Jesus' call to ministry. Such affirmation is so important for exercising ministry and leadership that Matthew makes sure that the voice speaks not only to Jesus, but to John and the multitudes: "*This* is my Son, the Beloved, with whom I am well pleased" (Mt. 3:17, emphasis added).[16]

Later, after his imprisonment, John the Baptist needed further affirmation about Jesus. In some remarkable texts John raises some serious questions about Jesus' ministry. The one who preached about a "Coming One" now questions the authority of the one who followed him into a significant preaching ministry: "Are you the one who is to come, or are we to wait for another?" (Mt. 11:3; cf. Lk. 7:19).

Significantly, John's disciples are the ones to take this question to Jesus, another demonstration that John's ministry had a large following even after this imprisonment. The book of Acts reminds us of John's popularity even after both Jesus and he have left the scene. John's followers only experienced "John's baptism" and not Jesus' (Acts 19:1–7). John had disciples close to him and "at a distance as well."[17]

Jesus' response to John's inquiry shows the parallel between his and John's ministry. The concern for the poor and the oppressed lies at the core of both their ministries, as Jesus revealed in his answer to John:

> "Go and tell John what you hear and see: the blind receive their sight, the lame walk, the lepers are cleansed, the deaf hear, the dead are raised, and the poor have good news brought to them. And blessed is anyone who takes no offense at me." (Mt. 11:4–6; cf. Lk. 7:20–23)

A preaching ministry with this kind of target audience (the poor, the lame, and the blind) in the kind of climate of abject oppression in which both John and Jesus ministered was bound to create controversy and "offense," even though it was just "the sort of activity Israel need[ed]."[18] Jesus' message to John, in effect, was: "Take no offense; I am following the same track of ministry you did."[19]

Thus Jesus paid great honor to a movement founder, John the Baptist, by following his lead, taking up the leadership mantel, and affirming a similar ministry. Jesus also affirmed that authentic, authoritative gospel leadership entails care for the poor and oppressed. John was about that; so was Jesus. The gospel record is consistent in this respect.

The Leadership of John and the Concern for the Poor

In the Q tradition, Jesus attested to the significant leadership of John. First, he affirmed that John was indeed a wilderness prophet, one who did not have all the trappings of the "elite" prophets extolled by the established leaders of the Israel:

> "What did you go out into the wilderness to look at? A reed shaken by the wind? What then did you go out to see? Someone dressed in soft robes? Look, those who wear soft robes are in royal palaces. What then did you go out to see? A prophet? Yes, I tell you and more than a prophet." (Mt. 11:7–9; cf. Lk. 7:24–26)

According to Jesus, as portrayed by Q, what made John "more than a prophet" was his ministry of preparation: "See, I am sending my messenger ahead of you," quotes Jesus, "who will prepare your way before you" (Mt. 11:10; Lk. 7:27; cf. Mal. 3:1; Isa. 40:3). However, even more than this preparation ministry, what defined John's greatness, Jesus asserts, was his singular identification with the poor and the outcast: "I tell you, among those born of women no one is greater than John the Baptist; yet the least in the kingdom of heaven is greater than he (Mt. 11:11; cf. Lk. 7:28). In an additional comment beyond the Q material, Luke clarifies this contrast between the greatness of John and the greatness of the "least in the kingdom:"

And all the people who heard this, including the tax collectors, acknowledged the justice of God, because they had been baptized with John's baptism. But by refusing to be baptized by him, the Pharisees and the lawyers rejected God's purposes for themselves. (Lk. 7:29–30)

Once again, a gospel writer probably exaggerates the role of the Pharisees because of post-70s realities, but the point is clear: John and Jesus ministered to the outcasts of their day in contrast to those in power, who failed at exercising such justice on behalf of the poor and oppressed. Another version of these words by Jesus about John makes the point about justice even more explicit:

Jesus said, "Why did you come out into the desert? To see a reed shaken by the wind? And see a man wearing soft clothing? See, your kings and your great ones are those who are wearing soft clothing, and they will not be able to know the truth." (Gospel of Thomas, Logion 78)[20]

Jesus affirmed that John was a great leader because of his attention to the "least in the kingdom," even to the point that "the least" became the greater. By contrast, as Thomas attested, "kings" and those normally considered "great" do not know the truth of what John and Jesus preached with regard to God, that is, God's justice. In a climate of sharp division between the peasantry at one end of the social economic spectrum and the established leadership at the other, these hard-hitting words, first by John and then by Jesus, created great controversy. Nonetheless, it's precisely their willingness to risk their lives for the truth of God–God's justice for the poor and oppressed–that made them great leaders. The gospel record points to the historical reality of these tendencies in the ministry of both John and Jesus.

Indeed, in the Q material Jesus goes on to lambaste his generation as a whole for rejecting the leadership of John, and by implication, that of Jesus as well:

"For John the Baptist has come eating no bread and drinking no wine, and you say, 'He has a demon'; the Son of Man has come eating and drinking, and you say, 'Look, a glutton and a drunkard, a friend of tax collectors and sinners!' Nevertheless, wisdom is vindicated by all her children." (Lk. 7:33–35; cf. Mt. 11:18–19)

Those in power rejected both John and Jesus, whether they freely ate and drank or whether they abstained, precisely because they made "friends" with outcasts. Yet, they were both "vindicated" by those in the know, the "children." Indeed, Jesus praised these "children" and seemed to identify them with the politically, economically, and socially powerless of his day: Jesus said, "I thank you, Father, Lord of heaven and earth, because you have hidden these things from the wise and the intelligent and have revealed them to infants" (Mt. 11:25; cf. Lk. 10:21).

Matthew makes this more explicit than Q when he adds to this context of discussing John's ministry a call to Jesus' audience:

> "Come to me, all you that are weary and are carrying heavy burdens, and I will give you rest. Take my yoke upon you, and learn from me; for I am gentle and humble in heart, and you will find rest for your souls. For my yoke is easy, and my burden is light." (Mt. 11:28–30)

Given the context of tremendous burden, financial and otherwise, for the poor and outcasts of Jesus' time, such a text clearly identifies Jesus (and John before him) with that very audience as the focal point of his ministry. He not only leads with John, but both took up the mantel of leadership for those to whom nobody else was paying attention—the poor and the outcast of Palestinian society under Roman domination. To drive this point home, Luke adds his own redaction to the words about John by including in the same context the story of "a woman of the city" who anoints Jesus' feet in the home of an established leader (a "Pharisee," cf. Lk 7:36–50). The established leader complains, "If this man [Jesus] were a [true] prophet, he would known who and what kind of woman this is who is touching him—that she is a sinner" (7:39). Jesus not only praises her for anointing his feet, but offers her forgiveness, a move which also sets off the ire of the elite sitting at the table with him: "Who is this who even forgives sins?" (7:48–49). Thus, again, like John, Jesus knows his ministry must be focused on the poor and the outcast, including rejected women, and in direct confrontation with those in power who directly or indirectly are the source of oppression for the "weary" and "heavy-laden."

One final example of how the leadership of John and Jesus relate also involves one of the many confrontational scenes Jesus had with the established leaders of his day. This one, attested in all three synoptic gospels, finds Jesus teaching in the temple when the "chief priests, the scribes, and the elders" conspire to ask Jesus a question to challenge him, "By what authority are you doing these things? Who gave you this authority to do them?" (Mk. 11:28; cf. Mt. 21:23; Lk. 20:2). Jesus' reply invokes the memory of John the Baptist: "I will ask you one question; answer me, and I will tell you by what authority I do these things. Did the baptism of John come from heaven, or was it of human origin? Answer me" (Mk. 11:30; cf. Mt. 21:24–25a; Lk. 20:3–4).

The leaders refuse to answer Jesus' question because of John's popularity. If his authority was from heaven, then why did they not believe John and prevent his death? If they thought his authority was humanly engineered, this would enrage the multitudes listening in on this conversation in the temple because they "all regarded John as truly a prophet" (Mk. 11:32b; cf. Mt. 21:26b; Lk. 20:6b). Jesus silenced the temple elite right on their own turf. He effectively took charge of the temple, and he did so using the still evident fascination with the authority and leadership of John the Baptist.

Thus, Jesus took up the leadership mantle in the tradition of John the Baptist. This tradition challenged those in power in his day and focused its attention on those to whom the powerful paid little attention–the abject poor, the socially rejected, including outcast women and the sick. These were the ones suffering most under the oppression of worldwide Roman imperialism and inattentive, local political and religious leadership. John's ministry produced a renewal movement within Judaism to prepare the people for a better day. Jesus followed suit after John's death and drew his own followers to the movement. After his death, these followers believed that Jesus himself had inaugurated that day in his life and ministry.

Who Leads with Jesus? His Disciples

Jesus also leads with his disciples. One of the first acts of his public ministry was to gather around himself a group of followers who would become movement leaders after his departure. What were these people like? The gospel witness makes a point that they were not necessarily the most exceptional people of the day.

The Call of the Disciples

In Mark and Matthew, Jesus' call to his disciples comes upon his return to Galilee, at the beginning of his proclamation about the reign of God. Whom does he call first? Humble fishermen!

> As Jesus passed along the Sea of Galilee, he saw Simon and his brother Andrew casting a net into the sea–for they were fishermen. And Jesus said to them, "Follow me and I will make you fish for people." And immediately they left their nets and followed him. As he went a little farther, he saw James son of Zebedee and his brother John, who were in their boat mending the nets. Immediately he called them; and they left their father Zebedee in the boat with the hired men, and followed him. (Mk. 1:16 20; cf. Mt. 4:18–22)

Two sets of brothers are called–Simon and Andrew, James and John. Thus, although both gospel texts make the point about James and John leaving their father (Mk. 1:20 and Mt. 4:22), it is significant that these disciples leave their families two-by-two, that is, not alone, but as a family pair. In subsequent texts, the commission passages, Jesus will also send them out two-by-two, although placing emphasis on the need to abandon family.

This initial call text also makes a point about mission. "Follow me, and I will make you fish for people" (Mk 1:17; Mt. 4:19). Thus, the very first gospel texts that mention the disciples describe how they follow a leader, that they are cognizant of a mission, and that they leave everything behind to follow that leader and carry out the mission he assigns.

Luke does not give us his first call passage until after Jesus has been initially rejected in his hometown of Nazareth (Lk. 4:16–30). There Jesus identified his mission with a prophetic call to preach good news to the poor and oppressed (4:18–20). Then he performed some healings and exorcisms to demonstrate this prophetic commitment to the masses (4:31–44). Thus when he chose his disciples, they, too, came from the masses. With a miraculous catch of fish, Luke dramatizes the call to mission, especially for Simon Peter (5:1–11). James and John also experienced the miracle of a catch at sea, which Jesus used to encourage them to leave everything and follow him. Once again, the focus also lies on how the first disciples were mere fishermen.

According to all three synoptic gospels, Jesus also called a tax collector to join his body of disciples (Mk. 2:13–17; cf. Mt. 9:9–13; Lk. 5:27–32). In Matthew's redaction, this tax collector is called Matthew, but in Mark and Luke he is Levi, a tax collector sitting at his booth, presumably collecting taxes. Levi, as a tax collector working for the Romans, was a hated figure in Palestine. Jesus, as with the fishermen, asked him to follow. Levi complied. Immediately, the scene shifted to dinner in the tax collector's house, along with many "tax collectors and sinners." Rather than separate groups of people, "tax collectors and sinners" could very well have referred to the same people. Tax collectors were "sinners" in the eyes of many in Jewish Palestine because of their association with imperial power and their overcharge of taxes or "tolls" to benefit their own pockets.[21] By associating with such people, and indeed including some of them among his disciples, Jesus conveyed a particular message: Not one of us is excluded from sinfulness, and at the same time not one of us is excluded from forgiveness and participation in God's new reign.

According to Luke, "the Pharisees and their scribes" (Lk. 5:30; see also Mk. 2:16; Mt. 9:11) challenged the disciples about Jesus' eating activity. This demonstrates the controversy Jesus engendered by his selection of disciples and of his table fellowship partners. In his reply, Jesus specifically referred to the lowly reputation among others of the tax collector turned disciple. His description could also be applied to the fishermen who became his disciples as well: "Those who are well have no need of a physician, but those who are sick; I have come to call not the righteous but sinners" (Mk. 2:17). To this Matthew adds the need for mercy toward these "sinners" (Mt. 9:12–13), and Luke, the need for repentance (Lk 5:31–32).

Thus the call to discipleship includes leaving everything behind, following Jesus, and accepting a mission. However, most striking are the constituencies from which these disciples emerge, including "lowly" fishermen and "disreputable" tax collectors. Next, we will look at the women disciples of Jesus, who represent another group of marginalized persons who became disciples in the Jesus movement.

Women Disciples of Jesus

For several decades now, biblical scholarship, in particular feminist biblical interpretation, has argued that the New Testament underplays the role of women in earliest Christianity. The fact that several stories about women survived redaction of the gospels indicates how active their role must have been.[22] A few of these texts provide some evidence for the leadership opportunities that might have been afforded women in the Jesus movement. Women play prominent roles in some of the healing stories in the gospels, in which leadership roles may lie behind the text. For example, the story about the Syrophoenician woman in Mark 7:24–30 (cf. Mt. 15:21–28) is quite striking. Not only did Jesus speak to a Gentile woman, but she also spoke back to him in a surprising way:

> But a woman whose little daughter had an unclean spirit immediately heard about him, and she came and bowed down at his feet. Now the woman was a Gentile, of Syrophoenician origin. She begged him to cast the demon out of her daughter. He said to her, "Let the children be fed first, for it is not fair to take the children's food and throw it to the dogs." But she answered him, "Sir, even the dogs under the table eat the children's crumbs." (Mk. 7:26–28)

Matthew's version, even more so than Mark's, records how taken aback Jesus was: "Then Jesus answered her, 'Woman, great is your faith! Let it be done for you as you wish.' And her daughter was healed instantly" (Mt. 15:28).

This story, which is none too flattering to Jesus, nonetheless survived the tradition. It seems that perhaps Jesus himself (and now the gospel communities) had to learn an important lesson about the extent of his ministry to both Israel and the Gentile world. Certainly that is the redactor's point—the gospel extends beyond Israel. More striking is that a woman, indeed a Gentile woman, becomes the vehicle, in this pericope, to teach such a lesson.

The story as it is presented in Matthew also points to a shortcoming among the male disciples (and thus a warning to the male readers of this gospel story). The male disciples at first called for Jesus to turn this woman away: "And his disciples came and urged him, saying, 'Send her away, for she keeps shouting after us'" (Mt. 15:23). But the woman will not be sent away. Both he and they learn the lesson of inclusion in the message about the kingdom of God, and, perhaps as well, about who should be allowed to lead in this kingdom.[23]

Luke offers the clearest example of a core group of women leaders in the Jesus movement. Luke narrates the stirring story about "a woman in the city, who was a sinner" and anoints the feet of Jesus in the home of an established leader of the community (Lk 7:36–50). The author follows this with a description of certain female supporters of Jesus:

> Soon afterwards he went on through cities and villages, proclaiming and bringing the good news of the kingdom of God. The twelve were with him, as well as some women who had been cured of evil spirits and infirmities: Mary, called Magdalene, from whom seven demons had gone out, and Joanna, the wife of Herod's steward Chuza, and Susanna, and many others, who provided for them out of their resources. (Lk. 8:1–3)

Although the redactor seeks to distinguish these women from "the twelve," their role as key supporters of the movement is clear. Several of the same women appear in the passion narratives as witnesses to the death and resurrection of Jesus (cf. Lk. 24:10). The reader must wonder how they could not be as authentic disciples as "the twelve" were, and, therefore, among those who became movement leaders after Jesus left the scene.[24]

Thus, in the triple tradition of the synoptic gospels, the resurrection narratives become the clearest instances of the importance of the witness of women disciples in the Jesus movement. While Peter and the male disciples failed miserably to support Jesus at the time of his death, the women took their places at the foot of the cross. They visited the tomb after three days and were charged to tell "his disciples and Peter" that the resurrection had taken place (Mk. 16:7). Mark leaves the women wondering and fearful whether or not they should tell the others (Mk 16:8, the more fully attested ending of Mark's gospel), but Luke describes how the women indeed "told this to the apostles" (Lk. 24:10c).

The latter interpreted the women's news as "an idle tale." They did not believe them until Peter saw the empty tomb himself (Lk. 24:10–12). Nonetheless, the gospel record does not hide the importance of female ministry in the earliest traditions of the Jesus movement, indeed at its most critical junctures. A fuller record would have included some of these women among the inner circle of Jesus' disciples, and therefore, among the first leaders of the movement.

Therefore, Jesus' disciples came from a broad and inclusive constituency, but especially people not normally represented in major religious movements. In many ways, the disciples of Jesus represented the target audience to which Jesus directed his ministry: social outcasts and the downtrodden, including women. I will discuss further the target audience for Jesus' ministry, but first we need to explore what their founder and leader commissioned these disciples to do.

Jesus Commissions the Disciples

The commissioning texts in the gospels provide significant material for reflection on the nature of the discipleship and leadership supported by both Jesus and the gospel communities that wrote about him.

THE COMMISSIONING TEXTS

First, let me note the immediate context of the three commissioning texts in the synoptic gospels. In Mark, Jesus has just been rejected in his hometown of Nazareth. He pronounced the famous words, "Prophets are not without honor, except in their hometown, and among their own kin, and in their own house" (Mk. 6:4). This did not leave too many familiar places for the prophetic leader to achieve honor. The text notes that Jesus "could do no deed of power there," and that "he was amazed at their unbelief." Then he called his disciples together, the special "twelve" who were his core movement leaders, and sent them out "two by two," with "authority (*exousia*) over the unclean spirits" (6:7). The gospel writer's implication is: If Jesus' leadership was not accepted too close to home, he would prepare a group of core leaders. He and they will go on the road with the message of renewal that perhaps others will accept.

In Matthew's gospel, the immediate context of the commissioning is also one of conflict and opposition, but this time with established leaders who question the constituents Jesus has in his leadership party and the healings that he performs. In Matthew 9:9–10, the tax collector Matthew (Levi) is called to discipleship, after which Jesus eats in his home, prompting challenges from opponents about Jesus' liberal table fellowship. To such opposition, Jesus declares, "Those who are well have no need of a physician, but those who are sick...For I have come to call not the righteous but sinners" (Mt. 9:12–13). Only Matthew narrates three controversial healings in this same context:

- the healing of a ruler's daughter, but not before healing a hemorrhaging woman who "touches" his garment (9:18–26)
- the healing of two blind men, who cannot keep quiet about what Jesus has done for them (9:27–31)
- the healing of a mute demoniac, which brought praise from the crowds, but scorn from opponents: "By the ruler of the demons he casts out the demons" (Mt. 9:32–34), an accusation that in other contexts Jesus strongly challenges (cf. Mt 12:22–37, Mk. 3:19–30, Lk. 11:14–23)

In Matthew 9, Jesus counters the accusations by sending out "the twelve" to carry out ministries similar to his own and also to face scorn, controversy, and rejection. Given the enormous needs of the masses, Jesus must enlist and commission them to carry out this difficult mission with him (and beyond him):

Then Jesus went about all the cities and villages, teaching in their synagogues, and proclaiming the good news of the kingdom, and curing every disease and every sickness. When he saw the crowds, he had compassion for them, because they were harassed and helpless, like sheep without a shepherd. Then he said to his disciples, "The harvest is plentiful, but the laborers are few; therefore ask the Lord of the harvest to send out laborers into his harvest."

Then Jesus summoned his twelve disciples and gave them authority over unclean spirits, to cast them out, and to cure every disease and every sickness. (Mt. 9:35–10:1)

Thus in Matthew, the commissioning takes place in a context that clearly defines the target audience for all disciples, including Matthew's readers. Disciples must have compassion for the "harassed and helpless," and, as in Mark, they must have the authority to "cure every disease and every sickness" afflicting such people. Moreover, the needs are so great and the needy so many that Jesus cannot go at it alone. He must commission the help of others who will follow in his footsteps. This type and scope of commissioning activity was not only operative in the movement of the earthly Jesus but also needed for Matthew's gospel community several decades later.

In Luke's gospel, Jesus sends the twelve with "power and authority over all demons and to cure diseases" (9:1), but he also sends "them out to proclaim the kingdom of God and to heal" (9:2). Thus Luke incorporates kingdom language, found elsewhere in Matthew and Mark, as a key ingredient of the message of Jesus, in the commissioning of the disciples. As in Mark, Luke immediately precedes his commissioning passage with Jesus' healing of two figures at the opposite ends of the social-economic spectrum—the daughter of a synagogue leader and a poor woman who could no longer afford doctors to heal her hemorrhaging. The disciples and Luke's readers must learn that their mission cannot exclude poor outcasts of any gender at the expense of catering only to those in power.

Luke and Mark also follow the commissioning of the disciples with questions from the Galilean Tetrarch Herod Antipas because all this activity surrounding Jesus and his disciples caused Herod to wonder:

Now Herod the ruler heard about all that had taken place, and he was perplexed, because it was said by some that John had been raised from the dead, by some that Elijah had appeared, and by others that one of the ancient prophets had arisen. Herod said, "John I beheaded; but who is this about whom I hear such things?" And he tried to see him. (Lk. 9:7–9)

With this passage, Luke follows his pattern from elsewhere in his gospel of setting the ministry of Jesus and his disciples against the larger context of established political and religious leaders and their negative reaction to the proceedings surrounding the Jesus movement (cf. Lk. 1:5; 2:1–2; 3:1–2).

ELEMENTS OF THE COMMISSIONING

Given these circumstances surrounding the commissioning of the disciples, what are some elements of the commissioning itself? In all three synoptic gospels, the ministry of the disciples is described in the language of wandering charismatics. As I discussed in the previous chapter, this indicates that such was the style of ministry of the first leaders of the Jesus movement. They traveled from place to place, depending on settled communities of believers for their room and board. Theirs was an itinerant ministry: "They departed and went through the villages, bringing the good news and curing diseases everywhere" (Lk. 9:6; cf. Mk. 6:12–13).

Upon returning, the commissioned disciples, called "apostles" (literally, "sent ones") by both Mark and Luke, reported to Jesus "all they had done" (Lk. 9:10; cf. Mk. 6:30–32). Jesus immediately takes them to a "deserted place" (Mk. 6:31), but they could not avoid the crowds (Mk. 6:32–34; cf. Lk. 9:10b–11). After an afternoon of preaching and healing, the crowds need to be fed. Jesus teaches his disciples that in their preaching and healing journeys they should have faith not only for their own provision, but also for that of the "multitudes." Thus Jesus "feeds the five thousand" and teaches his newly commissioned leaders a lesson about faith. By walking on water, performing various healings, and feeding another large crowd in the texts that follow, the gospel writers picture Jesus as continually trying to enhance the often-faltering faith of the commissioned (cf. Mt. 14:22–36; 15:29–39 and par.). Thus, while the disciples perform the activities Jesus commissions them to do, they are not always sure of the implications of their actions.

Matthew records some sobering warnings about the preaching and healing activity of the commissioned. After a word of judgment against towns that reject the commissioned disciples and their message, Jesus affirms that he sends the disciples "like sheep into the midst of wolves." Therefore, they ought to "be wise as serpents and innocent as doves" (Mt. 10:16). In this context, then, Matthew adds a warning about coming persecutions for those who would be faithful (10:17–25). Suffering and persecution at the hands of "governors and kings," as well as religious leaders (vv.17–18), will come; but wisdom and courage must prevail. The Spirit of God will help the persecuted disciples to say the right thing at the right time. They must endure to the end. Indeed, Matthew added to these warnings this saying of Jesus about the nature of teacher-student relationship:

> "A disciple is not above the teacher, nor a slave above the master; it is enough for the disciple to be like the teacher, and the slave like the master. If they have called the master of the house Beelzebul, how much more will they malign those of his household!" (Mt. 10:24–25)

Thus commissioned disciples and gospel readers alike must be aware that just as Jesus suffers rejection, his followers must suffer even more. This applies especially to those, like the commissioned disciples, who followed Jesus into roles of movement leadership. Matthew's commissioning passage turns into a full-fledged discourse on discipleship, including further warnings (Mt. 10:26–42). These are instructive for the author's views on leadership. He also follows Q at this point (cf. Lk. 12:2–9, 51–53; 14:26–27, 33). First, Matthew advises fearlessness and ongoing witness in the face of opposition and even death (10:26–33). Second, he acknowledges the division often caused by faith, including among family members (10:34–36). Thus, when family members oppose the movement, movement leaders and disciples must love the cause even more than their own family. This is stated in the strongest possible terms:

> "Whoever loves father or mother more than me is not worthy of me; and whoever loves son or daughter more than me is not worthy of me; and whoever does not take up the cross and follow me is not worthy of me." (Mt. 10:37–38)

However, this also means that such committed leaders and followers will always find an alternative home:

> "Whoever welcomes you welcomes me, and whoever welcomes me welcomes the one who sent me. Whoever welcomes a prophet in the name of a prophet will receive a prophet's reward; and whoever welcomes a righteous person in the name of a righteous person will receive the reward of the righteous; and whoever gives even a cup of cold water to one of these little ones in the name of a disciple—truly I tell you, none of these will lose their reward." (Mt. 10:40–47)

Thus Matthew identifies movement leaders with the movement founder, Jesus. Whoever welcomes and supports the itinerant minister, one who may have even been rejected by his family, does so as if it were Jesus. Thus a Matthean discourse that began with Jesus sending forth his disciples to carry out the same mission he came to carry out (10:1) ends with a clear message to Matthew's readers that even though Jesus is long gone, they still go out in Jesus' name, with his authority, on behalf of the same mission, and with the assurance of the Living Lord himself.

THE SECOND COMMISSIONING

In Luke's "Special Section"[25] of material unique to his gospel, we find a second commissioning passage. Luke indicates that upon Jesus' fateful decision to travel to Jerusalem to confront his destiny (Lk. 9:51–53), he once again commissions disciples, this time not just twelve, but seventy

(10:1–16). What is the significance of this second commissioning? Moreover, what does it teach us about leadership for Luke's gospel community?

First, a different kind of urgency surrounds this second commissioning. A dire warning against lackadaisical leadership precedes it. Such leadership does not count the cost, like the man who cries out, "I will follow you wherever you go" (9:57). Yet this man probably does not realize what Jesus reveals to him, "Foxes have holes, and birds of the air have nests, but the Son of Man has nowhere to lay his head" (9:58). In this context, Jesus calls for someone to follow him, as he did at the beginning of his career. However, excuses, even legitimate ones, are offered. Given the urgency, they just will not do:

> "Lord, first let me go and bury my father." But Jesus said to him,
> "Let the dead bury their own dead; but as for you, go and proclaim
> the kingdom of God." Another said, "I will follow you, Lord; but
> let me first say farewell to those at my home." Jesus said to him,
> "No one who puts a hand to the plow and looks back is fit for the
> kingdom of God." (Lk. 9:59–62)

Thus he will appoint seventy who can really do the job in this crisis situation. They receive instructions similar to the twelve with regard to the itinerant nature of their ministry (10:4–12; cf. 9:1–6) and the judgment that will accrue to those who reject these messengers. Indeed, Luke enjoins the Q tradition in citing woes to specific towns (10:13–15).

Returning to unique material, Luke describes the joyous return of the Seventy (10:17–20). Their ministries have been successful "over all the power of the enemy" (v. 19). Jesus commends them for this, but reminds them not to gloat over the fact "that the spirits submit to you." Rather they should rejoice in the eschatological security of commissioned disciples ("that your names are written in heaven"). In times of crisis, when earthly survival is not secure, especially for movement leaders who put their lives on the line on behalf of the gospel mission, heavenly assurance becomes a motivating factor and a final solace.

Nonetheless, as Luke draws on Q again, Jesus asserts one additional, vital element of vindication for movement leaders. The success of the Seventy, in times of crisis, upends the power of the powerful and enhances the power of the powerless:

> At that same hour Jesus rejoiced in the Holy Spirit and said, "I
> thank you, Father, Lord of heaven and earth, because you have
> hidden these things from the wise and the intelligent and have
> revealed them to infants; yes, Father, for such was your gracious
> will." (10:21)

Jesus turns to the disciples to reiterate this directly to them:

> "Blessed are the eyes that see what you see! For I tell you that
> many prophets and kings desired to see what you see, but did not
> see it, and to hear what you hear, but did not hear it." (10:23b-24)

Thus, understanding and insight about the reign of God has been
reserved for these select followers of Jesus, those commissioned to carry
on his ministry in good times and bad times. The wise and intelligent, the
prophets and the kings–that is, the established of this age–fail miserably in
comparison to the blessed disciples of Jesus, "infants" though they may be
in the eyes of those very same powerful forces.

In short, these passages of commission in the gospels depict some
important aspects of gospel leadership, including the need for an initial
core group of leaders that must not stop expanding into greater numbers
(from "the Twelve" to "the Seventy") because the need is great. The
opposition from powerful forces, including established leadership, will also
be great, but ultimately these passages show that the powerless will be
vindicated as more and more of the commissioned respond to their needs
even in the face of opposition and rejection. So the nature of this
commissioned leadership is charismatic and itinerant. Much faith is needed
because much suffering can be expected. Concern to feed the masses, both
physically and spiritually, must be in the forefront so they can be empowered
over the entrenched political and religious forces of the power elite.

The Disciples: Shortcomings and Failures

However, there is a flip side of this positive picture of the commissioned
leaders. In the gospels, the disciples of Jesus fairly consistently fall short of
the lofty goals Jesus sets for them. Called and commissioned from all walks
of life–including many from the bottom of the social-economic ladder–to
carry on the mission of Jesus and the kingdom of God, the disciples often
failed. They failed to properly understand and to properly carry out what
was expected. Moreover, the gospel record does not shy away from
depicting these failures and shortcomings.

Mark

Mark's gospel presents the harshest perspective on the disciples. In
several texts in which Jesus describes to his disciples some details about
the nature of his ministry, the disciples fail to understand, especially when
the description includes hardship and suffering. For example, according to
Mark, Jesus speaks in parables so that only authentic insiders can know the
truth. "To you has been given the secret of the kingdom of God, but for
those outside, everything comes in parables" (Mk. 4:11; cf. Mt. 13:11–12;
Lk. 8:10). However, Mark shows how Jesus consistently must interpret
parables for the disciples, even though–if they were truly insiders–they
should understand the meanings outright. Thus, in Mark, the disciples prove

to be outsiders to Jesus' true mission. Indeed, Jesus rebukes his disciples for their lack of understanding: "Do you not understand this parable? Then how will you understand all the parables?" (Mk. 4:13; cf. Mt. 13:18 and Lk. 8:11, where such a rebuke is not present).

Even after parables that explain the nature of the kingdom of God, with private interpretation for the disciples (Mk. 4:26–34), the disciples fail to understand. Then, when a storm hits the sea on which they are sailing, they call out to a sleeping Jesus, "Teacher, do you not care that we are perishing" (Mk. 4:38). Jesus calms the sea and rebukes the disciples, "Why are you afraid? Have you still no faith?" (v. 40). Jesus' true identity remains alien to them: "Who then is this, that even the wind and the sea obey him?" (v. 41). Jesus has high expectations for his disciples ("For to those who have, more will be given" [Mk. 4:25].) Yet, in Mark, they consistently fall short in understanding him.

Even after Jesus performs various healings (Mk. 5:1–43) and sends out "the twelve" to preach and heal by themselves (6:7–13), the disciples still do not understand. This remains the case even after Jesus feeds the five thousand (6:30–44) and walks on water (6:45–51a). "And they were utterly astounded, for they did not understand about the loaves, but their hearts were hardened" (6:51b–52). Mark's readers are left to wonder how these "hardened hearts" became the movement leaders when Jesus passed from the scene.

Indeed, after feeding another four thousand (Mk. 8:1–10), Jesus rails at the disciples for their lack of faith when they are short of some bread for a boat ride:

> "Why are you talking about having no bread? Do you still not perceive or understand? Are your hearts hardened? Do you have eyes, and fail to see? Do you have ears, and fail to hear? And do you not remember? When I broke the five loaves for the five thousand, how many baskets full of broken pieces did you collect?" They said to him, "Twelve." "And the seven for the four thousand, how many baskets full of broken pieces did you collect?" And they said to him, "Seven." Then he said to them, "Do you not yet understand?" (Mk. 8:17–21)

According to Mark, in fact they do not understand. The healing of a blind man after this incident highlights the disciples' own blindness (Mk. 8:22–26).

"WHO DO YOU SAY THAT I AM?"

The blindness of the disciples is evident even in their most lucid moments. Jesus asks them the most critical question to that point in the Markan narrative: "Who do people say that I am?" (Mk. 8:27). Peter gets it right: "You are the Messiah" (8:29). However, when Jesus explains the nature of his messiahship, that it will entail suffering and death, Peter rebukes Jesus (8:32). Jesus, in turn, strongly rebukes Peter: "Get behind me, Satan! For you are setting your mind not on divine things but on human things" (8:33). Jesus goes on to explain that authentic discipleship entails self-denial and willingness to lose one's life for the sake of the gospel (8:34–9:1). Matthew and Luke follow Mark quite closely at this point (cf. Mt. 16:24–28; Lk. 9:23–27). The gospel record did not deny the resistance on the part of Jesus' disciples to the sacrificial nature of his, and, therefore, *their* leadership.

Thus, the disciples lacked faith. When the disciples failed to heal a boy with an evil spirit, Jesus was not pleased: "You faithless generation, how much longer must I be among you? How much longer must I put up with you? Bring him to me" (Mk. 9:19; cf. Mt. 17:17; Lk. 9:41). Jesus promptly healed the boy, after he elicited a show of faith on the part of the boy's father, according to Mark's version of the story. In Mark and Matthew, the disciples asked why they could not heal the boy. In Mark, Jesus replied, "This kind can come out only through prayer" (Mk. 9:29). However, Matthew is more explicit about the real problem: "Because of your little faith" (Mt. 17:20a). Even faith as small as a mustard seed could have moved the "mountain" of such an illness (paraphrasing Mt. 17:20b). The story cries out for disciples with faith, given how Jesus continues to predict his impending death (Mk. 9:30–31). The disciples again fail to understand, and resist the idea that this could mark the ending of their engagement with this enigmatic leader: "But they did not understand what he was saying and were afraid to ask him" (Mk. 9:32). Both Matthew ("and they were greatly distressed," Mt. 17:23b) and Luke ("its meaning was concealed from them, so that they could not perceive it," Lk. 9:45) downplay the disciple's ignorance or resistance at this point. However, Mark immediately follows this pericope with further evidence of their extreme lack of understanding.

"WHO WILL BE THE GREATEST"

Despite Jesus' reference to himself as the suffering messiah, the disciples want to know who is the greatest in the kingdom of God (Mk. 9:33–34; cf. Mt. 18:1; Lk. 9:46). Jesus reacts with a measured response. He takes a child as an object lesson for his disciples: "Whoever welcomes one such child in my name welcomes me, and whoever welcomes me welcomes not me but the one who sent me" (Mk. 9:37). The Q tradition is more pointed in response to the disciples' search for greatness: "Whoever becomes humble like this child is the greatest in the kingdom of heaven" (Mt. 18:4) and "for the least among all of you is the greatest" (Lk 9:48c). The disciples need to understand the reversal of leadership roles that is to be expected in the reign of God that Jesus proclaims. The least become the greatest; greatness will entail sacrifice and service. "Whoever wants to be first must be last of all and servant of all" (Mk. 9:35).

Yet the disciples fail to comprehend this model of leadership. In Mark 10:13–16, they actually rebuke children for getting close to Jesus, this after Jesus had taught them that one must be like a child to be "great" in the kingdom of God. Now he must reiterate the teaching to his obstinate disciples: "Truly I tell you, whoever does not receive the kingdom of God as a little child will never enter it" (10:15). Mark (followed by Matthew and Luke) contrasts this second affirmation about being like children with the story of a rich man who cannot fathom giving up all his possessions to follow Jesus (Mk. 10:17–31 and par.). Thus, being like a child, and not like a rich man, is what secures the reign of God for those who would be disciples. However, the disciples' reaction to this is telling. They are "perplexed" that it is so hard for the wealthy to enter the kingdom of God (10:24). They become "greatly astounded" when Jesus suggests that "it is easier for a camel to go through the eye of a needle than for someone who is rich to enter the kingdom of God" (10:25). "Then who can be saved?" they ask themselves (v. 26).

At this point, however, Peter seems to understand: "We have left everything and followed you" (v. 28). Jesus affirms that this is indeed the way (vv. 29–30). Nonetheless, in this passage Mark has demonstrated the shock the disciples felt at the financial, as well as physical, sacrifices that must be made on behalf of the kingdom and its message. Both Mark and Matthew affirm a gospel saying, and a leadership principal, in this critical context: "But many who are first will be last, and the last will be first" (Mk. 10:31=Mt. 19:30; cf. Lk. 13:30).

SITTING WITH JESUS IN GLORY

For a third time in Mark's narrative, Jesus predicts his passion and death, and the disciples are "amazed" and "afraid" (Mk. 10:32–34). Yet, even after this some still misconstrue the nature of gospel leadership and seek great power in the kingdom to come:

> James and John, the sons of Zebedee, came forward to him and said to him, "Teacher, we want you to do for us whatever we ask of you." And he said to them, "What is it you want me to do for you?" And they said to him, "Grant us to sit, one at your right hand and one at your left, in your glory." (Mk. 10:35–37; cf. Mt. 20:20–21, where it is the mother of these disciples who asks for this favor)

Jesus launches into a discourse that clarifies, once again, the elements of gospel leadership. First, it entails suffering:

> "You do not know what you are asking. Are you able to drink the cup that I drink, or be baptized with the baptism that I am baptized with?" (Mk. 10:38)

The two disciples affirm their willingness to endure suffering for the sake of the kingdom (v. 39). However, Jesus clarifies the situation for them. Assigning hierarchy in the kingdom will not be his doing: "But to sit at my right hand or at my left is not mine to grant, but it is for those for whom it has been prepared" (Mk. 10:40; cf. Mt. 20:23, who adds, "prepared by my Father"). Then the other disciples grow angry with James and John because they assume that their boldness in asking will assure them some benefit. Thus Jesus clarifies a third point, offering this climatic statement of servant leadership:

> "You know that among the Gentiles those whom they recognize as their rulers lord it over them, and their great ones are tyrants over them. But it is not so among you; but whoever wishes to become great among you must be your servant, and whoever wishes to be first among you must be slave of all." (Mk. 10:42–44)

In other words, the disciples should not want leadership in the order of the Empire that oppresses them ("rulers" and "tyrants" who "lord it over them"). Rather, they should be willing to serve the people and in that way become "great." As one scholar writes:

> For servants of Christ, for those who follow him and are conformed to his death and resurrection, servanthood never means reduction in status. On the contrary, those who serve Christ find great power manifesting itself in their ministries.[26]

Such servant leadership should be christological in nature, that is, Jesus is the model: "For the Son of Man came not to be served but to serve, and to give his life a ransom for many" (Mk. 10:45). Servant leadership does not entail sitting on a throne. Rather, servant leadership becomes the lesson that the disciples must learn, both the disciples of Jesus and the disciples and readers of Mark's gospel. Matthew also follows this tradition very closely (Mt. 20:25–28). Luke sets the statement in a different context, but nonetheless is even more explicit about its meaning:

> A dispute also arose among them as to which one of them was to be regarded as the greatest. But he said to them, "The kings of the Gentiles lord it over them; and those in authority over them are called benefactors. But not so with you; rather the greatest among you must become like the youngest, and the leader like one who serves. For who is greater, the one who is at the table or the one who serves? Is it not the one at the table? But I am among you as one who serves." (Lk. 22:24–27)

Studies have shown that *diakoneō, the Greek verb behind "one who serves,"* may have referred not to "table service as such but a task or office of high status in which the servant is authorized to act as an emissary for a ruler or a divinity."[27] Thus Jesus offers his disciples a servant leadership that is noble because it comes from the directive of the Divine Creator. It is not self-serving, but other-serving.

LESSONS LEARNED?

Do the disciples finally learn these important lessons about the nature of gospel leadership? The picture in Mark is not good, especially when it comes to the passion narrative, about which I will say more in the next chapter. Judas, a disciple, betrays Jesus and turns him in for trial and execution (Mk. 14:10–11, 43–56, and par.). Before his arrest, Jesus wants to pray with his inner circle of disciples, but they fall asleep (Mk. 14:37–42; Mt. 26.40–46; cf. Lk. 22:45–46, who excuses the disciples–they sleep "because of grief"). When Jesus is arrested, the disciples flee (Mk. 14:50; Mt. 26:56). Peter, who has sworn not to abandon Jesus (Mk. 14:29–31 and par.), denies him three times outside the courtyard of the high priest (Mk. 14:53–72 and par.). His is a particularly vivid picture of a failed disciple: He feigns ignorance of Jesus; he curses; he swears; he breaks down and weeps (14:68, 71, 72).

Only the women disciples of Jesus are present when he dies. Yet, in Mark, at the resurrection scene, even they fail. The shorter, most probable ending of Mark's gospel shows the women frightened and fleeing from the empty tomb (Mk. 16:8). This, even though the young man at the tomb enjoins them to "go, tell the disciples and Peter" that Jesus had risen and was "going ahead of you to Galilee," to see them, "just as he told you" he would (Mk 16:7). The women tell no one, and thus ends the gospel of Mark.

The failure of the disciples thus becomes acute by the end of Mark's story. Of course, such ambiguity about their role fits Mark's overall purpose to challenge his readers to go beyond the failures of the original disciples, and their own, to exercise an effective servant gospel leadership in their day. Unlike the fleeing disciples and the uncommunicative women at the tomb, they must go forward and tell the story. They must not fail as disciples and movement leaders, even if the original disciples, in many ways, did so.

Failed Discipleship in Matthew, Luke, and Q

Matthew, Luke, and the Q tradition, as we have seen in certain instances above, are less harsh with regard to the shortcomings and failures of the disciples. Nonetheless, they do include certain unique features, which add to the general picture of how the disciples fall short in certain areas.

MATTHEW

Matthew combines several instances of the disciples' failures with those of the opponents of Jesus. Disciples fail to understand Jesus and his mission in ways similar to how his opponents fail to do so. For example, in a text that parallels Mark, Matthew's Jesus laments the testing of his ministry by established Jewish leaders ("the Pharisees"–Mt. 16:1–4; cf. Mk. 8:11–13). Jesus warns the disciples about "the yeast of the Pharisees and Sadducees" (Mt. 16:6). Yet, ironically, the disciples worry more about bread than about whether their leadership is what Jesus expects or is instead more like that of the established but neglectful leaders of the people (Mt. 16:7). Thus Jesus chastises them: "You of little faith, why are you talking about having no bread? Do you still not perceive?" (Mt. 16:8–9; cf. Mk. 8:17) Only Matthew goes on to clarify that it is "the teaching of the Pharisees and Sadducees" that ought to concern the disciples, not from where their next piece of bread will come (Mt. 16:11–12).

Similarly, in the context where the disciples have asked about who will be the greatest in the kingdom and Jesus offers a child as the model for such greatness (Mt. 18:1–5; cf. Mk. 9:33–37), Jesus also challenges anyone who causes these "little ones" to fall (Mt. 18:6–9; cf. Mk. 9:42–48). To this, Matthew adds a "woe" ("Woe to the world because of stumbling blocks!" [18:7]), which anticipates the woes against Pharisees and Sadducees in Matthew 23. Disciples should not identify themselves and their actions in any way with those who oppose the message and ministry of Jesus on behalf of "the little ones." Disciples need to have clear who the target audience is for their leadership–"the little ones"–a theme to which I will return below.

A second instance in which Matthew nuances the shortcomings of the disciples, besides relating them to the failures of the opposition, lies in the passage in which Peter declares Jesus as Messiah. Only Matthew adds Jesus' praise of Peter for this assertion:

> "Blessed are you, Simon son of Jonah! For flesh and blood has not revealed this to you, but my Father in heaven. And I tell you, you are Peter, and on this rock I will build my church, and the gates of Hades will not prevail against it. I will give you the keys of the kingdom of heaven, and whatever you bind on earth will be bound in heaven, and whatever you loose on earth will be loosed in heaven." (Mt 16:17–19)

Such effusive praise and enhancement of the leadership legend of the apostle Peter, however, also enhances the depth of his failures later on in the gospel record, including Peter's vehement denial, just a few short verses later, that Jesus will die:

> And Peter took him aside and began to rebuke him, saying, "God forbid it, Lord! This must never happen to you." But he turned and said to Peter, "Get behind me, Satan! You are a stumbling block to me; for you are setting your mind not on divine things but on human things." (Mt. 16:22–23)

Matthew tries to assuage Peter's failure to discern properly here by showing how Peter at least took Jesus "aside" to "rebuke" him. Nonetheless, Matthew did not completely hide that the gospel tradition recorded the failures of the disciples, including Peter, to understand the true nature of Jesus' earthly ministry. Matthew's community, too, needed to understand that disciples and leaders fail.

Nonetheless, Matthew presents a generally positive picture of discipleship in his gospel. Indeed, he ends with the commandment of the Risen Lord that the eleven disciples should "go therefore and make disciples of all nations" (Mt 28:19). In Matthew, discipleship is a good thing, worthy of engaging others, even if disciples have their faults.

LUKE

Luke is even more circumspect about the failures of disciples. After all, he wants to demonstrate to his audience, Theophilus and his followers (cf. Lk 1:1–4), that Jesus and the apostles were about the glorious business of spreading the good news about Jesus "to the ends of the earth" (Acts 1:8d). However, Luke includes some telling twists in his narrative that also challenge Theophilus and other readers to regard their leadership roles with care.

The most glaring comes in the placement of the passage about greatness in the kingdom. Only in Luke do we find this exchange between Jesus and the disciples about the nature of kingdom leadership as servant leadership in the context of the Last Supper. This represents a striking image, given the solemnity of the moment (Lk. 22:15–20). Jesus has just declared that he would be betrayed by one of his own (Lk. 22:21–23). Then in this incongruous moment the dispute arises among the disciples about who would be the greatest (22:24). A reader might wonder which is worse—the betrayer or the power-hungry. Jesus patiently teaches that, "the greatest among you must become the youngest, and the leader like one who serves" (22:26). He asserts that servant leadership describes the nature of his own work: "But I am among you as one who serves" (22:27c). Yet, in this context Jesus also praises the disciples for their steadfastness:

> "You are those who have stood by me in my trials; and I confer on you, just as my Father has conferred on me, a kingdom, so that you may eat and drink at my table in my kingdom, and you will sit on thrones judging the twelve tribes of Israel." (Lk. 22:28–30)

Luke invokes the Q tradition here, for this eschatological security and kingdom leadership for the disciples is also cited in Matthew, albeit in a different context (Mt. 19:28). Very little in Q seems to question the disciples' loyalty, certainly not as much as Mark does. Yet here in Luke, the placement of the disciples' misguided quest for power just before Jesus is handed over to those who wage unjust political power is a glaring example of how disciples might fail to fully comprehend the sacrificial nature of gospel leadership as Jesus expected it to be exercised.

Nonetheless, unlike Mark, Luke downplays the disciples' lack of understanding with regard to the parables (Lk. 8:9–11). And even if the disciples failed so miserably at the arrest, trial, and crucifixion of Jesus, at least the women disciples succeeded in reporting the message of the resurrection (which they failed to do in Mark). Luke had cited their ministry on behalf of Jesus earlier (Lk. 8:1–3), and he names virtually the same women again at the site of the empty tomb (24:1–11).

However, Luke does not want the disciples to be unaware of their responsibilities in this new reality called the kingdom of God. Theophilus and his fellow believers must realize the lowly status that can be expected in the leadership of gospel activities. Only Luke includes a pericope about a slave who should not expect table fellowship or even a word of gratitude for his service to the master (Lk. 17:7–10). In the same way, disciples should not expect much earthly reward for their service to the kingdom.

Shortly after this pericope, Luke writes extensively about the qualities needed for discipleship in the kingdom of God in material peculiar to Luke (18:1–14). First, he writes about a widow who persists in seeking justice from an unjust judge. Surprisingly, the judge grants her request. Similarly, God will grant justice to persistent prayers from his disciples. Can such faith be found? asks Jesus (18:1–8). Perhaps the original version of this story cried out for the just treatment of women and widows, but Luke uses it to encourage persistent prayer and faith from his readers.

A second story tells about a self-justifying Pharisee and a loathsome tax collector, both praying in the temple. The former thanked God for his exalted status. The latter prayed for forgiveness of his sins. For Jesus, and the author of Luke's gospel, the exalted will be humbled, and the humble will be exalted (18:9–14), an important lesson for disciples to learn.

Thus Luke challenges disciples toward high expectations. He follows these unique placements of material with the stories of disciples who want to keep children away from Jesus (18:15–17) and a rich young man who cannot bring himself to give away his possessions to follow Jesus (18:18–30). Disciples must understand fully their roles in God's kingdom and the sacrifices needed to fulfill those leadership roles. They must be like children in obedience, service, and sacrifice, or else, like the rich man, they won't experience the kingdom fully. When Jesus reiterates the fate that awaits him in Jerusalem (18:31–33), according to Luke, the disciples do not understand (v. 34). Yet, even a blind man can see that this Jesus is the "Son of David," a kingly agent of God (Lk. 18:35–43).

Significant Shortcomings, Great Expectations

The message Luke wishes to convey through his compilation of pericopes that includes material unique to him as well as material from the triple tradition is that disciples can and will fail, but Jesus still has high expectations for them. Indeed, this theme prevails throughout the synoptic gospels. Mark and Matthew, and to a lesser extent Luke and Q, highlight shortcomings and failures among the disciples; but these only enhance the great expectations Jesus has for them and that the evangelists have for their churches. The disciples of Jesus were weak in many ways, but even then God used them for great things, including spreading the good news about the kingdom of God in those early years of the movement. In the same way that Jesus had high expectations for his disciples, so, too, the gospel readers must have such expectations for themselves, especially those who lead among them.

Why these high expectations? Why must gospel leadership be so complex as pictured in the gospel record? Why not simply give us heroes vs. villains, with little ambiguity about each? I suspect that the nature of the target audience for the ministry of Jesus and his disciples lies at the heart of the conflicted picture we get of the leadership for this community. The target audience itself was a complex mix of the people represented by the gospel ascription "the least of these," the people nobody else–especially the established leaders of Palestine–was paying attention to. For these a committed, albeit complex and conflicted, group of leaders must be at the ready.

The Target Audience for Jesus' Ministry

The synoptic gospels present a varied picture as to the target audience to whom Jesus directed his message and ministry. Nonetheless, each of these gospels consistently includes one group in particular among those to whom Jesus focused his attention–the poor and the outcast, those suffering the most, those to whom nobody, not even the established political and religious leaders who *could* help, pays attention. Jesus identified with those who suffer, and, therefore, according to the gospels, became a great leader. When certain disciples questioned the validity of one who was not in their inner circle performing miracles and healings, Jesus refused to stop the individual. "Whoever is not against us is for us," claimed Jesus (Mk. 9:40). One who is "for us," said Jesus, is "whoever gives you a cup of water" in the name of Christ (Mk. 9:41). Matthew makes the ethical edge here more explicit: "And whoever gives even a cup of cold water to one of these little ones in the name of a disciple–truly I tell you, none of these will lose their reward" (Mt. 10:42). Thus, the "little ones" were the target of Jesus message and ministry. It should be the same for those who will follow him: the disciples who walked with him and the future leaders of the movement, including those reading these gospel texts decades later.

The Little Ones

Who were "these little ones?" Two incidents with potential leaders of the movement help to illustrate the constituents of Jesus' target audience. First, Jesus encounters a potential leader who fails to get the heart of Jesus' message, the so-called "rich young ruler."[28] He has fulfilled all the commandments, prospered financially, and wants to secure one last inheritance, the kingdom of God. Jesus challenges his understanding of the commandments and the appropriate use of his wealth: "You lack one thing; go, sell what you own, and give the money to the poor, and you will have treasure in heaven; then come, follow me" (Mk. 10:21; cf. Mt. 19:21; Lk. 18:22). Of course, the young man refuses, sad and in shock with the challenge of Jesus ringing in his ears (Mk. 10:22; Mt. 19:22; Lk. 18:23). He does not understand the connection between "inheriting the kingdom of God" and paying attention to the poorest of the poor in his society. His potential for gospel leadership ("Come, follow me," Jesus says, just like he did to his disciples), has thus been thwarted.

However, as we saw above, the disciples do not necessarily understand this point either. With reference to this young man, Jesus declares, "How hard it will be for those who have wealth to enter the kingdom of God!" (Mk. 10:23 and par.). The disciples are "perplexed" and "astounded": "Then who can be saved?" they wonder (Mk. 10:24–26). In an earlier incident, they too showed that they lacked understanding about the target audience for the ministry of Jesus, and eventually their own. People brought children to be blessed by Jesus, and the disciples rebuked them. Jesus in turn rebuked the disciples for their attitude, saying, "Do not stop them; for it is to such as these that the kingdom of God belongs. Truly I tell you, whoever does not receive the kingdom of God as a little child will never enter it" (Mk. 10:14b–15, and par.). With these two incidents, then, Jesus declared the economically poor and the otherwise defenseless as important constituents for his ministry and for that of anyone who would follow his lead. Yet potential, as well as future, leaders of the movement often faltered in understanding this fundamental aspect of their leadership.

Healings as a Sign

Jesus' healings also signal who constitutes his fundamental target audience, for he heals the most needy. For example, in rapid succession, Mark's gospel depicts Jesus healing a man with an unclean spirit (1:21–28), Peter's mother-in-law (1:29–31), a leper (1:40–45), and a paralytic who needs intervention from his friends to receive the healing (2:1–12). People with such ailments and need for healing were not usually the most prosperous of a community. The latter had greater access to authorized means of medicine. Thus, the people Jesus healed represented the most humble and the least attended, especially those like the leper and the man with the unclean spirit in the Markan passages.[29]

Yet, Jesus also heals the servant of a Roman centurion during this flurry of healings, according to the Q tradition (Mt. 8:5–13; Lk. 7:1–10). Interestingly, the centurion describes to Jesus his understanding of the typical expectations of leadership in his world. "For I also am a man under authority, with soldiers under me; and I say to one, 'Go,' and he goes, and to another, 'Come,' and he comes, and to my slave, 'Do this,' and the slave does it" (Mt. 8:9). Nonetheless, the man shows compassion for his servant and seeks his healing by means of another source of authority, Jesus of Nazareth. The latter, amazed at this show of faith by a non-Israelite, a Roman centurion, no less, declares the servant healed. Thus, this Roman centurion demonstrates that he understands the target audience for Jesus' ministry: persons like his servant–typically ignored by those in power, but not by compassionate people like Jesus–and hopefully persons like his disciples, and, ironically, persons like this representative of an oppressive regime. Established Roman and Jewish leaders have no excuse for ignoring the needs of the poor, the sick, the slave, and the conquered.

In a related story, Jesus encounters another recognized leader, Jairus the synagogue ruler (cf. Mk. 5:21–43; Mt. 9:18–26; Lk. 8:40–56). Similar to the Roman centurion, this Jewish leader also expresses faith in Jesus, requesting healing for his daughter. However, on his way to perform that miracle, Jesus stops to heal a woman, whom Jesus also calls a "daughter" (Mk. 5:34 and par.): Fearing recrimination, for she had a bleeding disease that made her "unclean" and unfit to be even seen in public, the woman felt that if she could only touch Jesus the miracle would happen. Despite her "clandestine" approach, Jesus healed her. Thus, in the midst of healing the daughter of a respected, accepted leader, Jesus stopped to show the main focus of his ministry, rejected persons like this "unclean" woman.

Tax Collectors and Others

Nonetheless, Jesus does include all kinds of people in his entourage and among those to whom he ministers, not just the poorest of the poor. It is curious to a reader of the gospels how often the evangelists make reference to "tax collectors" as a group; one even became a disciple (Mt. 9:9). These tax collectors, as we have seen previously, were well-off individuals, but nonetheless were hated by their Jewish countrymen as traitors to the community because they conspired with Rome in the collection and extortion of exorbitant amounts of tax money. Yet Jesus calls them to join him, ministers to them, as he did for Zacchaeus in the gospel of Luke (19:1–10), and even eats with them. How can this be?

Both healing the most unattended of society and eating with society's unacceptable are signs of the target audience for Jesus' ministry. In the context of calling and eating with a tax collector, Jesus declares, "I have come to call...sinners" (Mk. 2:17). John Dominic Crossan describes what Jesus does as "an open commensality, an eating together without using the table as a miniature map of society's vertical discriminations and lateral separations."[30] In this way, the gospel writer makes clear the broad spectrum of the audience to which Jesus ministers. "To touch a leper" or an unclean woman, or "to expel a demon" are all confrontational acts with which

Jesus creates around him a movement, "a community of the marginalized and the disenfranchised."[31]

Tax collectors, as well as the economically poor, represent social outcasts that must be brought into the "big tent" Jesus is creating for his movement.

A "Demoniac"

Another example illustrates the socioeconomic dimension of Jesus' choice of audiences. When he confronted the "Gerasene Demoniac" (cf. Mk. 5:1–20; Lk. 8:26–39; or the "Gadarene" demoniacs in Mt. 8:28–34), Jesus sent the "legion" of unclean spirits into a herd of swine. These rush down the side of a hill and perish in the sea, and the people from that region express concern with their economic well being, rather than with the health of the demoniac. They probably had every right to be upset, given the loss of their livelihood in those slain swine. However, Jesus would have none of that; his concern was more for this lost, tortured soul, than the lost swine and lost income. Lost, unattended souls comprised the audience his ministry targeted. By paying attention to people rather than possessions, his movement took a direct slap at the movement that oppressed his people, i.e., the Roman Empire and its "legions."[32] Whether the story was original with the historical Jesus or an early part of the tradition, the gospel witness makes this point evident for its readers. Followers of Jesus must take leadership in confronting evil in society by liberating and comforting those who suffer most from that evil.

This general picture of those whom Jesus included among his constituency, very much based on Mark's gospel, finds verification in the unique testimony of Matthew and Luke as well. In Matthew's genealogy, for example, the inclusion of several "disreputable" women, including Tamar, Rahab, and "the wife of Uriah" demonstrates, at an early point in this gospel, that outsiders, including Gentile women like these, were included among the target audience for the ministry of Jesus (cf. Mt. 1:3, 5, 6).

Poor, Grieving, Meek, and Hungry

Matthew's "Sermon on the Mount," almost universally accepted today as the values of the kingdom for all followers of Jesus, and even those that are not, sets the scene specifically between Jesus and the disciples: "When Jesus saw the crowds, he went up the mountain; and after he sat down, his disciples came to him. Then he began to speak, and taught them" (Mt. 5:1–2).

Yet, the audience for Jesus and these disciples ultimately includes those whom Jesus extols with the "beatitudes" at the beginning of his sermon:

> "Blessed are the poor in spirit, for theirs is the kingdom of heaven. Blessed are those who mourn, for they will be comforted. Blessed are the meek, for they will inherit the earth. Blessed are those who

hunger and thirst for righteousness, for they will be filled. Blessed are the merciful, for they will receive mercy. Blessed are the pure in heart, for they will see God. Blessed are the peacemakers, for they will be called children of God. Blessed are those who are persecuted for righteousness' sake, for theirs is the kingdom of heaven." (Mt. 5:3–10)

Jesus' disciples, both those in his initial inner circle and those who would become leaders in the movement, including Matthew's readers, needed to understand that the "poor," the grieving, the "meek," and those who hunger must be the focal point of the ministry. God wishes to bless them all. Disciples must, therefore, be "merciful," "pure of heart," and "peacemakers" in the midst of the violent world of the Roman Empire. Such attitudes might bring persecution upon them, but God and God's reign would prevail.

Economically Burdened

At the end of another long passage later in Matthew, after the Twelve have been commissioned, they must focus their ministry on this target audience from the Great Sermon:

"Come to me, all you that are weary and are carrying heavy burdens, and I will give you rest. Take my yoke upon you, and learn from me; for I am gentle and humble in heart, and you will find rest for your souls." (Mt. 11:28–29)

The peasant population of Jesus' time carried the greatest tax burdens of his day. This precipitated economic woes and physical ailments, and thus all kinds of "heavy burdens." To such needy people Jesus directed his ministry and directed his disciples to do the same.

Luke's gospel has similar emphases. Although his gospel apparently had the patronage of Theophilus, perhaps a well-to-do Greek Christian seeking to understand his newfound faith better (Lk. 1:1–4), this does not keep the author from confronting his readers with the need to pay attention to the poor. Only Luke has the song of Mary, the Magnificat, as we now call it, with its special focus on God's concern for the poor:

"My soul magnifies the Lord,
    and my spirit rejoices in God my Savior,
for he has looked with favor on the lowliness of his servant.
    Surely, from now on all generations will call me blessed;
for the Mighty One has done great things for me,
    and holy is his name.
His mercy is for those who fear him
    from generation to generation.
He has shown strength with his arm;
    he has scattered the proud in the thoughts of their hearts.

> He has brought down the powerful from their thrones,
>> and lifted up the lowly;
> he has filled the hungry with good things,
>> and sent the rich away empty..." (Lk. 1:46–53)

The "lowly," the hungry, and the poor will fare well by this God who puts "the proud," "the powerful," and the "rich" in their places. When Jesus bursts on the scene, according to Luke, his first message identifies the focal point of his ministry as well:

> "The Spirit of the Lord is upon me,
>> because he has anointed me
>>> to bring good news to the poor.
> He has sent me to proclaim release to the captives
>> and recovery of sight to the blind,
>>> to let the oppressed go free,
> to proclaim the year of the Lord's favor." (Lk. 4:18–19)

Like the prophet Isaiah, Jesus comes to confront the abuse of centralized power on behalf of those feeling the brunt of that power in an unjust way. Thus, they receive "release," "go free," and gain "the Lord's favor." God, through his agent, Jesus of Nazareth, will favor the "poor," "the captives," "the blind," and "the oppressed." This is not just random spiritualization, but actual concrete expectations of political and social, as well as spiritual, liberation for the oppressed peoples of Palestine. Such an agenda for the poor and oppressed must have been a prime message for Jesus. Moreover, it shines through in the gospel record as an ongoing expectation for gospel leaders following the Jesus tradition even after the fall of Jerusalem, when it would be expected that religious and political movements in Palestine and its surroundings would want to tone down anti-imperial rhetoric.

The Rejected

Jesus' "sermon" recorded in Luke 4:16–21 becomes programmatic for Luke's gospel. For example, only Luke has the parable of the good Samaritan (Lk. 10:25–37), which demonstrates how the focus of gospel ministry should include those often rejected by established religious leaders. However, the parable also shows that those who can carry out gospel ministry and leadership could very well be people whom we least expect, like the Samaritan of this story. Even a widow can confront the powerful in a claim for justice, as Jesus shows in the parable of the widow and the unjust judge (Lk. 18:1–8). He hopes that his disciples will always be like "babes" in their attitudes and in their actions toward their target audience, even as they return victorious from mission trips (Lk. 10:21). After all, they could easily lose their seats in the great eschatological banquet if they behave like the rich in earthly banquets. The latter quite easily invite their own, but lack space for those who cannot repay their hospitality, "the poor, the crippled, the lame, and the blind" (Lk. 14:7–14; cf. 14:15–24). Thus discipleship can be costly; one must be willing to identify with one's audience, which may entail giving up possessions and leaving behind ("hating") one's family, if need be, to serve "the lost" (Lk. 14:25–35; 15:1–32).

Luke and Possessions

The pericopes of Luke's gospel that deal with the theme of possessions are numerous and almost exclusive to this gospel. The necessary attention to those with few possessions becomes the requisite quality of gospel leaders, including the well-off, represented by Theophilus, the gospel's patron. Gospel leaders, unlike the established leaders of Palestine (often symbolized by "the Pharisees," Lk. 16:14), must not be "lovers of money," justifying themselves "in the sight of others" because of their possessions. Rather, priority lies in that "God knows [their] hearts." Dependence on possessions, "prized" as it is by human beings, "is an abomination in the sight of God" (16:15).

Luke drives home this point with the story of Lazarus and the rich man (16:19–31). On earth, clear distinctions exist between Lazarus, a poor man, and the unnamed rich man. By naming one and not the other, the story ascribes honor to the poor man in a striking reversal of the culture's honor-shame values.[33] Luke further emphasizes this role reversal by describing the chasm that exists between Lazarus and the rich man in the afterlife. Lazarus rests in luxury at the bosom of Abraham, while the rich man is tormented in Hades. Now, the rich man cannot pass over into the realm of Lazarus, just as Lazarus could not partake, except for crumbs, of the rich man's earthly context. Abraham reminds the rich man, "Child, remember that during your lifetime you received your good things, and Lazarus in like manner evil things; but now he is comforted here, and you are in agony" (16:25). From this story, Luke's readers would have understood that focus on possessions and neglect of the poor will be the downfall of any potential leader in the gospel movement. Moreover, in this life or the next, the poor will receive their reward. Woe to anyone–especially leaders, those in the best position to help the poor–who fails to do so.

In the parable of the ten lepers (17:11–19), the only one to come back to give thanks is a Samaritan, echoing the point from the parable of the good Samaritan–participation and leadership in the Jesus movement is open to all groups, including those least expected. As I previously noted, even tax collectors have access to this movement. In the parable of the Pharisee and the tax collector, the established leader prays haughtily, the hated tax collector humbly (18:9–14). According to Luke, with this story Jesus establishes an important principle for his movement: "For all who exalt themselves will be humbled, but all who humble themselves will be exalted" (18:14b). Thus another important quality for gospel leadership is extolled–humility instead of the constant search for honor and status, which is a *sine qua non* of secular leadership.

Another tax collector, found only in Luke, Zacchaeus, exemplifies the new attitude (Lk. 19:1–10). Zacchaeus "was a chief tax collector and was rich" (19:2). Therefore he was not a member of the peasant class, the most immediate constituents of the Jesus movement. Nonetheless, he wanted to see Jesus. When Jesus invites himself to Zacchaeus' home, others "grumble" because Jesus had "gone to be the guest of one who is a sinner" (19:7). However, despite his riches Zacchaeus demonstrates the quality of humility Jesus sought.

"Zacchaeus stood there and said to the Lord, 'Look, half of my possessions, Lord, I will give to the poor; and if I have defrauded anyone of anything, I will pay back four times as much'" (19:8). Pleased by this response, Jesus declares "salvation" for the man and his household, and includes him as part of his target audience "because he too is a son of Abraham" (19:9).

By showing his support for the poor, Zacchaeus secures his role in the Jesus movement, despite his wealth. Moreover, his wealth did not secure his leadership in Palestine. "He was rich, but because of his status as an outsider he did not belong to the elite;...he serves as an example of how tax-collectors and non-elite followed the will of God, while the leaders of the Jewish people did not"[34] As we shall see in the next chapter, the opposition of the established leaders to Jesus' ministry included their rejection of his target audience, including outsiders like tax collectors. Nonetheless, some well-to-do tax collectors and other "sinners" showed willingness to repent and use their substantial resources for the good in the Jesus movement, including care for the poor.

Thus, the synoptic picture as a whole, as well as message and material unique to each individual gospel, depicts this important quality of leadership in the Jesus movement: inclusion of and attention to the poor. In his own ministry, Jesus no doubt paid special attention in both his message and healing activity to those whom the established leadership of the day had neglected, the poor and oppressed people of Palestine. He gathered disciples, for the most part, from this group and instructed them to focus their ministry on their peasant peers. Among the disciples and among those whom he called into the movement from other groups, including tax collectors like Levi and Zacchaeus, some prosperous individuals may have taken part. However, even these tended to be outside the mainstream of Israel's elite socioeconomic groups and established leadership. Yet, for inclusion in the Jesus movement, one of the qualities leaders had to exhibit was concern for and action on behalf of the fundamental target audience for Jesus' ministry–the poor and oppressed. Finally, this message of attention to the poor does not get lost in the tradition by the time the evangelists compose their gospels. For Jesus and for the synoptic gospel communities, the poor constituted the main target audience of their ministry and leadership.

Conclusion

In this chapter, I have discussed the insiders of the Jesus movement—disciples and the poor—sources for leadership, and target of the ministry. Jesus, like John the Baptist before him, surrounded himself with disciples. They, alongside him and after his departure, would carry on a ministry similar to that of John: to challenge the established leaders of the day to a more attentive and inclusive ministry to the poor and oppressed of Palestine. Jesus chose disciples who, despite their humble backgrounds and significant flaws, would eventually best serve the target audience of Jesus' ministry, especially since for the most part they were from the same constituencies they would serve. The poor had no one else who would advocate for them, who would heal them in their time of dire need, given the neglect of those with official power to do more—the elite of Jerusalem.

In the chapter that follows, I will focus my attention precisely on these powerful leaders, many of whom the gospels record as the opponents of the Jesus movement. Whether Roman or Jew, the established leaders of the community failed their constituency and, therefore, garnered the attention of Jesus' message and activity, including his final activity in Jerusalem, the city from which the elite leadership of Palestine exercised their power over the entire land. Jesus' final confrontation with them constitutes the ultimate example of the sacrificial nature of his leadership.

3

Leadership in the Synoptic Tradition

Failure of Established Leaders

The Opponents to Jesus' Ministry

The established leaders of the Roman Empire and their colluders in Palestine became the direct opponents of Jesus during his lifetime. They had failed to respond to the needs of the poor in the countryside, who were the primary target audience of Jesus' ministry. We can see this in a variety of examples, from the beginning to the end of Jesus' ministry—from Galilee right up until his final ministry in Jerusalem and the temple, including the gospel passion narratives that describe his death. Indeed, the final confrontation between Jesus and his opponents in Jerusalem involved both Jew (the temple elite) and Gentile (the Roman overseers). This conflict precipitates Jesus' arrest, trial, and execution and thus exemplifies the ultimate sacrifice of leadership.

In the previous chapter I noted how the ministry of John the Baptist included a major word of protest against the established leadership of Galilee and Judea, including the priestly aristocracy in Jerusalem. Jesus followed in John's footsteps and also confronted the established leaders of the day.

Both John and Jesus did so out of a conviction that the leaders, both Roman and Jewish, had failed the oppressed masses of Israel's countryside.

Early in the Gospels

In the early parts of the synoptic gospels, confrontations with opponents abound. In Mark's gospel, consistent with its urgent tone, opponents challenge Jesus almost immediately. The crowds sense this opposition when they ascribe to Jesus and his teaching greater "authority" (*exousia*) than that of "the scribes" (Mk. 1:22). When faithful friends bring a paralytic to Jesus, not only does Jesus heal him; but he also forgives his sin, a blasphemous action in the eyes of the scribes (2:1–12). In the next pericope, these same "scribes of the Pharisees" (2:16) question how Jesus could have table fellowship with "tax-collectors and sinners" (2:13–17). Jesus replies, "I have come to call not the righteous but sinners" (2:17). Thus he implies that his opponents represent "the righteous," but the reader must conclude these established leaders are "righteous" only in their own eyes. In that way, they exclude themselves from the reach of the inclusive ministry of Jesus, a ministry offered to all who recognize their own sinfulness.

According to Mark, Jesus and the disciples continue to engender controversy with Israel's established leadership over such matters as fasting (2:18–22) and Sabbath observance (2:23–28). In each case, Jesus challenges the "conventional wisdom" of the religious powers of the day with new twists on old expectations: "No one puts new wine into old wineskins" (2:22), and "The sabbath was made for humankind, and not humankind for the sabbath" (2:27).[1] Jesus' insistence on performing acts of mercy on the Sabbath subverts the perverted interpretations of Sabbath observance. "Is it lawful to do good or to do harm on the Sabbath, to save life or to kill?" (Mk. 3:4). The deafening silence of his opponents both angers and grieves Jesus, "because of their hardness of heart" (3:5). When Jesus heals a man with a withered hand on the Sabbath, both religious and political leadership collude to bring Jesus down: "The Pharisees went out and immediately conspired with the Herodians against him, how to destroy him" (3:6).

Thus the gospels record early encounters of Jesus with those who would later conspire to put him to death. Among political powers, Jesus came to have the same reputation as John the Baptist, who had been beheaded for challenging Herod and his marriage practices (Mk. 6:14–29). To religious leaders, Jesus minced no words when he declared them "hypocrites" for worrying about whether the disciples washed their hands or not before table fellowship, citing "the tradition of the elders." Instead, Jesus cites the prophetic tradition of Isaiah to show the truncated and convenient interpretations of Jewish law by its current adherents: "You abandon the commandment of God and hold to human tradition" (Mk. 7:1–13). The crowds and his disciples hear Jesus say that it is what comes from within that can defile a person (7:14–23).

Early Confrontations in Matthew

Matthew's gospel includes most of Mark's early confrontation stories, but also follows Q in describing John's strong words against established leaders:

> But when he saw many Pharisees and Sadducees coming for baptism, he said to them, "You brood of vipers! Who warned you to flee from the wrath to come? Bear fruit worthy of repentance. Do not presume to say to yourselves, 'We have Abraham as our ancestor'; for I tell you, God is able from these stones to raise up children to Abraham. Even now the ax is lying at the root of the trees; every tree therefore that does not bear good fruit is cut down and thrown into the fire." (Mt. 3:7–10)

Matthew's indictment against Israel's established leadership is heightened by the fact that, by comparison, in Luke's redaction of Q the "Pharisees and Sadducees" become "the crowds" in this passage (Lk. 3:7–9). Moreover, Matthew follows this pattern throughout his gospel with several strong passages of rebuke against "Pharisees and Sadducees," especially toward the end of the gospel, as we shall see below.

The Sermon on the Mount

Matthew's teaching material demonstrates how Jesus challenged powerful forces in his day. Matthew contrasts the *dikaiosune* ("righteousness," "justice") expected of disciples with that practiced by existing leadership in the community: "For I tell you, unless your righteousness exceeds that of the scribes and Pharisees, you will never enter the kingdom of heaven" (Mt. 5:20). The justice to be practiced by legitimate leaders of the people had not been exercised by "the scribes and Pharisees." Matthew illustrates this in several ways in the Sermon on the Mount. First, the beatitudes present the merciful, the pure in heart, and the persecuted peacemakers–those who give attention to the poor, the grieving, the meek, and the hungry– and contrast them with those who persecute and falsely accuse them (Mt. 5:3–11). Merciful peacemakers are like the persecuted prophets of old (5:12). Indeed, they are like "the salt of the earth" and "light of the world" (5:13, 14).

In contrast, established leaders minimize the true meaning of the law, emphasizing only its extremes, i.e., murder, adultery, bearing false witness, and demanding an eye for an eye. According to Jesus, they forget the "spirit" of the law–reconciliation, faithfulness, integrity, nonretaliation, and love– even for one's enemies (Mt. 5:21–47). Established leaders have also failed to practice authentic piety. Piety in such spiritual exercises as almsgiving, prayer, and fasting should be private, not public, affairs. The authentically pious should not "trumpet" their almsgiving, not pray only by standing in "synagogues and street corners" with "many words" (6:1–8), and not fast with obviously "dismal" faces (6:16–18). The contrast between public and private sacred spaces suggests distinctions between those with more access to the public opportunities in temple, synagogues, and street corners, and those who must limit their practice of piety to their own, private spaces at home. According to Matthew's Jesus, established religious leaders relished these public opportunities to the detriment of their less powerful fellow countrymen and women, including the followers of Jesus. For Matthew, the less powerful group now included his own community, who perhaps had to stay at home to practice their piety, or do so in secret because of opposition. Matthew thus describes the opposition Jesus and his followers faced in his day in terms parallel to Matthew's own community.

Besides a penchant for publicly displayed piety, established leaders also offer harsh judgments for those they disagree with or find wanting in some shape or form:

> "Do not judge, so that you may not be judged. For the judgment you make you will be judged, and the measure you give will be the measure you get. Why do you see the speck in the neighbor's eye, but do not notice the log in your own eye? Or how can you say to your neighbor, 'Let me take the speck out of your eye,' while the log is in your own eye? You hypocrite, first take the log out of your own eye, and then you will see clearly to take the speck out of your neighbor's eye." (Mt. 7:1–5)

Apparently, opponents to Matthew's community "judged" them as outsiders to "mainline religion."[2] Invoking the memory of Jesus' own confrontation with opponents of his ministry, Matthew employs the harsh language of hypocrisy to challenge the religious leaders of his day, like Jesus did in his. In Jesus' day, "logs" in the eyes of temple leadership and the Roman military presence kept both groups from seeing their failure as leaders because they neglected the needs of the peasant masses in Palestine.

Thus Matthew calls for his readers to render their own judgments carefully about the authenticity of their leaders: "Beware of false prophets, who come to you in sheep's clothing but inwardly are ravenous wolves. You will know them by their fruits" (Mt. 7:15–16a). Eventually, authentically "good fruit" and "bad fruit" will be laid bare. "Not everyone who says to me, 'Lord, Lord,' will enter the kingdom of heaven, but only the one who does the will of my Father in heaven" (Mt. 7:21). For both Jesus and Matthew, established leaders were not producing good fruit on behalf of their followers, and they could expect eschatological judgment for themselves:

> "On that day they will say to me, 'Lord, Lord, did we not prophesy in your name, and cast out demons in your name, and do many deeds of power in your name?' Then, I will declare to them, 'I never knew you; go away from me, you evildoers.'" (7:22–23)

Therefore, leaders who refuse to employ their calling and their skills with honesty and integrity, especially on behalf of the outcasts of society, will be cast away from God's presence as "evildoers." Jesus thus ends his "Sermon on the Mount" in Matthew with a final word of warning. One must be not only a "hearer" of the word, but a "doer" as well (7:24–27), if one is to be a true "wise one." Such a challenge to the conventionally "wise" in Jesus' audience, as well as to Matthew's readers, must have presented a stern warning to those with political and religious power.

Healings and Warnings

The story of the Roman centurion represents an indictment by Jesus of Israel's established leadership. The centurion not only shows mercy by asking for the healing of his servant, but also understands the nature of Jesus' leadership and ministry:

> The centurion answered, "Lord, I am not worthy to have you come under my roof; but only speak the word, and my servant will be healed. For I also am a man under authority, with soldiers under me; and I say to one, 'Go,' and he goes, and to another, 'Come' and he comes, and to my slave, 'Do this,' and the slave does it." When Jesus heard him, he was amazed and said to those who followed him, "Truly I tell you, in no one in Israel have I found such faith." (Mt. 8:8–10)

Even a Roman centurion (at least one) understood the nature of leadership as taking care of the weaker ones among us. According to Matthew, Jesus had found no such understanding among the traditional leaders of Israel. More likely, Matthew's community confronted established religious leaders rejecting their movement and the type of leadership it offered.

For example, a scribe wished to follow Jesus, but Jesus doubted this established leader's commitment: "Foxes have holes, and birds of the air have nests; but the Son of Man has nowhere to lay his head" (8:20). The question before this "scribe"–could he live the sacrificial, itinerant life that Jesus and his most loyal followers from the countryside lived? Even those who already could be called disciples had to reorient their priorities if they wished to truly follow Jesus: "Another of his disciples said to him, 'Lord, first let me go and bury my father.' But Jesus said to him, 'Follow me, and let the dead bury their own dead'" (8:21–22). Both the scribe and the disciple needed to understand the harsh realities of gospel leadership and ministry. Matthew's community had the same need. Even when Jesus did a good thing, like heal a "demoniac who was mute," his opponents ranted, "By the ruler of the demons he casts out the demons" (9:32–34). Of course, part of the problem for his opponents was that Jesus elicited such exorbitant praise from those who benefited the most from such healing activity: "[T]he crowds were amazed [when the mute spoke] and said, 'Never has anything like this been seen in Israel'" (9:33b). Such praise represented a direct challenge to the established leaders of Israel, who should have been attending to such needy people long ago. No wonder they cried out in protest and attributed demon possession to Jesus even as he cast out demons.

Disciples and Opposition

Because of the opposition they would face, disciples were commissioned knowing that they must be "wise as serpents and innocent as doves." After all, they would be going out "like sheep into the midst of wolves" (Mt. 10:16). Thus Jesus warns his disciples on dealing with opposition:

"Beware of them, for they will hand you over to councils and flog you in their synagogues; and you will be dragged before governors and kings because of me, as a testimony to them and to the Gentiles." (Mt. 10:17–18)

Followers of Jesus, including those in Matthew's communities, must rely on the Holy Spirit to endure persecution from their opponents:

"When they hand you over, do not worry about how you are to speak or what you are to say; for what you are to say will be given to you at that time; for it is not you who speak, but the Spirit of your Father speaking through you." (10:19–20)

As in Mark, Matthew depicts how Sabbath controversies with opponents followed Jesus and the disciples everywhere they ministered, including early in the movement's history. When the disciples plucked grain to satisfy their hunger on a sabbath day, established leaders accused Jesus of being unlawful (Mt. 12:1–2). Jesus cited several examples to show the complete lawfulness of his Sabbath actions, including one unique to Matthew: "Or have you not read in the law that on the sabbath the priests in the temple break the sabbath and yet are guiltless?" (12:5). Thus Jesus directly challenged the elite temple leadership: "I tell you, something greater than the temple is here. But if you had known what this means, 'I desire mercy and not sacrifice,' you would not have condemned the guiltless. For the Son of Man is lord of the sabbath" (12:6–8). To demonstrate this new kind of authority, Jesus healed a man with a withered hand in the synagogue on the Sabbath (12:9–10, 13). He reminded his audience that many of them would save a sheep if it fell into a pit on the Sabbath. Therefore, Jesus declared, "How much more valuable is a human being than a sheep!" (Mt. 12:12a). Nonetheless, such humane attention to the neediest populations of Israel only served to seal the fate of Jesus, even early on in his career: "But the Pharisees went out and conspired against him, how to destroy him" (Mt. 12:14). All three synoptic gospels describe this early plot against Jesus (cf. Mk. 3:6; Lk. 6:11).

Luke and the Early Opposition to the Leadership of Jesus

Luke mutes some of the stronger warnings and early condemnations of the opponents of Jesus, but nonetheless subtly includes references to that opposition. For example, Mary's Song has the following words:

> "[God] has shown strength with his arm;
> > he has scattered the proud in the thoughts of their hearts.
> He has brought down the powerful from their thrones,
> > and lifted up the lowly;
> he has filled the hungry with good things,
> and sent the rich away empty." (Lk 1:51–53)

Such a description of the downfall of the mighty from a humble peasant girl at the outset of his gospel forewarns Luke's readers that the powerful and the elite of Jesus' time will not be the heroes of this story. Indeed, while emperors and governors issue decrees that move Nazarenes to Bethlehem, even if they are pregnant at such an inopportune time,[3] simple shepherds still celebrate the birth of "a Savior" (Lk. 2:1–20). Moreover, already at the outset the baby Jesus and the child Jesus invade the temple, in a sense, to declare it his own (2:21–52). The adult Jesus will return there toward the end of his life to reclaim it from those "who were selling things" and from "the leaders of the people" (19:45–48).

In addition, Luke includes this special teaching from John the Baptist about money, possessions, and justice, given to the people and their leaders:

> And the crowds asked him, "What then should we do?" In reply he said to them, "Whoever has two coats must share with anyone who has none; and whoever has food must do likewise." Even tax collectors came to be baptized, and they asked him, "Teacher, what should we do?" He said to them, "Collect no more than the amount prescribed for you." Soldiers also asked him, "And we, what should we do?" He said to them, "Do not extort money from anyone by threats or false accusation, and be satisfied with your wages." (3:10–14)

The actions of unjust leaders and soldiers precipitate such calls for justice.

Similarly, Jesus, as we saw earlier, identifies himself as a leader dedicated to justice for the poor and oppressed in his first public message according to Luke:

> "The Spirit of the Lord is upon me,
> > because he has anointed me
> > > to bring good news to the poor.
> He has sent me to proclaim release to the captives
> > and recovery of sight to the blind,
> > > to let the oppressed go free,
> to proclaim the year of the Lord's favor." (4:18–19)

On behalf of the poor, Jesus confronts the established leaders of his nation, for example, by "eat[ing] and drink[ing] with tax collectors and sinners" (Lk. 5:30) and also including them among his disciples. He also heals the needy on Sabbaths (6:1–11) and blesses them even though they are poor, "for yours is the kingdom of God" (6:20). Moreover, as in Matthew, blessings to the poor mean woes to the rich:

"But woe to you who are rich,
   for you have received your consolation.
Woe to you who are full now,
   for you will be hungry.
Woe to you who are laughing now,
   for you will mourn and weep.
Woe to you when all speak well of you, for that is what their
      ancestors did to the false prophets." (Lk 6:24–26)

Thus Jesus equates the current leadership of Israel with the "false prophets" of old. Both groups of leaders failed to distinguish between when to show mercy and when to abide by such matters as Sabbath laws. Usually in Jesus' time, those who obeyed these ritual rules to the letter of the law were the rich, the full or satisfied, and those who could laugh because life was good for them. Most such leaders could care less for the abject condition of the poor, those who hungered and those who mourned, as long as the rules were strictly heeded. Like John the Baptist, Jesus rejects this brand of leadership, even as proponents of the latter rejected John and now reject Jesus (7:30–34). Nonetheless, ultimately, "wisdom is vindicated by all her children" (7:35).

Luke turns to the story of "a woman of the city" (Lk. 7:36–37, RSV) as an example of how authentic wisdom, and therefore, genuine leadership, "is vindicated by all her [true] children," regardless of their status in society. This woman perfumes the feet of Jesus in the home of a presumably well-to-do Pharisee, a religious leader of the community. The host complains about this perfuming (7:39). In fact, however, as the host and a leader in the community, he had failed to show proper hospitality to Jesus by perfuming his dusty feet (7:44–46). It took a so-called, lowly "woman of the city" to lead the way in proper treatment of guests, even if the guest was a mere carpenter and traveling preacher. The community's established leaders had been short-sighted in forgiving this woman, who no doubt saw in Jesus one who could recognize her for who she was, just as much a child of God as the "Pharisees." Therefore, she too was worthy of forgiveness, which Jesus, in radical departure from what mere carpenters and traveling preachers should do, offered her (7:47–50).

Such just action on behalf of all peoples, women and men, engendered much support for Jesus and his ministry, including from many women who became leaders and supporters of his movement (Lk. 8:1–3). However, such action also further cemented the anger of the opposition toward Jesus, as noted in the reaction of the established leaders to his treatment of the "woman of the city": "Who is this who even forgives sins?" (Lk. 7:49b). Given the identity of Jesus as a mere carpenter and itinerant preacher, they cannot believe the authority he has taken for himself.

Thus in perhaps more subtle, but nonetheless concrete, ways in Jesus' early ministry, Luke demonstrates the confrontation of Jesus with his opponents, the established leaders of the community. All the gospels indicate that such confrontation was a fundamental reality Jesus faced from the first days of his ministry. The opposition only intensified when Jesus announced his intention to turn his mission toward the seat of power in Israel–Jerusalem.

Turn toward Jerusalem

All three synoptic gospels record a critical juncture in the ministry of Jesus when he announces a turn toward Jerusalem for one final journey (or the only journey as pictured in Mark and Matthew; Luke, of course, includes childhood visits to the temple in Jerusalem). In this journey, he will confront his opponents directly on their own turf, the center of power in Jerusalem, including the temple. By means of several pericopes along the way, the gospels depict how and why Jesus will face those opposed to his leadership agenda on behalf of the poor.

PREDICTIONS

In all three synoptics, the turn toward Jerusalem begins with a "passion prediction."[4] Peter has just confessed that Jesus must be understood as Israel's long-awaited Messiah (Mk. 8:29; Mt. 16:16; Lk. 9:20). Matthew includes a note of celebration for Peter's affirmation. Mark and Luke, however, turn immediately to Jesus' stern warning for the disciples not to tell anyone about this messianic identity. Why? The answer lies in a passion prediction that describes the messiahship of Jesus as a sacrificial one:

> From that time on, Jesus began to show his disciples that he must go to Jerusalem and undergo great suffering at the hands of the elders and chief priests and scribes, and be killed, and on the third day be raised. (Mt. 16:21; cf. Mk. 8:31; Lk. 16:22)

The confrontation with opposing leaders will be deadly. Such predictions of suffering and death bring a turning point in Jesus' relationship with his disciples and in his ministry. The various confrontations with local leadership described heretofore will culminate in an ultimate, fatal encounter in Jerusalem with the absolute leaders of the whole country. The second and third "passion predictions" reiterate some of these details. The third prediction in particular expands on the conspiracy of leaders that it will take to kill Jesus, as Mark and Matthew describe the collusion of Jerusalem's temple elite: "the Son of Man will be handed over to the chief priests and scribes, and they will condemn him to death" (Mt. 20:18b; cf. Mk. 10:33b). Luke focuses on the Roman involvement:

> "For he will be handed over to the Gentiles; and he will be mocked and insulted and spat upon. After they have flogged him, they will kill him, and on the third day he will rise again." (Lk. 18:32–33; cf. Mk. 10:33c–34; Mt 20:19)[5]

Thus, Jesus must go to Jerusalem and confront the entrenched leadership of the nation with his message of hope for the oppressed masses from the countryside, even though he will pay for such an act of sacrificial leadership with his death. However, his disciples consistently fail to understand this courageous act of leadership:

> The portrait of Jesus in the predictions is a witness to one unafraid to die, who knows the political and religious forces aligned against him, yet who resolutely pressed forward to the end. Mark draws the unforgettable picture of Jesus courageously walking ahead of his disciples as they journey to Jerusalem, while the disciples follow in fear and amazement [in Mark 10:32].[6]

Regardless of the actual historicity of these predictions in the form we have them in the gospels, this is how the gospel writers depicted for their readers that the leadership of Jesus must be understood, that is, in terms of service and sacrifice. As the journey unfolds, these aspects of leadership become more and more evident, until they are fully developed in the very scenes of the passion narratives toward the end of each gospel.

THE JOURNEY UNFOLDS

In addition to the predictions, each writer adds his own unique stamp to how the "journey to Jerusalem" unfolded, in particular with regard to Jesus' ongoing confrontation with his opponents in preparation for the final confrontation. Mark precedes the first passion prediction with a story about a blind man, whom Jesus heals gradually with saliva (Mk. 8:22–26). Symbolically, therefore, while the disciples testify to the messianic identity of Jesus, they fail to see a messiah that must die challenging the Jerusalem powers. Those powers themselves are completely blind to the possibilities of Jesus' leadership focused in particular on behalf of men and women like the healed blind man, that is, the neediest people of the community.

MATTHEW

Matthew incorporates just a few unique features in his depiction of this "journey to Jerusalem." After the second passion prediction, only Matthew records a question about Jesus and the temple tax. Matthew has already highlighted the emerging leadership of Peter. Jesus affirmed Peter as "the rock" for confessing the messianic identity of Jesus (Mt. 16:17–19). Thus, "the collectors of the temple tax" in this story come to Peter with the question: "Does your teacher not pay the temple tax?" (17:24). Peter immediately asserts, "Yes, he does." However, later Jesus asks Peter, "What do you think, Simon? From whom do kings of the earth take toll or tribute? From their children or from others?" (17:25). Peter replied that it was "From others," and thus Jesus affirmed, "Then the children are free" (17:26).

Now if the story ended here, this would be a rather radical approach to the overly burdensome taxation in first-century Palestine. Although this tax to support the temple had been generally popular in Palestine, coupled with a "double" taxation system on the temple as well as taxes to support the Roman forces, it was simply too much burden for the poorer constituents of the country.[7] Jesus and the gospel writers granted a role to appropriate taxation, but from the posture of freedom for all, not oppression of the masses in particular. Jesus gives Peter instructions for paying the tax, "so that we do not give offense to them." Peter was to "go to the sea and cast a hook; take the first fish that comes up; and when you open its mouth, you will find a coin; take that and give it to them for you and me" (17:27).

However, while Jesus expects his disciples to fulfill their obligations to the leaders of the state, he also expects the latter to exercise their leadership justly, respecting the "freedom" of their charges without oppressing them.

Freedom is the fundamental word: Jesus is free with respect to the temple tax and free with respect to subordination toward earthly rulers. Yet, at the same time, Jesus demonstrates free submission to the powers that be and their limited claim on humanity and the people of God.[8]

Thus Matthew depicts Jesus with a nuanced approach to the tax burden in Israel. Jesus focused attention away from collection to justice. Moreover, this story during "the journey to Jerusalem" prepares the ground for a similar but more intense confrontation directly with the taxing powers in both the temple and with the occupying forces in Jerusalem. For Matthew, the issue of taxation was a major point of contention in the relationship of Jesus to the established leaders of Jerusalem.

LUKE AND OPPOSITION ON THE ROAD TO JERUSALEM

Luke incorporates even more about the opponents of Jesus during the final journey to Jerusalem. A dozen or so pericopes or incidents in "Luke's special section" depict Jesus' confrontation with opponents of his ministry. Luke begins the section with an explicit statement that Jesus has "set his face to go to Jerusalem" (Lk. 9:51). Such determination caused an unwelcome reception among Samaritan villagers, accustomed as they were to bad treatment from Jerusalem (Lk. 9:52–56). Nonetheless, when a lawyer (in Greek, a *nomikos*, an interpreter of the law) seeking to "test" Jesus and "justify" himself, asked Jesus about inheriting eternal life and loving one's neighbor (10:25–29), Jesus tells a story in which he depicts a Samaritan as a hero. Two religious leaders of the community, a priest and a Levite, fail to help the victim of a robbery on the outskirts of Jerusalem. A Samaritan, like one of those who would not offer hospitality to a Jewish teacher like Jesus because of his determination to go to Jerusalem, nonetheless stops to help this needy individual (10:30–35). Thus Jesus teaches that the ultimate goal for political (lawyers) and religious (priests and Levites) leaders should be to show "mercy" (10:36–37). With the simple piety of the small-town girl Mary who sits at the feet of Jesus to learn–the pericope that follows the story of the good Samaritan (10:38–42)–Luke provides another marked contrast to the public arrogance of the "lawyer."

In this context of tests by opponents of Jesus and piety by his friends, Luke places the Beelzebul controversy from the triple tradition. Although Luke has "some" from among the "crowds" that question the legitimate source of Jesus' healings and exorcisms (Lk. 11:14–15), the tradition names established leaders, including "Pharisees" (Mt. 12:24) and "scribes" from Jerusalem (Mk. 3:22). They ascribe Jesus' power to "Beelzebul, the ruler of the demons" (Lk. 11:15b). In acknowledging another "test" from his opponents, Jesus counters with a proverbial saying: "Every kingdom divided against itself becomes a desert, and house falls on house" (11:17). Therefore, if Satan exorcises his own demons, he works against himself (11:18). By working with God, Jesus ushers in the kingdom of God (11:20). Then Luke takes the tradition one step further by identifying Jesus in this context with a "stronger man" who overtakes an existing but flawed authority:

> "When a strong man, fully armed, guards his castle, his property
> is safe. But when one stronger than he attacks him and overpowers
> him, he takes away his armor in which he trusted and divides his
> plunder. Whoever is not with me is against me, and whoever does
> not gather with me scatters." (11:22–23)

On the road to Jerusalem, according to Luke, Jesus used strong words like these against those who belittled his ministry of healing and attention to the most oppressed among them. He challenged his opponents to join him and to "gather," not "scatter." Yet, the opposition intensified the closer Jesus got to Jerusalem, and so did his words against opposing leaders. When he dined with a Pharisee who chastised him for not washing beforehand (11:37–38), Jesus lambasted all such leaders who pay more attention to external matters rather than practicing justice and authentic piety:

> "But woe to you Pharisees! For you tithe mint and rue and herbs of
> all kinds, and neglect justice and the love of God; it is these you
> ought to have practiced, without neglecting the others. Woe to you
> Pharisees! For you love to have the seat of honor in the synagogues
> and to be greeted with respect in the marketplaces." (Lk. 11:42–43)

Some established leaders might have asked, "What is leadership if not for honor?" For Jesus, it is much more than that. It is a matter of justice for the neglected. No one, not Pharisees, not "lawyers" who "load people with burdens" without lifting "a finger to ease them" (11:46), can escape the righteous anger of Jesus on this point–the need to practice justice to the neglected. Nonetheless, such strong indictments by Jesus on the road to Jerusalem resulted in stronger opposition and challenge:

> When he went outside, the scribes and the Pharisees began to be very hostile toward him and to cross-examine him about many things, lying in wait for him, to catch him in something he might say. (11:53–54)

Thus, while Jesus wins over the crowds, he also warns his disciples specifically about the false leadership they will face in their own ministries: "Beware of the yeast of the Pharisees, that is, their hypocrisy" (12:1).

However, Jesus also exhorts his followers not to be afraid of these leaders. "When they bring you before the synagogues, the rulers, and the authorities, do not worry about how you are to defend yourselves or what you are to say; for the Holy Spirit will teach you at that very hour what you ought to say" (12:11–12). Disciples need to be ready and watchful leaders (12:35–40), not like the rich fool who stored up his possessions, and ate and drank his days away, without concern to be "rich toward God" (Lk. 12:13–21). In contrast, disciples need not be anxious about earthly possessions, but sell them if necessary to "give alms" and store up "an unfailing treasure in heaven" (12:33). Thus "to whom much has been given, much will be required; and from the one to whom much has been entrusted, even more will be demanded" (12:48). The rich fool, and Jerusalem's leaders, failed to understand the serious responsibilities of leadership; disciples should not.

No Peace in Confronting Leaders

Because of the increasingly difficult breach between Jesus and his opponents, Luke declares that Jesus cannot be counted on to bring peace to his world, but rather division (Lk. 12:49–56). Those in power continually misinterpreted the work of Jesus, a point Jesus makes perfectly clear to them in the strongest possible terms: "You hypocrites! You know how to interpret the appearance of earth and sky, but why do you not know how to interpret the present time? And why do you not judge for yourselves what is right?" (12:56–57). Moreover, the Lukan Jesus in particular challenges *both* Roman and Jewish leaders. In this context (Lk. 13:1–9), only Luke makes reference to the historical event in which Pilate ordered the massacre of Galilean pilgrims in the temple district (13:1), and thus alerts the reader to Pilate's involvement in the crucifixion of Jesus later in the passion narrative. Although Jesus uses the story for a call to repentance, by including it Luke gives "no positive portrait…of Roman rule or their puppet representatives."[9]

In Luke's next pericope, Jesus indicts a Jewish leader. After Jesus heals a crippled woman on the Sabbath, the leader of the synagogue (*archisunagōgos*, "synagogue ruler"), was "indignant" (13:10–14). Jesus is equally indignant:

> "You hypocrites! Does not each of you on the sabbath untie his ox or his donkey from the manger, and lead it away to give it water? And ought not this woman, a daughter of Abraham whom Satan bound for eighteen long years, be set free from this bondage on the sabbath day?" (13:15–16)

Jesus' righteous indignation further cements the divisions his words and actions cause on the road to Jerusalem: "All his opponents were put to shame; and the entire crowd was rejoicing at the wonderful things he was doing" (13:17). Thus Jesus asserts a pattern of reversal: "Some are last who will be first, and some are first who will be last" (13:30). In Jerusalem, Jesus will show the way for "the last" to be considered first, even though it will cost him his life at the hands of those who are "first" now.

Another prelude to what awaits Jesus in Jerusalem according to Luke has the Pharisees warning Jesus to flee because Herod will kill him (Lk. 13:31). Yet, the Lucan Jesus refuses to back down:

> "Go and tell that fox for me, 'Listen, I am casting out demons and performing cures today and tomorrow, and on the third day I finish my work. Yet today, tomorrow, and the next day I must be on my way, because it is impossible for a prophet to be killed outside of Jerusalem.'" (13:32–33)

So Jesus laments for Jerusalem, the seat of power, because it kills its righteous prophets (13:34) and because its leaders fail to serve its most needy people. Jesus acts on behalf of these needy ones, whether on a Sabbath or not. In this way, he will silence the voices of protest:

> On one occasion when Jesus was going to the house of a leader of the Pharisees to eat a meal on the sabbath, they were watching him closely. Just then, in front of him, there was a man who had dropsy. And Jesus asked the lawyers and Pharisees, "Is it lawful to cure people on the sabbath, or not?" But they were silent. So Jesus took him and healed him, and sent him away. Then he said to them, "If one of you has a child or an ox that has fallen into a well, will you not immediately pull it out on a sabbath day?" And they could not reply to this. (14:1–6)

This dinner party among the elite provided an opportunity for Jesus to teach about the need for humility in leadership. He recommends that people not seek the most honored seats in the house, because "someone more distinguished" might displace them (14:8–9). Rather, guests should start from a "lowly" seat and then perhaps will be invited to move up and be honored in that way (14:10). Jesus summarized this important lesson in leadership with the aphorism: "For all who exalt themselves will be humbled, and those who humble themselves will be exalted" (14:11). Jesus gives further advice to his dinner hosts, the elite leadership of the people. They should not just invite to dinner people from their own socioeconomic level, especially because the latter can easily return the favor by inviting them over to their houses for dinner. Rather, "invite the poor, the crippled, the lame, and the blind," precisely those who "cannot repay you" (14:12–14). Jesus implies that although it is easier to be a leader among one's own kind, such is not the mark of a true, gospel leader.

The Cost of Discipleship and the Marks of Leadership

In the pericopes and parables that follow, Luke presents other marks of gospel leadership as taught by Jesus on the road to Jerusalem. Jesus expounds on the costs and sacrifices needed for true discipleship (Lk. 14:25–35) and presents three parables about lost things that are found by a persistent shepherd, a careful woman, and a forgiving father (Lk. 15:1–32). These three represent great examples of faithful people who exercised good leadership qualities by not refusing to give up on lost causes.

The last two parables of the special Lukan section summarize Luke's teachings about Jesus, his opposition, and his expectations for leadership. First, Luke offers the parable of the widow and the unjust judge (18:1–8). While the gospel writer signals that the story is about the "need to pray always and not to lose heart"(18:1), it proves to be more than that. A lowly widow cries out for justice to a man in a position of power. The judge "neither feared God nor had respect for people" (18:2b), but because of the woman's persistence he finally, though grudgingly, grants her justice (18:5). This is precisely the problem Jesus and his followers confront with their opponents, the religious and political leaders of the day. The people cry out for justice. Will their leaders grant it to them? "When the Son of Man comes, will he find faith on earth?" (18:6–8).

Second, the unique Lukan material concludes with the parable of the Pharisee and the tax collector. The story of two men praying in the temple exemplifies the problems Jesus finds on the road to Jerusalem. The elite leader, represented in the person of a Pharisee in Luke's redaction, prays with confidence that he is not a thief, a rogue, an adulterer, or the tax collector praying next to him (18:11). All the tax collector does is ask for mercy (18:13). Yet the latter is the one who goes home "justified" (*dedikaiōmenos*), declared righteous by God. On the road to Jerusalem, Jesus has wanted to teach his audiences, especially his disciples and followers, those who will be future leaders of the movement he has founded, that "all who exalt themselves will be humbled, but all who humble themselves will be exalted" (18:14b). Jesus has promulgated a reversal of values and opportunities for leadership.

In short, the stories from Mark, Matthew, and Q, and especially those from this special Lukan section, have shown us that Jesus' opponents, the elite leaders of the nation, especially those entrenched in Jerusalem, have failed. They have not humbled themselves enough to serve the poor and the needy in whatever ways necessary. They have refused to heed the call of first John the Baptist, and now Jesus of Nazareth, to exercise true, just leadership on behalf of their people. When Jesus finally arrives in Jerusalem with this leadership agenda and challenge, the opposition, both Roman and Jewish political and religious leadership, become even stronger, fiercer, and deadlier.

Jesus in Jerusalem

PRELUDE

The events immediately preceding Jesus' final arrival in Jerusalem effectively set the stage for the dramatic events that follow. In the triple tradition, Jesus heals a blind man from Jericho, a town on the outskirts of Jerusalem. Though blind, only he truly understands the mission of Jesus as he shouts to Jesus for mercy while others shout him down (Mk. 10:31–32; Mt. 20:48; Lk. 18:39). In addition, the story of Zacchaeus, also set in Jericho but included only by Luke, shows how even a "chief tax collector" can have a transforming encounter with Jesus, such that he desires to give ill-gained funds back to the poor (Lk. 19:1–10). Finally, Luke includes the parable of the pounds from the Q tradition in this context, with its object lesson that disciples must not squander the opportunities given to them to be productive leaders (Lk. 19:11–27; cf. Mt. 25:14–30). Luke offers a reason for this parable about a nobleman who gives his slaves ten pounds to invest while he is gone: "because [Jesus] was near Jerusalem, and because they supposed that the kingdom of God was to appear immediately" (19:11). The disciples needed realistic expectations and long-term commitments for what was to come.

With these stories, the gospel traditions set the stage for the details of Jesus' final ministry in Jerusalem and the passion narratives of his death. Both established leaders of Jerusalem *and* long-time followers of Jesus will be blind as the events of the passion unfold. Yet unexpected figures, like a blind man and a tax collector, understand. Disciples in particular needed to realize that this mission is for the long haul. Jerusalem will not bring quick fixes, but just the beginning, albeit a very tragic beginning, to a lifetime of service and sacrifice in gospel leadership for the kingdom of God.

ENTRY AND CLEANSING

The Jerusalem narratives begin with a triumphant entry (Mk. 11:1–10 and pars.) and a temple cleansing (Mk. 11:11 and pars.). There is remarkable coherence in the triple tradition as the story of the passion unfolds, with only a few features unique to Matthew, Luke, or Q. Matthew and Luke follow the Markan pattern fairly closely at this point, with a few exceptions.

The entry represents a provocative action on the part of Jesus, as he enters Jerusalem triumphantly like a conquering king, with the shouts of acclamation by the people welcoming him. Yet at the same time, by entering on a donkey Jesus signals the humility of his kingship, over prevailing notions of royalty and empire in his time. "Here authority and kingship are interpreted in terms of lowliness, service and peacemaking."[10] Moreover, such a humble, though provocative entry, sharply contrasts with the ultimate welcome he will be given in Jerusalem a short time later—arrest and execution. The protests of the "Pharisees" to the adulation Jesus receives, recorded only in Luke, presage this result, especially when, according to Luke, Jesus uses the occasion to predict the fall of Jerusalem (Lk. 19:39–44). Such words against Jerusalem and its leaders in the context of such a provocative act of entry must have further incensed the opponents of Jesus against him and in favor of a plot against his life.

The cleansing of the temple is the second major act Jesus undertakes upon his arrival in Jerusalem. More than any other act, it precipitates his ultimate arrest. In Mark, the cleansing waits for another day, but Matthew and Luke put it as an immediate action. Jesus overturns tables and drives out money changers and sellers of animals, both important activities for temple worship and sacrifices. However, for Jesus, the temple has become "a den of robbers," meaning not just petty thievery, but "violent corruption."[11] The misuse of the temple sacrificial system for the economic benefit of entrenched power fills this prophet from Nazareth with righteous indignation.[12] To demonstrate this, Jesus heals the blind and lame who come to the temple looking for relief, not more financial burden (Mt. 21:10–17; cf. Mk. 11:15–19; Lk. 19:45–46). Further, the gospels indicate the results of such provocative temple activity by Jesus: "The chief priests, the scribes, and the leaders of the people kept looking for a way to kill him" (Lk. 19:47). However, they did not dare act, initially because Jesus' teaching in the temple had "spellbound" the people and because the established leaders "were afraid of him" (Mk. 11:18). Nonetheless, their day would come.

Before it comes, Jesus symbolically takes over the temple and predicts its demise because of the failures of its leaders. In Mark, the cleansing of the temple is framed by the miraculous withering of a fig tree. First, Jesus predicts it (Mk. 11:12–14); then, it happens (Mk. 11:20–25; cf. Mt. 21:18–22, where both cursing and withering happen together, *after* the cleansing of the temple; Luke omits the story of the fig tree altogether). Thus Jesus symbolically cleanses the temple of its socioeconomic sinfulness through the physical act of turning over tables and driving out corrupt business people, even as he destroys a fig tree, symbol of Israel and its temple. Upon the death of Jesus, each gospel writer tells us, the temple curtain is torn in two (Mk. 15:38; Mt. 27:51; Lk. 23:45). "God ratifies his action by abandoning the Temple's inner sanctuary through a symbolic act of departure."[13]

Thus Jesus' actions of riding into Jerusalem and the temple district triumphantly with his followers, and of cleansing the seat of elite power in the temple, precipitate the plot against his life. The ensuing narrative in all three gospels traces his temple ministry and the emerging efforts to stop that ministry.

CONFRONTATION AND ETHICS IN THE TEMPLE

At the outset of Jesus' ministry in the temple, the temple elite ("the chief priests, the scribes, and the elders [of the people]") question the authority by which Jesus teaches and heals in the temple (Mk. 11:27–28 and pars.). Jesus replies with a question of his own regarding the ministry of John the Baptist and his authority. When the temple leaders cannot reply because of their concern for John's popularity as a martyred prophet in the people's eyes, Jesus also refuses to answer their question directly (Mk. 11:29–33 and pars.). However, he does reply after all, but only with a series of parables that contrast his leadership agenda with that of the temple elite.

In the parable of the two sons (Mt. 21:28–32) and the wicked tenants (Mk. 12:1–12; Mt. 21:33–46; Lk. 20:9–19), Jesus highlights the values of service, sacrifice, and sonship. In the first parable, two sons react differently to an offer of work in their father's vineyard. The first refuses, then changes his mind. The second accepts, but then reneges on his promise. Which is worse? It is worse for initial leaders who then change their ways when the going gets tough than for "tax collectors and prostitutes" who are reluctant at first but eventually do believe in the ministry of John and then Jesus? In the parable of the wicked tenants, again a vineyard is in question. This time its owner leased it to tenants who refuse to pay the owner his share of the produce. They beat or kill slave after slave until the owner sends his own son, whom he expects "they will respect" (Mk. 12:6 and pars.). However, the son, too, is killed.

Now, one would expect a story like this to be told from the perspective of the temple elite, many of them landowners themselves with sharecroppers to manage, and perhaps even abuse. However, the gospel redactor turns the tables on the leaders as Jesus provides his own interpretation of the parable with an ironic analogy: "Have you not read this scripture: 'The stone that the builders rejected / has become the cornerstone; / this was the Lord's doing, / and it is amazing in our eyes'?" The religious elite fail to see scripture fulfilled before their eyes, for they destroy the one who brings fulfillment (Mk. 12:10–11 and pars.).

Matthew is more explicit about the meaning of this "cornerstone" text from Psalm 118:

"Therefore I tell you, the kingdom of God will be taken away from you and given to a people that produces the fruits of the kingdom. The one who falls on this stone will be broken to pieces; and it will crush anyone on whom it falls." (Mt. 21:43–44 and pars.)

All three Gospels record the reaction of those in power to this application of the parable: "When the scribes and chief priests realized that he had told this parable against them, they wanted to lay hands on him at that very hour, but they feared the people" (Lk. 20:19 and pars.).

Nonetheless, the plot to entrap Jesus and have him arrested intensifies (Lk. 20:20 and pars.) because the temple leaders realize the implications of Jesus' teaching with these parables—he is attacking their failed leadership. They are the ones entrusted to care for the vineyard (the people of God), who have failed to heed the challenge from several parties to act as just stewards of this vineyard. Now the challenge comes from "the son of God," whom they will kill as well. The gospel tradition, of course, is reading back its theological understanding of what happened to Jesus, even as the gospel communities faced persecution from established religious and political leaders in their own day. Nonetheless, a similar principle prevails from Jesus' own time—failed leadership engenders injustice to God's people.

Thus, the next three pericopes of the triple tradition have Jesus being questioned by three different elite leadership groups about three different aspects of their common lives: taxation, theology, and ethics. First, "the Pharisees" and, according to Mark, "some Herodians" (Luke follows with "the scribes and chief priests" from the previous text, Lk. 20:19) question Jesus, "Is it lawful to pay taxes to the emperor, or not?" (Mk. 12:14d and pars.). The three different gospels acknowledge the "malice" (Mt. 22:18), "hypocrisy" (Mk. 12:15) and "craftiness" of the questioners. So Jesus replies with a bit of craftiness of his own. As he looks at a coin with the emperor's picture on it, he answers, "Give to the emperor the things that are the emperor's, and to God the things that are God's" (Mk. 12:17 and pars.). This reply silences his opponents, for now.

But what did Jesus mean by such a pronouncement? Scholars offer various interpretations.[14] In a world where the imperial option for taxation, and in some places even for worship, increasingly emerged as the only acceptable action by the masses, for Jesus to offer the option of dues owed to God, restores some balance. That's why he silences the temple leadership, who had colluded to dilute the option, indeed the priority, of giving to God God's due. One could give to Caesar his due as long as the responsibility to God was taken care of as a priority.[15] However, just to offer the option of God first and Caesar second creates an ongoing tension between the Jesus movement and the Empire. With his ascription of the God option, Jesus challenges temple leaders to examine their own views on the issue.

Moreover, the poorest of the poor still felt the pressure not only to give to God, to temple, and to Rome, but also to do all that and to eat as well, not at all an easy task in such a difficult subsistence economy.

In the next pericope, Jesus encounters another group of established Jerusalem leaders, the Sadducees. As we have seen, these leaders as a group, more than any other political and religious grouping in Israel, had turned away from fuller attention to the God of Israel to placate the Romans for their political and socioeconomic gain. Nonetheless, they opted to challenge Jesus with a theological question. Whose wife will a seven-time widow be in the afterlife after she marries each of seven brothers in this life (Mk. 12:18–23 and pars.)? Jesus confronts these leaders with his own theological perspective. Marriage does not matter in the afterlife and the resurrection, which are the real issues behind their questions because the Sadducees did not believe in the resurrected life in the hereafter as a scriptural teaching, as other Jews did (Mk. 12:24–32, and pars.). For Jesus, the Sadducees are wrong, and he tells them so in no uncertain terms: "[God] is God not of the dead, but of the living; you are quite wrong" (Mk. 12:27). Once again the crowds are astonished (Mt. 22:33), perhaps not so much at this theology, but at his strong stance against the politically powerful Sadducees. Even some scribes seem impressed: "Then some of the scribes answered, 'Teacher, you have spoken well.' For they no longer dared to ask him another question" (Lk. 20:39–40). No official leader of Israel and its imperial overlords, whether political or religious, was exempt from the challenge of Jesus and his renewal movement.

The third incident in this series of temple encounters involves a "scribe," according to Mark (Matthew calls him a lawyer from among the Pharisees, Mt. 22:34): "One of the scribes came near and heard them disputing with one another, and seeing that he answered them well, he asked him, 'Which commandment is the first of all?'" (Mk. 12:28).

So now Jesus is confronted with ethical questions. He replies by citing from the Torah: Love God above all else, and your neighbor as yourself (Mk. 12:29–31 and pars.; see Lev. 19:18; Deut. 6:4–5). In Mark, the scribe wholeheartedly agrees with Jesus and adds that this commandment "is much more important than all whole burnt offerings and sacrifices" (Mk. 12:33b). This perspective from at least one leader from the community places worship activity in the temple in its proper place and prompts Jesus to declare, "You are not far from the kingdom of God" (Mk. 12:34).

Nonetheless, most scribes and other political and religious leaders in Jerusalem are "far from the kingdom of God," according to Jesus, much to their chagrin. And this he teaches in the temple district, the seat of their leadership power:

> "Beware of the scribes, who like to walk around in long robes, and
> to be greeted with respect in the marketplaces, and to have the

best seats in the synagogues and places of honor at banquets! They devour widows' houses and for the sake of appearance say long prayers. They will receive the greater condemnation." (Mk. 12:38–40 and pars.)

Matthew has a longer condemnation and focuses with woes on the Pharisees (Mt. 23:15–36). In any case, these Jerusalem leaders have neglected their true allegiance to the people of God by being concerned more with outward appearance and less with just action on behalf of the poor, the widow, the sick, the needy, and other just actions that emerge from simple piety.

For these reasons, the synoptic Jesus cries over Jerusalem (Mt. 23:37–39; cf. Lk. 13:34–35) and predicts its downfall, as well as that of its famous, but now flawed temple (Mt. 24:1–3 and pars.). The only hope lies in those who give of themselves like the widow who gives her temple offering from her heart even though it is a relatively small amount (Mk. 12:41–42; Lk. 21:1–2). Jesus tells his disciples that this is how they ought to practice their gospel leadership in contrast to the entrenched temple leadership and their elite supporters:

> "Truly I tell you, this poor widow has put in more than all those who are contributing to the treasury. For all of them have contributed out of their abundance; but she out of her poverty has put in everything she had, all she had to live on." (Mk. 12:43–44)

It is fitting that a poor widow sets the prime example of discipleship and leadership as Jesus concludes his series of confrontations with the established leadership of the Jerusalem temple within earshot of their Roman imperial overseers. The widow has a dual role. She represents both those least attended in the Roman imperialism of Palestine, and the great truth the gospel record wishes to offer from these final days of Jesus in Jerusalem. Humble, self-giving hearts lead to good leadership in the gospel communities.

After these confrontations with the elite leadership of his day, Jesus turns from ethics to eschatology in his final critique of the temple and its leadership. Soon, however, these leaders will have had enough as they seek to have Jesus arrested.

FROM ETHICS TO ESCHATOLOGY

Many scholars read eschatological texts in the synoptic gospels in light of the post-70 era after the fall of Jerusalem and the destruction of the temple, as the evangelists respond to the needs of their own communities in that post-war era. Nonetheless, given his critical stance on the temple and its failed leadership, the historical Jesus probably envisioned a difficult future for Jerusalem, the temple leadership, and for the nation of Israel as a whole if the collusion with Roman imperial forces continued at the expense of continued oppression of the masses of the peasant poor in Palestine. As with the Dead Sea communities, John the Baptist, and others of his day, Jesus had to believe that God would intervene in some shape or form and radically change the plight of Israel for the better. In other words, Jesus was an eschatological prophet as well as a renewal movement leader and sage.[16]

For our purposes, the most pertinent aspects of the synoptic eschatological material are the words of exhortation to future disciples and leaders of the movement. The gospel writers depict Jesus giving warnings to his own disciples, but these are best read as warnings and exhortations to the current readers of the gospels in the aftermath of the Jewish Wars in the 60s and other subsequent imperial persecutions: "But before all this occurs, they will arrest you and persecute you; they will hand you over to synagogues and prisons, and you will be brought before kings and governors because of my name" (Lk. 21:12; cf. Mk. 13:9).

In light of such persecution, followers of Jesus, both present and future, ought to know that they will be protected. God will give them what they need to survive. Luke in particular emphasizes the ability to confront opposition: "For I will give you words and a wisdom that none of your opponents will be able to withstand or contradict" (Lk. 21:15). Thus, just as Jesus and his disciples confronted opposition as the passion neared, all gospel workers can expect persecution and difficulty, but also God's intervention on their behalf. Contemporary disciples may affirm, "Jesus experienced these. The first apostles did. We will." This, in a nutshell, is the synoptic message in the eschatological passages of the passion narratives.

Some details follow. First, all three gospels make clear reference to the fall of Jerusalem in 70 C.E., describing, for example, the "desolating sacrilege standing in the holy place" (Mt. 24:15; cf. Mk. 13:14) and especially "Jerusalem surrounded by armies" (Lk. 21:20). Gospel writers describe these as signs of the future return of the "Son of Man" (Mt. 24:30; Mk. 13:26; Lk. 21:27) and the final consummation of the kingdom of God (Lk. 21:31). Jesus may, or may not, have proclaimed an imminent return of "the Lord" and future realization of God's reign on earth, but certainly the gospel writers and presumably their readers did.

In any case, the belief in a future eschatological event influenced the exhortations to the community's future leaders. They were to be watchful: "Beware, keep alert; for you do not know when the time will come" (Mk. 13:33). They were to be on their best behavior:

> "Be on guard so that your hearts are not weighed down with dissipation and drunkenness and the worries of this life, and that day catch you unexpectedly, like a trap. For it will come upon all who live on the face of the whole earth. Be alert at all times, praying that you may have the strength to escape all these things that will take place, and to stand before the Son of Man." (Lk. 21:34–36)

These eschatological warnings and exhortations, then, did return ultimately to their ethical, earthbound implications. In his temple teachings, Jesus took his listeners (and the gospel writers their readers) from ethics to eschatology, and back again to ethics—albeit an interim ethic.

The Q tradition had similar concerns. Matthew in particular uses a variety of warnings and parables in the eschatological passages of the passion narrative, including warnings about the suddenness of the coming of the Son of Man (Mt. 24:37–41; cf. Lk 17:26–27, 30, 34–35, in a different part of his gospel narrative). Stories about a watchful house owner and a wise slave, which occur elsewhere in Luke's narrative, show up here in Mathew's eschatological discourse (Mt. 24:42–51; cf. Lk. 12:39–40; 42–46). Matthew also includes a parable about ten bridesmaids, five careless ones and five watchful ones, a story unique to Matthew, to warn his readers about being ready for eschatological fulfillment, "for you know neither the day or the hour" (Mt. 25:1–13, quote from v. 13). Similarly, Matthew inserts the parable of the talents, which Luke places earlier in his gospel (Lk. 19:12–27), in the passion narrative to illustrate the eschatological danger of not using our time and talents wisely. Thus, eschatological warning and exhortation from Jesus and the evangelists serve to prepare the present and future leaders of the movement to act wisely and faithfully. This applies especially in times of crisis (such as the passion for Jesus and his followers, and war for the gospel communities) during our earthly existence while we await God's final action on behalf of a future life and kingdom.

One final pericope from these synoptic eschatological discourses in the passion narratives illustrates well the focus on interim ethics. In the final judgment, after the return of the Son of Man, the distinguishing criterion for whether or not one will receive his or her final reward will be one's treatment of the poor and the hungry:

> "Come, you that are blessed by my Father, inherit the kingdom prepared for you from the foundation of the world; for I was hungry and you gave me food, I was thirsty and you gave me something to drink, I was a stranger and you welcomed me, I was naked and you gave me clothing, I was sick and you took care of me, I was in prison and you visited me." (Mt. 25:34–36)

The righteous wonder when they did this for "the Lord," and "the king will answer them, 'Truly I tell you, just as you did it to one of the least of these who are members of my family, you did it to me'" (Mt. 25:37–40). By giving life to the most needy, faithful, and just, believers will receive eternal life (25:46b). On the other hand, those who did not feed the hungry, quench the thirsty, clothe the naked, visit the sick and the imprisoned, and practice hospitality to the stranger will face eternal punishment (25:41–46a).

Therefore according to the gospel writers Jesus taught eschatology with strong ethical implications for justice. He did so in the temple, where his listeners included the elite leaders of the people, who had failed precisely at implementing justice and mercy on behalf of the poor and the needy:

> Every day he was teaching in the temple, and at night he would go out and spend the night on the Mount of Olives, as it was called. And all the people would get up early in the morning to listen to him in the temple. (Lk. 21:37–38)

Teaching in the temple was an activity ascribed to Jesus across the various gospel traditions. Moreover, the content of his teaching included attention to the poor and oppressed, whether he was teaching about current ethical practices or future eschatological expectations. These discourses and teachings, along with the symbolic acts of a triumphant, kingly entry and turning the tables over in the temple, no doubt solidified the opposition against Jesus and led to the conspiracy to arrest, try, and execute him. We now turn, therefore, to a discussion of the leadership aspects evident in the final passion narratives of the synoptic gospels.

Passion and Leadership

LEADERS AND DISCIPLES

In Matthew, Jesus announces the beginning of the end to his disciples this way: "You know that after two days the Passover is coming, and the Son of Man will be handed over to be crucified" (Mt. 26:2). Mark and Luke also note the Passover context at this point but concentrate on the actions of the "chief priests and scribes." They "were looking for a way to put Jesus to death" (Lk. 22:2a; cf. Mk. 14:1; Mt. 26:3–4). All three gospels note the leaders' caution because of all the pilgrims present during the Passover feast in Jerusalem: "Not during the festival, or there may be a riot among the people" (Mt. 26:5; Mk. 14:2). Luke generalizes the fear: "for they were afraid of the people" (Lk. 22:2b). Finally, Matthew is more specific about which leaders were involved in the conspiracy, mentioning "the chief priests and the elders of the people," all of whom met "in the palace of the high priest, who was called Caiaphas," to plot the arrest and killing of Jesus (Mt. 26:3).

These details show that the events surrounding the death of Jesus were rooted in a Passover context and the actions of the established leaders of the community. Their fear of the people speaks to their shortcomings as leaders of the people. Any threat from a popular leader such as Jesus jeopardized their own thin hold on authority, especially with their Roman overseers intent on keeping the "peace" at all costs.

Mark, followed by Matthew, further depicts the popularity of Jesus by recounting the story of his anointing at Bethany (Mk. 14:3–9; Mt. 26:6–13), a pericope that Luke places much earlier in his narrative to show the confrontation of Jesus with his opponents (Lk. 7:36–50). In the passion context, the text differs from Luke's in a variety of ways. Instead of the home of a Pharisee named Simon, as in Luke, the host is one "Simon the leper" (Mk. 14:3; Mt. 26:6). Therefore, instead of a Pharisee protesting the use of expensive ointment on Jesus' feet, "the disciples" (Mt. 26:8) or "some" (Mk. 14:4) protest the "waste." Further, Jesus interprets the anointing by the woman as a preparation of his body for burial (Mk. 14:8; Mt. 26:12). Jesus also says that as a result of this woman's action, her memory will live on (Mk.14:9; Mt. 26:13). Thus the beginning of the passion narratives shows that established leaders have failed to understand Jesus and even plotted his death. However, with this pericope the narratives also show that even future leaders of the movement were blinded at this critical juncture from understanding Jesus' fate. Nonetheless, a leper and, in particular, a simple woman with a jar of alabaster understand what is to come. Her actions, in fact, symbolize the heart of authentic gospel–service and sacrifice.

As if to further contrast the actions of the woman, the next pericope describes the failures of a specific disciple, Judas. For payment, he agrees to turn over Jesus "when no crowd was present" (Lk. 22:6b; cf. Mk. 14:10–11; Mt. 26:14–16). Thus the dilemma of the established leaders–arresting Jesus without arousing the ire of the crowds–has been resolved. An insider will betray his leader. A future leader, potentially, has failed at gauging the mission and purpose of the one he purports to follow. Later, in one strand of the tradition, we learn of Judas' own death by his own hand (Mt. 27:3–10). In both cases, that of the established leaders and that of the failed disciple, a lack of perception with regard to the mission and message of Jesus of Nazareth results in tragic circumstances. A misunderstanding about the nature of Jesus' leadership results in the untimely death of the disciple, Judas, and the unjust death of his teacher, Jesus.

"WHO WILL BE THE GREATEST?"

As if to highlight the problem of failed leadership, Luke inserts the critical debate among the disciples about "who would be greatest in the kingdom" in this most solemn of occasions as Jesus sits down to eat his final supper with his disciples. Jesus announces that he will be betrayed and predicts, once again, his impending death by establishing on this occasion, according to this gospel tradition, a memorial meal recollecting his death (Lk. 22:15–23). However, according to Luke, not only do the disciples wonder who it is among them that will betray Jesus (Lk. 22:21–23), but also who among them will "be regarded as the greatest [*meizōn*]" (Lk. 22:24). Thus Judas is not the only failed disciple at this critical point in the ministry of Jesus; they all are, especially as depicted by Luke. They all misunderstand the type of leadership that is expected of Jesus, and of them.

In responding to their inadvertent inquiry, Jesus reminds the disciples of the imperial way of leadership: "The kings of the Gentiles lord it over them; and those in authority are called benefactors [*euergetai*]" (Lk. 22:25). Jesus understood that in his world the recognition of doing good–benefaction–resulted from position in a hierarchy rather than actually doing any real good. In the Roman Empire, patronage, in which clients paid homage to their patrons above them in the social-economic scale, reigned as the means of exercising leadership.[17]

Jesus says to the disciples: "But not so with you" (Lk. 22:26). The alternative is to recognize for "greatness" those among them those who "become like the youngest [*neōteros*]." This echoes Jesus' earlier claim that to enter the kingdom of God one must be like "a child" (Lk. 18:17 and par.). During the "Last Supper," Jesus reminds his disciples that total dependence on God, like that of a child, must precede the search for greatness. Jesus furthers nuances this with the next simile: "and the leader [must become] like one who serves" (Lk. 22:26: *kai ho hegoumenos hōs ho diakonōn*). Thus the declaration reads like Hebrew synonymous parallelism: "To be great is to be like a child; to lead is to be a servant." The next verse affirms this sense with the rhetorical question: "For who is greater, the one who is at the table or the one who serves [*ho diakonōn*]? Is it not the one at the table?" (22:27a). Jesus describes normal circumstances in the imperial world of patron-client relations–"To be great is to be served." However, Jesus wants to model for his disciples a different approach: "But I am among you as one who serves" (Lk. 22:27b). "There is, then, a break with the patron-client relationship at its most crucial point: a service performed or a favor done shall not be transformed into status and honor."[18] Yet, even without "status and honor" in the world, Jesus practices authentic gospel leadership.

Therefore, Luke places this pericope about who is the greatest in the context just before the ultimate act of service–Jesus' death on an imperial cross. For Luke, such a context gives the debate among disciples about "greatness" much more import and impact. Jesus expected his disciples–and Luke expects his readers–to adopt this model of leadership:

> "You are those who have stood by me in my trials; and I confer on you, just as my Father has conferred on me, a kingdom, so that you may eat and drink at my table in my kingdom, and you will sit on thrones judging the twelve tribes of Israel." (Lk. 22:28–30)

Ultimately, servant leaders gain their "kingdom," not like the "kingdom of the Gentiles" (the Roman Empire), but directly from God. In such a kingdom, they will be able to "eat and drink" sitting at the table and even "sit on thrones judging the twelve tribes of Israel." But for now, they serve, and sometimes, like Jesus, they will be unjustly judged by Israel's and Rome's official, but deeply flawed, leadership.

Notwithstanding his high expectations, Jesus knows that his disciples will often fall short. Thus he warns Simon Peter about his imminent denial of ever having known Jesus (Lk. 22:31–34; cf. Mk. 14:26–31; Mt. 26:30–35). The fulfillment of this prediction later in the narrative (Mt. 26:69–75; Mk. 14:66–72; Lk. 22:63–65) proves to be a bitter moment for the one who the later church recognized as the key member of the original disciples. Yet, this all the more demonstrates the critical issue of how even failed disciples can emerge to become effective leaders in the movement. In addition, only Luke includes a somewhat obscure pericope in which Jesus also warns the disciples about his impending arrest and the persecution that is to follow. Previously, when they were commissioned to take the gospel forward, disciples did not need their "purse, bag and sandals." However, Jesus now says they will need those plus a sword (Lk. 22:35–36)! Luke cites a scripture (Isaiah 53:12b) about Jesus being "among the lawless," a reference to his impending arrest as a criminal of the state (22:37). When the disciples count among themselves "two swords," Jesus replies, "It is enough" (22:38).

How do we understand this difficult conversation, particularly with regard to questions about leadership? Most likely, Luke's point is that Jesus wanted his disciples to adopt a particular "attitude of mind," and not necessarily a concern for proper "equipment."[19] With opposition intensifying, gospel leadership will have to have "faith and courage which is prepared to go the limit."[20] Having purse, bag, *and* sword only metaphorically signals a shift in preparation for the rough going ahead. Again, the disciples misunderstood and produce actual swords. For Jesus, the conversation is over ("It is enough," v. 22:38b); they don't get it.[21] Later, when the disciples try to use these swords to defend Jesus (and themselves) at his arrest, Jesus rebukes them (22:49–51).

Thus in the final meal and in these final moments before Jesus is arrested, and as the events of the passion begin to unfold in a fast-paced manner, Jesus instructs his disciples on the nature of their future movement leadership. Service and sacrifice are the dominant themes of that leadership, just as they have been for Jesus. The disciples need to be properly prepared for the leadership they will undertake. What follows in the arrest, trial, and crucifixion of Jesus will serve as the ultimate model for them.

ARREST AND TRIALS

The arrest of Jesus (Mt. 26:47–56; Mk. 14:43–52; Lk. 22:47–53) is carried out by "a crowd with swords and clubs, from the chief priests, the scribes, and the elders" (Mk. 14:43; cf. Mt. 26:47, which adds "elders of the people" and eliminates "scribes"). Judas leads them to the site ("Judas, one of the twelve, was leading them" [Lk. 22:47]). All three synoptics report that when one of the disciples draws a sword to strike "the slave of the high priest," Jesus rebukes the swordsman (and according to Luke heals the injured slave, [Lk. 22:51; cf. Mt. 26:51–52, Mk. 14:47]). But he also rebukes the unjust and cowardly nature of his arrest: "Then Jesus said to them, 'Have you come out with swords and clubs to arrest me as though I were a bandit? Day after day I was with you in the temple teaching, and you did not arrest me'" (Mk 14:48–49a; cf. Mt. 26:55).

Luke specifies against whom Jesus directs these accusations: "the chief priests, the officers of the temple police [*strategous tou hiepou*], and the elders who had come for him" (Lk. 22:52). Jesus points out how they come with "swords and clubs," yet had refused to do so when Jesus was teaching publicly in the temple. Thus, according to Luke's Jesus, their "hour" to do this ghastly act demonstrated not legitimate authority but "the power of darkness!" (Lk 22:53).

Several trials and inquiries ensue at the hands of what Luke calls these "dark powers." First, the chief priests and scribes of the people accuse Jesus of having defamed the temple by predicting its destruction. Certainly his ministry in the temple and his challenges to the temple leadership lay behind these accusations as they filtered down through the tradition. Secondly, in the face of questions about his identity, Mark and Matthew report the silence of Jesus initially, but ultimately a messianic confession ("You have said so" in Matthew [26:64], and "I am" in Mark [14:62]). In Luke, to the question, "Are you, then, the Son of God?" Jesus answered, "You say that I am" (Lk. 22:70). In the synoptic record as a whole, such confessions garner accusations of blasphemy and a death sentence (Mk. 14:64; Mt. 26:65–66; cf. Lk. 22:71).

Yet the record of silence that the gospel tradition also includes probably speaks closer to the historical reality. Jesus stood accused of a temple ministry that challenged the entrenched powers of his day. In the gospels, Jesus speaks only to affirm his messianic identity. With his silence, however, he affirms his innocence. Moreover, "Jesus' silence convicts his accusers," both Jewish and Roman leadership.[22] If he can resist responding to their violent accusations with vehement protest, he has undermined their leadership and proven his own sacrificial, servant leadership. "[T]he motif of silence bears testimony to Jesus' attitude of resistance to and sovereignty over those who hold political and earthly power."[23]

PILATE

Silence continues when Jesus faces imperial power directly in the person of Rome's representative in Judea, the proconsul Pilate. Pilate's concern revolves around any potential threat to the emperor: "Are you the King of the Jews?" he asks Jesus. All three synoptic gospels record the same answer: "You say so" (Mt. 27:11; Mk. 15:2; Lk. 23:3), an ambiguous reply that seems to put the onus of the accusation back on the inquisitor. The synoptic tradition views Pilate as abdicating his power to please the crowds and the temple leadership. He even releases a real criminal in Jesus' place, Barabbas, whom Luke describes as an insurrectionist and murderer (Lk. 23:25). The crowds would rather have this one released than the one with a messianic identity and mission.

However, this scenario and view of Pilate reflects the later theological and polemical concerns of the gospel writers, including their own conflicts with Jewish synagogue leaders. Thus Pilate washes his hands of the blood of this "innocent" man Jesus in Matthew, the most polemical of the three synoptic gospels in terms of how it depicts the Jewish compatriots (cf. Mt. 27:24). Even worse in light of the subsequent disastrous centuries of Jewish-Christian relations, the crowds cry out with the unfortunate assertion, "His blood be on us and on our children" (Mt 27:25).[24]

Pilate gets off too easy in the gospels. We know from Josephus that Pilate was brutal in his retaliation and control of any uprisings against Rome's absolute rule.[25] We know that it would be impossible for any Roman official to release a violent insurrectionist, especially during the Passover feasts when Jerusalem filled with pilgrims, including many looking for any opportunity during this celebration of Israel's liberation from Egypt to assert similar freedom from Rome.[26] We know that execution on a cross–crucifixion–was a unique and horrific form of Roman imperial punishment. So that when Josephus writes that "Pilate...hearing him [Jesus] accused by men of the highest standing amongst us...condemned him to be crucified" (*Jewish Antiquities* 18.63[27]), we see both Pilate and the Jewish temple leadership at fault. However, it is ultimately Pilate's call. Given the tumultuous atmosphere of the Passover season in Jerusalem, he would not hesitate to quell any sign of revolt or resistance from any, even the most innocent of quarters, and to do so with quick and deadly force. The deadliest and most public of these forces, if not the quickest, was definitely crucifixion.[28]

Luke provides one more indication that in the end all of the official leadership of Palestine was engaged in and responsible for the execution of Jesus when, in his gospel account, Pilate sends Jesus to stand before a regional political leader, Herod, the tetrarch of Galilee (Lk. 23:6–16). Although Luke actually exonerates Herod, as well as Pilate, from the eventual execution of Jesus,[29] the presence of this leader in the passion narrative heightens the sense that all of the established political and religious leaders of Israel and of the Empire were involved in the trial, crucifixion, and death of an innocent leader of the masses, Jesus of Nazareth.

The Death of Jesus: Signs of His Leadership

The execution of Jesus involves, among other things, mocking and abuse. Mark, followed by Matthew, records the physical and verbal abuse Jesus endured from the Roman soldiers within the confines of "the governor's quarters [*praitorion*]" (Mk. 15:16; Mt. 27:27): "And they clothed him in a purple cloak; and after twisting some thorns into a crown, they put it on him. And they began saluting him, 'Hail, King of the Jews!'" (Mk. 15:17–18).

In the halls of official, Roman authority (a "praetorium"), mocking and abuse were inflicted upon another kind of leader, one who did not pretend to be "king of the Jews," as suggested by the mocking, but who did become a "servant king" in the eyes of those who followed him hereafter. Thus, once again the themes of a failed official leadership and a sacrificial servant leadership resound.

"Minor" characters in the events surrounding the crucifixion of Jesus highlight another theme—inclusiveness in leadership. The triple tradition speaks of Simon of Cyrene, a province of North Africa, whom the soldiers enlist off the street to help carry the cross for Jesus (Mk. 15:21; Mt. 27:32; Lk. 23:26). He becomes, for Luke's readers in particular, a kind of "model disciple," as he carries the cross, as Jesus asked his disciples to do (cf. Lk. 9:23; 14:27).[30] The point is intensified by the fact that by this time the immediate disciples of Jesus have disappeared from the scene.

Luke also includes a pericope in this context about grieving women whom Jesus "consoles" with warnings of worse days yet to come (Lk. 23:27–30), a clear reference from Luke to the fall of Jerusalem.[31] Luke also introduces the two criminals who will die beside Jesus at this point (Lk. 23:32). Thus, minor characters from the street, grieving women, and even hardened criminals will all have an opportunity to participate in Jesus' ultimate victory over death. "Today you will be with me in Paradise," Jesus promises one of the bandits who hangs next to him (Lk. 23:43b). Although mocked as "king of the Jews," nonetheless Jesus declares that there is room in the "real" kingdom of God for anybody, including those who will accept the role of humble, sacrificial servant leader as Jesus has.

During the crucifixion, mocking and verbal abuse by the crowds, but also by the soldiers and "leaders" [*hoi archontes*] (Lk. 23:35), prevails. One of the consistent themes in their taunts is, "He saved others; he cannot save himself. Let the Messiah, the King of Israel, come down from the cross now, so that we may see and believe" (Mk. 15:31b–32 and pars.). In mocking Jesus, the "leaders" from among the crowds belittle their own stature as leaders of the community. In Mark and Matthew, the mocking also includes references to Jesus' challenge of the temple: "Aha! You who would destroy the temple and build it in three days, save yourself, and come down from the cross!" (Mk. 15:29b–30; cf. Mt. 27:40). Later in the narrative, the temple is in fact symbolically destroyed: "Then Jesus gave a loud cry and breathed his last. And the curtain of the temple was torn in two, from top to bottom" (Mk. 15:37–38; cf. Mt. 27:50–51a; Lk. 23:45). Traditional theological interpretations have linked this act to the end of the sacrificial system of atonement and forgiveness. However, an early strand of the tradition also recognized in Jesus' ministry his challenge to the elite temple leadership and their failure to serve the oppressed peoples of Israel. Thus, their seat of power is torn in two, symbolizing direct access to God of those hitherto left out.

Such an interpretation is possible given the very next pericope in the triple tradition. A Roman centurion, called to carry out the execution ordered by the failed leadership, realizes the mistake: "Now when the centurion, who stood facing him, saw that in this way he breathed his last, he said, 'Truly this man was God's Son!'" (Mk. 15:39 and pars.). The failed Roman and Jewish leadership of Israel had executed the agent of God called to bring together the people of God from all walks of life. Looking on this grim scene, "from a distance," according to the triple tradition, were his followers from Galilee, especially the women, for the men had fled (Mk. 15:40–41 and pars.). Nonetheless, from among these "distant ones" would emerge the leaders of the movement beyond the scene at the cross.

Leadership in the Aftermath of Death: Burial, Resurrection, and Appearances

The aftermath of the crucifixion as described in all four gospels lacks consistency. Each gospel makes its own distinctive mark on the stories of Jesus' burial, resurrection, resurrection appearances, and final departure. Later editors of Mark's gospel even added a whole section based on the other three gospels (Mark 16:9–20). They could not accept Mark's rather open-ended original ending: "So they [the women at the tomb] went out and fled from the tomb, for terror and amazement had seized them; and they said nothing to anyone, for they were afraid (Mark 16:8).[32] John's gospel has extended post-crucifixion stories, well known in Christian tradition, including "doubting Thomas," Jesus' questions to Peter ("Do you love me?"), and the role of the mysterious "beloved disciple" present throughout the fourth gospel, and once again highlighted in the final chapters.

A LOYAL LEADER

Nonetheless, the synoptic tradition is consistent in three areas related to our topic of leadership. First, an established leader of the community actually comes out of hiding to at least secure proper burial for the martyred leader of the Galilean renewal movement. Joseph of Arimathea, according to Mark, was "a respected member of the council" (Mk 15:43a). Matthew calls him "a rich man" and "a disciple of Jesus'" (Mt 27:57). Mark and Luke describe Joseph's discipleship in terms of "waiting expectantly for the kingdom of God" (Mk 15:43b; Lk 23:51b). In addition, Luke posits that Joseph, "a good and righteous man" (instead of "a rich man" as in Matthew or a "respected" man as in Mark) "had not agreed to their [the council's] plan and action" (Lk 23:51a).

Thus we have the picture of an established leader who dares go to Pilate to ask for the body of Jesus to clean it, clothe it, and bury it in an appropriate tomb. Matthew writes that it was Joseph's "own new tomb" (Mt. 27:60; cf. Mk. 15:46, Lk. 23:53). The alternative was to let the crucified body rot on the cross and be eaten by the dogs.[33] Thus Joseph of Arimathea becomes a heroic figure in the stories surrounding the death and burial of Jesus. He shows his discipleship by seeking proper burial, "for to bury a person was to show honor to that person."[34] He facilitates the possibility of bodily resurrection because he secures safekeeping for the body, rather than have it succumb to the dogs. He does so at serious risk to himself, for "to honor a criminal in such an environment would be to expose one's self to suspicion and perhaps persecution for similar crimes."[35] Moreover, Joseph's actions contrast sharply with the prior actions of the temple leaders, who colluded with Rome to secure Jesus' execution. Matthew's account of a conspiracy by the chief priests and Pilate to secure the tomb from body snatching (Mt. 27:62–66) further highlights this collusion. In Joseph, we have a righteous leader, a model for what the temple elite should have been doing all along.

FAITHFUL WOMEN

Second, the strongest element about the resurrection, besides the notion of physical resuscitation itself, is the role of the women at the tomb. As we have noted, they are the only ones from among Jesus' followers who are anywhere near the scene of the cross. They are also therefore the only ones who come near the empty tomb on that fateful sabbath day. All three synoptic gospels name the women at the tomb, though including different people (Mt. 28:1; Mk. 16:1; Lk. 24:10). Mary Magdalene, perhaps the most significant female figure in the gospel stories besides Mary the mother of Jesus, is mentioned first in all three synoptic accounts. She represents, perhaps more than any other figure in the gospels, male or female, the transformative power of Jesus' ministry, especially with those whom everyone else had rejected Thus it is fitting that she, too, be present at this amazing story of transformation from death to life at the empty tomb.

Yet the women do not exactly shatter the world with their confidence about this matter, although readers can understand why. In Mark, as noted above, they flee the tomb with "terror and amazement" and fail to say anything to anyone about what they saw and heard (Mk. 16:8). Matthew goes beyond Mark with some further affirmation:

> Suddenly Jesus met them and said, "Greetings!" And they came to him, took hold of his feet, and worshiped him. Then Jesus said to them, "Do not be afraid; go and tell my brothers to go to Galilee; there they will see me." (Mt. 28:9–10)

However, Matthew further illustrates the difficulty with their testimony when he returns to talking about the "chief priests," who once again collude with Rome as represented, this time, by the soldiers guarding the tomb.

After the resurrection, the soldiers agree to tell a tomb-raiding story, and the temple leadership agrees to protect the guards from the wrath of the Roman governor (Pilate) because of the missing body (Mt 28:11–15).

So, in Mark, the women cannot tell their story out of fear. In Matthew, even when they do tell the story, the established leadership will conspire to label it a lie. In Luke, the disciples themselves have a hard time believing the women's story of a resurrected Lord:

> Now it was Mary Magdalene, Joanna, Mary the mother of James, and the other women with them who told this to the apostles. But these words seemed to them an idle tale, and they did not believe them. But Peter got up and ran to the tomb; stooping and looking in, he saw the linen cloths by themselves; then he went home, amazed at what had happened. (Lk. 24:10–12)

Luke adds the long story of two other disciples on the road to Emmaus meeting up with the resurrected Lord, who has to explain the scriptures to them so that they might understand what they had just seen and heard (Lk. 24:13–35). Similarly, Jesus appears to a group of all the disciples, where they touch him. Again he explains the scriptures to them so that they might understand, before charging them to "stay here in the city until you have been clothed with power from on high" (Lk 24:36–49).

Thus the women have a hard time being believed, but so does the Risen Lord himself. Yet, both the women and the disciples as a whole still represent the constituencies with whom Jesus served throughout his ministry. Regardless of their weakness in the eyes of others and despite the disbelief among themselves and others, Jesus will enlist the women and the disciples as movement leaders to carry the message of the kingdom forward.

A GREAT COMMISSION

Finally, the aftermath of the crucifixion and the resurrection includes a charge to these disciples who will be movement leaders. The charge is present obliquely in Mark's gospel. It lies in the encouragement of the women to go and tell others what they had seen, or not seen, at the empty tomb. They remain immobilized by the end of Mark's account (Mk. 16:8). The question for Mark's readers is whether they, too, will be so frightened with the power of the message that they will freeze and not move forward with it as leaders of the movement. Their task is not easy. Even those who were actual witnesses of these foundational events froze from fear. How much more so for those decades removed, still facing persecution as a result of their faith? Yet, lead in the propagation of the good news of Jesus they must. Such is the implication of the "open ending" of Mark's gospel. "[T]his ending is crafted to do much more than merely recall the disciples' failures. It is intended to move the hearers to respond, to excite the emotions on behalf of Jesus and the gospel message."[36]

Luke's charge is less subtle, but he still wants to leave the door open for the rest of the story. He ends his gospel with a foreshadowing of matters he will take up at the outset of his second volume of movement history–the book of Acts. So the disciples and leaders of the movement must be "witnesses" of what they have seen in the life of Jesus, as recorded in the gospel volume (Lk. 24:48; cf. Acts 1:8). To be such witnesses, they will need "power from on high," which they will receive by waiting "in the city" (Lk. 24:49; cf. Acts 1:4–5; 2:1–4). Luke ends his gospel where he begins his Acts, with the ascension of Jesus (Lk. 24:50–51; cf. Acts 1:9–11) and the disciples' decision to worship him, return to Jerusalem, and bless God in the temple districts (Lk. 24:52; cf. Acts 1:12–14). So, the leaders, whose founder the temple leadership rejected, do, in fact, symbolically take over that very same temple for their newfound worship of God in the name of their founder, Jesus of Nazareth.

Finally, Matthew offers a more direct charge to the disciples of Jesus who will become the movement's leaders. The charge enjoins both heavenly and earthly authority [*exousia*] to carry out the mission (Mt. 28:18). It entails duplication–disciples make disciples (28:19). And it makes an eschatological promise–the movement founder will be present–in spirit–with the movement followers and leaders (Mt. 28:20). For Matthew, teaching and making more disciples is the fundamental function of gospel leadership in the aftermath of the life and teachings of Jesus, even decades after the foundational events.

The aftermath of the death of Jesus, therefore, including his burial, resurrection, appearances, and ascension, reminds us of the themes of leadership prevalent throughout the gospel narrative. The story of Joseph of Arimathea reminds us of the failed leadership of Israel and Rome's imperial overseers. They could have relieved the oppression of the countryside, but failed to do so. That they killed one who offered to show the way demonstrates their tragic shortcomings. At least one member of established leadership came forward, if only a little too late, to bring final honor to this authentic leader.

The women at the tomb remind us of the insistence by Jesus on paying attention to those whom nobody, least of all the entrenched leaders of the people, had been paying attention to. Mary Magdalene, in particular, symbolizes not only the target audience of Jesus' ministry, but also the constituency from which the movement's leaders would come. The women took the lead in visiting the tomb and sharing the good news, even in the midst of fear and oppression. So should all leaders in the movement. And that is the lesson of the charges with which the synoptic gospels end their narratives. The "good news" of Jesus Christ would not be as good ultimately if it did not produce good leaders who will move the story forward and create other groups of the faithful. And so, a movement leader must be a witness to this good news, even decades after it first was told.

Summary and Conclusion

What have we learned about leadership from the model of Jesus in the gospels, and from the concerns of the gospel communities themselves in these last two chapters? First and foremost, attention to the poor is the fundamental quality of gospel leadership. Second, candidates for gospel leadership include all groups, especially the poor and outcast. Third, the gospel record emphasizes the sacrifice and service involved in gospel leadership.

Along with these basic elements, the synoptic gospels do not hide the shortcomings and failures of disciples in their early exercise of gospel leadership. Nonetheless, Jesus and the gospel writers still have high expectations for their leadership and the leadership of gospel readers. Moreover, the gospels teach that gospel leaders cannot be "lone rangers." Even Jesus needed a team, however flawed the team members happened to be. In addition, the egalitarian nature of gospel leadership in the early Jesus movement is still evident in gospel record. This remains true even though some note of hierarchy and official designations have already begun to set in, particularly with the language of apostleship and the attempted minimizing of female leadership (by speaking of the disciples as "the Twelve" and these twelve as men only).

Nonetheless, the gospel record points somewhat to an egalitarian approach to gospel leadership in the early Jesus movement. People from all walks of life, especially those least expected from the bottom of Roman imperial society, including the poor and women, join the movement and even exercise leadership in it. This picture needs to be tested out against what happens in the Pauline Christian movement, especially as the scene shifts from Palestine in the 20s and 30s to Paul's more Greco-Roman, Hellenistic, and urban context in the 40s and 50s. What happens to gospel leadership in those settings? Further, how does Paul's practice of leadership for his churches compare to that of the gospel writers of the 70s and 80s? To these questions and more, we now turn in the next several chapters.

4

Windows into Pauline Leadership

Introduction

We come now to a fundamental resource for a discussion of leadership in the New Testament–the life, ministry, and writings of the apostle Paul, a critical figure in the New Testament and earliest Christianity, second behind only Jesus himself. Paul's letters, the primary source for understanding his life and ministry, represent a form of his ministry to the congregations he founded. Therefore, the letters show how he exercised his leadership among the churches. Except for a few specialized scholarly studies on such related topics as apostleship and authority, only a few works have dealt extensively with the study of Pauline leadership.[1] In this chapter and the next two, I will only *begin* to rectify this situation. This chapter will offer a general study of leadership in Paul's letters. Chapter 5 involves a focused analysis on one aspect of leadership, namely, Paul's co-workers as leaders and his commendation of them. Chapter 6 is a case study of Paul's handling of a leadership crisis in Corinth, one of the congregations that best exemplifies Paul's leadership style, practice, and theology.

In the concluding chapter of this work, I will give attention to the pastoral letters, most likely not written by Paul, as a way of illustrating approaches to leadership in post-Pauline communities and the rest of the New Testament.

Windows into Pauline Leadership

What are some "windows" into understanding Pauline leadership as a whole? First, we should understand something about Paul's world, still the world of the Roman Empire that we outlined previously in chapter 1. However, some distinctive aspects of Paul's ministry in the Greco-Roman east, outside of Palestine, are worth discussing, if only briefly, to establish the immediate context in which Paul founds and leads his congregations. Second, a key to understanding Paul's leadership must lie in his own self-understanding. Clearly, his calling to be an apostle to the Gentiles (cf. Gal 1:16) functions as the fundamental *modus operandi* by which Paul conducts his ministry. He leads to the extent that he carries out his calling to preach the gospel to Gentiles and form communities of faith in the Gentile east. Of course, Jews like himself form an important part of the constituency in these churches. Indeed, the Jew-Gentile dynamic in his congregations constitutes a major challenge to Paul's leadership.

Third, Paul writes letters to these congregations during his prolonged absences from them. These letters basically provide *our* only window to his ministry to the churches he founded. As such what they show us specifically about Pauline leadership becomes our fundamental source for understanding leadership for Paul as a whole. Therefore, in this chapter, I will briefly review the content and structure of Paul's uncontested letters[2] from the perspective of leadership. This review will deal with three topics—Paul's world, his apostleship, and his letters—to illuminate some windows into Pauline leadership before entering into some detailed discussion of Paul's expectations for his leaders, found in the next chapter.

A Review of Paul's World

Paul's world was the urban context of the first-century Roman Empire in the eastern Mediterranean. It stands in contrast to the small-town or even rural feel of Jesus' world, as Wayne Meeks suggests:

> Paul was a city person. The city breathes through his language. Jesus' parables of sowers and weeds, sharecroppers, and mud-roofed cottages call forth smells of manure and earth, and the Aramaic of the Palestinian villages often echoes in the Greek. When Paul constructs a metaphor of olive trees or gardens, on the other hand, the Greek is fluent and evokes schoolroom more than farm; he seems more at home with the clichés of Greek rhetoric, drawn from the gymnasium, stadium or workshop.[3]

Meeks goes on to describe how Paul "depended on the city for his livelihood" by working as a manual laborer, a "tentmaker" according to the book of Acts (Acts 18:3). Moreover, the author of Acts also describes Paul as "a citizen of an important city," Tarsus in the Roman province of Cilicia, a major ancient urban center in the Greek east (Acts 21:39).[4]

What does it mean for Paul to have such influences from the city as part of his makeup and upbringing? As a Hellenistic, Diaspora Jew, rather than a Palestinian Jew, Paul's familiarity with Greek, Greek literary rhetorical strategies (Tarsus was known for its many rhetorical schools), and the Greek Bible of the Jews–the Septuagint–made him an ideal candidate to take the gospel to the Gentile world. As Calvin Roetzel writes:

> Although Jerusalem was no stranger to Hellenistic influence it is difficult to explain Paul's preference for the Septuagint, his familiarity with Stoicism, his facility in the use of idioms and rhetorical strategies, his close acquaintance with Hellenistic literary styles, and even his anthropology on the basis of an extended residence there.[5]

It makes more sense that Paul grew up and was trained in a major urban center of the Greek East, such as Tarsus.

This may also explain Paul's mission strategy. Just as Alexander the Great used urbanization to Hellenize eastern portions of the Mediterranean world, and as the Romans used Alexander's cities to facilitate Roman domination of their conquered regions, Paul evangelized by going to the great urban centers of the Roman Empire. A quick view of a New Testament table of contents confirms Paul's strategy. He (or his immediate followers) wrote letters to churches in the major cities of the Empire: Rome, Corinth, Galatia (a Roman province with various cities), Ephesus, Philippi, Colossae, and Thessalonica. Most of these churches Paul founded himself (Corinth, the Galatian churches, Ephesus, Philippi, Thessalonica). His emissaries may have been founded some (Colossae, cf. Col. 1:7), and missionaries not connected to the Pauline mission founded others (namely, the Roman churches, cf. Rom. 1:8–15). Although Paul did not found any churches in Rome, he knew many people who had traveled to the capital of the Empire from churches he had founded in the east (cf. Rom. 16:3–16) and planned to use Rome as a base of operations for a mission to Spain (cf. Rom. 15:22–24).[6]

Thus Paul's mission strategy was urban. His leadership was marked by the cities of the Roman Empire. What does this mean socially and theologically? First of all, social mobility in the urban centers of the Roman Empire had both positive and negative effects on the Pauline mission. Positively, it allowed for significant travel that facilitated evangelization by Paul and his associates. The need for good roads and good security so that Rome could receive goods and services it coveted from its conquered territories in the east also served the needs of travelers, Paul among them.[7] When Paul cannot himself travel to visit one of the churches, his associates, like Timothy, Titus, and Phoebe can (cf. 1 Thess. 2:17–3:6; 1 Cor. 4:17; 16:10–11; 2 Cor. 2:12–13; 7:5–7; Rom. 16:1–2). When Paul wants to connect to a church that is not his own, he can do so by sending greetings to previous participants in his mission who have traveled to a new locale (Rom. 16:3–16). Social mobility facilitates Paul's urban mission.

However, such mobility also meant that the cities of the empire had all kinds of social diversity. For the most part, the various groups were organized homogenously in voluntary associations, burial societies, trade organizations, and the like.[8] Whatever diversity they experienced revolved around the presence of rich benefactors who supported the organizing activities of the lower classes in exchange for receiving   honor from the membership for their presence and patronage . Otherwise, social classes stuck together in these groups and rarely interacted as equals with their patrons and clients.[9]

Nonetheless, the Christian communities founded by Paul tended to have significant social diversity. A study of the various individuals, both named and unnamed, in the Pauline letters shows that except for the very top and very bottom of the Greco-Roman social scales, most other groups were probably present in most Pauline churches.[10] While Paul himself argues that this should be the nature of the Christian church, in principle (e.g., "There is no longer Jew or Greek, there is no longer slave or free, there is no longer male and female; for all of you are one in Christ Jesus" [Gal. 3:28]), such diversity, in practice, was a source of conflict in churches. Social conflict in churches, therefore, came both as a result of Paul's message of egalitarian participation in the Christian community and as a result of the diversity inherent in the location in which his message was proclaimed–the city.

Moreover, many of these conflicts in the churches Paul started, as reflected in his letters, came about, as we shall see, over leadership issues. In certain instances, local church leaders attempted to replicate the patronage and hierarchy of the leadership in such ancient groups as voluntary associations. Leadership in these groups brought enhanced social status to those who served in such posts. Paul denounced those who replicated these outside models in several churches, most notably Corinth. Instead, Paul offered such theological leadership models as service, sacrifice, and especially "the cross" to undermine the status expectations of some leaders in his communities. The practice of leadership in the Roman cities, with a focus on status and hierarchy, served as the model being incorporated into the Pauline churches by some, but Paul rejected these models.[11] To illustrate this, we must highlight Paul's apostleship, which he also viewed in a different light than his constituents from the city did.

Paul's Apostleship

In terms of assignation, the term most closely associated with Paul's leadership is "apostle." The Greek root from the verb "*apostello*"–to send away–illustrates the missionary aspect of the term. An "apostle" is someone sent where no one else has gone. Paul himself alludes to this definition when he describes his ministry this way:

Thus I make it my ambition to proclaim the good news, not where Christ has already been named, so that I do not build on someone else's foundation, but as it is written,

"Those who have never been told of him shall see,
  and those who have never heard of him shall understand."
  (Rom. 15:20–21)

Paul also sees his apostleship as a call from God, given to him at his conversion. In Acts, Luke defines apostleship in terms of earthly knowledge of Jesus and direct call from him (Acts 1:21–26). In his letter to the Galatians, Paul emphasizes two matters: (1) the divine nature of his call and (2) its focus on the Gentiles. The book of Acts depicts Paul's conversion experience as a specific event based on a vision of the resurrected Lord (Acts 9:1–19; 22:4–16; 26:9–18). In his own description of the experience, Paul concentrates on his call to ministry, not the experience itself: "When God, who had set me apart before I was born and called me through his grace, was pleased to reveal his Son to me, so that I might proclaim him among the Gentiles, I did not confer with any human being…" (Gal. 1:15–16). For Paul, the important aspects lie in direct call (even if from a vision of the resurrected Lord), and the specialty and specificity of ministry–in his case, taking the gospel to Gentiles.

In his letter to the Romans, Paul explains this specificity of calling in a quite personal and emotional way:

For I am longing to see you so that I may share with you some spiritual gift to strengthen you–or rather so that we may be mutually encouraged by each other's faith, both yours and mine. I want you to know, brothers and sisters, that I have often intended to come to you (but thus far have been prevented), in order that I may reap some harvest among you as I have among the rest of the Gentiles. I am a debtor both to Greeks and to barbarians, both to the wise and to the foolish–hence my eagerness to proclaim the gospel to you also who are in Rome. (Rom. 1:11–15)

Paul did not found the Roman churches, but as "apostle to the Gentiles" he feels obligated to "share…some spiritual gift" with them, so that they each–apostle and church–might mutually benefit from the encounter.

Nonetheless, in his own churches Paul battled with the question of his apostleship–its nature, practice, and his identification with it. A reader can tell when Paul has to defend his apostleship with a church, often as early as the salutation in the letter addressed to that church. In each of his most contentious letters, 1 Corinthians, 2 Corinthians, and Galatians, he begins with his self-designation as an apostle: "Paul, called to be an apostle of Christ Jesus by the will of God" (1 Cor. 1:1); "Paul, an apostle of Christ Jesus by the will of God" (2 Cor 1:1); and perhaps his strongest: "Paul an apostle–sent neither by human commission nor from human authorities, but through Jesus Christ and God the Father, who raised him from the dead" (Gal 1:1). In each case, Paul uses the designation "apostle" as a way of identifying himself in addition to his name as author. In each case, Paul presents this apostleship as assigned by God, by the will of God through Christ, or as a calling and commission from both God and Christ. By implication in two of the salutations (1 and 2 Cor.) and directly in the third (Gal), Paul wants to distinguish the source of his call and commission as an apostle from any human source.

In Galatians, he proceeds to elaborate on that point, showing how during the first few years of his ministry he had relatively little contact with Jerusalem leadership, for example, and thus received calling and commission directly from God ("Am I now seeking human approval, or God's approval? Or am I trying to please people? If I were still pleasing people, I would not be a servant of Christ" [Gal. 1:10; cf. 1:11–2:21]).[12]

In less contentious churches, or those with whom he has a friendlier relationship, Paul designates himself as something other than an apostle. In Philippians, Philemon, and 1 Thessalonians, he is a "servant," a "prisoner," or just "Paul," (Phil. 1:1; Philem. 1; 1 Thess. 1:1, respectively). In each of these letters, he does not have to defend his apostleship or authority as the church founder, but rather seeks to resolve issues in the church from the posture of a leader with a firm hold on his congregation. He still has their attention. In Corinth and Galatia, the relationship between founder and congregation has suffered for a variety of reasons, and Paul has to reestablish his authority and his apostleship.

The remaining uncontested Pauline letter, Paul's letter to the Romans, also has a designation of Paul as apostle: "Paul, a servant of Jesus Christ, called to be an apostle, set apart for the gospel of God" (Rom. 1:1). Again, Paul projects the aspects of divine call ("set apart" by God) and divine mission (apostle "for the gospel of God") in this salutation. However, the Roman "house churches" (cf. Rom 16:3–16) represent congregations Paul did *not* found. Thus in Romans 15:22–24 Paul indicates that for "many years" he has wanted to visit Rome, implying that churches had been founded there years before he ever wrote or visited. Under these circumstances Paul need not reestablish his apostleship with his own, contentious churches, but rather establish it for the first time with churches that do not know him and his version of the gospel. Thus he expounds at length his gospel, "asking that by God's will I may somehow at last succeed in coming to you" (Rom. 1:10). He longs to see them "so that I may share with you some spiritual gift to strengthen you–or rather so that we may be mutually encouraged by each other's faith, both yours and mine" (1:11–12). There is some controversy in Rome, but it remains unrelated to Paul's leadership of them. He will address Jew-Gentile conflict in the churches there, for he needs the unity of these churches for the support of his ministry to Spain (Rom. 15:24).

Thus, Paul provides his Roman readers with a full accounting of his gospel in light of God's work in Christ on behalf of both Jew and Gentile. Given his apostolic calling, Paul highlights the work of God for the Gentiles, but reminds the latter not to forget Israel's role in salvation history (cf. Rom. 9–11; 15:14–21). Therefore, he is Paul, "apostle," sent by God (1:1), "a minister of Christ Jesus to the Gentiles in the priestly service of the gospel of God" (15:16).

Apostolic identity is thus important to Paul, whether he is defining it, defending it, or introducing it. However, for most of his communities, Paul proposes a particular kind of apostleship and leadership with which many of them are not familiar, or which they refuse to accept. What are the models of apostleship that Paul puts forward to his communities?

The most formidable model has to do with Paul's image of the "suffering apostle." When the Corinthians debate over who should be their leader–Paul, Apollos, Cephas, or Christ (1 Cor. 1:12)–Paul wonders if their search for a leader is not bound up with their search for glory: "Already you have all you want! Already you have become rich! Quite apart from us you have become kings! Indeed, I wish that you had become kings, so that we might be kings with you!" (1 Cor. 4:8). What they do not seem to understand is that apostles like himself and others actually achieve little earthly glory in the exercise of their ministry: "For I think that God has exhibited us apostles as last of all, as though sentenced to death, because we have become a spectacle to the world, to angels and to mortals" (1 Cor. 4:9).

When the Corinthians see Paul suffering as a result of his apostolic ministry, they wonder if he is an authentic leader. Paul has to remind them that he will do whatever it takes to create and nurture Christian communities like those he has founded in Corinth:

> For though I am free with respect to all, I have made myself a slave to all, so that I might win more of them…To the weak I became weak, so that I might win the weak. I have become all things to all people, that I might by all means save some. I do it all for the sake of the gospel, so that I may share in its blessings. (1 Cor. 9:19, 22–23)

Nonetheless, the Corinthian rejection of Paul's leadership intensifies, especially under the influence of outside agitators (Paul calls them "false apostles" and "super-apostles," cf. 2 Cor 11:13; 12:11). In a subsequent letter, Paul has to remind them once again that his lowly worldly status as an apostle is actually a job description for the position:

> But whatever anyone dares to boast of–I am speaking as a fool–I also dare to boast of that. Are they Hebrews? So am I. Are they Israelites? So am I. Are they descendants of Abraham? So am I. Are they ministers of Christ? I am talking like a madman–I am a better one: with far greater labors, far more imprisonments, with

countless floggings, and often near death. Five times I have received from the Jews the forty lashes minus one. Three times I was beaten with rods. Once I received a stoning. Three times I was shipwrecked; for a night and a day I was adrift at sea; on frequent journeys, in danger from rivers, danger from bandits, danger from my own people, danger from Gentiles, danger in the city, danger in the wilderness, danger at sea, danger from false brothers and sisters; in toil and hardship, through many a sleepless night, hungry and thirsty, often without food, cold and naked. And, besides other things, I am under daily pressure because of my anxiety for all the churches. Who is weak, and I am not weak? Who is made to stumble, and I am not indignant? If I must boast, I will boast of the things that show my weakness. (2 Cor. 11:21b-30)

For Paul, the marks of a "true apostle" must be found in the effectiveness of his ministry among them in spite of these hardships (2 Cor. 12:12), not in his physical appearance or health, social status, or oratorical skills ("lofty words or wisdom," 1 Cor. 2:1; cf. 2 Cor. 10:10). Actually, Paul argues, "whenever I am weak, then I am strong" because God's grace and Christ's power reveals itself in just such situations of vulnerability and danger, as he works "for the sake of Christ" (2 Cor. 12:9–10).

Thus Paul identifies his apostleship with "the sufferings of Christ" (2 Cor. 1:5). As Christ suffered and died, the apostle is willing to risk illness and death to share the new life in Christ with those who would believe (4:8–12). He therefore relates apostleship and leadership in terms of the model of the cross and the crucifixion of Jesus. To use the symbol of the cross as a model of his apostleship struck his congregations, especially in Corinth, as odd: "For the message about the cross is foolishness to those who are perishing, but to us who are being saved it is the power of God" (1 Cor. 1:18). At least that is what he hoped: that the message of the gospel– "Jesus Christ, and him crucified" (1 Cor. 2:2), that it's simplicity–would be sufficient to convince believers of the nature of apostleship, ministry, and leadership as well:

When I came to you, brothers and sisters, I did not come proclaiming the mystery of God to you in lofty words or wisdom. For I decided to know nothing among you except Jesus Christ, and him crucified. And I came to you in weakness and in fear and in much trembling. My speech and my proclamation were not with plausible words of wisdom, but with a demonstration of the Spirit and of power, so that your faith might rest not on human wisdom but on the power of God. (1 Cor. 2:1–5)

For Paul, believing in the crucifixion of Jesus Christ as the fundamental avenue of divine action on behalf of human salvation has implications for how the gospel is preached and lived out. The accepted and expected standards of power–human wisdom and social status–did not transfer into the practice of gospel ministry and leadership. Rather, total dependence on God and the power of God's Spirit were the means of acquiring and building faith.

Thus Paul relates the cross to his own apparent "weakness" in the eyes of some in his congregations. Paul sees himself as the "embodiment" of this strange reversal that is the cross of Christ.[13] However, it is not just Paul's apostleship that stands mirrored in the message of the cross. He expects all his followers to understand any suffering and persecution they undergo in light of the cross of Christ.

The cross of Christ serves as a potent symbol for community formation. It provides, for example, a profound theodicy, enabling the churches to come to terms with the experiences of persecution and suffering, by seeing such experiences as analogous to, and therefore associated with, the suffering of Christ (e.g., 1 Thess. 2:14–16; cf. 1:6; Rom. 5:1–5; 8:28–39).[14]

Therefore, when Paul describes his apostleship in terms of suffering, he identifies with the suffering and crucified Christ on the cross and expects a similar identification from churches. On similar grounds, furthermore, in places like Corinth he defends the presence and leadership of those from the underside of the social hierarchy of the city:

> Consider your own call, brothers and sisters: not many of you were wise by human standards, not many were powerful, not many were of noble birth. But God chose what is foolish in the world to shame the wise; God chose what is weak in the world to shame the strong; God chose what is low and despised in the world, things that are not, to reduce to nothing things that are, so that no one might boast in the presence of God. He is the source of your life in Christ Jesus, who became for us wisdom from God, and righteousness and sanctification and redemption, in order that, as it is written, "Let the one who boasts, boast in the Lord." (1 Cor. 1:26–31)

Given the diversity of social classes in the Pauline churches, to identify the heart of the gospel message with the shameful symbol of a Roman cross, reserved for slaves and criminals, must have been empowering to lower social class members in Paul's congregations:

> For such as these the symbol of the cross must have been very potent: it gave them access to an alternative source of power based upon an ideology which taught that the first would be last and the last first, that he who suffered most gained most, that the "weak" had precedence over the "strong."[15]

So Paul's view of apostleship not only served to identify his own leadership with that of Christ, but to empower all believers to take up leadership roles in the church based on a similar model, regardless of their socio-economic status. This Paul tried to do again and again as he wrote letters to his congregations as a form of his preaching and ministry to them.

Paul's Letter-writing as a Window into His Leadership
The Character of the Letters

In the history of the study of Paul's letters, a distinction has often been made between Paul's letters as private correspondence and as public correspondence. On the one hand, Paul writes letters to a specific group of people, or in one case to a specific individual (Philemon).[16] On the other, these letters have far-reaching, *public* implications, beyond the specific group that Paul had initially intended to reach. His letters were circulated, collected, preserved, and centuries later became part of the Christian canon, for Christians of all generations to read, interpret, and follow.

Nonetheless, even though in one sense their public nature became a subsequent phenomenon, in another, Paul himself knew that he was not writing private correspondence, *per se*, for a variety of reasons. First of all, Paul wrote these letters to a group of people—the church as a whole—not individuals.[17] Paul expected his letters to be read publicly, in the context of the church coming together (1 Thess. 5:27; cf. Col. 4:16). Even in the one letter directed at an individual, Philemon, he addresses the entire community from the outset as a way of putting pressure on Philemon to respond positively to Paul's appeal (Philem. 2). Thus because Paul writes to entire congregations, his letters cannot be considered, strictly speaking, private correspondence.

Further, the matters with which Paul deals are of such wide-ranging import—matters of theology, ideology, and ministry to communities struggling with the interpretation of a newfound religion—that they cannot be considered simply the "private 'real letters' of ordinary people preoccupied with everyday concerns" as argued by Adolf Deissmann in an earlier generation.[18] Given the concern to exhort and advise his congregations with elaborate, complex literary productions, Paul's letters have more in common with the literary and philosophical letters of Greece and Rome than with the thousands of short, to-the-point, business-like letters that Deissmann studied and compared to Paul.[19] Thus, public matters of worship, the moral life, and apostolic authority are in view in Paul's letters, more so than private matters such as eating, shelter, and one's livelihood or business, as in the many papyri letters.

Third, Paul's letters presuppose a public presentation of Paul's message—the gospel. Although not fully recoverable, at the heart of much of Paul's message in his letters is his public proclamation of the gospel—what he believed, what he proclaimed, and what he wanted his followers to practice and proclaim in their own right. Indeed, one could argue that Paul's letters represent the follow-up to his "evangelistic preaching" that formed the communities he writes to in the first place. His letters represent his "pastoral preaching," the "ministry of encouragement" that Paul must exercise once his communities have formed and begun to experience the implications of his gospel in their life together.[20]

For these reasons, letter writing is a window into Paul's ministry and leadership. The letters not only became "public documents" generations after Paul passed from the scene, but also were intentionally written to minister to groups of people struggling with what it meant to be a believer in Jesus Christ, especially in the way that their founder and leader expected them to be. In fact, Paul's elaborate use of the letter genre served as such a model that he began what became the "apostolic letter tradition" in Christianity for centuries to come.[21] To minister to and lead congregations by means of the letter format became the *modus operandi* of bishops and pastors in the second and third centuries of the church and beyond.

The Purpose of the Letter

Why did Paul write letters? "The letter aims to substitute presence for absence."[22] Paul exercises his leadership in time of need for his congregations, even when he cannot be there, by means of the letter. In Corinth, he makes this explicit. When the congregation needs to discipline a wayward brother, Paul invokes his authority for them to do so in solemn assembly, even though he will not be there, physically:

> It is actually reported that there is sexual immorality among you, and of a kind that is not found even among pagans; for a man is living with his father's wife. And you are arrogant! Should you not rather have mourned, so that he who has done this would have been removed from among you?
>
> For though absent in body, I am present in spirit; and as if present I have already pronounced judgment in the name of the Lord Jesus on the man who has done such a thing. When you are assembled, and my spirit is present with the power of our Lord Jesus, you are to hand this man over to Satan for the destruction of the flesh, so that his spirit may be saved in the day of the Lord. (1 Cor. 5:1–5)

In fact, Paul will be there, with full authority, as their apostle and leader. The letter, 1 Corinthians, makes this possible.

One would think, nonetheless, that Paul would always prefer to be physically present with his congregations in time of need, rather than write letters. His other option is to send envoys. He often does, with Timothy or Titus as his favorite alternates. When he cannot visit the church at Thessalonica himself, he sends Timothy:

Therefore when we could bear it no longer, we decided to be left alone in Athens; and we sent Timothy, our brother and co-worker for God in proclaiming the gospel of Christ, to strengthen and encourage you for the sake of your faith, so that no one would be shaken by these persecutions. (1 Thess. 3:1–3a)

However, he would have preferred going himself: "For we wanted to come to you—certainly I, Paul, wanted to again and again—but Satan blocked our way" (1 Thess. 2:18). When Timothy visits and returns with news from Thessalonica, Paul still cannot visit in person, so he writes a letter (1 Thessalonians): "But Timothy has just now come to us from you, and has brought us the good news of your faith and love. He has told us also that you always remember us kindly and long to see us—just as we long to see you" (1 Thess 3:6).

Thus, it would seem that writing a letter is a third preferred option for Paul to exercise leadership among the churches he began. First, he seems to prefer to visit himself. If he cannot, he will send an envoy as a second preferred option. If all else fails, then a letter will have to suffice.[23] This would seem logical. However, Paul's letters contain indications that an apostolic visit was not always the best option. After a "painful visit" to Corinth, between the writings of 1 and 2 Corinthians (2 Cor. 2:1–2), Paul actually chooses to write a letter as the next best option (2 Cor. 2:3). However, even this letter turns out to cause "pain" for it becomes a letter of "tears" for both Paul and the Corinthians (2 Cor. 2:4). In fact, the best option in this case was to send Titus as an envoy to bring reconciliation between founder and congregation (2 Cor. 2:12–13; 7:5–16). Thus, Paul's letters are one of several options available to him to exercise his leadership among churches—he can visit; he can send an envoy; or he can write a letter, depending on what would work best given time and circumstances. Nonetheless, the fact remains that we can only know this today by means of the letters that Paul did write. The question remains then, why did he write them?

Calvin Roetzel cites three main reasons for Paul's letters:

1. to rehearse past experiences with his readers in order to console them in times of distress
2. to exhort and advise them toward a particular action or set of actions in times of confusion and misconduct
3. to defend his ministry against internal or external opposition[24]

Thus Paul's letters have hortatory, polemical, and apologetic functions.

The letters are also, of course, theological documents. However, as many have argued, Paul was a "task theologian." In J. Christiaan Beker's terms, Paul's letters represent a "contingent" response to a "coherent" theology.[25] Paul has a core theology, around such issues as God, Christ, the cross, salvation, the Spirit, the Christian life, and the "coming triumph of God" (eschatology, sometimes in apocalyptic terms); but he rarely if ever expounds these themes systematically. Rather, he will pick and choose and apply from his storehouse of developing theological truths to minister to the immediate needs of his communities, based on the crisis or issue that confronts them (and their relationship with Paul in many instances) at the moment of the writing of the letter.

Thus, to the extent that Paul's letters are theological documents, it is "praxis" theology that concerns Paul and his readers, for the most part. Such praxis theology entails theological reflection for faithful action in the interim, between the Christ event of death and resurrection and the Christ return in the impending future (the *parousia*). Paul writes letters, in other words, to help his followers "walk between the times."[26]

Therefore, in what follows, I want to review briefly each of the uncontested letters of Paul, to outline the concerns found therein, and how Paul exercises his apostolic leadership to his congregations by exhorting, consoling, advising, defending, and theologizing.

Paul's Letters from the Perspective of Leadership

1 Thessalonians

Paul's first extant letter, written sometime in the early fifties C.E. according to most date reckonings,[27] 1 Thessalonians contains all of the letter-writing goals—remembering, consoling, exhorting, and theologizing. Paul reminds the Thessalonians of their acceptance of the gospel message and the missionary behavior in their midst (1:5–10; 2:1–12). He exhorts them to continue their journey of faith in the midst of opposition and persecution (2:13–16; 3:1–5). He reminds them of the holy behavior and love expected of Christ believers (4:1–12), and he consoles them as they grieve for lost loved ones (4:13–18). In this last section, Paul also consoles by doing theology, in this case an apocalyptic theology of the end times, in which Christ will return, the dead in Christ will arise, and, "together" with the living, "be with the Lord forever" (4:14–18).

The letter concludes with several general exhortations, including the exhortation to "respect those who labor among you," a reference, no doubt, to local church leaders (1 Thess. 5:12–13), to which we will return in the next chapter. Suffice it to say here, that who better to carry out the exhortations and expectations that Paul has for his congregation, than those who already practice hard work and admonishment among the Thessalonians. "Esteem them very highly in love *because of their work*," writes Paul (5:13a, emphasis mine). Already they practice what Paul preaches, so they merit recognition as leaders. Moreover, because Paul is distant and this letter will not suffice in his mind, nor did Timothy's brief visit, Paul must rely on local leaders to console, exhort, teach, and advise, in his and his associates' stead, especially in the apparently delicate situation of the Thessalonian church.

In addition, Paul apparently feels the need to defend his and his associates' behavior among the Thessalonians. At the outset of the letter, Paul expresses his concern that the Thessalonians remember the missionaries' integrity and the power of their ministry:

> because our message of the gospel came to you not in word only,
> but also in power and in the Holy Spirit and with full conviction;
> just as you know what kind of persons we proved to be among
> you for your sake. (1 Thess. 1:5)

Paul picks up again on this theme of leadership integrity in 1 Thessalonians 2, recounting his and his associates' sacrificial service (2:1–2), their honesty, and their divine calling (2:3–4). They showed loving concern for the Thessalonians, "like a wet-nurse nursing her own child" (1 Thess. 2:7, my translation) and "worked night and day" so as not to be a financial burden to the Thessalonians (1 Thess. 2:9). For Paul, these were signs that even though he and his associates had perhaps left their newfound congregation before the appropriate time, they were not "fly-by-night" roaming preachers who started a community and then, when the going got tough, left it alone to face persecution. Rather, they showed integrity every step of the way. Even now, as far away as they were, they still cared for the well-being of the community. By sending Timothy to find out about the condition of the community and subsequently writing this letter as a follow-up to that visit, Paul showed this ongoing concern for the community (1 Thess. 2:17–3:10).[28] Thus he puts himself in a position to remind, exhort, and advise them, and to commend other, local leaders who can do the same in his absence (1 Thess. 5:12–13; see my discussion of this passage of commendation in the next chapter).

1–2 Corinthians

The Corinthian correspondence depicts a much stormier relationship between Paul and several factions in that church, compared to Paul's relationship with the Thessalonians. According to Acts, Paul spent some eighteen months establishing and nurturing this congregation. After that, probably around 54 C.E., he penned the Corinthian letters. Both letters demonstrate that Paul's leadership was always in question there. In 1 Corinthians, indeed, division over acknowledged leaders apparently precipitates a series of problems in the community (1 Cor. 1:10–12). Further reading shows that Paul himself lies at the center of the controversy:

> When I came to you, brothers and sisters, I did not come
> proclaiming the mystery of God to you in lofty words or wisdom.
> For I decided to know nothing among you except Jesus Christ,

and him crucified. And I came to you in weakness and in fear and in much trembling. My speech and my proclamation were not with plausible words of wisdom, but with a demonstration of the Spirit and of power, so that your faith might rest not on human wisdom but on the power of God. (2:1–5)

Some in Corinth have trouble with the nature of Paul's leadership. So, he must defend it, with such statements as:

What then is Apollos? What is Paul? Servants through whom you came to believe, as the Lord assigned to each. I planted, Apollos watered, but God gave the growth. So neither the one who plants nor the one who waters is anything, but only God who gives the growth. The one who plants and the one who waters have a common purpose, and each will receive wages according to the labor of each. For we are God's servants, working together; you are God's field, God's building. (1 Cor. 3:5–9)

Paul had to defend this servant perspective on leadership throughout his relationship with the Corinthians. We will explore this further in chapter 6, arguing that a key to understanding all of the Corinthian correspondence is Paul's defense of his ongoing leadership role with Corinth, even when absent.

In 2 Corinthians, for example, the matter becomes so serious that Paul must send an intermediary, Titus, to bring about reconciliation with the Corinthians (2 Cor. 1–7). Titus does so well that Paul appoints him to lead the delegation to Corinth to complete his collection for Jerusalem (2 Cor. 8–9). However, by the time of Titus's collection visit, a group of outside agitators had apparently exacerbated the leadership questions in Corinth so that Paul must once again defend his leadership, this time with some rather strong, rhetorical attacks on his opponents (2 Cor. 10–13).[29]

Thus, the consistent theme of Paul's leadership defense throughout 1–2 Corinthians explains many, if not all, the exhortations and problem-solving efforts that Paul must undertake throughout his relationship with this congregation. He rarely consoles or advises calmly. Rather he must exhort, correct, defend, and, of course, theologize, often with extreme passion. His theology, especially in 1 Corinthians, revolves around the correction of over-realized eschatology on the part of some Corinthians. Thus he reminds them of the *teologia crucis*–the suffering aspect–of gospel leadership:

Already you have all you want! Already you have become rich! Quite apart from us you have become kings! Indeed, I wish that you had become kings, so that we might be kings with you! For I think that God has exhibited us apostles as last of all, as though sentenced to death, because we have become a spectacle to the world, to angels and to mortals. (1 Cor. 4:8–9)

He also reminds them that a future resurrection is yet to be experienced (1 Cor. 15). In 2 Corinthians, when he thinks that his problems with them have been resolved through the reconciliation efforts of his envoy Titus, Paul theologizes that reconciliation lies at the heart of what God had done for the world in Christ (2 Cor. 5:18–20). The text is a marvelous example of Paul's theology in the service of his ministry and leadership.

Galatians and Romans

Romans and Galatians represent the height of Pauline biblical theological reflection. Nowhere else does he rely as heavily on Israel's traditions to make his arguments as he does in these two letters. For Paul in Galatians and Romans, the Torah and the Prophets presaged the nature of the gospel message in Christ and of "justification by faith" as the means by which God carries out the divine plan of salvation for all.

Nonetheless, in both letters Paul's leadership is also in question. In one case some in the church doubt his apostolic credentials (Galatians). In the other the readers have no direct experience of those credentials and how Paul embodies them (Romans). Thus, in both cases Paul employs extensive biblical theology to defend (Galatians) and showcase (Romans) his gospel and thereby reestablish (Galatians) and establish (Romans) his leadership.

In Galatians, Paul not only expounds on his theology of justification by faith by teaching about Abraham, faith, God's promises, Christ, and the law (Gal. 3:6–29); he also demonstrates his calling to teach on these matters by recounting his biography: his divine call (1:13–16); his dependence on God, not on human intervention (1:1, 17–24), even that by the Jerusalem church leaders (2:1–10); and his consistent defense of his apostolic calling to deliver a law-free gospel to the Gentiles (2:11–21). He denounces those leaders who introduce a "false gospel" to his Galatian congregations (1:6–9; 3:1; 5:7–12; 6:11–13, 17). In short, Paul not only uses Jewish scriptural and Greek cultural (cf. Gal. 4:1–11) traditions to make his case in Galatians, but he also speaks to his leadership calling, practices, and pastoral character (on the latter, cf., in particular, Gal. 4:12–20).

Romans represents an altogether different approach because Paul did not found any of the house churches in Rome (represented by the several house church leaders Paul greets in Rom 16:3–16). He has apparently not ever visited Rome, at least not as an evangelist, and the churches in Rome know him only by reputation. So, what kind of letter does he write?

Scholars have debated for ages "the purpose of Romans."[30] Is it Paul's singular systematic theological statement about his gospel? Or, to cite Beker again, is Romans still a "contingent" response to a contextual situation, albeit based on a "coherent" but underlying core theology? The answer may lie somewhere in between, but closer to a typical Pauline letter than a surface reading might reveal. Romans is certainly the most elaborate statement of Paul's gospel, with the heart of the letter focusing on biblical and theological warrants for "the righteousness of God" on behalf of humanity exercised through the agency of the Christ event–death and resurrection (an argument especially promoted in Rom. 1:16–8:39). Nonetheless, certain indications show that Paul seeks to establish not just his theology, but his leadership among the Romans by "shar[ing] with you some spiritual gift to strengthen you" and "reap[ing] some harvest among you as I have among the rest of the Gentiles" (Rom. 1:11, 13).

As "apostle to the Gentiles," Paul feels that even though he did not found the churches in Rome, he has a right, indeed a responsibility, to minister to their needs. As the narrative of Romans unfolds, it becomes clear that problems of division between Gentile and Jew persist in the Roman congregations. Paul, therefore, constructs his Romans theology around a reminder that God's salvation plan chronologically begins with the people Israel and that Gentiles, who now apparently comprise a majority of the Christians in Rome, have been "grafted" into God's plan like "wild olive shoots" (Rom. 11:17). Thus, when Paul succinctly defines his gospel at the outset of the letter, the attempt at coherence has a contingent flavor: "For I am not ashamed of the gospel; it is the power of God for salvation to everyone who has faith, *to the Jew first and also to the Greek*" (Rom. 1:16, emphasis mine). Paul repeats this theme of Jewish historical precedence in God's salvation plan several times throughout the letter (e.g., Rom. 2:9–10; 3:1–2; 9:4). He wants to remind his Gentile believers, even in the Roman churches that he did *not* found, that the gospel is for all, both Jew and Gentile, and that, therefore, Gentile majorities in Rome ought not oppress Jewish minorities, especially those in the Roman Christian house churches.[31]

Thus, once again, Paul uses the letter format, even with churches that do not know him personally, to exhort appropriate behavior. Even though he is not the founder of those communities, Paul attempts to bring about reconciliation of divided parties in the local Christian communities. To do so, he theologizes about the righteousness of God through Christ available to all who believe. Indeed, it can be argued that justification language in Romans includes not only "right relationship" vertically with God, but right relationships horizontally, especially with fellow believers, both Jew and Gentile. Such a reading includes the culminating moment in Paul's argument: "Therefore, since we are justified by faith, we have peace with God through our Lord Jesus Christ" (Rom. 5:1).[32] The results of justification include *eirenē*, "peace," with both God and fellow human beings.

Paul is the type of leader who does not shy away from an opportunity to heal a divided community, even one not his own. He does this for pragmatic reasons, as well as ministerial and theological ones. He plans to complete his work in the east, and travel west to Spain to proclaim the gospel in those virgin territories of the Roman Empire. However, he needs the support of the Roman churches for this mission (Rom. 15:23–24). Financial support from a unified church in Rome would be much better than from a divided one. Thus he writes one letter (Romans), sends one envoy to read and interpret the letter (Phoebe, Rom. 16:1–2),[33] and greets all the local house church leaders in one sweeping paragraph, including those who know him from their mission work together in the east (Rom. 16:3–16). *And* he presents a gospel that serves all, both Jew and Gentile in the church, so they should be unified, with no one group looking down on the other.

In this way, Paul seeks to secure a stronger base of operations for his mission to Spain *and* to fulfill his apostolic call "to bring about the obedience of faith among all the Gentiles for the sake of his name" (Rom. 1:5). Gentiles in Rome should feel obligated to seek unity with their Jewish Christian brothers and sisters, and, indeed, with all Jews, for:

> They are Israelites, and to them belong the adoption, the glory, the covenants, the giving of the law, the worship, and the promises; to them belong the patriarchs, and from them, according to the flesh, comes the Messiah, who is over all, God blessed forever. Amen. (Rom. 9:4–5)

For this cause, Paul will take up the leadership mantel of his gospel, even with churches for which he is not directly their apostle. His letter to the Romans is an excellent example of this all-encompassing sense of calling and commitment.

Philippians and Philemon

Finally, we come to two letters that represent Paul's engagement with much more friendly congregations, over whom his apostleship seems to have a firm hold, and for whom, at the same time, he exhibits a gentler, friendlier spirit.

The dating and precise situations behind these letters are difficult to ascertain. Only one thing is certain—Paul is imprisoned. It could be a Roman imprisonment, as traditionally assumed, or one of several other imprisonments that Paul experienced (cf. 2 Cor. 11:23).[34] At any rate, how Paul continues to exercise leadership over his congregations from the situation of imprisonment becomes a major consideration with both these letters.

In Philippians, Paul follows a classic rhetorical deliberative argument to persuade the Philippian congregants toward a particular mode of behavior, stated clearly in the *propositio* of the letter:

> Only, live your life in a manner worthy of the gospel of Christ, so that, whether I come and see you or am absent and hear about you, I will know that you are standing firm in one spirit, striving side by side with one mind for the faith of the gospel. (Phil. 1:27)[35]

Paul repeats this central exhortation toward unity and steadfast faith in the face of opposition (cf. Phil. 1:28) at various key points throughout the argument (2:1–4, 2:12–16; 3:1; 4:1) and recapitulates it in a final exhortation at the end of the letter (4:4–9).[36]

At the heart of the exhortation, Paul cites examples ("proofs" in the *probatio* section of the letter) of leaders who have overcome suffering and opposition to maintain faith and accomplish the gospel mission. These include Jesus, as the example *par excellence*, described as one

> who, though he was in the form of God,
>> did not regard equality with God
>> as something to be exploited,
> but emptied himself,
>> taking the form of a slave,
>> being born in human likeness.
> And being found in human form,
>> he humbled himself
>> and became obedient to the point of death. (Phil. 2:6–8)

Such humble sacrifice on behalf of the community is what Paul requires of leaders and all believers in Philippi.

However, Jesus is not the only example. Paul himself, "poured out as a libation over the sacrifice and the offering of your faith," still is "glad and rejoice[s] with all of you" (2:17). Similarly, Timothy and Epaphroditus have given of themselves for the good of the community and the cause of the gospel (2:19–30). In the next chapter, I shall return to Paul's commendations of Timothy and Epaphroditus. Suffice it to say here that they play an important role, along with the testimonies to Jesus and to himself, in Paul's efforts to exhort the Philippians toward maintaining unity and faithfulness in their own situation of stress. In other words, Paul cites the commitment of strong leaders to exact commitments from leaders and believers alike in Philippi: "Brothers and sisters, join in imitating me, and observe those who live according to the example you have in us" (Phil. 3:17). Euodia and Syntyche are examples of leaders in Philippi who need to be brought together for the unity of the church to be maintained over the long haul (cf. Phil. 4:2–3).[37]

Thus, even as a prisoner, Paul maintains his leadership concerns over his gospel communities, Philippi included. In the beginning of the letter, he describes his own joy even in the midst of a difficult imprisonment because the gospel is still being preached:

> I want you to know, beloved, that what has happened to me has actually helped to spread the gospel, so that it has become known throughout the whole imperial guard and to everyone else that my imprisonment is for Christ; and most of the brothers and sisters, having been made confident in the Lord by my imprisonment,

dare to speak the word with greater boldness and without fear. (Phil. 1:12–14)

While, it is true that some proclaim the gospel to spite Paul and mock his lack of effectiveness because he is in prison (Phil. 1:15–17), at least, to date, they are getting the message straight despite their questionable motivations (1:18).[38] Thus, Paul even rejoices when others preach the gospel and take advantage of his imprisonment to do so. In this way, Paul shows the Philippians what he means by faith in the midst of opposition. As their leader, he models for them what he wants them to do.

Further, in the section that shows his love and warm connection to the Philippians (the "pathos" aspect of his letter *exordium* or introduction[39]), Paul suggests that he would rather survive his Roman imprisonment and have another opportunity to minister to the Philippians (1:19–26). Death in Christ would be a welcome outcome to his imprisonment, but time and ministry with the Philippians is necessary and most acceptable:

> For to me, living is Christ and dying is gain. If I am to live in the flesh, that means fruitful labor for me; and I do not know which I prefer. I am hard pressed between the two: my desire is to depart and be with Christ, for that is far better; but to remain in the flesh is more necessary for you. Since I am convinced of this, I know that I will remain and continue with all of you for your progress and joy in faith, so that I may share abundantly in your boasting in Christ Jesus when I come to you again. (1:21–26)

In this way, Paul further cements his relationship to the Philippians and his leadership among them, even though he is in prison. If and when he gets out, he assures the Philippians, he still has some ministry to offer them on behalf of their "progress and joy in faith."

Thus Paul's letter to the Philippians is an excellent example of how Paul uses the letter format[40] to solidify his leadership among churches, even in a church that is very loyal to him, as the Philippians are by all indications. (They send an offering [Phil. 1:5; 4:10–20]; they also send one of their leaders to minister to Paul [2:25–30].) As we shall see in the next chapter, several passages in Philippians also show what Paul expects of other leaders in his missionary network.

In Philemon, Paul is even more forthcoming in his exercise of leadership with a "friendly" church, even though he tries to be very subtle about it. One major question in studying Philemon is that of the intended recipient(s). Paul mentions several recipients in the letter's opening: "Paul, a prisoner of Christ Jesus, and Timothy our brother, To Philemon our dear friend and co-worker, to Apphia our sister, to Archippus our fellow soldier, and to the church in your house" (Philem. 1–2). Because he is mentioned first,

Philemon has been the presumed primary letter recipient. (When the letter moves to the thanksgiving in verses 4–7, Paul has a single individual in mind.) However, at least one scholar has argued for Archippus as the letter's main target because he is mentioned last, followed by the reference to the church that meets in his house.[41]

However, the more important point is that Paul sets a larger, public context for his comments and request to one individual (assumed as Philemon in my analysis below). Although the matter would seem to be a private one (apparently, the handling of a runaway slave), by invoking the names of other leaders of the community (Apphia, Archippus), as well as the church as a whole, Paul puts additional pressure on Philemon to comply with his request.

What does Paul want? This provides another subject of hot debate in the interpretation of this letter. Several alternatives suggest themselves. Paul returns a runaway slave, Onesimus, so that his master, Philemon, might forgive him (not punish him with death as was his right) and receive him as a "beloved brother" (Philem. 16). Or, Paul requests that Philemon not only forgive Onesimus, but set him free: receive him "no longer as a slave but more than a slave, a beloved brother" (Philem. 16). Whether through simple forgiveness and restoration or through outright manumission, perhaps Paul also wants Philemon to return Onesimus so that he might minister to an imprisoned Paul: "I wanted to keep him with me, so that he might be of service to me in your place during my imprisonment for the gospel" (Philem. 13). However, Paul would not keep Onesimus without Philemon's "consent" (v. 14). Thus, with this letter, he returns the now "useful" Onesimus to his rightful owner.

Alan Callahan represents another possibility. Perhaps the figurative language in the letter is not the familial language ("brother"), but rather the slave language, and Paul is calling for two brothers "in the flesh" (v. 16b) to be reconciled to each other: "Perhaps this is the reason he was separated from you for a while, so that you might have him back forever, no longer as a slave but more than a slave, a beloved brother—especially to me but how much more to you, both *in the flesh* and in the Lord" (Philem. 15–16, emphasis mine).[42] That Philemon and Onesimus were warring real-life brothers and leaders in Paul's Christian communities who needed to be brought back together, I tend to doubt. Nonetheless, the theme of reconciliation, of which Callahan reminds us, is clearly an important theme in this letter and thus corresponds to Paul's similar concerns in his other letters, such as 1–2 Corinthians, Galatians, and Romans.

In addition, Callahan is also right to highlight the leadership status of both Philemon and Onesimus, whether or not theirs was a master-slave relationship or an actual sibling relationship. First of all, Paul describes Philemon as a loving and faithful leader of the community he serves (Philem. 5).[43]

Through Philemon's ministry "the hearts of the saints have been refreshed" (Philem. 7). Under Paul's tutelage Onesimus, too, has emerged as a "useful" instrument in the gospel mission:

> I am appealing to you for my child, Onesimus, whose father I have become during my imprisonment. Formerly he was useless [*achreston*] to you, but now he is indeed useful [*euchreston*] both to you and to me. I am sending him, that is, my own heart, back to you. I wanted to keep him with me, so that he might be of service to me in your place during my imprisonment for the gospel. (Philem. 10–13)

Later, Paul furthers his play on words with Onesimus's name, which means "useful" or "beneficial," by concluding his appeal to Philemon with, "Yes, brother, let me have this benefit [*onaimen*] from you in the Lord!" (Philem. 20). Onesimus, slave or not, has become an important player in the Pauline mission.

Finally, what can we say of Paul's own leadership as demonstrated in this letter—his subtle yet firm handle on what he wants Philemon to do? By including Philemon's fellow church leaders (Apphia and Archippus), as well as the whole church, Paul puts added pressure on Philemon to respond positively to Paul's request (Philem. 2). Further, Paul claims that he can exercise a measure of authority over Philemon, but would rather "appeal" to him so that he might comply voluntarily (Philem. 8–9, 14). Paul wants Philemon to "consent," not to be "forced" (14).

By the end of the letter, Paul makes clear the kind of response he expects from Philemon. He cites their relationship as "partners" (*koinonos*), which means they have a mutual responsibility to watch out for each other's well-being. This is one way Philemon can fulfill his side of the partnership equation—"welcome [Onesimus] as you would welcome me" (Philem. 17b). As an incentive to Philemon, Paul offers to pay back any debt or wrongdoing Onesimus owes to Philemon (Philem. 18–19a). However, Paul takes it right back with this not-so-subtle reminder: "I say nothing about your owing me even your own self" (19b). Because Philemon owes his spiritual well-being to the ministry of Paul, Paul can now exact from him this startling request of, at the very least, forgiveness for a runaway slave, and maybe even his manumission.

We may not know exactly what Paul wanted Philemon to do, but we do know Paul fully expected Philemon to comply. Having moved from "appeal" language (9) to accounting language ("debt"; "benefit" [18–20]), at the very end Paul lets "the cat out of the bag," rhetorically, with the language of obedience: "Confident of your obedience [*hupakoe*], I am writing to you, knowing that you will do even more than I say" (21). Perhaps, given the overwhelming nature of slavery in Roman times, Paul cannot say outright, "set Onesimus free." However, by receiving him as a "brother"

(16), Paul really does expect Philemon to do "more than" what was normally expected, maybe even set him free.[44] Paul places further pressure on Philemon's obedience when he promises to visit soon: "One thing more–prepare a guest room for me, for I am hoping through your prayers to be restored to you" (22).

This letter, short as it is, reflects many elements of the complex nature that is Paul's leadership. He praises leaders, in this case both Onesimus and Philemon, for their service to the saints and to Paul. He shows his dependence on them–Philemon in the local congregation, Onesimus directly with Paul during the latter's imprisonment. Subtly at first, but very directly by the end of the letter, Paul shows he sees his leadership over churches as wide-ranging. He can exact compliance with theological truth (e.g., Galatians) as well as moral behavior (1 Corinthians 5–7), and even with such apparently "mundane" matters as the status of a slave (Philemon). Yet, the relationship of "brothers" and "sisters" in this new family of God makes our treatment of each other not so mundane. Thus forgiveness, reconciliation, and maybe even breaking with the excepted norms of the Empire (setting free instead of putting to death a runaway slave) are the new orders of the day. In Philemon, and indeed in all his letters, Paul directs his considerable leadership skills, including exhortation and persuasion, toward life for a new day.[45]

Paul's Letters as Instruments of His Leadership–Concluding Remarks

Thus we have seen how Paul's letters go to considerable lengths to demonstrate Paul's leadership over his congregations. He does indeed exhort, advise, persuade, and theologize with his letters. When a letter will not suffice, he sends an envoy or goes himself. In either case, he defends his right to exercise leadership because these churches were founded by him and his immediate co-workers, or others in his network, or, as in the case of the Roman churches not founded by him, because he needs them for his ongoing Gentile mission.

The letters are literary windows into Paul's leadership. However, they are not the only windows, as we have seen throughout this chapter. Paul uses every available resource in his world, the world of the Roman Empire, to advance his cause, the cause of the gospel of Jesus Christ. He feels a calling for this task, especially as it relates to the Gentile mission. Because that mission breaks new ground, Paul considers it apostolic, in a way that is different from the original disciples and apostles who ministered with the living Jesus, but nonetheless still apostolic. Paul is apostle to the Gentiles.

Paul also defines leadership as a whole among churches in a way quite distinctive from the generally expected norms in the Greco-Roman world. Many in the churches he begins identify leadership with power and glory. Paul consistently identifies the tasks of leadership with service and sacrifice.

Not only that, but he expects his leaders–those who travel with him and those who serve the churches–to exercise a similar form of leadership. At the heart of the gospel message, for Paul, lies the cross of Jesus Christ, the ultimate symbol of service, sacrifice, commitment, and also an anti-imperial posture (although this is not always explicitly stated as such). Gospel leadership needs to be just as grounded in service, sacrifice, commitment, and distinctiveness from business as usual in the Empire. Whenever Paul's leadership is challenged in the churches, he invokes these symbols of the cross, of service, and of sacrifice to defend the nature of his leadership.

In our next chapter, we explore how Paul expects similar leadership criteria from his leaders. Then we will turn, in a subsequent chapter, to a case study of leadership in one specific Pauline congregation–the Corinthians.

5

Paul's Leaders

The Study of Paul's Co-workers

Over the years Pauline studies have included various efforts to explore the nature and function of Paul's co-workers and associates. In 1971, E. Earle Ellis published a very influential article entitled "Paul and His Co-Workers,"[1] in which he discussed the quantity and quality of the named associates in the Pauline mission, including those mentioned in both Acts and Paul's undisputed and disputed letters. Ellis pointed out that "in the Book of Acts and the canonical literature ascribed to Paul some 100 names, often coupled with assorted titles, are associated with the Apostle."[2] Ellis noted that most of these were Paul's "co-workers in the Christian mission." Paul ascribed various "titles" to them. Ellis deduced that "if one eliminates those with general or no designation and those who appear only in Acts, there remain thirty-six persons associated with Paul under nine designations."[3] After these initial calculations, Ellis proceeds to discuss these designations more closely, including the most frequent: *synergos* (co-worker), *adelphos* (brother or sister), *diakonos* (servant) and *apostolos* (apostle or messenger). He especially notes the frequency of the term *adelphos* that Paul ascribes to many of his associates. Ellis suggests that Paul, more often than not, used this term specifically for his co-workers and associates rather than generically for all believers as traditionally understood.[4] This argument occupies a large portion of this essay, although more attention could have been paid to the actual people carrying this and other "titles," as well as to their role in the Pauline mission.

Bengt Holmberg contributed another important work exploring Paul's leaders. Holmberg writes specifically about the distribution of power in the Pauline churches.[5] He goes beyond Ellis's description of the "nine categories" to actually discuss in more detail the persons whom Holmberg argues were the closest associates of Paul, including Titus, Timothy, Silas, Apollos, and Barnabas.[6] Each of them, in their own way, had an important impact on the conduct of Paul's Gentile mission.[7] However, Holmberg relies heavily on the accounts in Acts to fill descriptions of these individuals, especially Apollos and Barnabas. What Paul actually said about them in his letters is much more limited than the fuller description Holmberg provides. Nonetheless, Holmberg's account gives us some insight into what Paul expects from his associates.

First of all, Paul had certain expectations of his "children" in the new assemblies he founded. To have such expectations and convey them to the churches was in itself "an exercise of power."[8] Second, Paul exercised this "power" in a variety of ways, including through his "representatives," especially his closest associates, Timothy and Titus. Holmberg describes how Paul commended these individuals to his churches as being "helpers" of Paul and that Paul expects his churches to receive them as they would receive Paul, that is, with "recognition," "obedience," and "financial support."[9]

When Wayne Meeks summarizes the "governance" patterns of Pauline churches, he divides the types of Pauline leaders into three: apostles, fellow workers, and local leaders.[10] Paul, of course, is the preeminent apostle in his churches. Others exercise various degrees of influence in the Pauline churches. These include the Jerusalem apostles and "the apostles of the churches," who are the more or less authorized representatives of Pauline and other assemblies (cf. Phil. 2:25; 2 Cor. 8:23). Among the major aspects of his apostleship Paul sees his role as a model of the faith for others to imitate. His "fellow workers" follow suit. They are closely associated with Paul and have various degrees of dependence on him. Among the closest are Silvanus, Timothy, and Sosthenes, all of whom Paul names as coauthors of one or more of his letters. Timothy travels to Thessalonica and Corinth on Paul's behalf and stands ready to travel to Philippi during one of Paul's imprisonments (Phil. 2:19). Silvanus helps Paul establish the church at Corinth (2 Cor. 1:19). Titus another "fellow worker" (2 Cor. 12:18; Gal. 2:1,3; 2 Tim. 4:10; Titus 1:4) helps Paul resolve conflicts with the Corinthians (2 Cor. 2:13; 7:6–16) and is a major player in organizing the Corinthian contribution to Paul's all-important Jerusalem collection (2 Cor. 8:16–24).

Others are more independent of Paul, but nonetheless exercise important leadership in the Pauline mission, some over long periods of time such as the missionary couple, Prisca and Aquila (Rom. 16:3–4; Acts 18:2, 26). Finally, local leaders emerge in Paul's churches. When Paul discusses their roles, he focuses on their gifts and functions rather than any titles or offices they hold locally. Some of these local leaders become envoys or "apostles" of their churches to Paul and subsequently become Pauline co-workers (e.g., Epaphroditus, in Phil. 2:25–29; 4:18). Others start their own assemblies as part of the overall Pauline mission; they become "missionary founders" (e.g., Epaphras, Col. 1:7–8; 4:17).

All of these various types of leaders are windows into Paul's practice of leadership. In the previous chapter, I argued that Paul employed a variety of means to exercise his leadership, including his letters and a financial relationship of some sort with at least some of his churches.[11] In this chapter I want to concentrate on Paul's leaders and what they show us about leadership in the Pauline communities. Moreover, I want to acknowledge that much of Paul's discussion of his leaders occurs in the context of commending them to his assemblies. Commendation was actually a widespread practice in the Greco-Roman world, with its own conventions and expectations. Paul employs this practice to recognize the contributions of co-workers and local leaders in his assemblies.

The Commendation of Leaders in Paul's Churches

In his study of Pauline power, Bengt Holmberg observed, "Paul recommends [Timothy and Titus] to the churches by means of letters of introduction (*epistolai sustatikai*) incorporated in his epistles, and this fact alone tells us that his position is above that of those addressed and of his assistants."[12] In fact, elite leaders in Greco-Roman society wrote letters of commendation to promote patron-client relations. Richard Saller, a noted historian of ancient patronage, argued that "scholars have not always taken sufficient notice of the Republican tradition of recommendations."[13] Patrons would write letters of commendation to their peers on behalf of protégés and others whom they hoped to promote to positions of power within the imperial hierarchy. Only sporadically has New Testament scholarship taken note of the fact that Paul, in the context of letters to his assemblies, wrote commendations for various leaders, including close associates and local church leaders.[14] Thus, Pauline commendations represent a window into Paul's leaders and Pauline leadership in general.

Commendation in the Roman Empire

The political and social elite, in particular, practiced commendation in the Roman Empire. The models for writing commendation letters included such Roman luminaries as Cicero (106–43 B.C.E.), Pliny (ca. 61–ca. 120 C.E.), and Fronto (ca. 100–ca. 166 C.E.), all of them connected directly to emperors. From all of them we have an extensive collection of commendation letters. Fronto, the teacher of the emperor Marcus Aurelius, considered himself a loyal critic of the Ciceronian traditions in letter writing, and sought to improve the tradition. However, "Cicero and Fronto's *commendationes* to provincial governors look very much alike." Such similarity suggests that "exchange relationships remained essentially unchanged from the Republic" to the Empire.[15] Thus patronage and its principle vehicle of communication, the commendation letter, were significant instruments for a long period of time in the cohesion and durability of the ruling class of the Roman imperial order.

A letter from Cicero's collection shows very well the nature of Roman commendation letters. Cicero endorsed a candidate for a consulship as a "most admirable and gallant of citizens [*optimus et fortissium civis*]; a man of great influence [*summa auctoritate*] and soundest sentiments [*optime sentiens*]." Cicero concluded that people like this were "leaders of public policy [*auctores consili publici*]." He decried the paucity of such character traits in most other Roman consular candidates.[16] However, at the end of the letter, Cicero also shows how the commendation letter was an exchange of power between those already in power. He wrote:

> For myself, I never fail, and I never shall fail, to protect those dear to you: and whether they appeal to me for advice or whether they do not, I can in either case guarantee my love and loyalty [*benevolentur fidesque*] to yourself.[17]

Cicero's personal relationship to the letter recipient, as well as to the subject of the letter, stood behind the dynamics of this commendation letter. Patron-client relations were motivated by persons of similar aristocratic status supporting each other and their clients and protégés. The message of each commendation letter tended to be: "this man is a friend or client of mine and hence of worthy character."[18] In many ways, leadership depended upon one's connections in the social hierarchy.

Similarly, Pliny wrote to the Emperor Trajan in support of a good friend:

> As a result of your generosity to me, Sir, Rosianus Geminus became one of my closest friends; for when I was consul he was my quaestor. I always found him devoted to my interests and ever since then he has treated me with the greatest deference...I therefore pray to you to give your personal attention to my request for his advancement; if you place any confidence in my advice you will bestow on him your favor. He will not fail to earn further promotion in whatever post you place him...I pray you, Sir, most urgently to permit me to rejoice as soon as possible in the due promotion of my quaestor—that is to say in my own advancement in his person.[19]

One immediately notes that the loyalty and "deference" of Geminus to Pliny made possible this endorsement to the Roman Emperor. In other words, Pliny and Geminus had a patron-client relationship. However, Pliny's relationship to the Emperor also helped. Pliny had not failed to make good recommendations to the Emperor in the past; so the latter could assume that this one should be no different because Pliny had gained the Emperor's "confidence." Yet, the passage concludes noting that a promotion for Pliny's client meant "advancement" for Pliny himself. Thus, the status of patrons benefited from the enhanced status of their clients. Although Pliny referred to Geminus as a "close friend," the latter's deference and dependence on Pliny's largesse for his leadership advancement definitely made Geminus the client in this relationship of patronage. Moreover, a letter of commendation made possible both Geminus *and* Pliny's status enhancement. Thus, the commendation letter in Roman imperial practice was a tool of patronage, status, and leadership.

The Form and Structure of Commendation

An important aspect of the use of commendation was its form and structure. Chan Hie-Kim has studied the form and structure of Greco-Roman letters of commendation and suggests several fundamental elements in all such letters. The letter writer usually began by identifying the subject of the commendation, usually by name and also with some reference to the subject's family or household relationships. The writer then indicated the qualities that commended this individual, including personal, social, and financial criteria—what character traits he or she had; what family, business, and political connections they bore with them; and the state of their, or their family's, economic well-being. Wealth and patronage connections were critical commendation criteria in most Greco-Roman commendations among the elite. Toward the end of the letter, the writer made the formal commendation request. This request usually entailed some kind of general hospitality, employment opportunity, and/or advancement in rank or status. In addition to the elite Roman literary letters by Cicero, Pliny, and Fronto, Kim studied many Greek-language commendations from the Hellenistic and Roman imperial periods in particular. Many of these merely commend an envoy, including slaves and freed persons, as they carried out business transactions on behalf of their masters or patrons.[20]

Paul's Commendations

Paul's commendations of leaders have similar elements to those of Greco-Roman commendation letters. He identifies the leaders he wishes to commend, by name in all but one instance. He cites the criteria that commend these individuals, i.e., their "credentials." And he makes a request on behalf of these individuals to the letter recipients, namely the congregation to which Paul is writing. Thus Paul's commendations, in terms of structure, parallel the structures of typical Greco-Roman letters, both the private papyri letters Kim studied and the more universally known, literary ones by Cicero, Pliny, and Fronto. However, differences abound, particularly with regard to whom Paul commends, their apparent status in the larger society, and the reasons or criteria Paul employs for commending them. In what follows, I will review the major commendations in the uncontested Pauline corpus and discuss the leadership criteria Paul employs to commend these individuals to his churches. In this way, we can ascertain the character and function of Paul's leaders and add to our picture of Pauline leadership in general.

PAUL'S SELF-COMMENDATIONS

First, however, I must note that Paul commends himself, his apostleship, and his leadership in a few instances, mostly in defense of his ministry. Such "self-commendation," including the commendation criteria of his own ministry, illuminates what Paul expected of his commended leaders. In writing to the Corinthians after a disastrous visit and "painful letter" (2 Cor. 2:1–4), Paul describes his frustration with the apparent Corinthian insistence on letters of commendation that should have accompanied Paul's missionary activity:

> Are we beginning to commend ourselves again? Surely we do not need, as some do, letters of recommendation to you or from you, do we? You yourselves are our letter, written on our hearts, to be known and read by all; and you show that you are a letter of Christ, prepared by us, written not with ink but with the Spirit of the living God, not on tablets of stone but on tablets of human hearts. (2 Cor. 3:1–3)

Some in Corinth expect Paul, like other leaders in the Greco-Roman world, to travel with letters of commendation from others to ratify Paul's leadership among them. Paul insists, however, that the authenticity of his ministry comes not from written letters but from the spiritual success his ministry has demonstrated among the Corinthians themselves–"you are a letter of Christ, prepared by us." Several times throughout 2 Corinthians, Paul questions why he should have to commend himself: "We are not commending ourselves to you again, but giving you an opportunity to boast about us, so that you may be able to answer those who boast in outward appearance and not in the heart" (2 Cor. 5:12; cf. 4:2; 6:4; 10:12, 18; and 12:11). For Paul, any commendation of his leadership must come from the actions, motivations, and results of his ministry, not from a written letter from external patrons.

Yet, in effect, Paul proceeds in large portions of 2 Corinthians to offer a self-commendation of his ministry.[21] First, he defends his ministry as the ministry of a new covenant (3:4–18). Then, he sees his ministry as a "treasure" (4:7) that he holds by the "God's mercy" (4:1). Yet, God chooses to carry out this ministry of the new covenant in "clay jars" (4:7), weak human beings, so that ultimately it is God who is commended by it, not

God's "clay jars." In fact, these "jars" suffer as they carry out this ministry, and thus Paul offers as a fundamental criterion of his leadership the first of several "hardship lists" in canonical 2 Corinthians:

> We are afflicted in every way, but not crushed; perplexed, but not driven to despair; persecuted, but not forsaken; struck down, but not destroyed; always carrying in the body the death of Jesus, so that the life of Jesus may also be made visible in our bodies. For while we live, we are always being given up to death for Jesus' sake, so that the life of Jesus may be made visible in our mortal flesh. So death is at work in us, but life in you. (2 Cor. 4:8–12)[22]

Paul makes the connection between his suffering for the cause of Christ and the criteria for his self-commendation more explicit in a second "hardship list":

> But as servants of God we have commended ourselves in every way: through great endurance, in afflictions, hardships, calamities, beatings, imprisonments, riots, labors, sleepless nights, hunger; by purity, knowledge, patience, kindness, holiness of spirit, genuine love, truthful speech, and the power of God; with the weapons of righteousness for the right hand and for the left; in honor and dishonor, in ill repute and good repute. (2 Cor. 6:4–8a)

Thus Paul offers a "biography of reversal"[23] in his self-commendation. Instead of the positive criteria expected in Greco-Roman commendation, such as good health, ample wealth, and great family connections, Paul surprises his readers with pictures of "afflictions, hardships, [and] calamities." For Paul, his authority is best expressed by "the dialectical, even at times paradoxical pattern by which he tries to employ the fundamental proclamation of Christ's death and resurrection as a paradigm of authentic power."[24] Paul proclaims that, like Jesus,

> We are treated as imposters, and yet are true; as unknown, and yet are well known; as dying, and see—we are alive; as punished, and yet not killed; as sorrowful, yet always rejoicing; as poor, yet making many rich; as having nothing, and yet possessing everything. (2 Cor. 6:8b–10)

This self-commendation supports a "ministry of reconciliation" (2 Cor. 5:18–19). Believers become "ambassadors for Christ," even though Christ, "who knew no sin," was made "to be sin" that "we might become the righteousness [or "justice," *dikaiosunē*] of God" (5:20–21). So, as Christ suffered unjustly, Paul believes this, too, is part of his ministry. Hardship, ironically enough, commends him.

The irony is even more explicit in 2 Corinthians 10–13, where Paul must defend his ministry against outside agitators, whom he condemns as "false apostles" (11:13) and satirizes as "super-apostles" (11:5; 12:11). Several times he refers to the commendation of these opposing leaders:

> We do not dare to classify or compare ourselves with some of those who commend themselves. But when they measure themselves by one another, and compare themselves with one another, they do not show good sense. (10:12)

When Paul wants to discuss the commendation of his ministry, he must rely on the commendation of God: "'Let the one who boasts, boast of the Lord.' For it is not those who commend themselves that are approved, but those whom the Lord commends" (10:17–18).

Yet, what God commends seems so unlike that which larger Greco-Roman circles commend. Paul turns to "a little foolishness" to describe that which commends him. He will not accept that he is in anyway "inferior" to opposing leaders in Corinth (11:5–6). Their focus on financial issues and Paul's rejection of financial support from the Corinthians should not undermine his gospel. "Did I commit a sin humbling myself so that you might be exalted, because I proclaimed God's good news to you free of charge?" (11:7). Paul did not accept support from the Corinthians so as not to be a financial burden (11:8–9), he says.[25] Such refusal, however, should not disqualify him from rightful leadership of the community he established and that he loves (11:10–11). Moreover, his qualifications entail his willingness to forego honor and position among other Jewish Christian missionaries. ("Are they Hebrews? So am I. Are they Israelites? So am I. Are they descendants of Abraham? So am I." [11:22].) Once again, he describes his leadership in negative terms: "Are they ministers of Christ? I am talking like a madman–I am a better one: with far greater labors, far more imprisonments, with countless floggings, and often near death" (2 Cor. 11:23).

Paul then describes the various beatings, shipwrecks, dangers, toils, hardships, sleepless nights, hunger, thirst, and anxiety he has endured on behalf of his churches (11:24–28). In all of this, however, he has depended on God to carry out the gospel mission. Thus, Paul "will boast of the things that show [his] weakness" (11:30). "For," he writes later in the letter, "whenever I am weak, then I am strong" (12:10). Leadership that ultimately depends on God fosters strength rather than weakness.

Commendations in the Greco-Roman world, including self-commendation, invoked high status, patron-client ties, and financial wherewithal. Apparently, some in Corinth, those who sought to depose Paul's apostleship and install "super-apostles," invoked the same qualities as well. Paul must commend himself, and ultimately God, to forestall such an action that in his estimation could be detrimental to the gospel witness in Corinth. He does so by siding with the "foolishness" and "shame" of the cross, rather than with the glory of the "super-apostles." Peter Marshall writes, "When Paul commends his apostleship in 2 Cor. 10–12 and the

Corinthian letters generally, he mainly draws upon conventional notions of shame rather than of honour, and upon terms which denote inferior rather than superior status."[26] Does Paul expound similar qualities when he commends other leaders to his congregations?

The Commendation Passages

Paul writes commendation in six of the seven uncontested letters. Interestingly, Galatians represents the only letter that does not contain commendation. Commentators regularly note that Galatians, likewise, does not contain a thanksgiving in its structure. Rhetorically, the absence of thanksgiving *and* commendation speaks to the serious concerns Paul has about theology and leadership in this community. In addition, among the disputed letters, only Colossians, the contested letter with the most Pauline epistolary features, has commendation (Col. 4:7–9). Therefore, commendation of leaders is a regular, if not regularly recognized, feature of a Pauline letter.

First Thessalonians contains one commendation to leaders of his congregations (1 Thess. 5:12–13). First Corinthians has two in one passage (1 Cor. 16:15–18). In 2 Corinthians Paul commends a set of envoys to the Corinthians for the purposes of the Jerusalem collection (2 Cor. 8:16–24). Philippians, although a short letter, has three commendation passages for four people: Timothy (Phil. 2:19–24), Epaphroditus (Phil. 2:25–30), and Euodia and Syntyche (Phil. 4:2–3). Paul begins the long set of greetings at the end of his longest letter, Romans, with the commendation of Phoebe (Rom. 16:1–2). As we shall see below, structurally Philemon has all the features of commendation, and, therefore, represents the only full commendation letter in the Pauline corpus. In what follows, I will take each of these commendation passages in turn, review their commendation elements, and most importantly discuss what they teach us about Paul and his leaders.

1 Thessalonians 5:12–13

I have already noted the probable circumstances surrounding 1 Thessalonians in chapter 4, previously. I pointed out that one of the ways Paul consoles the young persecuted assembly in Thessalonica and exercises leadership over them from a distance is to encourage recognition of hard-working local leaders: "I exhort you, brothers and sisters, to respect those who labor among you and help you in the Lord and admonish you. Esteem them highly in love because of their work. Be at peace among yourselves" (1 Thess. 5:12–13, author's translation).

STRUCTURE

The commendation structure of identity, criteria, and request is clearly discernible in this pericope, although Paul does not identify those being commended by name. Rather, the criteria commending them identifies who they are. Therefore, Paul commends those who labor, help, and admonish the community. He exhorts the community to respect them and esteem them highly "because of their work."

Paul employs three participles to identify the local leaders and describe their work on behalf of the community. Elsewhere, I have called these the "participles of service."[27] Each of them reflects a different aspect of *diakonia* (service) that these leaders exercise for the Thessalonian community. The first participle is *kopiōntas* ("those who labor"). The root word is the noun *kopos*–"labor," or usually more specifically, "hard labor."[28] The term is used throughout 1 Thessalonians as Paul discusses his ministry, that of his missionary colleagues, and what he expects of believers in Thessalonica:

> You remember our labor and toil [*ton kopon hemōn kai ton moxthon*], brothers and sisters; we worked night and day, that we might not burden any of you while we proclaimed to you the gospel of God. (1 Thess. 2:9)

This passage refers specifically to manual labor that Paul engages in outside of the ministry in order not to be a financial burden to the ministry. However, later in the letter he refers to the whole ministry in Thessalonica as a "labor":

> For this reason, when I could bear it no longer, I sent [Timothy] to find out about your faith; I was afraid that somehow the tempter had tempted you and that our labor [*kopos*] had been in vain. (1 Thess. 3:5)

Thus *kopos* refers to hard work on behalf of the gospel. Not only Paul, but his missionary associates as well have carried out such labor. Paul expects the same from local leaders that emerge from his faith communities.

The second participle, used less frequently by Paul, is more difficult to translate. *Proistamenous* comes from the verb *proistēmi,* which literally means "place first" and thus often refers in Greek literature to "presiding" or "leading." Therefore, the *Revised Standard Version* translated the term in 1 Thessalonians 5:12 as "those who...are over you" and the *New Revised Standard Version* uses "those who...have charge of you." However, the term also carries an alternative meaning, also used frequently in the literature: "to be concerned about," "to care for," "to help."[29] In Romans 12:8, for example, Paul lists various gifts available to the church, including "the one who contributes, do so liberally, the one who gives aid (*proistamenous*) do so with zeal, and the one who shows mercy, to do so with cheerfulness" (my translation). The confluence of these three gifts of service (contributing, helping, and showing mercy) in Romans 12 strengthens the translation in the triad of 1 Thessalonians 5:12–those who labor, help, and admonish. All three are indicative of the service these individuals practice in the community. Paul wants to commend such service to the rest of the community.

However, this does not mean that *proistamenous* does not also carry the original sense of leadership in this context. Rather, a leader in the Pauline communities must be one who labors, helps, instructs, and serves on behalf of the community. Only in that way does a person demonstrate his or her leadership.

In most cases *proistēmi* seems to have sense (a) "to lead," but the context shows in each case that one must also take into account sense (b) "to care for." This is explained by the fact that caring was the obligation of leading members of the infant church.[30]

Thus, through this commendation that appears in one of his earliest letters, Paul introduces the notion that leaders in his assemblies must demonstrate their care and concern for the community if they expect Paul to commend them as leaders.

The third participle of service, *nouthetountas*, continues in this vein. The root word, the verb *noutheteō,* means "to counsel about avoidance or cessation of an improper course of conduct, "to admonish," "warn," or "instruct."[31] One interpreter suggests that the term refers to teaching that is "addressed to the will" rather than to the mind, with the intention of changing behavior.[32] Just after the commendation, Paul exhorts the entire community to "admonish [*noutheteite*] the idlers" among them (1 Thess. 5:14). Thus Paul seems to strengthen the hand of community leaders by encouraging all to cooperate in correcting and instructing those who are not doing their share. Indeed, "beloved" (*adelphoi*) should also "encourage the faint hearted, help the weak, be patient with all" (5:14). In other words, these are community responsibilities that some have already begun to practice (5:12). For the latter, commendation is merited (5:12–13); but all are invited to help, the implication being that they, too, could receive leadership commendation.

THE REQUEST

The final aspect of this commendation is the formal commendation request. The request comes in two parts here—*eidenai* ("recognize") those who labor, help, and admonish you (5:12) and *hēgeisthai* ("esteem") them very highly because of their *ergon* ("work").[33] Awareness and recognition is what Paul wants for the emerging local leaders in Thessalonica. With a different term (*epiginōskō),* but a similar root meaning as here (*oida*–to know), Paul also commends recognition of leaders in 1 Corinthians (1 Cor. 16:15–18). He also wants them to be honored ("esteemed").

Many Roman commendation writers sought honor and status for their protégés and clients. For example, Fronto requested "not only protection but advancement and honor"[34] for one Julius Aquilinus. Yet here Paul does not seek "advancement" in a social hierarchy but rather "the highest regard" for persons who have "worked" for the well being of the community. *Ergos* ("work") is another term like *kopos* ("labor") and *diakonia* ("service").

We shall see in other commendations that Paul uses such terms to describe his gospel mission and ministry. Paul describes his colleagues in the ministry as *synergoi* ("co-workers"). Paul urges recognition and the highest respect for leaders in the community, not because of their status or titles, but "because of what they do," their hard work on behalf of the gospel community.

The final phrase of this commendation passage, "Be at peace among yourselves" (5:13b), may actually introduce the general, community exhortations that follow (thus, "Be at peace among yourselves. And we urge you, beloved, to admonish the idlers, encourage the faint hearted, help the weak, be patient with all of them" 5:13b-14.[35] However, it also might be a request for "peace" between leaders and the rest of the community and thus an extension of the commendation. Perhaps Paul commends emerging leaders in the community because of some resistance to them. Paul includes a call for peace at the end of the commendation because he expects "good relations between the church leaders and the rest of the Christian community."[36] Commendation helps the leaders do their work in the community better.

SUMMARY

This initial commendation demonstrates that Paul employs the basic structural elements of commendation. He identifies the leaders, in this case by citing their credentials. The credentials include three aspects of their work for the gospel community–hard labor, caring concern, and good instruction. Because of such efforts (*ergos*), the leaders merit recognition and esteem from the community. Indeed, they lead because they care, incorporating the dual meaning of a key term in this commendation, *proistamenous*. As we shall see, the thrust of this passage, the qualities of Paul's leaders, will be echoed in subsequent commendations.

1 Corinthians 16:15–18

This passage toward the end of 1 Corinthians would seem to follow a pattern of ending Pauline letters with commendations, final exhortations, travel plans, and greetings, as in 1 Thessalonians.[37] However, the mention of Stephanas at the outset of the letter (1 Cor. 1:16) as one of the few people that Paul baptized in this community strategically sets up this endorsement at the end of the letter. Even though he follows typical epistolary formulations, nothing in Paul is without rhetorical import.

The commendation of Stephanas and his household in 1 Corinthians 16:15–18 is actually two commendations in one, as noted by Kim's structural analysis.[38] Twice Paul follows the identity, criteria, and request model in this passage. Nonetheless, the dual commendation has a "singular emphasis on Stephanas."[39] He is mentioned by name twice in the passage. His "household" (16:15) presumably including "Fortunatus and Achaicus," persons named specifically at the outset of the second commendation along with Stephanas (16:17), comprises the other subject of the commendation:

> Now, brothers and sisters, you know that members of the household of Stephanas were the first converts in Achaia, and they have devoted themselves to the service of the saints; I urge you to put yourselves at the service of such people, and of everyone who works and toils with them. I rejoice at the coming of Stephanas and Fortunatus and Achaicus, because they have made up for your absence; for they refreshed my spirit as well as yours. So give recognition to such persons. (1 Cor. 16:15–18)

FIRST COMMENDATION: VV. 15–16

The first commendation focuses on the "household of Stephanas" and their "service" (*diakonia*) to the "saints," Paul's frequent assignation for believers, those called out from the world to be "saints of God," (cf. Rom. 1:7; 16:2; 1 Cor. 1:2; 2 Cor. 1:1; Phil. 1:1; Philem. 4). Paul notes that Stephanas and his household were the "first fruits" (*aparchē*) or "first converts," as the NRSV suggests, of the Corinthian *ekklēsia*. In another letter, Paul sends greetings to Epaenetus, a believer residing in Rome, but who had been Paul's "first convert [*aparchē*] in Asia for Christ" (Rom. 16:5). Paul also uses the term with reference to Christ's resurrection as the "first fruits" of all believers' future resurrection (1 Cor. 15:20, 23).[40] Thus the term carried important theological weight for Paul. "First fruits," like Christ's resurrection and like initial converts in a region, could be expected to produce positive results for the gospel community.

Thus, Stephanas was a key figure in the Corinthian church. He was a "first fruit," baptized by Paul, and a "householder" who may have opened his home to Paul and provided financial support to him and the community as a whole.[41] Nonetheless, as he did with the Thessalonian leaders, Paul here focuses his commendation on the service of Stephanas to the community, as well as to Paul.

Stephanas and his household have "devoted themselves [*etaxan eautous*] to the service [*diakonian*] of the saints" in Corinth. The verb *tassō* refers to being placed in a "fixed spot," thus being appointed. However, in its reflexive form, as here, the term refers to a self appointment, usually by means of some kind of activity, either work or service. For example, in both Plato's *Republic* (2.371c) and Xeno's *Memorabilia* (2.1.11), a form of *tassō* is related to *douleia* (servanthood) or *diakonia* (service). Thus "to assign oneself" is to "devote oneself to a service."[42] This is the mark of Stephanas's leadership in the Corinthian community—devotion to service on behalf of "saints."

The commendation request on behalf of Stephanas and his household also invokes service: Because of the service of Stephanas, the Corinthian believers should therefore (*hina*) "devote themselves [*hypotassesthe*] to such people and all those who work together [*synergounti*] and labor [*kopiōnti*]" (16:16). Paul offers a play-on-words with forms of *tasso*. Not only Stephanas and his household must serve the community, but the community must respond in kind to the servant leadership of Stephanas. The verb *hypotasso* appears frequently in Paul with reference to submission to God, or to the law or to the will of God (1 Cor. 15:27–28; Rom. 8:7; 10:3), or to government authorities or church prophets (Rom. 13:1; 1 Cor. 14:32). Only here in 1 Corinthians 16:16 does Paul use it with reference to the relationship between a church and those who serve it.[43] Because of the emphatic "and you also should *hypotassesthe*," the NRSV is probably right to translate the term here not as "submit yourselves" to Stephanas, but to *also* "put yourselves at the service" of Stephanas in anything he has need of. In this commendation, Paul pursues reciprocity of service for his leaders, not just blind submission by others. This holds even in this case, where Stephanas has status as a "first fruit" and a "householder."

In addition, Paul calls for exemplification in this commendation request. The community ought not just "serve" Stephanas and company, but "everyone who works and toils" for the cause of the gospel (16:16b). When Paul did not indicate the names of the leaders of the Thessalonian community, he may have wanted to open up the opportunity for leadership to *all* who labor, help, and instruct the community. In 1 Corinthians 16:16, Paul is more explicit. Anyone who follows the example of Stephanas and the others in their service, work, and hard labor for the church merits the recognition Paul requests for them. Thus Paul commends reciprocity, mutual service, and exemplification, following the examples set by others, in congregational leadership.[44]

SECOND COMMENDATION: VV. 17–18

In the second commendation, Paul names two of Stephanas's household members–Fortunatus and Achaicus. Both names have been linked to slave names because they seem to be "nicknames" (the terms, respectively, connote "Lucky" and "the Greek").[45] At any rate, the important aspect of this second commendation is that now Paul praises these individuals for their ministry to and presence with Paul:

> I rejoice at the coming of Stephanas and Fortunatus and Achaicus, because they have made up for your absence; for they refreshed my spirit as well as yours. So give recognition to such persons. (1 Cor. 16:17–18)

The presence (*parousia*) of these individuals with Paul has brought joy (*chairō*,–"I rejoice") and much-needed "refreshment" (*anepausan*) to Paul. They have "made up for [the] absence" [*aneplerōsan*] of the Corinthians as Paul finds himself far removed from them (probably being in Ephesus

[1 Cor. 16:8]). However, their present ministry to Paul is nothing new, he asserts, for besides "refreshing" Paul's tired spirit, they have done the same in the past to the Corinthians ("for they refreshed my spirit as well as yours," 16:18a). Thus, for this further proof of their *diakonia* to the gospel community, including the community's founder, Paul reiterates his commendation: "Give recognition [*epiginōskete*] to such persons" (1 Cor. 16:18b), echoing the commendation request of 1 Thessalonians 5:13. Besides supporting the leadership of Stephanas and members of his household (including perhaps slaves!), this final recommendation repeats the exemplification of 16:16. Leaders who "serve" and "refresh" like Stephanas, Fortunatus, and Achaicus merit recognition for their leadership and also are worthy of "imitation," a term that Paul does not use here or in any of his commendations, but certainly lies behind several of them, including 1 Thessalonians 5:12–13 and 1 Corinthians 16:15–18.[46]

SUMMARY

Our findings in 1 Corinthians 16:15–18 parallel some of the results in the commendation of 1 Thessalonians 5:12–13. In both cases Paul exhorts recognition of leaders who have served the local gospel mission with hard work and caring concern, even "refreshment." In both cases, Paul is less concerned with the social status of his commended leaders than with what they have done positively on behalf of the gospel community. We do not know anything about the social status of the Thessalonian leaders; their names are not even mentioned. We do know that Stephanas is a householder, who may own slaves (perhaps Fortunatus and Achaicus). So Stephanas may be a man of some means.[47] However, unlike typical Roman imperial commendations, Paul does not focus on socioeconomic factors. Rather, his commendation criteria cite matters of service, work, and concern for the church community. In addition, in both 1 Thessalonians and 1 Corinthians, Paul establishes the commended leaders as models for others to follow. Stephanas and his household members, in particular, exemplify how other members of the community can expect leadership recognition. In 2 Corinthians, Paul also commends a group of exemplary leaders.

2 Corinthians 8:16–24

Strictly speaking, 2 Corinthians 8:16–24 represents the "commendation of envoys," a somewhat different ancient convention that focused on "commissioning" and "sending" rather than "commending" and "recognizing" (cf. Phil. 2:19–24; 1 Thess. 3:1–10; 1 Cor. 4:17). Nonetheless, commendation of the envoys could also be incorporated into an envoy passage, as is the case in 2 Corinthians 8.[48]

As noted earlier, I support the integrity of 2 Corinthians 1–9, partially on the grounds that Paul's reconciliation with the Corinthians, described in chapters 2 and 7, allows Paul to turn his attention to the collection for

Jerusalem in chapters 8 and 9.[49] After reminding the Corinthians that the Macedonians have already contributed to the collection (2 Cor. 8:1–15), Paul describes his plans for completing the contribution of the Corinthians for this cause. He will send them an "advance team" to prepare them to give. Three people constitute the leaders of this team, and Paul wishes to clarify their credentials for this important task. Thus, he commends them to the Corinthians.

TITUS–2 COR. 8:16–17

Each envoy has a different set of leadership qualities that commends him for the task of the collection. Paul has already described Titus as a successful ambassador of reconciliation between an apostle and his community (cf. 2 Cor. 2:12–13; 7:6–16). Thus, it is logical that Titus should take on this next important task: "So that we might urge Titus that, as he had already made a beginning, so he should also complete this generous undertaking [i.e., the collection] among you" (2 Cor. 8:6).

The qualities that commend Titus for the collection effort include the same eagerness for (2 Cor. 8:16) (*spoudē*) the well-being of the Corinthians. This echoes the qualities Paul mentioned in previous commendations–the caring concern (*proistamenous*) of the Thessalonian leaders and the devoted service (*diakonia*) to the community by Stephanas and his household members. Just as Titus accepted the previous assignment to heal the rift between Paul and the Corinthians, he now accepts, with great earnestness (*spoudaioteros*), the assignment to return to Corinth and bring about completion of the Corinthian contribution to the Jerusalem collection (8:17).

"THE FAMOUS BROTHER"–2 COR. 8:18–21

However, Titus will not travel alone. With him, Paul sends "the brother who is famous [*epainos*–also meaning "praised," "honored," or "commended"] among all the churches for his proclaiming the good news" (8:18). This individual seems to have an independent and highly respected ministry, apart from Paul. Indeed, "since this famous brother has built his reputation on the gospel, that is, on preaching and missionary work (verse 18), he is presumably not a local leader but someone widely recognized in all the major cities, someone perhaps not unlike Paul himself."[50] However, despite the envoy's status in the movement, Paul does not name him, as he does Titus. He refers only to his notoriety and his appointment by the churches.

Two factors converge here. First, Paul needs this well-known, but independent preacher as part of the team to lend integrity to the process of the collection, especially to the already suspicious Corinthians. Paul makes that clear in the next sentence: The famous brother

> has been appointed by the churches to travel with us while we are administering this generous undertaking...We intend that no one

should blame us about this generous gift that we are administering, for we intend to do what is right not only in the Lord's sight but also in the sight of others. (8:19b, 20–21)

Having a member of the team appointed not by Paul, but by the churches, and a highly respected, independent missionary at that, lends support to the cause of this collection that is intended "to show our goodwill" (verse 19), between Paul's "diaspora,"[51] Gentile believers and the "mother" church in Jerusalem.

However, a second factor drives this Pauline pragmatism. While the brother is "famous" and appointed by the churches, he shall remain nameless in this passage because Titus, Paul's named associate, will, as a representative of Paul, be the head of the delegation. In that way, it will be clear to all, especially the Corinthians, that this "generous undertaking," the collection, remains a "generous gift that *we* [read 'Paul,' emphasis author's] are administering" (verse 20). Titus is also part of that "we," at Paul's request, but not the "famous brother." Yet, the brother will travel to Corinth, with Paul's full commendation, and also that of his (the brother's) churches.

"THE APPROVED BROTHER"–8:22

The third "brother" is also unnamed but has less of a wide-ranging reputation than the "famous brother." His description puts him closer to Titus and probably part of Paul's immediate team in some form. He has *spoudē*, earnestness, like Titus, and has "great confidence" in the Corinthians, like Titus now has (8:22; cf. 7:15–16). Above all, Paul has "tested" and thus approved [*edokimasamen*] him over time. Paul often uses *dokimos* and related terms to refer to a period of testing and approval that all of God's servants, including himself, need to undergo in the gospel mission (cf. 1 Thess. 2:4; Phil. 2:22; 2 Cor. 13:5).

This third brother has gone through this testing period in the gospel mission and proven himself. This also shows that he is closely tied to Paul, and is not an independent operator like the "famous brother." The third brother also remains nameless, like the famous brother. However, he depends more on Paul, and now Titus, for his leadership assignments than the famous brother does.

SUMMARY OF QUALIFICATIONS OF THE ENVOYS AND THE COMMENDATION REQUEST–8:23–24

Paul reiterates the qualities of his envoys (8:23) in the context of making the formal commendation request (8:24). However, in this summary he concentrates singularly on his lead envoy, Titus: "As for Titus, he is my partner [*koinōnos*] and co-worker [*synergos*] in your service; as for our brothers, they are messengers [*apostoloi*] of the churches, the glory of Christ" (8:23).

As a "partner" and "co-worker" of Paul, Titus clearly belongs to Paul's inner circle of missionary colleagues. Paul reserves the term *koinōnos* for those who have entered into a partnership of give and take with Paul on behalf of the gospel mission (cf. Phil. 1:5, 7; 4:15; Gal. 2:9).[52] Moreover, with such designations Paul marks Titus as the leader of this expedition to Corinth. Again, only Titus is named, and only he is called a partner and co-worker of Paul. In addition, the other two brothers are in this summary statement lumped together as one ("as for our brothers…"). Paul does refer to them as *apostoloi*, but this means "messengers" or "envoys" (literally, "sent ones"), not the more formal title of "apostle" that Paul reserves for himself and the Jerusalem leaders (as well as, perhaps, for some other leading missionaries like Junia and Andronicus, [Rom. 16:7]). For example, Paul also refers to Epaphroditus as an *apostolos*, in a context where he clearly means an "envoy" from the Philippians to him (Phil. 2:25).

Thus, the commendation criteria highlight the leadership of Titus and the support ministry of the other two brothers, including the one who is more independent of the Pauline mission and yet well known in his own right among the churches—presumably, of the Pauline region.[53] Paul wants to make sure that the Corinthians realize that the brothers are subordinate to Titus, and, therefore, to Paul, in this venture. Yet, he also refers to the brothers as "the glory of Christ" (8:23, *doxa Christou*).[54] The apostles belong to the churches; but it is these apostles, not the churches (at least not here), that are the "glory of Christ." Hans Dieter Betz offers a parallel to this text to suggest that the past ministry and future action of these messengers has brought and will bring glory to Christ:

> And we have received the man in a friendly manner, and because of the glory [*doxan*] that have been bestowed on him before and because of his genuine goodness we have also given a favorable hearing to him with regard to the things he asked for.[55]

Betz concludes from this second century B.C.E. citation that *doxa Christou* characterizes "the function the two brothers were to perform in Corinth."[56] Their actions will bring glory to Christ.

Thus, the Corinthians should make no mistake. These two individuals provide important leadership to the collection team. However, the Corinthians should be clear that Titus, on Paul's behalf, is the "leader of the leaders." With this point made evident, Paul turns to the commendation request: "Therefore openly before the churches, show them the proof of your love and of our reason for boasting about you" (2 Cor. 8:24). Paul had previously asked the Corinthians to show their love to Paul and the Pauline mission by means of cooperation with the Jerusalem collection (8:7, 8). Now, with the arrival of these tried, tested, and appointed envoys, led by the trusted Pauline associate, Titus, the Corinthians should prepare to cooperate fully:

But I am sending the brothers in order that our boasting about you may not prove to have been empty in this case, so that you may be ready, as I said you would be…So I thought it necessary to urge the brothers to go on ahead to you, and arrange in advance for this bountiful gift that you have promised, so that it may be ready as a voluntary gift and not as an extortion (9:3, 5).

Sze-kar Wan notes the difficulty of the tasks before these envoys:

This cannot make for a tranquil time for the Corinthians, and the collection could be seen not as a free-will offering but, as Paul anticipates it in 9:5, as "an extortion." All this cannot but result in an exceedingly difficult job for Titus and the two brothers. They are charged with bringing the collection to completion *before* Paul comes and therefore in his absence; as Paul's representatives, they will bear the brunt of the Corinthians' invectives…[T]hey will have to play both fund managers and skilled negotiators.[57]

Moreover, if 2 Corinthians 12:17–18, where Paul asserts that his envoys, including Titus, were not received well by the Corinthians, happened subsequent to the writing of 2 Corinthians 8:16–24, we must agree with Wan that "the mission of the delegates failed."[58]

Nevertheless, Paul invested his authority in these individuals, especially Titus. He uses commendation to cite their qualifications for this delicate task, including love and concern for the Corinthian community, earnestness for the success of the collection for the church in Jerusalem, and a measure of respect among all the churches in the Pauline region. Moreover, Paul shows his dependence on other leaders for important aspects of his ministry.

SUMMARY

Thus, this important envoy passage in 2 Corinthians has taught us several aspects of Paul's leaders and leadership. First, parallels continue with previous commendations, both in terms of similar structure (identification, qualifications, recommendation), but the passage is more important in terms of the consistent quality Paul expects of church leaders, whether local or sent ones. The Thessalonians helped the community, and Stephanas served it. Similarly Titus and the brothers have earnest concern (*spoudē*) for it. Such care, service, and genuine interest are *sine qua non* of gospel leadership in Paul's assemblies.

Second, the commendation of envoys in 2 Corinthians 8 highlights Paul's dependence on his associates. Without Titus, we learn from 2 Corinthians 1–7, Paul could not be reconciled to the Corinthian church. And now, he needs Titus again to lead the delegation that he hopes will complete the Jerusalem collection with one final, major congregation, the Corinthians. We learn throughout Paul's letters that his mission could not succeed without a team of leaders as his close associates and supporters.

At the same time, however, Paul trusts his closest associates like Titus (and Timothy) more than any others. He will need other members of the Corinthian collection team, including a well-known preacher apparently independent of the Pauline mission, to lend integrity to the enterprise. However, while commending the two brothers, as well as Titus, for their prior leadership in the church and the Pauline mission, Paul names only Titus. Only Titus is called "partner" and "co-worker." The others are important and necessary, but this aspect of the Pauline mission, like others, must be accountable to Paul and his direct representatives. This demonstrates an important and intriguing aspect of Paul's leadership–he needs his associates not only to help him do the work but also to help him maintain or regain his authority, especially over conflict-ridden assemblies like the Corinthians.

Finally, and related to this last point, are the literary and rhetorical strategies that Paul employs to exercise leadership. When he rhetorically leaves out the names of the Thessalonian leaders he commends in 1 Thessalonians 5:12–13, he sends a message to all the Thessalonians: "If you work hard, help out wherever needed, and admonish those in need of it, you, too, deserve leadership recognition." In the commendation of Stephanas and his household, such leadership opportunity is made explicit: "Give recognition to such persons" (1 Cor. 16:18). However, Paul also strategically set up Stephanas for this leadership recognition by naming him earlier in the letter as one of the few baptized by Paul (1 Cor. 1:16). Paul needed such a rhetorical move–foreshadowing his commendation of Stephanas early in the letter–because he needed loyal leaders to help bring unity in Corinth.

Similarly, Paul needs Titus, who has already had success negotiating with the Corinthians, to take the lead in his next assignment, although this time he cannot go it alone. Strategically, Paul needs an endorsed team for the collection. To keep his leadership in Corinth intact now that Titus has helped restore it, Paul needs that very same, close associate at the head of the team. So, rhetorically, he identifies only Titus by name, several times, and the others only by reputation.

Therefore, Paul uses commendations in powerful, thoughtful, and strategic ways to endorse his leadership, his leaders, and his mission. This becomes very evident in the letter to the Philippians, in which Paul actually uses commendation three times to exercise leadership even with this beloved community.

Philippians

In my earlier discussion of Philippians, I noted that the *probatio* of Paul's rhetorical argument in the letter included examples of gospel leaders who had lived their lives "in a manner worthy of the gospel" (Phil. 1:27), which is Paul's central exhortation in this letter. Among these examples are Jesus, Paul, Timothy, and Epaphroditus. The passage on Timothy has the characteristics of the commendation of envoys, similar to 2 Corinthians 8:16–24, because Paul plans to send Timothy to the Philippians on his behalf (Phil. 2:19). The passage describing the leadership of Epaphroditus concludes with a commendation of his ministry (2:29–30). After a section in which Paul discusses the effects of refusing to accept and follow his exhortations (3:1–21), Paul begins the final exhortations of his letter with an exhortation to two divided leaders in the church, which includes their commendation (Phil. 4:2–3). In what follows, I will analyze each of these three commendations in order to illuminate the leadership qualities of one of Paul's closest associates, Timothy, and three Philippian leaders, Epaphroditus, Euodia, and Syntyche.

TIMOTHY–PAUL'S BELOVED "SON"–PHIL. 2:19–24

Since Paul is in prison, possibly facing execution (Phil. 1:19–26), he cannot visit the Philippians; but he does want to send a close associate, Timothy: "I hope in the Lord Jesus to send Timothy to you soon, so that I may be cheered by news of you" (2:19). Paul proceeds to describe Timothy's qualities as an associate and envoy of Paul. First of all, Timothy exhibits the kind of genuine concern for the well being of the Philippian community that Paul expects of his leaders (2:20). In this sense, Timothy is like Paul; they are *isopsuchoi*–"like-souled."[59] Indeed, Paul laments that many leaders look after their own interests (2:21a). Perhaps he has in mind the rival preachers he describes at the beginning of the letter (1:15–18), or opponents disrupting the Philippian church unity (3:2, 18–19). Timothy, however, is like Jesus (2:21b), as they both "look not to [their] own interests, but to the interests of others" (2:4). We have seen this trait of unselfish concern for the well being of the gospel community in other commended leaders, including the Thessalonians, Stephanas, and Titus.

Second, Paul praises Timothy for his "proven character" or "worth" (*dokimos*, 2:22a). Paul commended the tried and tested character of the second brother he was sending to Corinth along with Titus (2 Cor. 8:22). Demonstrated leadership over time was an important mark of service in the Pauline gospel mission. Paul Sampley writes:

> In Paul's picture of things, some people emerge over time as the ones who have proved themselves. "Tried and true" is a good translation of the term *dokimos* because it suggests a testing and a proving true in and through the test.[60]

Paul says that Timothy has passed such a test and demonstrated his "worth." Paul's use of *dokimos* to describe leaders like Timothy "suggests a certain *gravitas* that a person establishes over a period of time and through heavy responsibilities or in a rugged trial."[61]

Paul describes the specific circumstances surrounding the development of Timothy's character in very personal terms: "But Timothy's worth you know, how like a son with a father he has served with me in the work of the gospel" (2:22). A commendation letter from Pliny to the Emperor Trajan serves as a good parallel to this text. Pliny praised the son of a long-time associate as "an honest, hard-working young man," much like Timothy. The son's hard work, according to Pliny, has made the young elite "well-worthy of his excellent father."[62] Thus by being such a good worker, the young man has served to enhance his father's reputation. By contrast, Paul praises Timothy for serving the gospel together with Paul, not serving Paul and enhancing Paul's reputation, although certainly having an associate that works so well with Paul enhances the latter's reputation among his churches. That is why Paul can send Timothy to the Philippians in the first place. In Paul's estimation, Timothy models well what the Philippians need to be and do. Nonetheless, "Paul says Timothy has served with him, not served him, in the cause of the gospel."[63]

For these reasons–Timothy's concerns for the Philippians, his proven character, and service with Paul in the gospel–Paul feels confident to send Timothy to Philippi (Phil. 2:23a) so that Timothy might bring good news about the community back to Paul (2:19b). This is something Timothy did for Paul frequently, i.e., visit churches when Paul could not (cf. 1 Thess. 3:1–10; 1 Cor. 4:17; 16:10–11). However, Timothy will not go just yet. Paul needs to wait until he knows the results of his trial ("as soon as I see how things go with me," 2:23). Paul needs his most trusted associate by his side when the results come in. Thus, this commendation of Timothy reveals perhaps more than any other reference to Timothy in the Pauline corpus how closely tied Timothy's leadership was to Paul's. However, if Timothy, like Titus, was traveling to all these Pauline churches on Paul's behalf (Thessalonica, Corinth, Philippi, at least), then Paul's confidence in his leadership skills was significant.

EPAPHRODITUS: MESSENGER OF THE PHILIPPIANS TO PAUL– PHIL. 2:25–30

Epaphroditus will go back to the Philippians. Unlike Timothy, who travels on behalf of Paul, Epaphroditus came from them. This passage of commendation distinguishes itself for the dual description of Epaphroditus as both a leader in Philippi and as their messenger to Paul in the midst of his imprisonment. Thus Paul refers to Epaphroditus as "*my* brother and co-worker and fellow soldier, *your* messenger and minister to my need" (Phil. 2:25, author's emphasis). Some reflection on these assignations will help us understand the leadership qualities of Epaphroditus.

We have already noted, with E. Earle Ellis, how often Paul uses the assignations of "brother" and "co-worker" for members of his mission team, as well as for some local congregational leaders. Epaphroditus's apparent status as a leader in the assembly at Philippi does not preclude that Paul also considers him a "co-worker," especially now that he has been present with Paul. Indeed, Paul adds another, related ascription: *sustratiōtes*–"fellow soldier," "a military term to describe those who fight side by side."[64] Paul often refers to his ministry with such military imagery (cf. 1 Cor. 9:7; 2 Cor. 10:3, 4). With this description, Paul asserts that Epaphroditus has faced the conflicts and battles of the gospel ministry. One of these has been an illness, which Paul discusses in subsequent verses. But in general, as one of those ministering to Paul in the context of his imprisonment under Roman guard (whether in Rome or the provinces), Epaphroditus has seen up close the vicissitudes and hardships of the gospel mission as practiced by Paul and his team. As a co-worker and fellow soldier, Epaphroditus has experienced the type of life Paul also instructs the Philippians as a whole to expect: "For [God] has graciously granted you the privilege not only of believing in Christ, but of suffering for him as well–since you are having the same struggle that you saw I had and now hear that I still have" (Phil. 1:29–30).

Paul then turns (Phil. 2:25) to designations that show the connection of Epaphroditus to his home church, the Philippians. He is *their* "messenger" (*apostolos*) and "minister" (*leitourgos*) to Paul. We saw in 2 Corinthians that Paul designated the two brothers who comprised the collection team to Corinth, along with Titus, as *apostoloi* of the churches. By this he meant that unlike Titus, who represented Paul, the two brothers represented the churches. Similarly, Epaphroditus is the Philippians' representative to Paul during his time in prison. They, not Paul, have sent him. He is, therefore, their *apostolos*–appointed messenger. Later in the letter we read that Epaphroditus delivered an offering from the Philippians to Paul (Phil. 4:18). This was the immediate reason for his trip, but, apparently, he decided to stay longer.[65]

The second designation, as the *leitourgos*, servant or minister, of the Philippians to Paul, perhaps describes what Epaphroditus did when he stayed with Paul. The term bears a more cultic sense of service than *diakonia*. Paul has already hinted at the meaning of service as *leitourgia* when he described his own ministry: "But even if I am being poured out as a libation over the sacrifice and the offering [*leitourgia*] of your faith, I am glad and rejoice with all of you" (Phil. 2:17).

Sacrifice lies behind this kind of service. "Paul is borrowing temple sacrificial language and employing it metaphorically" to explain the nature of his ministry.[66] Epaphroditus has joined him in this understanding of the sacrifice involved in the Pauline mission. Paul's imprisonment and Epaphroditus's illness are immediate examples of this type of service. We saw in Paul's self-commendation that suffering like Christ is inherent in gospel leadership.

Thus, with these assignations, Paul has brought the Philippian leader directly into the fold of his immediate missionary team. Epaphroditus is a brother, co-worker, fellow soldier with Paul. The Philippians sent him as their apostle and minister to Paul. His apostleship and ministry have been integrated into Paul's mission, which is carried out with hard work, in spite of conflict, and with service and sacrifice. Along these lines, Paul next discusses Epaphroditus's serious illness: "He was indeed so ill that he nearly died" (2:27a). Yet, Epaphroditus showed his true, apostolic mettle. He was "distressed" because the Philippians had heard of his illness. Some commentators suggest that Epaphroditus was more distressed because his illness precipitated his departure from the Pauline mission and therefore constituted a failure for this Philippian envoy. He feared going back to his church.[67] However, the Philippians probably needed him as much as Paul did. If disunity is a problem in this church, as the central exhortation suggests (Phil. 1:27; cf. 2:1–4; 4:2–3), then Epaphroditus's absence may have left "a power vacuum."[68] Paul encourages his return, not only to ensure his ongoing good health, but also to deliver this letter and exercise his leadership in the Philippian assembly.

Thus Paul writes this commendation of Epaphroditus so that Epaphroditus would be honored in his home church and "to enable Epaphroditus to be of some ongoing ministerial use in Philippi as a respected leader."[69] The commendation request at the end of the passage demonstrates this: "Welcome him then in the Lord with all joy, and honor such people, because he came close to death for the work of Christ, risking his life to make up for those services that you could not give me" (2:29–30).

Paul reiterates the criteria that commend Epaphroditus—his sacrificial service (*leitourgia*) to Paul and the gospel mission, and his work (*ergos*) on behalf of the cause of Christ. Such language echoes the commendation of both the Thessalonian leaders and Stephanas and his household. Paul more explicitly here introduces a criterion that he cites in his self-commendation—risk and hardship. Epaphroditus, with his travels to Paul's location, with his deathly illness that resulted from it, all in an effort to deliver the Philippians' offering to Paul ("a fragrant offering, a sacrifice acceptable and pleasing to God," 4:18), has risked his life to complete the *leitourgia* of the Philippians to Paul (2:30). People like these in the gospel mission merit honor (2:29). Again Paul employs the commendation of a hard-working and sacrificial leader to encourage others to join the leadership ranks.

The commendations of Timothy and Epaphroditus exemplify, therefore, the type of leadership Paul expects of those engaged in the gospel mission. They care about the community and the mission. They serve Paul. They serve with Paul. And they serve communities they are sent to and sent from. They sacrifice, risk, get sick, get well, and try again. They are apostles, co-workers, and servants. They are examples. Paul makes this explicit: "Brothers and sisters, join in imitating me, and observe those who live according to the example you have in us" (Phil. 3:17). Paul is to be imitated in his leadership agenda and approach, but not only him. His leaders, like Timothy and Epaphroditus, also become examples. However, what happens when exemplary leaders have problems? The final commendation passage in Philippians engages that scenario.

EUODIA AND SYNTYCHE–PHIL. 4:2–3

Several factors converge to suggest the degree of import of Paul's commendation of Euodia and Syntyche in the overall argument of his letter to the Philippians. First is its place. This passage is traditionally believed to be at the beginning of the *peroratio* of the rhetorical argument–the final recapitulation. More likely, it forms its own pericope at the end of the long set of proofs, both positive and negative, with regard to the central exhortation in which Paul seeks community unity and steadfastness in the face of opposition (1:27–30). Carolyn Osiek suggests the passage in Philippians 4:2–3 is the culmination of the argument that begins at 2:1.[70]

Second, a large part of the evidence for such an assessment lies in what Paul requests of Euodia and Syntyche: "I urge Euodia and I urge Syntyche to be of the same mind [*to auto phronein*] in the Lord." The same phrases are found in 2:2 ("make my joy complete: be of the same mind") and 2:5 ("Let the same mind be in you that was in Christ Jesus"). The topic of unity goes back to the original exhortation ("standing firm in one spirit, striving side by side with one mind [*mia psychē*] for the faith of the gospel," 1:27b). The examples of unity and steadfastness cited in 2:5–30 and Paul's reflection on how to overcome the negative example of opponents in 3:1–4:1 leaves only a very specific, but serious, example of disunity to be overcome. That is the apparent rift between Euodia and Syntyche.

> That such a direct exhortation to individuals in a group communi-
> cation is virtually unprecedented in Paul's letters...attests to the
> importance of these women and Paul's concern that they could
> make the general appeal for unity in this letter of no effect unless
> they too accepted its lessons.[71]

Some would argue that the whole letter is headed in their direction, and the "general communication" toward unity rhetorically sets up the specific one.[72]

Third, like Timothy and Epaphroditus, Paul also commends Euodia and Syntyche (4:3), after urging their unity (4:2). Chan Hie-Kim identifies the three-fold commendation structure: "(a) introduction/identification: 'I appeal to you, true yokefellow;' (b) credentials: '[they] have struggled with me...and the rest of my co-workers;' and (c) request: 'help these.'"[73] Commentators have no definitive answer for who the "true yokefellow" (*gnesie syzyge*–"loyal companion" [NRSV]) might have been. Suggestions range from somebody actually named Syzyge (but no such name has been found in antiquity) to Epaphroditus, the probable letter carrier. However, if such were the case, why would Paul address him in the second person as if he were already present at Philippi and reading the letter for the first time? Whoever the individual was, as a "loyal companion," he or she probably was included among the co-workers Paul also mentions here. In other words, Paul asks another congregational leader to help bring unity between two other leaders.

How do we know Euodia and Syntyche were leaders? The two commendation criteria help us see that. First, Paul affirms that "they have struggled beside me in the work of the gospel." He employs the verb *synathleō*, which means "contend" or "struggle along [with someone]."[74] In all the New Testament, we find this specific term only here and in Phil 1:27. There Paul describes the "manner of life' (RSV) that believers should find "worthy of the gospel of Christ" (RSV) as "striving side by side [*synathloutes*] with one mind for the faith of the gospel." Given that Philippians 1:27 introduces the unity theme in the rhetorical argument of the letter, it is significant that Paul should repeat a key term from that text here in chapter 4 at this point in the argument. Not only have these two women leaders joined Paul at some point personally, it seems ("they have struggled beside me"), but his call for their unity evokes the unity exhorted for the whole congregation at 1:27 as well as at 2:1–5 and 3:15. "Paul's entreaty to them is one of the final instances of *phronein*-related words in the letter."[75] Thus, the unity Paul requested for the congregation as a whole must be exemplified in the first instance by its leaders. Euodia and Syntyche, given their disagreement, represent important individuals in Paul's request for unity. They have struggled beside him in the gospel, and therefore their local leadership in Philippi must set the standard for unity. Unfortunately, it does not. Thus Paul must exhort them, and he does so by commending their leadership and, like other commendations in Paul, citing relevant criteria.

Second, Paul refers to Euodia and Syntyche as his "co-workers": "They have struggled beside me in the work of the gospel, together with Clement and the rest of my co-workers" (4:3). The simplest reading of the grammar suggests that Paul refers both to Clement and Euodia and Syntyche as co-workers. Literally, they "have strived with me and Clement and the rest of my co-workers." The "me" (Paul), "Clement" and "the rest" are all in genitive forms related to the verb "struggle." So Paul makes the work of Euodia and Syntyche equivalent to Clement and all other co-workers. They have been and continue to be his co-workers, a term, as we have seen throughout this chapter, that identifies the bearer with the closest of Paul's mission associates and church leaders.

Inclusion in such a group of Paul's associates and leaders also bears witness to the importance of this passage in the rhetoric of Philippians. Most commentators agree that the particular nature of the relative pronoun that introduces the clause about their apostolic labors is not a simple relative but a categorization. The two women are pointed out as belonging in the special category of Paul's co-workers, along with Clement. This too suggests that theirs is not a petty quarrel with no impact on the community, but the central focus of disunity.[76]

Paul also includes Euodia, Syntyche, Clement, and all co-workers "in the book of life" (4:3c), which "reflects an old tradition, especially amenable to apocalyptic theology, that a list of the names of those to be saved is kept in heaven."[77] Paul asserts that because of their leadership in the gospel mission, his co-workers–including Euodia and Syntyche–can be assured of inclusion in this eschatological book.

Thus, Euodia and Syntyche represent important leaders in the Pauline mission in general and in the life of the Philippian church specifically. Their disunity, whatever its specific nature, presents a problem for Paul's search for unity in the Philippian assembly. If these two women leaders cannot "agree" with each other, how can Paul get the whole congregation to "agree"? In fact, the general exhortation earlier (1:27; 2:1–5; 3:15) could serve to set up this specific and most important one at the end of the letter before the final exhortations, which begin at 4:4.[78]

The commendation of Euodia and Syntyche has a unique structure. The focus is not on their leadership credentials, but on the problem of their disunity. Nonetheless, as a commendation of leaders, the passage invokes qualities we have noted in other commendations, albeit with different language, tied more to the immediate rhetorical situation of Philippians. That situation is Paul's exhortation toward unity in the face of opposition. To "struggle" for the gospel corresponds to earlier commendation language of "hard labor" (*kopos*), "work" (*ergon*) and "service" (*diakonia*). Taken together these terms reflect the intensity and urgency of the gospel mission in which Paul and his leaders are engaged. Carol Osiek suggests that Euodia and Syntyche may be among the "bishops and deacons" that Paul mentions at the outset of the letter (1:1). These apparent "offices" may have been emerging at this early stage perhaps only in Philippi.[79] Paul commends Euodia and Syntyche, however, as he did others, for how they functioned in the church, not the titles they may have carried.

Phoebe–Romans 16:1–2

Structurally and linguistically, the commendation of Phoebe at the end of Paul's letter to the Romans has very clear parallels to Greco-Roman commendations. Chan Hie-Kim outlines the elements of this commendation quite nicely:

a. identification: "I commend [*synistēmi*] to you Phoebe,

b. credentials: our sister who has been a servant [*diakonos*] of the church at Cenchreae,

c. request: so that you might receive [*prosdexēsthe*] her in the Lord, in a manner worthy of the saints, and help [*parastē te*] her in whatever matter [*pragmati*] she may have need.

b'. credentials: For she also has been a patroness [*prostatis*] of many and also of me."[80]

This is the only time Paul introduces a commendation with the actual term "commend" (*synistēmi*), although he uses cognates several times with reference to commendation letters (2 Cor. 3:1), self-commendation of himself and others (2 Cor. 6:4; 10:12), and what type of leaders God commends (2 Cor. 10:18). Phoebe's commendation also utilizes several other typical commendation terms: "receive" (*prosdexēsthe*), "help" (*parastēte*) and "matter" (*pragmati*). We also find a designation Paul has used for other commended leaders–*diakonos* ("servant") and one that is completely new in the noun form–*prostatis* ("patroness," "benefactor," or in some translations, "helper"). How do this commendation and these commendation terms help us understand Phoebe as a leader of the Pauline mission? I will first discuss her role at the church of Cenchreae and then turn to her relationship with Paul. Finally, I will look at Paul's request for her to the Romans.

PHOEBE OF CENCHREAE

Cenchreae was a port city near Corinth. Thus, if Paul is writing to the Romans from Corinth, as we can deduce from Romans 15:26 and 16:23, Phoebe is a leader of a nearby house church, the one in Cenchreae. She is also most likely the letter bearer for this important letter to the Romans. What is Phoebe's role in Cenchreae? Paul calls her a *diakonos*, a term he uses of himself and Apollos (1 Cor. 3:5) and, apparently, of a group of leaders in Philippi (Phil. 1:1, including perhaps Euodia and Syntyche). For the most part, Paul focused the term *diakonos* on the function of service rather than some official role. "What then is Apollos? What is Paul? Servants [*diakonoi*] through whom you came to believe, as the Lord assigned to each. I planted, Apollos watered, but God gave the growth" (1 Cor. 3:5). Thus, "when Paul applied [the term *diakonos*] to himself and to his co-workers, the preaching of the gospel is central."[81] Phoebe, as a *diakonos* of Cenchreae, may have had a preaching ministry; certainly she was a leader in the community.

Paul describes his opponents in Corinth, who were itinerant missionaries of some kind, as *diakonoi* (2 Cor. 11:23). He declares that God has made him and his associates "competent" to be "ministers of a new covenant [*diakonoi kainēs diathēkēs*]" (2 Cor. 3:6). In this way, Paul makes clear that *diakonoi* represented "an important designation in the Pauline mission."[82] Again, whatever her specific duties, Phoebe was an important leader of the church at Cenchreae.

PHOEBE THE PATRONESS

Yet, her role seems to transcend what she did for the local church. For Paul also calls her a *prostatis* of many, including himself (Rom. 16:2). The noun *prostatis* is a cognate of the verb *proistēmi*, which means both "preside" and "help," as we saw earlier in our discussion of 1 Thessalonians 5:12–13. Some translations of Romans 16:2 opt for "helper" (RSV), "great help" (NIV), or even "good friend" (TEV). However, again as with *diakonos*, and the refusal to translate it as "leader" or "minister" as is done when it refers to Paul, one suspects a hesitancy among translators with regard to overstating the role of a female leader in Paul's churches.

The noun *prostatis* has a history of association, albeit limited, in ancient usage with the practice of patronage. Indeed, in the region of Corinth we have evidence of the term being applied to a well-to-do woman of great respect, Junia Theodora. An inscription in her honor read:

> ...the council and people of Telemessos decreed...: since Iunia Theodora, a Roman, a benefactress of the greatest loyalty to the Lycian federation and our city has accomplished numerous benefits for the federation and our city...displaying her patronage (*prostasian*) of those who are present...it is decreed that our city...to give honor and praise for all the above reasons to...Iunia Theodora and to invite her...to always be the author of some benefits toward us...in return our city recognizes and will acknowledge the evidence of her goodwill.[83]

An earlier papyri document of the second century B.C.E. discusses the legal patronage of a mother's fatherless son. The mother requests legal responsibility and supervision of her son; she wants to be her son's *prostatis*.[84]

Thus Paul describes his relationship with Phoebe in terms that directly invoke the language of patronage and benefaction. Some scholars argue that perhaps Phoebe may have been on a par with Junia Theodora, or close to it, in terms of her wealth and benefaction, both in Cenchreae as a whole, but especially toward the Christian assembly that met there.[85] However, we have no evidence that Phoebe's benefaction was directed at any entity other than the church at Cenchreae. Moreover, as Justin Meggitt argues, Phoebe could be a supporter of the church at Cenchreae and of Paul's mission overall, without necessarily being very wealthy or "an elite patron."[86] Rather, as an independent woman, perhaps even widowed since no husband is mentioned, Phoebe seems to have devoted her time, energy, and whatever financial means she did have available to this new religious movement, the *ekklēsia* of Jesus Christ and its local expression found in the port city of Cenchreae. As Meggitt puts it, "Clearly Phoebe was a crucial figure in the early Pauline communities. The apostle's vocabulary makes this unequivocal, but her significance cannot be assumed to be a consequence of her wealth."[87]

So, Phoebe was a local leader of the church at Cenchreae and a leader in the Pauline movement. The commendation request Paul makes on her behalf to the Romans lends credence to this broader role. It is a conventional request in many ways, but it also conveys hints of Paul's broader agenda in this letter to the Romans. Paul may very well have needed the assistance of this leader from Cenchreae to carry out his agenda, especially since she had on occasion, it seems, taken on broader responsibilities in the Pauline mission. "She has been a benefactor of many and of myself as well" (Rom. 16:2c).

The language of the request speaks of "general assistance," as in typical Greco-Roman commendations: "help her in whatever she may require from you" (Rom 16:2b).[88] Robert Jewett has suggested, however, that Paul has more in mind in his commendation request than general assistance or hospitality. He bases this on the fact that Paul follows the general request with a "causal clause"[89] that ends the commendation with Phoebe's status as a patron of Paul and of his mission ("for she has been a benefactor of many and of myself as well")[90]. Jewett argues that to understand Paul's request we must take into account the context before and after the commendation of Phoebe. Before the commendation, Paul describes his plan to travel to Rome so the Roman house assemblies might support a mission to Spain (Rom. 15:23–24, 28–29). After the commendation, Paul greets twenty-six individuals by name and several others by designation (a sister, a mother), in addition to families and house churches, presumably led by some on the list (Rom. 16:3–16). Jewett suggests that by greeting these individuals, some of whom Paul knows personally and some known to him by reputation only, "Paul in effect takes the first step toward recruiting them for Phoebe's patronage."[91] The strategic presence of the commendation of Phoebe between these passages sets her up, argues Jewett, as a patron of the Spanish mission. Paul's extended description of her reinforces this theory. He describes her not only as a "sister" and "saint" worthy of proper treatment, as any believer would be, but also a congregational leader (*diakonos* of Cenchreae) and, most telling, a "patron" of the Pauline mission. She will help organize this mission, initially, by approaching the Roman Christians on Paul's behalf for their support.

In fact, Jewett argues in another essay that Paul's letter to the Romans as a whole should be read rhetorically as "an ambassadorial letter." As such, the letter advocates for the unity of Jew and Gentile and all house churches (hence the specific greetings to five house churches in Rom. 16:5, 10, 11, 14, 15) under the "righteousness of God" so the mission to Spain can be carried out successfully.[92] The commendation of Phoebe as a patron of Paul and his mission in the east extends her missionary leadership to this new Pauline endeavor in Spain. Hers is a "diplomatic mission" preparing the way for Paul who will come after he delivers the Jerusalem collection (Rom. 15:25–29). The "matter" (*pragma*) with which the Roman assemblies should help Phoebe actually involves the preparations for the Spanish mission.

In full detail, Jewett's reading may be too elaborate for the available evidence. However, throughout Paul's letter to the Romans, he argues long and hard for the unity of Jewish and Gentile believers because such is the nature of the gospel and the "righteousness of God." This is seen in the entire argument of Romans 9–11 as well as at the purpose statement of the letter at 1:16–"For I am not ashamed of the gospel; it is the power of God for salvation to everyone who has faith, *to the Jew first and also to the Greek*" (emphasis author's). The result of this argument, if not its only culminating purpose, could be greater facility with the plans for the Spanish mission, including identifying Phoebe and the local leaders in the Roman churches as leadership for the mission (Rom. 16:1–7).

PHOEBE'S LEADERSHIP

Jewett's conclusion that the whole elaborate theological argument of Romans 1:16–15:13 culminates with commendation and greeting may be putting too much burden on Romans 16. However, I must note some critical factors with regard to Phoebe's leadership that Jewett's extensive argument suggests. First, we must remember that if Phoebe is not the "patroness of the Spanish mission," she is at least the bearer of this letter, and as such, someone who will read it to the various house churches greeted in 16:3–16. Such reading would no doubt entail some interpretation, explanation, and background. Therefore, in effect, Phoebe does become a "patroness" of Paul's mission in Rome, including the Spanish mission that Paul highlights in the Roman letter. The role of letter bearer makes Phoebe an important figure for the whole enterprise of sending, reading, and putting into effect the exhortations of the letter to the Romans. Her patronage, that is, support of the Pauline mission, and thus her leadership, includes the ministry of interpretation of the Pauline message and mission.

Second, Paul commends Phoebe. As a patroness of Paul's ministry, *she* should be commending *Paul,* as patrons in Roman imperial society normally do. Scholars have described the relationship between Paul and Phoebe as "mutual patronage."[93] Paul has depended on the ministry of Phoebe in Cenchreae and elsewhere. Perhaps now Phoebe needs Paul's support as he sends her to Rome because, as some have suggested, Phoebe may be traveling on personal business (the *pragma*). Paul uses the occasion of her trip to send the letter along with her.[94] However, Jewett is right in arguing that some attention has to be paid to her role in Paul's request to the Romans for support for the Spanish mission. If not the primary reason for the whole letter, certainly Phoebe as letter bearer would have an opportunity to explain the Spanish mission even further on Paul's behalf. If she did have some economic means and had been a prior financial supporter of the Pauline mission in the east, she could allay any Roman fears about investing in Paul.[95]

At any rate, in commending Phoebe Paul inverts the expected practices. A "client" commends a "patron." Meggitt suggests that such "departures from the convention of patronage should alert us to the fact that Phoebe did not actually fulfill the traditional role of a patron."[96] In fact, in most commendations patrons are not directly called "patrons," but only by implication.[97] Thus, in employing this language, Paul quite possibly "intended to pay Phoebe a powerful, public compliment, and to indicate to the Roman Christians something of her importance to the church at Cenchreae."[98]

Having commended Phoebe for her leadership in Cenchreae, through service and benefaction, whatever specific shape these may have taken, now Paul wants the group of churches in the capital of the Roman Empire to extend this leadership recognition to Phoebe even though he did not found these churches. In addition, Paul quite possibly commends Phoebe not just to recognize her past leadership but also to provide opportunity for it to be exercised yet again. Certainly Phoebe would read and interpret the long, complex Roman letter she bears. Perhaps she would also help the Roman believers see how they might begin to carry out Paul's request for support in the Spanish mission. If all this is so, Phoebe had quite a leadership agenda on her plate.

The Letter to Philemon: Commending a Slave

Paul's brief letter to Philemon reflects on the gifts and qualities of three, and not just one, Pauline leader. Paul commends Onesimus, the main subject of the letter, but he does so on the basis of self-commendation and also with praise of Philemon, the letter's recipient.

Technically, according to Kim, the commendation of Onesimus comes toward the middle of the letter.[99] After a typical epistolary beginning, including a thanksgiving for letter's recipient (Philem. 4–7), Paul finally identifies the person to be commended: "I am appealing to you for my child, Onesimus" (v. 10). He then cites the person's credentials: "Formerly he was useless [*achrēston*] to you, but now he is indeed useful [*euchrēston*] both to you and to me" (v. 11). The play on words with the modifiers "useless" and "useful" also reflects the meaning of Onesimus's own name—"beneficial." Toward the end of the letter, Paul makes a more direct play on words in his final appeal to Philemon: "Let me have this benefit [*onaimēn*] from you in the Lord" (Philem. 20). Apparently, Onesimus has become true to his name, a useful benefit to both Paul and Philemon. Thus Paul makes this commendation request: "So if you consider me your partner, welcome him as you would welcome me" (v. 17).

Such a generalized request seems straightforward enough. We have seen such requests for hospitality in Greco-Roman commendations and in Paul. Yet the surrounding clues in Philemon point to a more complex matter, especially the texts immediately preceding the formal commendation request:

> Perhaps this is the reason he was separated from you for a while, so that you might have him back forever, no longer as a slave but more than a slave, a beloved brother—especially to me but how much more to you, both in the flesh and in the Lord. (Philem. 15–16)

Traditionally, Paul's references to slavery in this text have been interpreted to mean that Onesimus was a slave, indeed a runaway slave, because "he was separated from [*echōristhē*]" Philemon for a while (v. 15). In addition, Onesimus may have run away with either some debt or stolen goods or money, for Paul asserts, "If he has wronged you in any way, or owes you anything, charge that to my account" (Philem. 18). With the "conversion" of Onesimus while with Paul ("my child, Onesimus, whose father I have become during my imprisonment," v. 10), Onesimus has become "useful" and "of service" to Paul (v. 13), and, therefore, Philemon, as well. Knowing that he must send the slave back to his master ("I preferred to do nothing without your consent, in order that your good deed might be voluntary and not something forced," v. 14), Paul does so, but not without appealing to Philemon to receive Onesimus back, "no longer as a slave but more than a slave, a beloved brother" (v. 17).[100]

This basic narrative structure for the story of Philemon still leaves us with some fundamental questions. What does Paul mean by "no longer as a slave, but... a beloved brother"? What does Paul really want from Philemon? What does "welcoming" a runaway slave, if in fact Onesimus was such, entail? Does it entail forgiveness and reconciliation ("as a beloved brother...in the Lord," v. 16b), or does Paul also want the manumission of Onesimus ("no longer as a slave, but more than a slave, a beloved brother...both in the flesh and in the Lord")?

These questions have challenged commentators for centuries, and I do not intend to solve them here. I do want to explore the leadership of Paul, Philemon, and Onesimus reflected in this short, but complex letter, and perhaps in that way shed some light on possible answers to some of these questions.

THE SELF-DESIGNATIONS OF PAUL

The letter begins with greetings from Paul, who designates himself a prisoner [*desmios*], not an apostle or even a "servant" as he does in his other letters (cf. 1 Cor. 1:1; 2 Cor. 1:1; and Gal. 1:1 for "apostle"; Phil. 1:1 for "servant"; Rom. 1:1, where he is both). Such a designation as prisoner represents both the physical reality of Paul's current location–a Roman prison (whether Rome, Ephesus, or some other specific locality does not concern us here),[101] –and his decision to focus on that fact as a rhetorical strategy for this current letter.

First, physically Paul's power as apostle and itinerant missionary are limited. Paul is imprisoned. That is, Paul is substantially powerless as regards the basic issue of his own physical location. Paul, whose calling is by nature, peripatetic, cannot leave his present place of residence.[102]

Second, in verse nine he is not only a prisoner, but also a *presbutēs*, "old man."[103] Thus he focuses either on his advanced age, or, more likely, his advanced stature in the gospel because of his experience–an "elder."[104] In so doing, Paul highlights qualities that show his vulnerability and his durability. Paul puts forward neither apostolic pretensions nor traditional formulae to recommend himself to his addressees. Paul's status as prisoner and "ambassador" carries weight in his rhetorical strategy. Perhaps he has chosen this course because neither tradition nor apostolic status held the promise of persuasion.[105] If, in fact, he must commend a slave, Paul will show that he, too, serves the gospel from a position of weakness in the eyes of the world, as we saw in the study of Paul's self-commendation.

Later in the letter Paul uses other designations and some indicators of his authority. He writes that he is "bold [*parrēsia*] enough in Christ to command" Philemon's compliance with his request (v. 8). However, he would rather "appeal...on the basis of love" (v. 9). Sandra Polaski writes, "While Paul eventually invites Philemon into a set of power relations based on love and personal regard, he alludes in this verse to a set of relations grounded quite differently, with a legal or quasi-legal tone."[106] Polaski ponders whether Paul offers these options for "rhetorical affect" or whether he really does have the option of "commanding."

Although he does not cite it directly, Paul probably has his apostolic role behind this option, his role as founder of the churches in the region of Philemon's leadership even if not the very house church that Philemon leads.[107] This may be asserted from Paul's final request at the end of the letter after his appeal for Onesimus has been laid forth. Paul requests that Philemon "prepare a guest room" for him (v. 22). Such a request both shows Paul's leadership role with Philemon's church (the apostle will come to visit and stay in the church leader's house), and puts pressure on Philemon to comply with Paul's request on behalf of Onesimus. Paul will be there soon (he hopes) and will see if Philemon has responded positively.

Paul also calls himself a "partner" (*koinōnos*) with Philemon. Indeed, he does so at the precise point of his commendation request: "So if you consider me your partner, welcome [Onesimus] as you would welcome me" (v. 17). To be a partner with Paul is to be joined in the gospel enterprise in a mutual relationship of give and take.[108] Paul and Philemon "have participation with one another" in the mission of the gospel. This will not be the case, says Paul, if Philemon does not accept Onesimus.[109] Paul puts further rhetorical pressure on Philemon by reminding him that not only is Paul Onesimus's "father" in the faith (v. 10), but Philemon "owes" Paul his "very self," presumably a reference to Philemon's own conversion by means of Paul's ministry.[110] All these designations point, ultimately, to the fact that Paul does have significant leverage with Philemon. Although he says he makes his appeal on the basis of "love" (v. 9), Paul, in the final analysis, is "confident of [Philemon's] obedience" and that Philemon "will do even more than [Paul] say[s]" (v. 21) because of this leverage.

THE LETTER RECIPIENTS

In the greetings section of the letter (vv. 1–2), Paul greets not only Philemon, the presumed recipient that Paul starts to address individually in the thanksgiving of verses 4–7,[111] but also Apphia and Archippus. Each of them also has their own designations, some of which we have seen previously in Pauline commendations. As he did with Phoebe, Paul calls Apphia "our sister." We are not told enough else about her to determine her role in the church. We have no way of knowing for sure whether or not she was the wife of the one of the other two, as some have suggested. Still, her inclusion in the greetings probably means she had some leadership status in the church. Just as with Epaphroditus, Paul calls Archippus "our fellow soldier [*systrapatiōtes*]," showing his willingness to struggle along with Paul for the cause of the gospel.

However, Paul reserves his highest accolades for Philemon, whom he designates as "our dear friend and co-worker," Paul's favorite designation for his closest associates, as we have seen elsewhere. Again, the fact that he is named first along with his designation as a "co-worker" and not just a brother or fellow soldier, probably means that Philemon is the primary recipient and also the householder in whose home the church meets. The latter represents the fourth recipient of Paul's greeting–"and the church [that meets] in your ['singular'] house" (Philem. 2). Although the collective, plural greeting in Philemon 1b–3 is followed by singular thanksgiving to one individual in Philemon 4–7, rhetorically Paul invites those greeted initially, including the church, to "listen in" on his appeal to the assembly's house church leader, Philemon.

> …[T]he multiple addressees of the letter are strong evidence that Philemon is more than a private letter, that it does not merely reflect power dynamics at work between Paul, Philemon and Onesimus but also offers insight into Paul's perception of his own place within the network of young churches.[112]

Although the matter may be private, the relationship of Philemon and Onesimus, with Paul stepping in between them, as he did in the rift between Euodia and Syntyche (Phil. 4:2–3), has communal implications (as did the situation of Euodia and Syntyche). Thus Paul includes others in the conversation. However, as indicated by the thanksgiving section that follows, Philemon, and then later Onesimus, form the focal point of the letter's exigence.

THE QUALITIES THAT COMMEND PHILEMON

In the thanksgiving (Philem. 4–7), Philemon emerges as a classic Pauline leader in terms of the qualities that Paul extols. First, Paul praises Philemon for his "love and faith," fundamental Christian virtues in Paul's theology. Philemon focuses these values on both Jesus Christ and "all the saints" in the house assembly that meets in his home (Philem. 5). Further, Philemon, like other Pauline leaders, shares his faith such that others learn about "all the good" to be done "for Christ" (v. 6). Having faith and love, and then sharing it, brings great "joy" and "encouragement" to Paul because Paul's ultimate concerns with regard to the faith communities he founded are being addressed: "the hearts of the saints have been refreshed through you, my brother [Philemon]" (v. 7). Why does Paul praise Philemon so effusively?

First, it reflects the qualities Paul expects of his leaders. Love and caring for the community of saints marks Paul's leaders as exemplified in the Thessalonians in 1 Thessalonians 5:12–13, Stephanas and his household in 1 Corinthians, Timothy and Epaphroditus in Philippians, and Phoebe in Romans.

Second, this thanksgiving, like others in Paul (see, for example, 1 Cor. 1:4–7; 1 Thess. 1:2–10), sets the tone for future actions on the part of the letter recipient so that the latter will demonstrate these very same qualities in how he responds to Paul's request.[113] Philemon has refreshed "the hearts of the saints." He should also "refresh" Paul's "heart in Christ" (v. 20) in the matter of his relationship to Onesimus. Just as Philemon's love has brought "much joy and encouragement" to Paul (v. 7), so should he provide one more "benefit" to Paul (v. 20a) by receiving Onesimus as if he were Paul (v. 17). Paul praises Philemon for "the sharing [*koinōnia*] of [his] faith" (v. 6). Therefore, if Philemon is to be an authentic "partner" (*koinōnos*) of Paul, he needs to exercise hospitality to Onesimus (v. 17). Finally, Philemon is a "dear friend and co-worker" of Paul (v. 1). Paul sends Philemon someone who has become Paul's "child" even during Paul's imprisonment (v. 10). Onesimus has become Paul's "own heart [*splanchna*]" (v. 12), and Paul would have liked to keep him near him during this time of imprisonment so that Onesimus might "be of service" (*diakonē*) to Paul in Philemon's place (v. 13).

Thus the qualities that commend Philemon become the basis of Paul's commendation request on behalf of Onesimus. "Paul establishes good will between himself and Philemon by praising Philemon's past behavior, highlighting those qualities upon which he will draw to make his case."[114] In fact, the qualities that commend Onesimus parallel, and even surpass, the qualities of Philemon. "Philemon is Paul's brother and fellow-worker, but Onesimus is closer to Paul than that: he is Paul's child and a part of Paul's self."[115] This puts further pressure on Philemon to comply with Paul's request because, if in fact Onesimus is a slave, "the terms" by which Paul commends Onesimus gives the latter "the place of favor over his master."[116]

The Qualities that Commend Onesimus

At some point Onesimus had become "useless" (*achreston*) to Philemon, but now he had become "useful" (*euchrestōn*), both to Paul and Philemon (v. 11). The Greek terms are often used in opposition to each other and, as noted above, represent a play on words with Onesimus's name, which means "beneficial." Traditionally, the content of Onesimus's "uselessness" is related to his presumed status as a runaway slave ("Perhaps this is the reason he was separated from you for a while," v. 15a) and the possibility that he stole money from Philemon or at least owes him a debt ("If he has wronged you in any way, or owes you anything, charge that to my account," v. 18).

However, now Onesimus is beyond such problems. Like Timothy (cf. 1 Cor. 4:17; Phil. 2:22), he has become a "child" of Paul in the faith (v. 10). He has become so dear to Paul ("my own heart," v. 12) that Paul wanted to keep Onesimus with him, but not just out of pity or emotion. Onesimus had become useful to Paul and of such "service" (*diakonē*) that Onesimus could stand in Philemon's place while Paul is imprisoned ("I wanted to keep him with me, so that he might be of service to me in your place during my imprisonment for the gospel," v. 13). In this case, Onesimus parallels the qualities that commended Timothy's leadership to the Philippians: "But Timothy's worth you know, how like a son with a father he has served [*edouleusen*] with me in the work of the gospel" (Phil. 2:22). Paul uses more servile language (*douleō*–serve like a slave) for the ministry of himself and Timothy than he does for Onesimus (*diakonia*–service, ministry). If Onesimus was a slave, the use of a Pauline term for ministry in the gospel–*diakonia*–with reference to Onesimus and his work for Paul, instead of a form of the term often reserved for the enslaved–*doulos*–may be intentional on Paul's part. Using a form of *diakonia* adds significance to the role of Onesimus and his leadership.[117]

Onesimus has become useful to Paul and Philemon as a *diakonos* in service to Paul during the latter's imprisonment. Ultimately, I think, Paul would like Onesimus returned to Paul to continue that *diakonia*, but he would rather have Philemon agree to that voluntarily (vv. 13–14). Paul closes out his appeal by implying that he wants more than a mere "welcome" (v. 17): "Confident of your obedience, I am writing to you, knowing that you will do even more than I say" (v. 21). Such confidence (*pepoithōs*) of some extra efforts in Philemon's response could refer to Paul's desire to have Onesimus back with him, or could refer to the manumission of Onesimus, if indeed he was a slave, or it could refer to both. In either case, Paul has affirmed for his readers, especially Philemon, the emerging leadership qualities of Onesimus.[118]

PAUL'S REQUEST AND THE LEADERSHIP OF PHILEMON AND ONESIMUS

With the commendation of Onesimus, the implied commendation of Philemon, and his own self-commendation, Paul has furthered our understanding of his approach to leadership, especially with regard to different social classes within his assemblies. It does seem probable that Onesimus was a slave, notwithstanding the cogent arguments of Allen Callahan to the contrary. Such status makes easier sense of several elements in the letter, including the critical text: "Perhaps this is the reason he was separated from you for a while, so that you might have him back forever, no longer as a slave [*doulos*] but more than a slave, a beloved brother– especially to me but how much more to you, both in the flesh and in the Lord" (vv. 15–16). Nonetheless, as Callahan argues, "brother…both in the flesh and in the Lord," seems to point to Onesimus and Philemon as actual, blood brothers, for whom Paul wants to bring reconciliation ("welcome him as you would welcome me," v. 17). If such were the case, the slave language would be figurative: Philemon refers to Onesimus as a slave only metaphorically because of their rift.[119] For a variety of reasons, however, it is more likely that Onesimus was a slave and Philemon his master. First, Paul implies a physical separation between Philemon and Onesimus, with "he was separated from you from a while." When that is combined with the debt that somehow Onesimus has incurred (v. 18, although Callahan suggests that Paul has a hypothetical situation in mind and not an actual occurrence)[120] "it is difficult" not to conclude "that there is something wrong between Philemon and Onesimus." Moreover, "the legal language by which Paul tells Philemon to charge anything to his account is more than raising a possibility contrary to the fact."[121] Onesimus, either in terms of actual goods, services, or cash, or in terms of honor, perhaps because he ran away, owes Philemon a debt. Third, in several ways Paul emphasizes how much authority Philemon has in this situation. Paul could command Philemon, but he prefers to appeal (vv. 8–9). Paul would rather keep Onesimus with him, but not without Philemon's consent (vv. 13–14). Paul asks Philemon to prepare a guest room for him in his house, implying, along with the content of his greetings and thanksgiving, that Philemon is a house church leader. For these reasons–Onesimus's "separation," his debt, and Philemon's apparent position of authority–it seems that the traditional view that Onesimus was a slave and Philemon his master is most likely accurate. Given that probability, three things need to be said about Paul and leadership in this letter to Philemon. First, Philemon, although a house church leader and perhaps a slaveholder, still has some lessons to learn about the gospel. As Norman Petersen has shown us, for Paul the realm of the Spirit and the church with the various new roles and expectations ("father," "child," "brother," "partner," "elder," "co-worker," etc.) now supercedes the realm of the "flesh" and the "world" with its roles, statuses, and expectations (including those of slave, householder, slave owner, debtor, prisoner, etc.).[122] Paul asks Philemon to live out his faith and love in this realm over against business as usual in Greco-Roman society, whether as a master punishing a slave or as a wronged brother reconciling with his estranged brother (to follow Callahan's interpretation). Moreover, as a "brother" of Onesimus, "both in the flesh [the realm of the world] and in the Lord [the realm of the Spirit and the church]," Philemon must realize that "the social role 'brother' and the social roles 'master' and 'slave' are in fact incompatible."[123] Therefore, "Paul's line of argument strongly suggests that the only acceptable action would be for Philemon to free his slave."[124]

This does not necessarily mean "that Paul had a single, comprehensive rule on the legal status of slaves as such."[125] However, as the need arose, as it did in this case between Philemon and Onesimus, Paul drew out the implications of the gospel, including "that the norms of life 'in Christ' required the renunciation of the slaveholder's legal prerogative over the slave."[126]

Second, Paul continues to exercise his leadership over his churches. In fact, "Paul has put all of his apostolic authority at stake for the sake of this runaway slave."[127] He employs a very careful rhetorical strategy, which speaks to the delicate situation before him. It sounds like Paul wants Philemon to do two things—one very radical and another very self-serving for Paul—manumit Onesimus and return him to Paul so that he might join the associates serving Paul during his imprisonment. To accomplish these requests, Paul uses all the rhetorical strategies at his disposal, including praising Philemon's leadership, commending Onesimus, and reminding Philemon of his responsibilities and indebtedness to Paul. In the end, even preparing a bed for Paul's impending visit is a further inducement for Philemon to comply with Paul's request. Paul's leadership, while subtle, is on full display in this short, but powerful letter.

Finally, Paul's letter to Philemon adds other members to Paul's long list of associates, co-workers, and local church leaders, some of whom we have studied in this chapter. Among local church leaders, Paul presents not only Philemon here, but also Apphia as a "sister" and Archippus as a "fellow solider." Moreover, Paul enlists these individuals plus the entire church to listen in on this conversation with Philemon and, therefore, presumably, to apply pressure themselves on Philemon to do his "duty" (v. 8). They, along with Philemon, should also learn these lessons about leadership, including that the new realm of church and Spirit is the locus of their exercise of leadership. In addition, whether or not Onesimus is a slave, a new or renewed leader has emerged from the dynamics of this personal and communal conflict, a conflict about what to do about an estranged "brother" and/or "slave." In the midst of such a conflict, a "useless" individual in the eyes of some, including at least one church leader, Philemon, has emerged, through his relationship with Christ and Christ's "ambassador" (the variant reading of *presbutēs* in v. 9), the apostle Paul, such that now Onesimus is "useful," a "benefit," and a servant. In short, a "slave" has become a leader.[128]

Conclusion: Leaders and Leadership in the Pauline Mission

These, then, are Paul's leaders; among them are some of the more, well-known names in Pauline studies—Timothy, Titus, Philemon—and some not so well-known names—Stephanas, Epaphroditus, Euodia, Syntyche, and Phoebe. Some slaves may appear among these commended leaders—Fortunatus, Achaicus, and Onesimus. Some leaders remain nameless—the Thessalonian leaders and the two "brothers" enlisted for the Jerusalem collection in Corinth. And these are only the names that appear in Paul's commendations. Ellis and others have reminded us of how long the list is. However, I chose to concentrate on those leaders who appear in commendation passages because of some common elements that can help us build a cohesive picture of leadership in the Pauline mission.

One of the major contributions commendations make in our understanding of Paul's leaders has to do with the qualities Paul commends in them. At the outset of this chapter I noted how typical Greco-Roman commendations promoted credentials related to family ties, economic status, and patronage connections. By contrast, Pauline commendations concentrate on such qualities as hard work, service, and concern for the community. Consistently, Paul uses such terms as *ergos* (work), *kopos* (hard work, labor) and *diakonia* (service, ministry) to praise his leaders, both those who are close associates or part of his immediate missionary team, and local leaders who have emerged during and after Paul's initial ministry in the particular congregation being addressed. Paul also relates these qualities to the intensity and urgency of the gospel he proclaims. These are the qualities necessary in light of the gospel mission and the urgency Paul feels about it. Paul needs leaders ready to sacrifice all for this gospel and the communities founded on its basis.

Thus specifically Paul will praise several of his leaders for qualities of risk and sacrifice that they have been willing to suffer on behalf of the gospel and the gospel community. Of course, Paul does not do this without setting a tone himself. Thus, in his self-commendations Paul discusses at length the suffering and sacrifice he has undertaken throughout his ministry. When he calls for believers to "be imitators of me, as I am of Christ" (1 Cor. 11:1), such exhortation includes more than how Paul preaches, conducts his personal spiritual life, and solves problems in the local congregation. Such exhortation also shows how he suffers hardship for the cause of Christ. Leaders that "came close to death for the work of Christ" (Phil. 2:30) and "risked their necks" for Paul and his mission (Rom. 16:4) are exemplary models, worthy of imitation. They have become like Paul, who wrote to the Philippians: "Brothers and sisters, join in imitating me, and observe those who live accordingly to the example you have in us" (Phil. 3:17).

Paul also depends on these leaders he commends. He cannot work alone. Indeed, without Titus, he could not be reconciled to the Corinthians and attempt to complete their contribution to the Jerusalem collection. Without Timothy, he could not receive news about the Thessalonians (1 Thess. 3:1–10), including the leaders he subsequently commends (1 Thess. 5:12–13). He wishes he could keep Onesimus with him and probably wants Philemon to send him back (Philem. 13). Epaphroditus not only delivered an offering from the Philippians to Paul, but also ministered to Paul while present with him during his imprisonment (Phil. 2:25, 30). And Phoebe not only carried Paul's letter to the Romans, but also probably prepared the way in some form for Paul's future arrival and his future mission to Spain (Rom. 16:1–2). Each of these individuals, and many others, had an impact on Paul's ministry, facilitated his ministry to congregations, and in general functioned as important team members in the Pauline mission. Paul depended on them.

Paul indicates several times that true gospel leaders must be *dokimos*– "tried and true." Whether "approved by God" (1 Thess. 2:4), the churches (Phil. 2:22), or by Paul (2 Cor. 8:22), leaders in the Pauline mission go through a time of testing by means of various experiences to demonstrate their ongoing worthiness for the ardent task that is gospel leadership and ministry. Again, enduring hardships is a key component of this testing, even for Paul and his missionary colleagues:

> But though we had already suffered and been shamefully mistreated at Philippi, as you know, we had courage in our God to declare to you the gospel of God in spite of great opposition…, just as we have been approved [*dedokimasmetha*] by God to be entrusted with the message of the gospel, even so we speak, not to please mortals, but to please God who tests [*dokimazonti*] our hearts. (1 Thess. 2:2, 4)

Paul encourages his troublesome Corinthian believers to "test" (*dokimazete*) themselves in their relationship to Christ and Paul. Leaders in the Pauline mission "test themselves" by engaging directly in the trials and tribulations of gospel ministry. When they have survived these various "tests" and still stand firm on behalf of the gospel, Paul considers them *dokimoi*–approved leaders.

Commendations also help us see, perhaps more than any other Pauline literary motif, the role and impact of female leadership in the Pauline mission. The key figures of any discussion of women's ministry in Paul– Phoebe, Euodia, and Syntyche–are referenced in commendation passages. Along with his male leaders, Paul recognizes the importance of several female leaders in his churches and overall mission by commending them. Both Phoebe in Cenchreae and Rome and Euodia and Syntyche in Philippi have ministries both in and beyond their local settings as co-workers "together with" Paul. Their critical role in Paul's leadership efforts is clear. Phoebe will have an impact on Paul's efforts in Rome, whether by carrying, reading, and interpreting Paul's letter to the Romans; by helping to make preparations for the Spanish mission; or both. Paul's efforts to promote unity in Philippi could be derailed by the division of the local leaders Euodia and Syntyche. In addition, leaders who carry letters, travel as envoys, or otherwise do ministry (*diakonia*) on Paul's behalf have an impact on the Pauline mission as further interpreters of the gospel that Paul proclaims. Anytime someone travels on behalf of the mission–and many of those commended by Paul, whether female or male, do just that–they exercise their influence, hopefully positively, as Paul expects, but perhaps on occasion negatively. At any rate, such envoys, letter carriers, and missionaries must be considered leaders in the Pauline mission.

Paul's intimate style with several of his leaders as gleaned through these commendations deserves mention. Timothy and Titus are obviously close to Paul; one can tell this in the way he commends them. Timothy, Paul says, is "like a son with a father" in their mutual service for the gospel (Phil. 2:22). Paul distinguishes Titus from other envoys to Corinth: "As for Titus, he is my partner and co-worker in your service; as for our brothers, they are messengers of the churches…" (2 Cor. 8:23). Nonetheless, Paul also exhibits closeness to several other leaders he commends. He has previously baptized Stephanas and his household in Corinth, and Stephanas and company have served the community well. Therefore, Paul feels close enough to him from among all the Corinthian leaders to promote his leadership recognition before signing off at the end of Paul's first letter to the Corinthians. The illness of Epaphroditus, which he contracted as a result of his ministry to Paul (Phil. 2:30), has Paul so worried that he is relieved when Epaphroditus is well enough to go back to Philippi (2:27–28). Paul evokes emotive language as he expresses his joy at Epaphroditus's impending return:

> He was indeed so ill that he nearly died. But God had mercy on him, and not only on him but on me also, so that I would not have one sorrow after another. I am the more eager to send him, therefore, in order that you may rejoice at seeing him again, and that I may be less anxious. (Phil. 2:27–28)

As noted earlier in this chapter, Paul also expresses appreciation for the ministry of Philemon and calls him his "dear friend, "co-worker," "partner," and "brother" (Philem. 1, 17, 20), all significant terms of endearment and mutuality. However, Paul employs even more intimate terms with reference to Onesimus, whom he calls his "child" and his "own heart" (Philem. 10, 12), as well as a great "benefit" to Paul's ministry (11, 13, 20). For Paul to express greater closeness to Onesimus, an apparent slave, than to the slave's master is not only a striking rhetorical move, but also a sign of the relationships Paul appreciates with his co-workers and leaders.

This brings me to three final points about Paul and leadership as expressed through the commendation of his leaders. First, to reiterate a previous point but with a different focus: Paul viewed his calling and mission as a *diakonia*–a ministry or service that entailed sacrifice and commitment. By commending leaders who practiced *diakonia* on behalf of the gospel communities, Paul highlights the very focus of his calling, that is, he interprets his proclamation of the gospel and all that follows as his *diakonia* to God. Gospel leaders must have a similar sense of calling and ministry, a similar *diakonia*.

Second, the context for exercising this *diakonia* leadership entails another key Pauline term in Greek—*koinōnia*, understood as fellowship, communion, or partnership. Paul expects his leaders to exercise their ministries in and for the community and as part of a team. They should be in partnership—in *koinōnia*—not just with Paul, but also with each other, with their congregations, and with the Pauline mission as a whole. This is why the Jerusalem collection is so important for Paul. It is a *diakonia*—a ministry—that expresses the *koinonia*—the partnership—of Paul's Greek churches, all of them, with the Jerusalem wing of the church (cf. Gal. 2:9–10). The collection models the unity and partnership Paul pursues as a leadership goal for himself, his leaders, and his congregations.

Finally, because patronage and social status play such an important role in typical Greco-Roman commendations, it is worth asking about their role in Paul's commendations. With Paul these elements do not seem to be as prominent a feature. Paul never directly cites the family roots or social status of the leaders he commends. As far as we can tell, none of the Pauline leaders, or any other members for that matter, are politicians or office-holders. Such positions were reserved for the imperial and provincial elite.[129] One could infer from the fact that some of the leaders appear to be homeowners, slaveholders, or patrons that many of them did have high social status in "secular" Greco-Roman society. However, Justin Meggitt argues against assuming that home ownership and other such indicators among Pauline Christians are automatically signs of high social status. Pauline Christians in general "shared fully in the bleak material existence that was the lot of the non-elite inhabitants of the Empire."[130] Moreover, home and slave ownership and such activities as travel and hospitality were not limited to the elite. "A Christian having a 'household' cannot serve as *probable* indicator of elevated social status at all." People from all walks of life, unfortunately, owned slaves in ancient society, including other slaves.[131]

Yet, even if at least some of the persons named and unnamed in Pauline churches, including some of those commended, had some significant economic means and social status, what's impressive is that Paul does not refer to these as vehicles for leadership recognition. Rather, the qualities I mentioned above—hard work, sacrificial service, and genuine concern for the community—dominate the discussion and not much else. Paul's leaders could be from among the elite in secular society, but more likely than not, they were not. And this is not the usual case in matters of leadership in Greco-Roman society, certainly not as exemplified in typical Greco-Roman commendations.

Jesus and Paul

The matter of social status, as well as the issues of intimacy and team ministry, in Pauline leadership compare favorably to what we see in the leadership exemplified in the Jesus movement and the gospels. The disciples, in particular, do not seem to come from the social elite of their day, but rather, as I noted in previous chapters, from among the target audience of Jesus' ministry–the poor and the outcast. Jesus and the early Jesus movement certainly showed the "intimate community" that he fostered and that his followers promoted in those early years, with such fundamental features as itinerancy, self-sacrifice, and hospitality.[132] Paul's closeness to his co-workers parallels the intimacy of Jesus with his disciples and of early Christian itinerant preachers with their converts. Finally, both Jesus and Paul promoted team ministry. Leaders should be part of groups that foster learning and support for each other, especially in times of crisis and need. These are important lessons from Jesus and Paul that merit further investigation in the final two chapters of this book.

6

Problems in Leadership

Corinthian Correspondence

Introduction

A final window into understanding the nature of leadership in the Pauline communities entails a case study in Paul's Corinthian correspondence. Widely studied and long-hailed as a productive window into Pauline studies as a whole, 1 and 2 Corinthians clearly address various aspects of leadership, both problems concerning it in the community and articulations on Paul's part. In this chapter, I propose to bring these various strands of problems and solutions together into a selective reading of 1 Corinthians through the lens of leadership questions, with a briefer accounting of the issue in 2 Corinthians. I will argue that there is a common thread of the various problems Paul addresses in both these letters, and that that thread has to do with misunderstandings of the nature of gospel leadership as Paul practices and teaches it.

Corinth as a City

The Corinth that Paul evangelized in the early 50s C.E. was a major urban center of the Roman Empire. Classical scholars refer to it as "Roman

Corinth." Classical Corinth lay dormant for one hundred years after its destruction in 146 B.C.E. until Julius Caesar rebuilt it as a retirement haven for his military veterans in 46 B.C.E. Roman Corinth developed a reputation for having a mixed constituency, with veterans and former slaves ("freedmen") seeking refuge and economic development. As a port city on the Aegean Sea, Corinth became economically prosperous and in many ways a "noveau riche" city. It was also a diverse city. Economically, it featured a thriving tourist and service economy tied to the various athletic games hosted by the city. Socially, it housed various ethnic and racial groups including Romans, Greeks, Egyptians, Syrians, and Jews. Religiously, it incorporated a wide range of gods and cults in the city's religious landscape, including Aphrodite, the goddess of love; Neptune, the god of the sea; and Asclepius, the god of healing.[1] When the Romans rebuilt the city in the latter half of the first century B.C.E.., they added the Roman imperial cult to this mix in a major way.[2]

Despite this diversity, like any Greco-Roman city, Corinth placed limits on the inter-mingling of these various socioeconomic, ethnic, and religious groups. In particular, patrons controlled economic activity from their vantage point at the very top of the socioeconomic ladder. Freed persons and slaves depended on their patrons and masters for access to jobs and status within the city. Vocational, religious, and social associations met homogeneously, but only with the economic support of elite patrons. Burial societies, trades groups, and religious cults depended on financing by an upper echelon of elite and wealthy individuals, especially in a city like Corinth, where there was so much economic activity and so many diverse social and religious groups. In short, especially under Roman imperial control, a strict hierarchy of leadership controlled economic and social movement in the major port city that was Corinth.[3]

Paul and the Corinthian Correspondence

Into this diverse and prosperous city came the apostle Paul in the early fifties C.E. He established the Corinthian *ekklēsia*, the community of believers in Christ Paul called an "assembly," like the democratic assemblies of classical Corinth. After a period of time in the city, Paul continued his missionary journeys and later wrote several letters to the Corinthians, and they to him.[4]

In his first extant letter, known as canonical 1 Corinthians, Paul ostensibly addresses a litany of seemingly unrelated problems–division in the church (1 Cor. 1–4); incest (5:1–13) and sexual immorality (6:12–20); believers taking other believers to secular courts (6:1–11); misunderstandings about marriage, singleness, and asceticism (7:1–40); questions about food offered to idols (8:1–11:1); women praying in assembly without veils (11:2–16); and abuses in the ritual meal of the community–"the Lord's supper" (11:17–34). Paul also deals with problems with spiritual gifts, especially speaking in tongues (12:1–14:40), and the Corinthian understanding of the resurrection (15:1–58). Paul hears about these problems through reports from various members of the assembly (1:11) and also through a letter from the congregation (7:1). So he writes 1 Corinthians, which is actually at least the second letter he wrote to them (cf. 1 Cor. 5:9), to respond to these various problems, promising to visit them at a later date (4:18–21; 16:5–9).

Paul did visit the Corinthians subsequent to writing 1 Corinthians, but that visit, described at the beginning of canonical 2 Corinthians, was not a happy one (2 Cor. 2:1–11). He refers to it as a "painful visit" (2 Cor. 2:1), in which, it seems, Paul had a serious confrontation with one individual in particular (2:5–10a). Subsequent to this "painful visit," Paul wrote another letter, described as a "letter of tears," in an attempt to remedy the disastrous results of the "painful visit" (2:3–4). Eventually, however, Paul's close associate Titus brings about reconciliation between Paul and his Corinthian assembly (2 Cor. 2:12–13; 7:5–16). When Titus returns from his visit to Corinth with good news of Corinthian reconciliation with Paul (7:5–7), Paul writes 2 Corinthians. He describes his joy at the reconciliation, explains the nature of his ministry in terms of reconciliation (2 Cor. 3:1–6:13), and makes plans for Titus's return with a delegation that will complete Paul's collection for the Jerusalem believers with the Corinthian contribution (2 Cor. 8:1–9:15).

Second Corinthians 10–13 represents a problem in the compositional integrity of canonical 2 Corinthians. After all the positive elements of reconciliation described throughout 2 Corinthians 1–9, 2 Corinthians 10–13 begins with:

> I myself, Paul, appeal to you by the meekness and gentleness of Christ–I who am humble when face to face with you, but bold toward you when I am away!–I ask that when I am present I need not show boldness by daring to oppose those who think we are acting according to human standards. Indeed, we live as human beings, but we do not wage war according to human standards; for the weapons of our warfare are not merely human, but they have divine power to destroy strongholds. We destroy arguments and every proud obstacle raised up against the knowledge of God, and we take every thought captive to obey Christ. We are ready to punish every disobedience when your obedience is complete. (10:1–6)

It seems that Paul is back at "war" with the Corinthians, given all the military imagery invoked in this passage. In the remainder of the section, Paul vigorously defends his ministry, in particular against outside agitators whom he calls derisively "super-apostles" (11:5) and "false apostles" (11:13). Thus, most scholars agree that 2 Corinthians 10–13 represents a fragment from a separate letter by Paul, most likely after he wrote 2 Corinthians 1–9, or perhaps before, including the possibility that it represents in part the "letter of tears" Paul describes in 2 Corinthians 2:4.[5]

However one works out the compositional issues in 1–2 Corinthians, one thing is certain: The correspondence between Paul and the Corinthians reflects a long, stormy relationship between apostle/founder and congregation. Moreover, I would argue that many of the problems between apostle and assembly are to be found in a fundamental disagreement between Paul and some in Corinth about the nature of gospel leadership. In the remainder of this chapter, I will trace this argument through a number of the key passages in 1 Corinthians, especially 1 Corinthians 1:10–4:21. Subsequently through this case study I will draw out some implications for our understanding of leadership in Paul, specifically, and leadership in the New Testament in general.

1 Corinthians 1–4 and the Problems of Leadership

The Parties Involved

After typical Pauline epistolary greetings and thanksgiving, which, nonetheless, already alert us to what's coming with regard to Paul's apostleship (1:1) and the Corinthian preoccupation with spiritual gifts (1:5–7), Paul jumps right into the first of many issues he must confront in this correspondence. However, the problem of division among leaders in Corinth, and how Paul deals with it, actually sets the tone for the other problems he discusses, both in terms of how they are related to leadership and how Paul responds to them.

Initially, Paul describes the problem as a matter of disunity, similar to his descriptions elsewhere in his letters (Phil. 1:27; 2:2; Rom. 15:5):

> Now I appeal to you, brothers and sisters, by the name of our
> Lord Jesus Christ, that all of you be in agreement and that there
> be no divisions among you, but that you be united in the same
> mind and the same purpose. (1 Cor. 1:10)

Literally, the Greek reads, "that you all say the same thing and that there be no *skismata* ['divisions,' 'dissensions'] among you," echoing language particularly from his letter to the Philippians (see Phil. 4:2–"I urge Euodia and I urge Syntyche to be of the same mind [*to auto phronein*] in the Lord"). Thus, it sounds like familiar territory for Paul and his churches.

However, immediately Paul specifies the circumstances surrounding the disunity and divisions:

> For it has been reported to me by Chloe's people that there are
> quarrels [*erides*] among you, my brothers and sisters. What I mean
> is that each of you says, "I belong to Paul," or "I belong to Apollos,"
> or "I belong to Cephas," or "I belong to Christ." (1:11–12)

The divisions or dissensions are related to "quarrels" over leaders. Apparently, some identify themselves with (literally "are of") Paul, others with Apollos, and still others with Cephas, the Aramaic name for the apostle Peter (cf. Gal. 2:6–14). Some shun these human leaders altogether and align themselves solely with Christ. Further, these alignments appear to be tied to which human leader baptized whom, for Paul adds:

> Has Christ been divided? Was Paul crucified for you? Or were you baptized in the name of Paul? I thank God that I baptized none of you except Crispus and Gaius, so that no one can say that you were baptized in my name. (1:13–15)

The term "divided" (*memeristai*) suggests divided "parties," including political parties. Thus L. L. Welborn translates 1:13a as, "Has the body of Christ been split into parties?"[6] Scholars have debated long and hard over the nature of these Corinthian "parties." Some have argued for a literal understanding with indeed four "parties" (Paul, Apollos, Cephas, and Christ) and that the division was more likely over doctrinal issues. Others have suggested three "parties"–those of Paul, Apollos, and Cephas–and that Paul introduces Christ to illustrate the absurdity of these divisions. Still others have suggested that the division is over Paul and Apollos, because these two names appear several times in the rest of the letter (3:5–9; 4:6; 16:12), while not so for Cephas/Peter, an original apostle and traveling missionary of the Jerusalem church, with whom Paul had a run-in early in his ministry (Antioch, cf. Gal. 2:11–14). Some have even suggested that no such actual parties existed and that Paul speaks metaphorically here.[7]

A variation on this last theme is that Paul is really the lightening rod for the Corinthian conflicts. In 1 Corinthians 1–4, Paul quickly changes positions or emphases. First, he mentions four "parties." Then he discusses the nature of leadership in terms of servanthood illustrated by two of these individuals–himself and Apollos (3:5–9). Finally, he describes apostleship with himself as the lead example in 1 Corinthians 4:1–21. "[A]lthough [Paul] *begins* his response by taking on the distortion of the gospel and the church revealed by these quarrels, he *concludes* the argument by defending his apostleship and his authority over [the Corinthians]."[8] Thus, regardless, of whether there were all these actual parties, the one thing most scholars agree on is that a significant group of leading members in Corinth opposed Paul and his leadership. A close look at the argument in 1 Corinthians 1–4 shows this to be the case.

Gospel and Sophia

After introducing the theme of division over leaders, Paul takes a surprising turn in his response. He introduces a discussion of *sophia*–wisdom–and contrasts it with the gospel of the cross Paul has proclaimed in Corinth.

> For Christ did not send me to baptize but to proclaim the gospel,
> and not with eloquent wisdom, so that the cross of Christ might
> not be emptied of its power. For the message about the cross is
> foolishness to those who are perishing, but to us who are being
> saved it is the power of God. (1 Cor. 1:17–18)

Apparently, some in the church in Corinth identified the gospel with
sophia logou–"wisdom of the word" or "eloquent wisdom." Stephen Pogoloff
has argued that "*logos* and *sophia*" referred not just to Greek philosophy in
general, but Greek rhetoric and what it demonstrated about the user's social
status.[9] Thus in Corinth a group of individuals were enamored of oratory
adornments in speech to the extent that it showed the elevated educational
and social status of the orator, in this case the founder and leader of their
religious community. When Paul turns to discuss his own oratorical skills
(2:1–5), he says that they did not measure up to the expectations of some
among the Corinthians. Perhaps such perceived shortcomings lead to these
divided groups as some sought out more eloquent leaders to whom they
could attach themselves. At any rate, Paul takes up the argument against
his own failings in this area.

Paul and Rhetoric

Paul compares the content of his gospel message to issues of form and
rhetoric. Paul's gospel requires "cruciformity," that is, "conformity to the
crucified Christ."[10] However, because Roman crucifixion was such an
"insidious and intimidating instrument of power and political control," to
identify with "a crucified political criminal and his cross" seemed the height
of folly and scandal to both Jews and Greeks:[11]

> For Jews demand signs and Greeks desire wisdom, but we proclaim
> Christ crucified, a stumbling block to Jews and foolishness to
> Gentiles, but to those who are the called, both Jews and Greeks,
> Christ the power of God and the wisdom of God. For God's
> foolishness is wiser than human wisdom, and God's weakness is
> stronger than human strength. (1:22–25)

Therefore, in effect, Paul asks why the *ekklēsia* should conduct its
ministry with worldly "sages," "scribes" and "debaters." "Has not God made
foolish the wisdom of the world?" (1:20). In fact, Paul goes on to argue, the
ekklēsia should depend on the leadership of those who have actually been
called to be part of the gospel community, regardless of their status in the
world:

> Consider your own call, brothers and sisters: not many of you
> were wise by human standards, not many were powerful, not many
> were of noble birth. But God chose what is foolish in the world to
> shame the wise; God chose what is weak in the world to shame

the strong; God chose what is low and despised in the world, things that are not, to reduce to nothing things that are, so that no one might boast in the presence of God. (1:26–29)

Scholarship about this text has tended to concentrate on the "some" implied by the "not many," that is, if most of the believers in Corinth were not of the well-educated, politically powerful, and well-born, then at least *some* were, and therein lies the problem that Paul confronted. Well-to-do leaders wanted to exercise "secular" power based on status in the gospel community, but Paul wanted the community's leadership (and his own) to be exercised based on calling.[12]

Given the abject poverty of the vast majority of people in the Greco-Roman world, Justin Meggitt has questioned whether there could be any members of the elite in Pauline communities, especially based on texts from such highly rhetorical contexts as 1 Corinthians 1:18–31.[13] However, Wayne Meeks's suggestion that "status inconsistency" could be the experience of some leaders in the Corinthian context might help explain the situation. Referring to the lack of evidence to show that Corinthian leaders could be well integrated into the larger society, Meeks writes:

> We would avoid these contradictions if we recognized that "the strong" of the Corinthian congregation are inconsistent in status. They enjoy a high rank in some dimensions, such as wealth, identification with the Latin elements in the colony, support by dependents and clients, and in one or two cases perhaps also civic office, but they may be ranked lower in others, such as origin, occupation or sex. Such people would share many of the attitudes, values, and sentiments of unambiguously higher social levels yet still lack status crystallization.[14]

I agree with Meggitt that perhaps wealth and civic office elude most, if not all, of Pauline believers. However, at least some in Corinth feel the need to exercise leadership in the Pauline community as they would if they had leadership status in the outside world. Their status inconsistency outside the Christian community encourages the search for status enhancement inside the community. This Paul must rebuke because of its detriment to other members of the community, who have little or no status outside or inside the Corinthian *ekklēsia*. Yet, within the community, they should be reckoned with on community decisions and attitudes because "God chose what is foolish in the world to shame the wise; God chose what is weak in the world to shame the strong" (1:27).

Thus, the Pauline *ekklēsia* may have had no top elites from Corinthian society (as Meeks suggests–no one from "the extreme top"),[15] but still have people without elite status in the outside, "secular" world (to use Clarke's term)[16] who want to exercise leadership within the church in a "secular" way. Those are the models they have seen. Now, in the Christian *ekklēsia*, they have a place to practice such leadership. Later in the letter, Paul writes, "Be imitators of me, as I am of Christ" (11:1). The Corinthians should not imitate the secular world in matters of faith and practice, including leadership.

Thus, from the outset of 1 Corinthians Paul addresses these issues. Whether or not there were actual high status elites in the Corinthian community, Paul writes that some from among them were behaving as such, and, therefore, acting "fleshly" even though they are "spiritual":

> And so, brothers and sisters, I could not speak to you as spiritual people, but rather as people of the flesh, as infants in Christ. I fed you with milk, not solid food, for you were not ready for solid food. Even now you are still not ready, for you are still of the flesh. For as long as there is jealousy and quarreling among you, are you not of the flesh, and behaving according to human inclinations? For when one says, "I belong to Paul," and another, "I belong to Apollos," are you not merely human? (3:1–4)

Although Paul addresses the entire congregation ("brothers and sisters") at this point, he has in mind especially those practicing leadership in a "fleshly" way by taking sides with leaders, especially Paul and Apollos. Paul even challenges those who would claim allegiance to *him* because they, too, are wrong-headed in their approach.[17] In effect, Paul argues, "If you came into the community as 'are nots' in the eyes of society, then exercise leadership as such, trusting in God and not boasting in yourselves, your status, and your power."

The Practice of Gospel Leadership by Paul

Paul himself practices leadership in this way, as he turns to apparent accusations against the nature of his ministry and proclamation among the Corinthians:

> When I came to you, brothers and sisters, I did not come proclaiming the mystery of God to you in lofty words or wisdom [*hyperochēn logou hē sophias*]. For I decided to know nothing among you except Jesus Christ, and him crucified. And I came to you in weakness and in fear and in much trembling. My speech and my proclamation were not with plausible words of wisdom, but with a demonstration of the Spirit and of power, so that your faith might rest not on human wisdom but on the power of God. (2:1–5)

Paul again establishes a dichotomy between *sophia* and the message of the cross, this time applying it to his own ministry. In his proclamation of the gospel in Corinth he depended not on "eloquent speech" to get his message across, in a way that would enhance his own status.[18] Rather, he allowed the power of God to be exhibited in the Spirit, so that the faith of the Corinthians would be based on God and not on the person of Paul. Further, such an approach in his proclamation was important as a way to exemplify the nature of the gospel. If Paul came to them "in weakness and in fear and in much trembling," rather than with "plausible [*peithois*– persuasive] words of wisdom," then the Corinthians would better understand that his message was in essence about nothing more than "Jesus Christ, and him crucified," or as Michael Gorman translates, "I decided to know nothing among you except Jesus Christ–that is, Jesus Christ *crucified.*"[19]

In other words, how can one proclaim a suffering, crucified Lord as the crux of faith, but do so in a way to exalt oneself, the proclaimer rather than the proclaimed? "Professional rhetors often affected weakness in an ironic method 'by which one urbanely displayed one's own skill by affecting the lack of it.'"[20] Thus Paul did not lack for rhetorical skill, but in light of Corinthian emphasis on rhetoric for the sake of status, he (rhetorically) eschews focus on form for the sake of content. A rhetor of great skill, but "serious about his philosophy," Dio Chrysostom, put it this way:

> My purpose…was…[not] to range myself beside those who habitually sing such [exalted] strains, whether orators or poets. For they are clever persons, mighty sophists, wonder-workers; but I am quite ordinary and prosaic in my utterance, though not ordinary in my theme."[21]

Paul did not proclaim an "ordinary" theme to the Corinthians, although some now question his "ordinary" presentation.

Paul has another challenge to those who question his leadership. He questions the leaders they wish to model themselves after: "Yet among the mature we do speak wisdom, though it is not a wisdom of this age or of the rulers [*archontōn*] of this age, who are doomed to perish" (2:6). The *archontes* Paul refers to here were probably human rulers, rather than spiritual or demonic forces.[22] Again, Paul distinguishes between "the wisdom of this world" and the "wisdom of God," this time as represented by leaders. The "wisdom of this world" as practiced by its leaders actually crucified the Lord Jesus· "But we speak God's wisdom, secret and hidden, which God decreed before the ages for our glory. None of the rulers of this age understood this; for if they had, they would not have crucified the Lord of glory" (2:7–8).

In the context of Roman Corinth, Paul verbally challenges the "wisdom" of a Roman crucifixion. If some in Corinth want to model their leadership after the "wisdom of this world," they run smack into a serious contradiction of their faith, for the "rulers of this age" who practice such wisdom had a direct hand in the crucifixion of their Lord. Thus, the mythological language with which Paul discusses the death of Jesus serves clear rhetorical purposes in 1 Corinthians, effectively extending the significance of Jesus' death at the hands of "the rulers" so as to determine how citizens of a flourishing Roman colony, hundreds of miles distant from dusty Judea, ought to conduct themselves toward the "scheme of this age, which is passing away" (7:31), on the one hand, and toward the "have-nots" in their own community (11:22) and in Judea itself (16:1–4).[23]

Corinthian church leaders ought not to model their practices after the ruling order of Rome, especially in their treatment of fellow believers, including their founding apostle.

The Spirituality of Gospel Leadership

One reason for the distinctive behavior of all believers, especially leaders, resides in their distinctive spirituality:

Now we have received not the spirit of the world, but the Spirit that is from God, so that we may understand the gifts bestowed on us by God. And we speak of these things in words not taught by human wisdom but taught by the Spirit, interpreting spiritual things to those who are spiritual. (2:12–13)

Paul believed and taught his converts that "the link" between them and God was the Spirit. "To the believer all of what God might believe is potentially available through the Spirit." Thus, one does not need to depend upon human learning or reason to understand God's purposes in the believer's life. "The believer may know God because the believer has the Spirit, not because he or she has received some advanced course in esoteric human rhetoric or wisdom."[24] Paul once again challenges the apparent "sophistic" ideology of some leaders in Corinth. He "contrasts ordinary human understanding through persuasion with understanding through the spirit of God."[25] Paul suggests that the Corinthians as a whole, whatever leadership party they were ascribing to, including his own, are not behaving as people of the Spirit (3:1–5).

The Fundamental Nature of Gospel Leadership

Thus, he turns to a truly spiritual understanding of the nature of leadership in his estimation—servanthood. "What then is Apollos? What is Paul? Servants [*diakonoi*] through whom you came to believe, as the Lord assigned to each" (3:5). Paul offers an inversion of their understanding of the nature of their leaders. For, rather than consider them powerful sages or patrons of some sort, their leaders should be viewed as servants of the gospel. These servants themselves do as God assigned to them, and their ultimate reward comes not from honor bestowed by their followers, but by the quality of their work before God.

Moreover, God, not the workers, is ultimately responsible for the growth in the Christian assembly. "I planted, Apollos watered, but God gave the growth. So neither the one who plants nor the one who waters is anything, but only God who gives the growth" (3:6–7). The leaders, then, are equal. Not only are they mere servants, they are equal partners in the gospel enterprise. Paul thus trivializes the Corinthian factionalism by modeling leadership equality, specifically between Apollos and himself:

> In 3:5–17 Paul demonstrates the need and possibility for Corinthian unity by appealing to the concord which exists between himself and Apollos, one of the leaders to whom some kind of allegiance was also paid. He uses their relationship as a paradigm for Corinthian unity rather than a cause for division (1:12; 3:4, 22; 4:6; 16:12).[26]

Besides the metaphor of menial service, Paul also employs farming and building metaphors, both for the work of the leaders in the assembly and the nature of the assembly itself: "For we are co-workers [*synergoi*] with God; you are God's field, God's building" (3:9, author's translation). A gospel leader can be a "master-builder"(*architektōn*), but if such, should build wisely (3:10a). In Corinth, Paul was the builder who laid the "foundation," but he realized that others would build on it (3:10b). However, these should do so carefully as well (3:10c). Paul warns about using the wrong "material" for this building job: "wood, hay, straw" instead of "gold, silver, precious stones" (3:12). Eschatological judgment awaits those who build badly (3:13–15). Thus, Paul issues a warning about the bad leadership that has taken hold in the Corinthian assembly. He returns to the problem of human wisdom as the guiding light of some Corinthian leaders to drive home this point:

> Do not deceive yourselves. If you think that you are wise in this age, you should become fools so that you may become wise. For the wisdom of this world is foolishness with God. For it is written,
>
> "He catches the wise in their craftiness,"
> and again,
> "The Lord knows the thoughts of the wise,
>   that they are futile."
> So let no one boast about human leaders. (3:18–21a)

The "human leaders" in Corinth should be considered mere "servants," because they are equal in importance as they do the work of God in the faith community, even as God does the important work of spiritual growth. They must also build the community carefully, or else face judgment. Therefore, the community should not "boast" about its leaders. Relying on the various gifts of rhetoric and human wisdom for assessing the value of leaders belies ultimate dependence on God by leaders and community alike.

Indeed the nature of the faith community requires the kind of careful, caring leadership Paul describes in these texts. Besides being the "field" of God and of God's co-workers as well as the building upon which the "foundation [that] is Jesus Christ" is established (3:11), the community is the "temple" (*naos*) of God's Spirit (3:16). Paul pronounces another strong word of judgment against anyone who would not take seriously this divine nature of the *ekklēsia*: "If anyone destroys God's temple, God will destroy that person. For God's temple is holy, and you are that temple" (3:17). A later reference to the individual believer's body as the "temple of the Holy Spirit" (6:19) should not take away from the clear reference to the importance of collective expression of faith represented by the Corinthian *ekklēsia*. Reading 3:16–17 by means of 6:19

> is all the more unfortunate because [3:16–17] is one of the few texts in the NT where we are exposed both to an understanding of the nature of the local church (God's temple indwelt by his Spirit) and where the warning of v. 17 makes it clear how important the local church is to God himself [sic].[27]

Thus, Paul heightens leadership responsibility by describing the *ekklēsia* as the "dwelling place" of God.

Paul concludes the section by once again alluding to the foolishness of factionalism. How could various parties of the "dwelling place" of God say they belong to human leaders? "For all things are yours, whether Paul or Apollos or Cephas or the world or life or death or the present or the future—all belong to you, and you belong to Christ, and Christ belongs to God" (3:21b–23). Paul inverts the Corinthian attitudes toward leadership. Believers do not belong to leaders. Leaders belong to believers because believers belong to Christ and ultimately even Christ responds to God. "Christ is functionally subordinate to God, just as the leaders serve the followers and are functionally subordinate to them, though they are also ontologically equal with them."[28]

Because the focus of gospel leadership, according to Paul, entails the tasks of nurturing and building a community of faith, hierarchy is less important than faithfulness to the task. Even Christ responds to God, as do believers in Christ and their leaders. Leaders should not take advantage of their success in ministry to foster their own following, and believers should not expect to enhance their social, "secular" status by attaching themselves to particular leaders. To avoid such leadership principles and practices, Paul deliberately employs "non-status leadership vocabulary" (i.e., "agricultural, artisan, and household imagery") and focuses "not on who [the leaders] are, but rather on what their task is."[29]

The Leadership of Apostles

The general references to leaders in 1 Corinthians 3:5–23, as exemplified by Paul and Apollos, after the specific reference to Paul's own leadership in 1 Corinthians 2:1–5, brings Paul back to a discussion of apostleship in general in 4:1–21. However, as the passage unfolds, it is clear Paul has his own apostleship in mind, as well as the Corinthian interpretation of it. Benjamin Fiore compares 1 Corinthians 3 and 4 as a "covert allusion" to the Corinthian leaders (1 Cor. 3:5–23), with a specific explanation in terms of Paul's apostleship (1 Cor. 4:1–21).[30] Ancient rhetorical figures of covert allusion involved making oblique or veiled references to delicate subjects, sometimes so as not to offend one's audience.[31] Paul's delineation of the servant nature of the gospel leadership of Apollos and himself in 1 Corinthians 3:5–23 subtly undermines the secular approach of leadership by some in Corinth. However, Paul uncovers his meaning in 1 Corinthians 4, explicitly addressing the problem leaders of Corinth:

> I have applied all this to Apollos and myself for your benefit, brothers and sisters, so that you may learn through us the meaning of the saying, "Nothing beyond what is written," so that none of you will be puffed up in favor of one against another. (4:6)

Paul references the problem of divided parties on the basis of favored leaders as a matter of arrogance (to be "puffed up," *physiosthe*). Despite the potential resistance of these leaders to his exhortation, he will not hold back his critique at this point in the argument. The subtle allusions to their wrongheaded approach to leadership in 1 Corinthians 3:5ff, by analogy to the right approach to leadership, namely, that of Paul and Apollos, as well as other "servants," becomes more explicit in the argument of 4:1–21.

First, Paul applies the servanthood motif to apostleship in general, including his. However, he employs two terms distinctive from those he used in 3:5–9. "Think of us in this way, as servants [*hypēretas*] of Christ and stewards [*oikonomous*] of God's mysteries" (4:1). Why does Paul use *hypēretas* instead of *diakonoi,* as he did in 3:5? The context for the metaphor changes more specifically to the household setting. One type of household servant is the *hypēretes,* a household slave, who, nonetheless, "willingly learns his task and goal from another who is over him in an organic order but without prejudice to his personal dignity and worth."[32] Thus one can easily see the connection between God and apostle in such a model. However, to employ *hypēretes* in this context of defending apostolic leadership is striking.

So is Paul's use of the next term *oikonomos,* household "steward," someone more in a position of leadership within the Greco-Roman household, but still a low status servant. In some cases, stewards were slaves as well.[33] Although *oikonomos* did not necessarily designate a slave, in the context of Paul's self-description as *diakonoi* and *hypēretai* in 1 Corinthians 3:5 and 4:1–2, it should be read as referring to slave stewards.[34]

Thus a household steward may be a slave placed in this administrative position of trust ("it is required of stewards that they be found trustworthy [*pistos*–'faithful']" [4:2]). However, the fact remained that they belonged to a pecking order in a well-to-do Greco-Roman household, and usually toward the lower end of that pecking order. For example, one ancient author, Artemidorous, writes about "different kinds of slaves in what seems like an order of ascending status": after "servers (*therapontes*) comes "underlings or helpers (*hyperetai*) and "stewards (*oikonomoi*)."[35] Thus both terms from 1 Corinthians 4:1–2 appear with reference to lowly household servants. Paul has contrasted his leadership in ways that may have shocked his readers in Corinth. In fact, the readers, especially the elite leaders among them, may have been questioning Paul's leadership precisely for these reasons. However, Paul claims such judgment matters little to him in the larger context of his ministry:

> But with me it is a very small thing that I should be judged [*anakritho*] by you or by any human court. I do not even judge myself. I am not aware of anything against myself, but I am not thereby acquitted. It is the Lord who judges me. (4:3–4)

L. L. Welborn suggests that Paul's opponents in Corinth wanted to "judge" or "interrogate" Paul as if in a court. "Paul's language in 4:1–5 leaves little doubt that his opponents sought to examine his credentials in quasi-judicial proceedings."[36] I question whether the Corinthians had actual court proceedings in mind for Paul, or even "a kind of ecclesiastical court."[37] Certainly they doubted and questioned the legitimacy of Paul's authority in their midst, and so Paul uses the figurative language of the courtroom to describe their ill-conceived judgments of Paul.

Paul responds first by describing the "irrelevance"[38] of any interrogation by Corinthian leaders: "But with me it is a very small thing that I should be judged by you or by any human court" (4:3a). Then he employs eschatology to solidify his position against any Corinthian critique:

> It is the Lord who judges me. Therefore do not pronounce judgment before the time, before the Lord comes, who will bring to light the things now hidden in darkness and will disclose the purposes of the heart. Then each one will receive commendation [*epainos*, praise] from God. (4:4b-5)

Placing his apostleship in an eschatological context of divine judgment makes Paul's position "unassailable."[39]

As servants and stewards of God, Paul, other apostles, and other preachers of the gospel, such as Apollos, cannot receive their assessment from fellow human beings or a judicial court because "they have a responsibility to God. They are employees of God, and not of the Corinthian congregation."[40] Paul thus "transfers this discourse" about leadership "from the human to the divine sphere: only God will interrogate and judge him."[41] Paul demonstrates that the wisdom and judgment of the Corinthian factions has been "faulty"[42] because they lack an appropriate eschatological vision.

Not that the Corinthians lacked an eschatology. "Already you have all you want! Already you have become rich! Quite apart from us you have become kings! Indeed, I wish that you had become kings, so that we might be kings with you!" (4:8). Some in Corinth apparently believed that the eschaton had already arrived. Thus they were acting "fulfilled" (*kekoresmenoi*), "rich" (*eploutēsate*) and "kingly" (*ebasileusate*). Yet, Paul asserts, "the kingdom [*basileia*] of God depends not on talk but on power" (4:20). The Corinthian eschatology overreached because it was based on earthly "boasting" (4:7), a consistent problem in Corinth (1:29, 31; 3:21).

However these terms ("fulfilled," "rich," "kings") have social as well as theological content. They parallel previous ascriptions Paul makes of some in Corinth, namely the "wise," the "powerful," and the "well-born" (1:26; cf. 1:20). Indeed, Paul makes this parallel explicit: "We are fools for the sake of Christ, but you are wise in Christ. We are weak, but you are strong. You are held in honor, but we in disrepute" (4:10). The contrast between terms describing some Corinthians and those describing apostles is striking:

You are *phronimoi* [wise] in Christ...we are *mōpoi* [fools] for Christ
You are *ischuroi* [strong]...we are *astheneis* [weak]
You are *endoxoi* [honored]...we are *atimoi* [dishonored].[43]

A study of these terms in their Hellenistic context demonstrates their social content. The *phronimoi* are equivalent to the *sophoi* in 1 Corinthians 1:26. They are "those who possess the *sofia tou kosmos*," and who "are members of the educated/cultured...circle, those who belong to the social elite."[44]

The *ischuroi* parallel the *dunatoi*, the "powerful" of 1:26. This represents "a technical term for political power derived from economic muscle" and thus denotes "people of influence."[45] Ramsey MacMullen referred to the *dunatoi* as "magnates,"[46] or, as Pogoloff puts it, "landlords whose economic, political and legal power dominated the life of the poor."[47]

Finally, the *endoxoi* ("honored") of 1 Corinthians 4:10 parallel the *eugeneis*, the "well-born" of 1:26. These were "people of esteemed families, of high birth, to whom a suitable conduct—we can even say a suitable character—should correspond."[48]

Paul critiques the Corinthian elite, not so much for achieving these indicators of high status, because most likely few of them actually did. He criticizes them for aspiring to such status and its indicators and for attempting to use leadership in the gospel community as a means toward such achievement. "Already you have all you want! Already you have become rich! Quite apart from us you have become kings!" (4:8a). Paul decries their status aspirations in ironic tones ("Indeed, I wish that you had become kings, so that we might be kings with you!" [4:8b]) by contrasting these status indicators with the perceived status of apostles like himself in the secular realm, which is to say, their lowly status:

> For I think that God has exhibited us apostles as last of all, as
> though sentenced to death, because we have become a spectacle
> to the world, to angels and to mortals…To the present hour we are
> hungry and thirsty, we are poorly clothed and beaten and homeless,
> and we grow weary from the work of our own hands…We have
> become like the rubbish of the world, the dregs of all things, to
> this very day. (4:9, 11–12a, 13b)

Before God, apostles are missionaries and founders of new communities
of faith in Christ, but before the *cosmos* they have exhibited all the qualities
and activities of low status: hunger, poverty, violence, homelessness, and
menial manual labor. In short, they have become nothing more than street
rubbish for the cause of the gospel. This negative, hyperbolic description[49]
is set up precisely as a contrast to the high status expectations of Corinthian
leaders.

Paul contrasts the apostles' weakness with the strength of "certain"
people at Corinth. His assertion of his authority and his call to imitation
are directed at those "certain ones" who judge their own positions by normal
criteria of social status. "Paul targets the ones on top: the wise, rich, strong,
and free."[50]

A Concluding Parental Plea

Paul concludes his argument for appropriate understanding of the
nature of gospel leadership with a generalized plea to the entire Corinthian
community (1 Cor. 4:14–21). He turns from the ironic tones of 4:8–13,
which he had directed at the elite Corinthian leaders, to more a familial
tone as he addresses the community as a whole:

> I am not writing this to make you ashamed, but to admonish you
> as my beloved children. For though you might have ten thousand
> guardians in Christ, you do not have many fathers. Indeed, in
> Christ Jesus I became your father through the gospel. I appeal to
> you, then, be imitators of me. (4:14–16)

With this conclusion Paul seeks to "reestablish [his] authority among
the Corinthians" as a whole.[51] He does this with "fatherly" tones that remind
the Corinthians of his role as founder in contradistinction to any and all
teachers or "guides" (*paidagōgos*) that they might have. "In Greek and Roman
society, the father held the authority, in no uncertain terms, whereas slaves
were usually charged with the tasks of disciplining and cleaning up after
children, with the 'guardian' (*paidagōgos*) picking up where the wet nurse
and nanny left off."[52] Thus Paul clearly sets himself up as the sole human
authority over the Corinthian situation in light of factions over other leaders
and teachers.

Paul further makes this point by calling for the Corinthians to "imitate"
him (4:16). Thus he is not only their founder but also the prime exemplar

for their practice of faith and leadership going forward from their acceptance of Paul's gospel message about Christ Jesus. This imitation is tied to his parenthood. "Paul calls for imitation…as a consequence…of his fatherhood of the community in Christ."[53] Paul, who himself imitates the ways of Christ (4:17; 11:1), expects the same behavior from believers in his assemblies, especially leaders. Paul asserts that he writes this not for their shame, but for their admonishment, which Gordon Fee describes as instruction that leads to change.[54] Specifically, Paul "has in mind the pattern of patient suffering just laid out (vv. 8–13)"[55] as the model for leadership he hopes they will all adopt. To imitate Paul, therefore, "refers to his moral way of life and his ministerial lifestyle, which he has just described in 4:9–13.[56] Of course, this passage detailing apostolic sufferings is a direct response to some in Corinth assuming triumphalistic perspectives on leadership, including the search for status through human wisdom, which Paul has been discussing since first describing the problem of division over leadership in 1:10.

To aid in showing the need for change of attitudes and behavior, Paul will send one of his close associates, Timothy, "to remind you of my ways in Christ Jesus" (4:17). Timothy not only goes in Paul's stead in the interim until Paul himself can go (4:19a), but he, too, represents the kind of servant leadership Paul wants the Corinthians to practice, for he "is my beloved and faithful child in the Lord" (4:19b). In other words, as a "child" of Paul, like the Corinthians, Timothy has been faithful in imitating Paul and his "ways in Christ," including in matters of leadership. Toward the end of the letter, Paul again takes up the embassy of Timothy and writes, "he is doing the work of the Lord just as I am" (16:10b). In sending Timothy and then promising a visit himself, Paul seeks to strengthen his admonition for the Corinthians to fix their leadership ways.[57]

Finally, Paul returns to the harsh tones he had earlier reserved for the select few in Corinth causing leadership problems: "But some of you, thinking that I am not coming to you, have become arrogant [*ephusiōthesan*]. But I will come to you soon, if the Lord wills, and I will find out not the talk of these arrogant people but their power [*dunamin*]" (4:18–19). Paul had already referred to opposing leaders in Corinth as "puffed up" or "arrogant" (*phusiōsthe*). Moreover, these terms are connected to Paul's earlier admonishments about "boasting in human leaders" (3:21; cf. 1:12, 29, 31), "but now Paul makes clear that he refers to actually, not just potentially, arrogant persons."[58] Those who have been resisting Paul's leadership and his approach to leadership in terms of service and sacrifice for the gospel and gospel community must be called to task. "For the kingdom of God depends not on talk but on power" (4:20). Paul rarely used the term "kingdom of God," but his use here indicates that the Corinthians knew about it. Thus verse 20 "serves as a summary recapitulation of his whole argument since 1:17–18."[59]

The Corinthian love of mere rhetoric or words, "a falsely placed trust in eloquent wisdom (1:17–20; 2:1–5)"[60] for the sake of status enhancement over service and sacrifice, the real "power" of the gospel, leads to a final warning from Paul: "What would you prefer? Am I to come to you with a stick, or with love in a spirit of gentleness?" (4:21). Paul's previous paternal language at the outset of this passage (4:14) shows he would rather come with a "a spirit of gentleness." He hopes this letter and the sending of Timothy can avoid the other approach, to come "with a rod of discipline,"[61] an attitude he showed with the ironic tones of 4:8–13. Either way, the matter was serious. It involved a clear understanding of the sacrificial nature of gospel leadership. Such sacrificial leadership may lead to lowly status in the eyes of the world outside the gospel community. In fact, in Paul's case it did lead there, much to the dismay of some in Corinth. As such, this serious matter demands serious action from Paul.

Summary of 1 Corinthians 1:10–4:21 and Transition to Rest of Letter

The care with which Paul addresses the problem of division over leaders in 1 Corinthians 1:10–4:21 belies the terminal treatment of an isolated problem from which Paul must move on now to other issues within the Corinthian community. Rather, the issue was serious and pervasive. The question of the nature of gospel leadership was fundamental to the gospel itself. Christ lies at the heart of the gospel message. Christ was a servant who died on a Roman cross. Gospel leadership needs to model such sacrificial service; it must be "cruciform." The problem with Paul and his leadership in the eyes of some in Corinth was that it lacked the glamour that they looked for in their leaders, a glamour that would add to their status in the larger society. This also affected the way these local leaders treated the "are-nots," the lower status believers among them. This created the disunity and discord that existed in the community.

Paul fights against this wrongheaded leadership in a variety of ways. He describes the spirituality of authentic gospel leadership, and the failure of "human rulers" the Corinthian elite wish to emulate as those who crucified Jesus. Paul distinguishes between human understanding of gospel and leadership ("wisdom") and spiritual understanding. His best explanation for spiritual understanding of leadership comes out in the metaphor of service. He warns against those who would undermine the servant aspect of leadership and boast in anything other than their dependence on God, who causes growth in the gospel community, which Paul variously views as God's field, God's building, God's temple, and God's household. With these metaphors, Paul exemplifies the importance of *ekklēsia*, the ground on which gospel leadership takes place. Appropriate care must be taken to lead the church rightly or judgment awaits. Leaders belong to the assembly and its various members, not members to the leaders. Thus throughout 1 Corinthians 1–4, Paul inverts the expected modalities of leadership, including among apostles. While some leaders in Corinth revel in eschatological glory as already rich, fulfilled "kings," apostles like Paul suffer in mistreatment and poverty for the cause of the gospel. "What kind of leaders could these be?" ask some in Corinth. Again, Paul talks about service and stewardship in a household as marks of apostleship. However, no human judgment, but only divine, can be ascribed to such leadership. So Paul offers parental advice: "Mend your leadership ways, or the real eschaton will catch up with you."

The fact that Paul will send his envoy to teach about his "ways in Christ Jesus" and that he himself will come to visit, hopefully with "gentleness" and not "with a stick," points to a future development in this problem. As Richard Horsley suggests, "the stern, paternal, threatening plea to change their ways (v. 21) both concludes his long opening argument and sets up the rest of the body of the letter, which addresses problematic views and behaviors among the Corinthians."[62] Margaret Mitchell concurs and actually relates what is to come to Paul's exhortation toward imitation in 4:16 ("I appeal to you, then, be imitators of me.") We have already seen that such imitation refers to Paul's servant leadership. Thus,

> The call for imitation in 4:16 points both backward and forward. For each of the comparisons in 4:1–13 by which the Corinthians fared so badly, they are to seek to emulate Paul's behavior. Each type of behavior there, we noted, is an example of humility and self-effacement as opposed to fractious boasting and self-interest seeking. Throughout 1 Corinthians Paul will present himself as the opposite of a factionalist, in regard to each of the contested issues championing in himself the conciliatory position. 4:16 serves to introduce the predominant rhetorical strategy of the proof sections to follow, a strategy already explicitly used in the first proof section.[63]

Paul calls for imitation of himself not just in the problem he has discussed in 1 Corinthians 1–4, but in those that will proceed from here in the rest of the letter. Mitchell argues that in each case he will illustrate how these problems relate to the problems of factionalism. I would like to suggest that the problem of misunderstanding about the nature of gospel leadership lies behind these divisions and that in many, if not all, of the problems Paul delineates in the rest of the letter, the wrongheaded attitude about gospel leadership can be detected as well. I now turn to a brief discussion of this thesis in several of the passages that follow in 1 Corinthians.

Leadership and the Litany of Problems in Corinth

The rest of 1 Corinthians can be neatly and broadly divided into five sections: Problems of Sexuality and Marriage (5–7), Problems of Food Offered to Idols (8–10), Problems of Worship (11–14), the Resurrection

(15), and Concluding Matters (16). Such a neat structure belies several problems, including the issue that at 7:1, Paul turns to concerns that have been raised in a Corinthian letter to him ("Now concerning the matters about which you wrote...") rather than matters that have been reported to him by personal visitors or church representatives (such as "Chloe's people," 1:11 and perhaps Stephanas, 16:17).

Immorality

The issue that immediately follows Paul's long argument about division over leaders comes from an in-person report to Paul, rather than written correspondence: "It is actually reported that there is sexual immorality among you..." (1 Cor. 5:1). The matter has to do with a believer who has been "living with his father's wife," most clearly understood as a sexual relationship between a son and his stepmother, presumably after his father's death. When Paul writes that this act is "of a kind that is not found even among pagans" (5:1b), he suggests a wide-ranging condemnation of such a sexual relationship—the "cohabiting of father and son with the same woman"—not just among Jews, but among Greeks and Romans as well.[64] It was incestuous.

Even worse for Paul was the reaction of some in the church with regard to the actions of this believer: "And you are arrogant! Should you not rather have mourned, so that he who has done this would have been removed from among you?" (5:2). Many in the Corinthian assembly have refused to do anything about the "immoral brother," and Paul decries their inaction. In this passage he calls for the individual's excommunication from the community, "so that his spirit may be saved in the day of the Lord" (5:5b). The eschatological judgment that Paul warned would come upon bad workers and "builders" in God's gospel community in Corinth (3:10–15) will be visited upon this "brother...who is sexually immoral" (5:11).

Could this individual be a leader of the church? Moreover, could those who in particular are looking the other way at his behavior be part of the anti-Pauline leadership pool in Corinth? Several factors point in this direction. First, Paul calls the people tolerating this behavior (v. 2) "arrogant" (*pephusiomenoi*), the same term he used to describe those who have questioned his leadership in the previous passage (4:18, 19; cf. 4:6). Moreover, we have seen how those "arrogant" or "puffed up" ones are also those who have been "boasting" about their ties to sophistic human leaders (3:21; 1:31). It is not just coincidental that Paul begins to address various problems in the Corinthian community, including this one about an "immoral brother," by referring to a group of "arrogant" individuals. These are the ones who probably boast about their spiritual status as "fulfilled," as "rich," and as "kings" (which in turn heightens their social status). Therefore, they feel at ease when perhaps one of their own partakes in sexual behavior that is at odds with acceptable mores. After all, the "kingdom" has already come. Why should such behavior matter?

Moreover, if in fact this individual were one of "their own" socially, perhaps it would be difficult for them to sanction him. John Kingman Chow employs social network theory to argue in favor of the social ties between the "arrogant" and the "immoral brother."[65] First, Chow wonders why this man might be so interested in the wife of his presumably deceased father. Could it be that matters of inheritance (more so than love!) were at issue? Roman law allowed widows to take their dowries to another family if an appropriate suitor was not available within her dead husband's family. Could keeping the money within the family, at the cost of accusations of incest, be part of the scandal Paul rails against in this passage?

If so, why do Corinthian leaders accept the situation? Besides their triumphant spirituality and over-realized eschatology, a fellow believer with a lucrative dowry could mean some additional patronage for the *ekklēsia*. Moreover, how could they challenge a budding social elite, someone with whom their association could add to their own social status in the larger Corinthian community? "That the Corinthians continued to accept (proudly even! [5:2]) a sexually immoral person in their midst despite Paul's instruction in the previous letter (5:1–2, 9) suggests that he was someone of importance for the group."[66] Further, Paul's reference together to both the "sexually immoral" *and* the "greedy" among them as people to be avoided by the believing community (5:9–11) suggests some measure of economic status for the "immoral brother," maybe even a patron of the community. "The man may have been a member of the elite and a major patron of their community since the church had not acted against him. As such, they could not afford to criticize him and therefore lose his patronage."[67]

For these reasons, the problem of the immoral brother was probably linked to the problem of leadership that Paul has just discussed at length in 1 Corinthians 1–4. Like-minded leaders have rejected Paul's leadership on spiritual, social, and financial grounds. For similar reasons, when one of their own persists in immoral behavior, the Corinthian leadership elite refuse to take action. As he did in the previous passage of his letter (4:16–21), Paul lays claim to his apostolic authority to rectify a bad situation gone worse and to make a point about the true nature of gospel leadership. So, "as if present" he "pronounce[s] judgment" on the situation and calls the entire assembly, including the poor, as one, to do the same when they come together as a community (5:3–5). In so doing Paul opposes the socially elite leaders and their loyal followers. If the assembly does not obey Paul, those who "boast" about their relationship to this man do not do a "good thing" (5:6) because "a little yeast leavens the whole batch of dough." Although it is one group of believers supporting this one wayward individual, the whole assembly is affected, socially elite and nonelite alike. Thus the social divisions exhibited in this community as described by Paul in the previous section (1:10–4:21) continue to affect it in other matters besides their allegiance to various leaders. In fact, the group that questions the leadership of Paul because he does not exhibit the types of social status indicators that could enhance their own status is at it again with regard to the immoral brother. He is one of them, and Paul is not. For Paul, these persons represent bad gospel leadership.

Taking Believers to Court

As he completes his argument about driving out the immoral brother from the community because it is the believers who judge "those who are inside" (5:12), Paul reminds the community that judging or being judged by outsiders to the community is not within their purview, but rather "God will judge those outside" (5:12–13). This ends direct discussion of one problem while introducing another, but related, issue: believers taking other believers to outside courts to settle disputes. While it is difficult to determine what these disputes were about, Paul is again more outraged about the action than about the reasons for the action:

> When any of you has a grievance against another, do you dare to take it to court before the unrighteous, instead of taking it before the saints? Do you not know that the saints will judge the world? And if the world is to be judged by you, are you incompetent to try trivial cases? Do you not know that we are to judge angels–to say nothing of ordinary matters? If you have ordinary cases, then, do you appoint as judges those who have no standing in the church? I say this to your shame. Can it be that there is no one among you wise enough to decide between one believer and another, but a believer goes to court against a believer–and before unbelievers at that? (1 Cor. 6:1–6)

With these words, Paul celebrates the status of the *ekklēsia* in the eschatological judgment of God, while challenging the status of those who would initiate these court proceedings, whatever the litigation entailed. Paul makes a distinction between the realm of God, the church and its believers, and the realm of the "outsiders."

> Paul rebukes the Corinthians for taking their "insider" problems to secular "outsider" courts to secure justice. According to Paul, this is a violation of the sanctity of the church community (6:6). As in ch. 5, the underlying principle at work in this argument is the clearly drawn boundary between the insiders [the saints], and the outsiders (here called…"unjust," or…"unbelievers").[68]

Initiating court proceedings in the Roman world was a matter of status. Roman law favored the elite in such cases because they were the ones who elected judges in the first place.[69] To bring cases to court and win them enhanced the social status of the litigants. Roman imperial society understood that only the social elite could initiate court cases. The elite held every advantage in a court proceeding because their reputations were at stake. Judges, in many instances their social peers, would lean over backward on behalf of the plaintiff in a civil case, usually an elite patron, rather than the defendant, usually a lower status individual. Thus, "the Graeco-Roman world of legal suits was a world where the socially inferior were severely disadvantaged."[70]

Paul decries this practice among some in the Corinthian community. Moreover, every indication points to another instance of the social elite among the Corinthian believers once again acting in a "fleshly" way to enhance their status in the larger society. By going to court, they were taking advantage of their fellow believers, most likely of low social status. The "arrogant" challenged the leadership of Paul and have permitted one of their own to participate in an illicit relationship. Now those same "believers" humiliate fellow believers in open, public, secular court cases. "I say this to your shame," Paul cries out (6:5a).

In invoking the language of honor/shame and wisdom ("Can it be that there is no one among you wise enough to decide between one believer and another…?" 6:5b), Paul mocks those Corinthian leaders who sought honor by means of attaching themselves to leaders who exhibited eloquent wisdom. Moreover, Paul was not one of these. Once again, in this context, Paul reminds them of a better way to exercise their leadership: "In fact, to have lawsuits at all with one another is already a defeat for you. Why not rather be wronged? Why not rather be defrauded? But you yourselves wrong and defraud–and other believers at that" (6:7–8).

With these words, Paul echoes his earlier apostolic hardship list (4:9–13). He invites the Corinthian leaders who oppose him and who have introduced these litigations to secular courts to practice, instead, authentic gospel leadership that may include shame in the eyes of the outside world but will bring honor in God's eyes.

Paul also reminds these leaders how they now practice and live in anticipation of a new realm–"the kingdom of God" (6:9; cf. 4:20). As such their former manner of life, which included for "some" of them immorality and idolatry of all types, including economic sin ("thieves, the greedy,…robbers," [v. 10]), has been transformed under the authority of Christ with the power of the Spirit (v. 11). Thus Paul has hopes for these status-hungry leaders in the Corinthian assembly, along with everybody else in the community, to live out their new life in Christ.

Sexual Immorality

And so, Paul calls everyone in Corinth, but especially those who are mouthing his slogans back to him, to a more complete life of moral uprightness, in particular by putting an end to participation in *porneia* (6:12–20), most likely a reference to prostitution rather than sexual immorality in general.[71] Apparently some in the community were going to prostitutes and claiming the freedom to do so, "Do you not know that your bodies are members of Christ? Should I therefore take the members of Christ and make them members of a prostitute [*pornēs*]?" (6:15). Paul rejects such activity with an emphatic *me genoito* ("Never!"). What lies behind this second instance of sexual impropriety in this section (1 Cor. 5–6)?

Dale Martin suggests a fundamental ideological difference between Paul and some in Corinth with regard to their understanding of the human body (*sōma*). The Corinthian elite, who Martin calls the "strong" following Paul's ascription in 1 Corinthians 8–10, represent those in Corinth "who to a great extent controlled their own economic destiny" as opposed to those who had to depend on the well-to-do for jobs and livelihood.[72] This latter group, by all indications in the text (e.g., 1 Cor. 1:26; 11:22), probably included the majority of the believers in Corinth.

The "strong," despite constituting only a small minority, nonetheless exercised great of influence in the Corinthian church, as we have seen. Their worldview included an attitude toward the physical body, *sōma*, quite different from Paul's. They apparently considered the body and bodily activities such as sex and eating as *adiaphora*–indifferent matters with regard to faith and practice. Other matters, such as "mind" and "heart" mattered more. "Paul takes issue with corporeal hierarchy of upper-class ideology, substituting in its place a topsy-turvy value system," based on "the logic of apocalypticism and the loyalty to a crucified messiah."[73] Thus the spirituality of the Corinthian elite denies that the body, along with the spirit, "is the place of divine service."[74]

The attitude toward going to prostitutes was one of these disagreements between Paul and the Corinthian elite about what constituted *adiaphora*. Paul argues strongly against *porneia* because the believer's body is now attached to Christ and, therefore, cannot be also attached to a prostitute: "Do you not know that whoever is united to a prostitute becomes one body with her? For it is said, 'The two shall be one flesh.' But anyone united to the Lord becomes one spirit with him" (6:16–17). Therefore, Paul concludes, "Flee prostitution [*porneian*]" (6:18a, author's translation).

But who participated in such activity? Certainly, those who held to these views could be expected to participate in them. The Corinthian slogans at the beginning of 6:12–20 were probably the product of "a general deprecation of the body [that] enjoyed wide currency among the educated elite of Greco-Roman society."[75] So here we have the specter of leaders in Paul's Corinthian community "becoming as one" with prostitutes.

Participating in prostitution in Roman Corinth was often the activity of the social elite because of the opportunity for enhancing status that it provided. Craig de Vos points out how marriage and cultic engagement were means of enhancing status in the Greco-Roman world.[76] Related activities included members of the elite, including the *paterfamilias*, the heads of Greco-Roman households, frequenting prostitutes. However, this was not cultic prostitution, as in Classical Corinth, but rather prostitution associated with elite dinner parties in Roman Corinth during Paul's period.[77] Thus gluttony and prostitution become associated with each other, certainly in Paul's mind as he not only debunks one Corinthian maxim, "All things are lawful for me" (1 Cor. 6:12a), but also another, "Food is meant for the stomach and the stomach for food" (6:13a). The latter will draw his attention at length in 1 Corinthians 8–10.

These maxims illustrate another aspect of this problem of sexual immorality in Corinth. Ultimately, it's about freedom and authority. The Corinthian elite believed they were free to participate in prostitution. In similar fashion their brother was free to cohabitate with his stepmother (1 Cor. 5); other brothers were free to initiate court proceedings against fellow believers (1 Cor. 6:1–11); and still others were free to eat meat offered to idols in elite temple feasts (1 Cor. 8–10). "All things are permissible [*exestin*] to me" (6:12, author's translation; cf. 10:23). They think they have the authority,[78] indeed the spiritual authority given their ideology about the physical body, to participate in prostitution, eat food offered to idols, and the like. As the Greek philosopher, Dio Chrysostom wrote, "Who needs more steadfast control than he to whom all things are permitted."[79]

Paul counters with a strong spiritual theology that undermines the presumed authority of the Corinthian leaders espousing this ideology:

> Or do you not know that your body is a temple of the Holy Spirit within you, which you have from God, and that you are not your own? For you were bought with a price; therefore glorify God in your body. (6:19–20)

Paul refuses to dichotomize between body and spirit. In the Christian community, there is no room for individualized exercise of rights without concern for the larger whole, which is "the temple of the Holy Spirit" (cf. 1 Cor. 3:16–17). Therefore the answer to the slogan, "All things are lawful for me" (6:12) is, "You are not your own" (6:19).[80] The Corinthian elites, the self-appointed leaders and trendsetters of the community, were wrong in their assessments about the body, both how they use their individual bodies and what is good for the well-being of the corporate body.

Thus, 1 Corinthians 6:12–20 depicts one of several "secular practices" that Christian leaders in Corinth viewed as "status symbols."[81] Moreover, the passage and the two that preceded it reflect a "crisis of authority" in Corinth by those "puffed up" against Paul on matters of sexuality (5:1–13; 6:12–20) and also litigation (6:1–11).[82] These were areas in which the status and authority of the Corinthian elite could be enhanced, but such actions put them in direct challenge with Paul's mores and, therefore, his authority. Based on his Jewish cosmology and his gospel sense of community edification, Paul wants the elite Corinthian leaders to take seriously the role of body, both individual and corporate, in their Christian self-understanding.

In Paul's Corinthian *ekklēsia,* "Christians were simply following the secular mores of the elite of Corinth."[83] For Paul, this was unacceptable, especially among the leaders of the community.

Immorality, Litigation, and Idolatry

The corporate impact of the behavior of some elite leaders in Corinth becomes even more evident when Paul addresses another apparent disagreement about *adiaphora* (indifferent things)—eating food offered to idols. Paul first discusses marriage and celibacy, issues raised in a letter from the Corinthians to Paul (1 Cor. 7:1–40). These matters are, nonetheless, probably connected in some form to the problems of sexual immorality in 1 Corinthians 5 and 6.[84] Paul then returns to another matter directly related to the hubris of elite members of the church who probably also exercised some leadership in the community. This is the matter of participating in socially elite meals in pagan temple districts (1 Cor. 8–10).

As Gerd Theissen has pointed out, meat offered to idols (1 Cor. 8:13) was a delicacy that only well-to-do patrons partook of as a sign of honor.[85] Apparently, some Corinthian leaders partook of this meat and did so "in the temple of an idol" (8:1; 10:20–22). Paul, in ironic tones, refers to these leaders as "Anyone who claims to know something" (8:2).

John Kingman Chow shows how these dining habits very well could have been the practice of those same influential patrons who opposed Pauline leadership (1 Cor. 4:18–19), allowed the immorality of one of their own (1 Cor. 5), and took their fellow, but poorer, church members to court (6:1–11). Participating in temple district meals was a means of maintaining and enhancing social class networks, argues Chow, and therefore a matter of patronal rights and "business as usual."[86]

In 1 Corinthians 8–10, his response to this problem, Paul addresses the implications of the gospel with regard to "business as usual" among influential leaders within the church. The latter were in fact "sinning against their brothers and sisters," to paraphrase Paul (8:12) and were refusing to acknowledge it. Paul's response—in 1 Corinthians 9 in particular—provides further evidence that church leadership in Corinth has gone astray because of their efforts to enhance patronage networks in the world outside the church. On the surface, Paul in 1 Corinthians 9 merely provides an example of leadership that does not use its freedom in a way that would harm the weak (8:13; 9:1, 4–5). However, the rhetorical impact of the passage points to a defense of Paul's leadership approach. Paul will not eat anything if it causes harm to a brother or sister. He will deny himself marriage and a salary, and would rather work at manual labor to be able to preach the gospel at no cost to his audience. Ultimately, because of such a stance, the Corinthian patrons do not view Paul as a viable leader. In their view he does not take their patronage, but rather works at menial, dishonorable jobs.[87] Again, Paul presents a perspective of gospel leadership that entails hardship. In 9:27, he talks about "punish[ing] [his] body" so as not to be "disqualified."

In short, Paul wants the Corinthian leaders who tolerated immorality, initiated court cases, and participated in temple meals to "punish their bodies," like Paul, and not partake of those practices. Such practices may have enhanced their status in the outside world, but did more harm than good to the gospel and to the nonelite members of the Christian community. With regard to the temple meals, Paul writes, "You cannot drink the cup of the Lord and the cup of demons. You cannot partake of the table of the Lord and the table of demons" (1 Cor. 10:21). In other words, participation in God's new community implies a different relationship to outside associations. Regardless of social status matters, every believer, especially the leader, must think first of one's new associations and relationships within the Christian community. The believer must first consider the Lord's supper and whose body we eat there. Such consideration may lead to practices diametrically opposed to "business as usual."

The Problem of the Lord's Supper

Perhaps the clearest instance of division caused by wrongheaded, status-hungry leadership in all of 1 Corinthians comes when Paul returns to a discussion of ritual eating and the Lord's supper in 1 Corinthians 11:17–34. The abuses Paul describes in this passage depict division between "the haves" and "the have-nots" of the Corinthian community as a source of serious conflict.[88] Paul argues that the Lord's supper is for the whole community ("when you come together as a church" [11:18]), but once again powerful Corinthian patrons engage in "business as usual." Class-specific meals are taking place (11:20–21). The reference to "those who have nothing" (11:22) signals that well-to-do members of the community (including perhaps patrons of the *ekklēsia*) have their elaborate main meal, including drink. Meanwhile, the poorer members of the community (including perhaps clients and slaves of these same patrons) have to wait for these elite feasts to be over; or they have to come late from their menial labor and chores for the elite, only to be denied a main meal. They participate only in the ritual piece of bread and cup of wine of the communion meal (11:21–22).

In this passage, Paul offers the words of institution (the tradition) for two purposes. The traditional teachings remind the Corinthians of the true meaning of the meal (11:23–26). They also pronounce judgment (11:27–32) on those who would partake of the meal without considering the well-being of the entire community (referred to as "body" in 11:29).

In hindsight from the perspective of our early twenty-first–century sensibilities, Paul did not go so far as to try to completely break down the long-held, deeply seated social divisions. At the end of the passage he writes,

> So then, my brothers and sisters, when you come together to eat,
> wait for one another. If you are hungry, *eat at home*, so that when
> you come together, it will not be for your condemnation. (11:33–
> 34a, emphasis author's)

Paul seems more concerned with the assembly of believers as they gather
for worship than with the possible opening up of the homes of the patrons
to regular egalitarian meals for the entire community. He suggests that
they have their class-specific parties at home, but not as part of what they
do as a whole community in worship. Something is wrong and contradictory
to the spirit of the ritual meal if only the elite eat well when the whole
community–the social elite and the poorer members of the community–
both gather for worship.

Regardless of our desire for Paul to have done or said more in this
instance, he does challenge to a certain extent the typical patterns of ancient
patronage and class division. Even for the socially unequal to celebrate a
ritual meal around the same table in the same social space presented a
radical departure from business as usual. Thus, as Chow suggests, in
challenging immorality, litigation, and idolatry, Paul questions the "status
quo" in Corinth and the "socially powerful" who maintained it and profited
from it.[89]

This social and cultural analysis of the dynamics that took place between
Paul and the Corinthians, as reflected in 1 Corinthians, leads to one point.
Failures of local leaders from the more elite classes helps explain several, if
not all, of the problems that persisted in this community. As Gerd Theissen
suggests with regard to the Lord's supper passage, the problems of 1
Corinthians 11:17–34 were not just theological (i.e., the meaning of the
meal), but social as well, perhaps even predominantly social.[90] Two different
groups–the elite and the nonelite, patrons and clients, some relatively well-
to-do individuals and families and the rest, mostly all poor–belong to one
single community or association, a rarity in ancient Greco-Roman society,
as I noted earlier. This created an inevitable climate of conflict. This conflict
impacted not just the practice of the Lord's supper, but other matters as
well. It caused division between a core group of leaders seeking to use the
Corinthian gospel community for their own social status enhancement and
those whom they left behind, the "not many wise, powerful and noble" of
this prosperous and diverse Greco-Roman city.

Other Matters

Do passages in 1 Corinthians that we have left unexamined also exhibit
connections to the problems of leadership delineated in the passages above?
For example, what about the problems of marriage and celibacy Paul
discusses in 1 Corinthians 7? In addition, the problems of worship–first
women in worship (11:2–16), and then abuse of gifts in worship, especially

the gift of tongues (12–14)–occupy a large portion of the text of 1 Corinthians. Are they, too, in some shape or form related to the core issues of leadership seen elsewhere in the letter?

At least two of these problems are linked to the role of women believers in the community. Antoinette Wire has argued that women prophets, in fact, are leaders in the congregation and, therefore, behind the problems of both their role with unbelieving husbands (7:1–24) and whether some of them should remain unmarried or not (7:25–40). In addition, many of them were praying and prophesying in community worship, and some in the community wanted them to at least wear signs of authority over their heads–veils (1 Cor. 11:2–16).[91] Paul agrees with the latter position because he wants such cultural practices as the women wearing veils to help secure order and decorum in community worship. However, he does not stop these women from praying and prophesying during the community's worship, unless, like he discusses later in the letter, some among them disrupt worship, like the prophets who speak out of order or those who practice ecstatic speech without interpretation. In that case these disruptive women must be silent and "ask their husbands at home" (1 Cor. 14:26–36).[92]

Disorder also plagues the use of the gift of tongues in worship. As with veils, Paul wants a control of this gift as well. He provides a rationale for its orderly use by enhancing the value of all other gifts, especially love (1 Cor. 12:31–13:13). Yet, it is quite possible that speaking in tongues represents another attempt at status enhancement, perhaps even by the same people who seek leadership by other signs of status as well, although the latter is difficult to tell. At any rate, ecstatic speech was one of those gifts, as it was in other ancient religious expressions, that anyone in Corinth who wanted to could use to enhance their spiritual and, therefore, social status.[93]

Leadership in 2 Corinthians

Even a surface reading of 2 Corinthians shows that questions about leadership continue to plague the relationship between Paul and the Corinthians. In fact, that the problems in this area persist provide further indication that misunderstanding about the nature of gospel leadership lies at the heart of dysfunctions in the Corinthian assembly. After writing 1 Corinthians, Paul visits and has an unpleasant encounter with a member of the community (2 Cor. 2:1–11). We do not know if this individual was a leader, indeed perhaps one of the elite leaders Paul challenged in 1 Corinthians on a variety of issues. In any case other leaders in the community did not seem to support Paul sufficiently in this encounter, because he had to leave suddenly and then refused to return until the matter was resolved: "So I made up my mind not to make you another painful visit" (2 Cor. 2:1).

Paul's apostleship is so challenged at this point in Corinth that it takes the intervention of an envoy, Titus, to secure some reconciliation between

Paul and the Corinthians (2 Cor. 2:12–13; 7:5–16). Thus 2 Corinthians shows how Paul invests leadership in his surrogates. In fact, without them he could not successfully lead his congregations in their faith development and in his mission. Although he is pleased about this reconciliation with his difficult Corinthian congregation, Paul will not take any chances in his letter to them after Titus has reported the good news. Paul reminds them about the nature of his ministry as a "new covenant" with God (2 Cor. 3:6) and as a "treasure" that God has given even to the least powerful, those who are like "clay jars." In this way, it is made "clear that this extraordinary power [to exercise ministry] belongs to God and does not come from us" (2 Cor. 4:7).

This community and its leaders have taken advantage of Paul several times. He wants to be clear (once again) that gospel leadership entails hardship and sacrifice (2 Cor. 4:8–12). Nonetheless, he is so pleased with how Titus has been able to reconcile the Corinthians to Paul that he describes the nature of the gospel in terms of reconciliation: "In Christ God was reconciling the world to [God]self, not counting their trespasses against them, and entrusting the message of reconciliation to us" (2 Cor. 5:19). Thus Paul concludes that gospel leaders are "ambassadors for Christ" (5:20), just like Titus was an "ambassador" of reconciliation between Paul and the Corinthians.

Yet, despite Paul's repeated efforts and this successful intervention by Titus, the problems of leadership apparently resurfaced with this community, this time around the issues of the collection for Jerusalem. Paul concluded his "letter of reconciliation"[94] (2 Cor. 1–7) with instructions for a monetary gift he was collecting from his Greek-speaking assemblies for believers in Jerusalem (2 Cor. 8 and 9). This included sending Titus, along with two other "brothers," back to Corinth to prepare them for Paul's return and the completion of the collection.[95] However, it seems that outside missionaries, whom Paul sarcastically refers to as "super-apostles" and also "false apostles" (2 Cor. 11:5, 13), agitated local Corinthian leaders to raise questions about the nature of this offering and about Paul's financial dealings in general (2 Cor. 11:7–11). Paul defends not only his leadership and integrity but also that of Titus: "I urged Titus to go, and sent the brother with him. Titus did not take advantage of you, did he? Did we not conduct ourselves with the same spirit? Did we not take the same steps?" (2 Cor. 12:18).

Thus Paul wrote a letter, most likely subsequent to the reconciliation letter of 2 Cor. 1–9, of which we have a long fragment in 2 Cor 10–13. This letter is very personal, very angry, very defensive of Paul's leadership, and very virulent in its attacks on Paul's opponents, who this time, unlike in 1 Corinthians and 2 Corinthians 1–9, constitute outside leaders encroaching on Paul's "territory" and challenging his apostolic leadership of the Corinthian assembly. Paul's "fool's speech" in 2 Cor. 11:16–30, while dripping with irony and sarcasm, once again shows Paul's conviction that gospel leadership entails service and sacrifice: "Are they [the opposing leaders] ministers of Christ? I am talking like a madman–I am a better one: with far greater labors, far more imprisonments, with countless floggings, and often near death" (2 Cor. 11:23). Paul proceeds with another of his long hardship lists (third in all of 2 Corinthians, fourth in 1–2 Corinthians) that show what type of leader he is–one who suffers for the cause of Christ, even if others view such sacrifice as shameful rather than honorable.

When Paul writes to the Roman assemblies sometime after his encounters with the Corinthians, he indicates that he is in Achaia and that he is ready to finally deliver the collection from his congregations to the Jerusalem saints (Rom. 15:25–26). Most scholars assume that he writes from Achaia's provincial capital, Corinth, and that the completed collection includes a gift from Corinth. Thus, Paul somehow reached some kind of resolution of his difficulties with the Corinthians. This no doubt entailed some more diplomacy and thus some more gifts of leadership that Paul and his associates practiced and perfected time and again in their gospel mission. However, by the end of the first century, depending on dating, we read of more leadership problems in the Corinthian church. This time older leaders of the church were challenged by a younger group, and the author of 1 Clement writes in defense of the older leaders.[96] Thus, it seems, leadership continued to be a problem for this early Christian community.

Conclusion of Corinthians Case Study

In conclusion, then, my analysis of select passages in 1 Corinthians and briefly of the argument of 2 Corinthians as a whole suggests that leadership was a key problem in Paul's relationship with this assembly. In Weberian terms, Paul was a charismatic leader who organized his gospel converts into communities of faith. The leadership of this community emerged naturally from the community's own constituency, but some of those leaders, indeed a significant core, if not high number, needed correction, according to their founder, as to what was the appropriate nature of leadership in a gospel community. Because Paul's communities were from mixed social strata, problems arose in the ongoing relationships of the members of the community. Patrons behaved like patrons, and expected clients to behave like clients. Paul argued that this should not be the case, especially because there is a heavenly patron to whom we all equally belong. "For it is not those who commend themselves that are approved, but those who the Lord commends" (2 Cor. 10:18).

Further, Paul's responses to the problems of leadership conflict between himself and certain influential patrons and leaders, both from within and outside his Corinthian congregation, might have had some impact on the leadership of the so-called "have-nots." For, if Paul challenged the leadership of some persons of higher social status, especially when they mistreated those of lower status, he may have, thereby, enhanced the leadership opportunity within this congregation for persons from lower social economic groups. Indeed, Paul probably supported the leadership of the client classes in his church over at least some from the patron classes because the former had proven to be correct about the matters that had been reported to Paul. It was wrong to tolerate division between rich and poor in the church (1 Cor. 1:26–31), to ignore the immoral actions of a believer, regardless of his social standing (1 Cor. 5), and to take other believers, most especially the poor, to court (6:1–11). It was wrong to partake of pagan ritual meals simply to enhance one's social standing in the outside world. It was wrong to abuse one's poorer brothers and sisters at the Christian ritual meal. Those of lower social status had been more readily forthcoming in questioning these matters and therefore Paul empowered them for leadership, whether directly or indirectly:

> ...members of the household of Stephanas...have devoted thems-elves to the service of the saints; I urge you to put yourselves at the service of such people, and of everyone who works and toils with them. (1 Cor. 16:15–16)

Presumably, "members of the household of Stephanas" included not just the head of the household, but also his associates, clients, and slaves, men and women, all of whom served the gospel community, as well as shared their thoughts and insights about what was wrong and right about it.

Thus, on matters of empowering *everyone* for leadership and service in the gospel community and the gospel mission, including the poor, both Jesus and Paul seemed to agree. I will elaborate on this and other concluding matters in the summary analysis that follows.

Conclusion

Summary of Leadership in Jesus and Paul

I began this book considering the importance of understanding the nature of religious leadership in our day and age, and suggesting that a biblical perspective might help since so many people turn to the Bible for so many reasons. Two of the most important figures in the Bible—Jesus and Paul in the New Testament—certainly were leaders of their respective religious movements and merit close attention in our quest for models of leadership. I have suggested elsewhere that in our post-September 11, 2001, world, religious leadership has and should continue to weigh in with their perspectives on how to move forward from those tragic events toward a more just and peaceful world, even as political and military leaders offer their own answers to the crisis.[1] In what follows I will summarize our findings from our study of leadership of Jesus in the gospels and Paul in his letters. I will do so in dialogue with our concerns about modern-day religious leadership, especially in the midst of the crisis caused by the tragic events of September 11, 2001.

Jesus–Leadership in Response to Imperial Domination

The historical Jesus exercised leadership in the midst of the domination system that was the Roman Empire. Rome carried out its imperial domination by extreme oppression of the poorest of the poor, including heavy tax burdens on the peasant population of Palestine. Rome did this in collusion with Israel's elite leadership—both political and religious. As a result, various grassroots resistance and reform movements emerged throughout the period of the early Empire in and around first-century C.E. Palestine. The leaders of such movements included "bandits," "prophets," and "messiahs." These, in one form or other, tried to respond to the imperial oppression hoisted upon the Palestinian countryside. They resisted Roman domination either through social banditry, religious renewal movements, or outright revolt. Religious renewal movements included, for example, the communities represented by the Dead Sea Scrolls with their messianic expectations. The outright revolts, prefigured by violent forays in earlier decades, issued into full-fledged war in the late 60s C.E., culminating in the horrific sack and destruction of Jerusalem by Roman forces in 70 C.E.

Within this context of domination and resistance, we find the leadership of John the Baptist and later, one of his followers, Jesus of Nazareth. John the Baptist challenged the entrenched powers of his day because of their oppression of the masses in Palestine. The gospels record John's challenging words to official leaders of Palestine, whether religious, financial, or military

197

leaders. To all of them, John the Baptist pronounced a word of judgment and justice. In particular, the word of justice entailed attention to those with less by those with more. Indeed, such a cry for justice by the "voice in the wilderness" eventually led to his death at the hands of those political leaders whom he denounced. John founded; and Jesus, his follower and successor, enhanced this reform movement that paid attention to the poor and oppressed. Indeed, such attention was a fundamental criterion of leadership that both John and Jesus proclaimed. Like John, Jesus was executed for proclaiming this message of justice.

When time came for Jesus to take over the leadership mantle from John, John raised questions about Jesus' commitment to the cause of justice. Jesus replied by recounting his acts of compassion for the poor and oppressed. Thus, in many ways, but especially in this concern for those to whom nobody else paid attention–the poor in Roman-dominated Israel–Jesus followed in John's footsteps.

However, Jesus did not carry out his mission alone. He gathered a group of followers–the disciples. One of the fascinating aspects of the stories about Jesus and his disciples was that they were not the "cream of the crop" from among Israel's constituencies. Rather, they included working-class fishermen, hated tax collectors, and women disciples in a society that undermined the leadership of women. Because of this constituency, the established leaders of the community questioned the presence and the quality of such leaders among Jesus' supporters.

In fact, the disciples, the future leaders of the movement, came from among the target audience for Jesus' ministry, such as the peasants of the countryside and the overtaxed working class of the local fishing and building trades. Jesus himself was a carpenter. Thus, John Dominic Crossan has referred to the Jesus movement as "a kingdom of nobodies." Ironically, much of the gospel record depicts the failure of the disciples to fully understand Jesus and his ultimate mission during his time with them. When Jesus spoke in parables to outsiders to see if they really understood the heart of his message, he had to interpret not only for them, but also for his disciples. When Jesus calmed a storm in their presence, the disciples stood amazed, wondering who this strange and powerful leader might be. Jesus wondered about them too, however, because repeatedly in the gospels the disciples lacked the vision and faith to rightly perceive the true nature of the mission of Jesus. They even failed to see to whom the heart of Jesus' message was directed–their very own people. Jesus rebuked a "rich young ruler" who wanted to become a disciple, but only on his own terms. The disciples could not understand how Jesus could reject him. After all, they claimed, if a rich man cannot enter the Kingdom, who can?

Jesus had some news for these future movement leaders: Many who are first today will be last tomorrow, and those who are considered the last today will be first tomorrow. Such striking reversals in the Jesus movement came because all-out commitment was needed for leadership in this movement, even if it came from those at the bottom rung of the social ladder. The rich young ruler lacked that commitment, exemplified by his unwillingness to give of himself and his possessions to the poor and oppressed in Palestine. Thus, Jesus must rely on the poor themselves. Even if some of them also failed to understand completely, at least they had commitment. Peter, one of the leading disciples and seemingly the most committed of all, often failed to understand that Jesus had to face the ultimate sacrifice for the cause. Jesus had to rebuke Peter several times. Nonetheless, Peter's consistent failures did not preclude him from ultimately being a major movement leader in the aftermath of Jesus' departure from the scene.

Besides surrounding himself with a team, even though team members tended not to be from among the elite leaders of the community, Jesus also gave these committed followers a clear mission to carry out. This mission was intimately tied up with Jesus' concern for the poor and oppressed of Palestine. Their mission included living the life of itinerant preachers or "wandering charismatics," who should not worry about possessions but must depend on their constituencies for physical needs. In this way, the disciples could best identify with the target audience of Jesus and their ministry—the poor, peasant population among Palestine's people. By healing physical maladies and exorcising evil spirits, they symbolically challenged the powerful human forces that controlled and oppressed the lives of the masses.

Given the radical nature of this mission, however, the disciples could not expect a grand and glorious reception. Rather they endured ignominy. Some disciples wanted to sit in the seat of honor next to Jesus when the Kingdom came. This was their expectation for all their trouble on behalf of the messianic mission that Jesus had presented to them. They wanted glory and power. However, this contradicted the very nature of their mission—a challenge to the hegemony and power of their oppressors. So Jesus consistently set them straight. Jesus elaborated on the nature of their mission as one of sacrifice. They, like him, must serve and not expect to be served. Indeed, several times Jesus suggested that such service might entail the ultimate sacrifice of death because the nature of their leadership went counter to business as usual in the Roman Empire. Otherwise, they risked repeating the same mistakes of their oppressors and becoming oppressors themselves. "Lording over" their charges was not the way of the gospel, but rather servanthood was. To be first, to be a leader, entailed the sacrifice of service on behalf of those most in need.

Ultimately, the gospels teach us that Jesus himself had to sacrifice it all for the cause of his gospel. He gathered, commissioned, and trained a team of future leaders. Their training came as Jesus modeled for them a ministry of service and sacrifice for the "least of these" among their peers in Palestine. Jesus thus taught his disciples that their ultimate victory depended upon their treatment of those whom nobody else in the Empire was paying attention to, even if it meant dying for such a cause.

Jesus showed the way toward this vision, not only by healing and preaching to the neglected masses, but by challenging their oppressors right in their own seat of power. At last during the Passover feasts, Jesus entered Jerusalem for the last time, to the cheering throngs of his many followers and supporters. When he did so, the eyes and ears of the Roman and Jerusalem elite perked up with concern. Then he entered the Jerusalem temple, the seat of Jewish exercise of power, and turned over the tables of the money changers, merchants, and tax collectors. In so doing Jesus challenged the financial, religious, and political foothold of the Empire over his people. He drew the wrath of those in power, and their plot to kill him intensified. Both the Roman forces, represented by the proconsul Pontius Pilate, and the Jewish hierarchy of the city, those whose seat of power was the temple, colluded in the arrest, trial, and execution of Jesus.

Despite the horrific death Jesus suffered at the hands of the Roman military forces and of those who colluded with them from among the temple elite, his followers picked up where he left off after his death. They believed in his ultimate vindication by means of resurrection and return, even though most had initially fled the scene of his crucifixion (all except the women disciples, the gospel accounts agree). Nonetheless, despite this initial fear, the disciples, women and men, came forward to carry on the traditions that Jesus left for them: those of preaching, teaching, and caring for the "least of these" within the world of the Roman hegemony in Palestine. They, too, faced sacrifice and persecution; but they remembered the words of Jesus with regard to the nature of gospel leadership: "For the Son of Man came not to be served but to serve, and to give his life a ransom for many" (Mk. 10:45).

Thus, the key to the leadership of Jesus was that he carried out his mission in direct contrast to the established leadership of his day. He followed John the Baptist, chose his own disciples, and trained and commissioned them with the express purpose of providing relief to those who were suffering the burdens of a failed religious and political leadership.

Therefore, anytime Christians ask themselves what kind of religious leadership they want, especially in times of crisis, like those faced now in the aftermath of September 11, 2001, a christological question needs to be asked: Who is attending to the poor and oppressed? What in our actions and policies is creating more or less justice, or injustice? Can we, dare we, rise to the occasion, even ride against the tide, and call for, ultimately, attention to those whom nobody else pays attention to in our society, in our world? Dare we demand that this be the clarion call of gospel leadership, whether it be politically or religiously acceptable in mainstream circles? To invoke the name of God and not call for justice to the neglected masses is to shortchange a christological definition of leadership.

Thus, for example, it may be that the U.S. response to the September 11 attacks with a "war on terrorism" is justifiable on some political level or maybe even moral level in the eyes of some, but *not* without a consistent, accompanying question: What is demanded from us on behalf on those who suffer ongoing persecution, poverty, rejection, and turmoil? Without such a question, our leadership–religious, but also political–is not complete, not if we are to learn some lessons from the leadership of Jesus as portrayed in the gospels.

Summary of Leadership in Paul

Historical Setting

Paul's ministry took place in the same climate of Roman imperial hegemony in which Jesus carried out his ministry, except that Paul (among others, less well-attested) took the Jesus movement out beyond the immediate beginnings in Palestine into large areas of the Empire. In particular, Paul devised a strategy in which he preached and established Christian communities in the major cities of the Roman Empire. Paul's mission, it seems, benefited from several aspects of the Roman imperial hegemony–good roads with military security, prosperous cities, individuals with financial means–to support and enhance his gospel mission.

Also, like Jesus, Paul did not go about his mission alone. He surrounded himself with a group of associates, whom he regularly referred to as co-workers and partners. Paul depended upon these men and women to help him nurture and instruct the congregations he founded. This study has described the qualities Paul expected of these leaders and showed that Paul did not rely on typical Greco-Roman expectations of class and status to select his associates or to endorse their leadership to his churches. Rather, like Jesus, Paul selected and endorsed leaders from among those whom he served. He expected them, as he did of himself, to disinterestedly serve the Pauline congregations, even to the point of sacrifice and risk.

Defending Leadership

Paul alludes to the nature of his leadership in a variety of places in his letters. Throughout his ministry he found himself defending the nature of the Pauline mission, including himself and his associates. In these self-defenses, Paul shows how he and his missionary associates were willing to suffer on behalf of the gospel mission. Therefore, Paul also expected any new leaders who emerged in his congregations to confront similar mistreat-ment on behalf of the gospel with courage and integrity. Integrity represented an important emphasis at several points in Paul's letters. For example, he wrote to the Thessalonians that neither "deceit," "impure motives," or "trickery" motivated the Pauline missionary enterprise, but rather the desire to serve God's people. Thus, ultimately, God motivated the Pauline mission, not personal gain or greed (cf. 1 Thess. 2:1–6).

Several passages in Paul's letters refer to his and his associates' love for their constituents. Their love and concern was "like a wet nurse caring for her own children" (1 Thess. 2:7, author's translation). Paul and his associates loved their churches so much that oftentimes they did manual labor to support the ministry and not be a financial burden. Thus in Paul's ministry, issues of suffering, integrity, and finances confronted his missionary efforts, and therefore demanded a defense, which he provided again and again. He affirmed honest efforts in doing God's will through his preaching ministry, through his genuine love for his converts–including not wanting to be a financial burden–and through his willingness to confront opposition in all shapes and forms. Paul expected similar actions and attitudes from the leadership of his associates, fellow-workers, and local congregational leaders.

Defining Leadership

Paul not only defended his leadership, but he also defined it. He did so incorporating theological reflection. For example, the Corinthian correspondence shows how gospel leadership must be defined in terms of both human humility and divine power. If the power of God, and not just human ability, did not lie behind Paul's missionary efforts, he wrote to the Corinthians, the enterprise would fail. Paul also defined leadership in terms of servanthood, much like Jesus did. He called Apollos and himself "servants" through whom the Corinthians came to believe (1 Cor. 3:5). Gospel leaders, as servants of God, each has a role to play in the gospel mission, but only God provides growth. Reward for gospel service depends not on who is on top, but who carries out his or her role according to the common purpose–the gospel mission. This vision represents a somewhat upside-down expectation for leadership compared to the hierarchy of the Roman imperial society in which Paul's congregations were imbedded. Nonetheless, an upside-down leadership, with God at the top, and everyone else equal servants of Gods' divine purpose, functioned as the *modus operandi* in Paul's vision of leadership for his congregations and the gospel mission.

Of course, that was not everyone's vision for leadership in Paul's congregations. For example, as we saw, some in Corinth sought more status out of their role as leaders of a Pauline congregation, an approach Paul mollified by citing apostolic suffering, again and again. In particular, Paul used several "hardship lists" throughout his correspondence to correct any overly glorified vision of gospel leadership by local leaders.

Commending Leadership

Paul used unique criteria to commend his leadership and that of his co-workers, associates, and local leaders. While others in the Roman world depended on commendation letters to support their leadership, Paul depended on the actual existence of a thriving gospel community to demonstrate the authenticity of his own ministry. "You yourselves are our letter," he wrote to the Corinthians (2 Cor. 3:2). He showed how any competence for his leadership came from divine prerogative and the presence of God's life-giving Spirit. In commending his leadership, Paul wrote that he depended on God for his assignment as an apostle and missionary. Suffering was an integral part of the nature of his leadership on behalf of the gospel communities, and his love and concern for these communities overruled any personal gains or interests that he or any gospel leader might seek from such an assignment. For Paul, gospel leadership was about service, even if that service entailed suffering, hard labor, and criticism from those who misunderstood the nature of the ministry. The ministry may not bring much earthly glory, but satisfaction was derived from knowing one was responding to God's call, serving with God's power, and would be rewarded with eternal life. Therein lay the authority for exercising gospel leadership—divine call, divine service, and divine reward.

In commending and developing other leaders, Paul expected no less from those who served with him and those who emerged into leadership from among the constituents of his congregations. In all but one of Paul's uncontested letters (Galatians), we saw how Paul commended local leaders and/or his associates to his congregations. These commendation passages, like similar commendations in the Greco-Roman world, provided a window into the qualities Paul expected of his church leaders. These very much paralleled what Paul expected of his own leadership.

In commending local church leaders, Paul focused on their hard work and service for the church. Local church leaders in Thessalonica proved their leadership skills by means of their hard labor, admonishment, and work in the congregation over a period of time. Therefore, they should be recognized for what they were already doing. Leadership recognition was not *ex nihilio*, but came from having a track record.

Similarly, when Paul sought out loyal leaders in the turmoil that was the Corinthian congregation, he turned to proven commodities. Stephanas and others in his household from the very beginning had demonstrated their loyalty to Paul and to the gospel by means of their service to the gospel community in Corinth. Indeed, the gospel community should serve them because they had served Paul, the community, and the cause of the gospel. In fact, Paul asserted that anyone who put themselves at the service of the church ought to be recognized as leaders in the community.

Paul also recognized the risks the associates and envoys undertook on behalf of the gospel mission. For example, Epaphroditus became gravely ill when he traveled from Philippi to minister to Paul during the latter's imprisonment. Thus, Paul commended Epaphroditus for his sacrificial service because his illness demonstrated his commitment to the gospel mission (Phil. 2:25–30). He deserved leadership recognition. Whether immediate associates and co-workers of Paul, or envoys sent by his churches, all these leaders share a common commitment to the gospel, the gospel community, and the specific expression and activity of it in the Pauline mission.

The Pauline mission included various women leaders that Paul also commended at critical points in his letters. When the Philippian church needed examples of good leaders who would follow the Pauline injunction to "live your life in a manner worthy of the gospel of Christ" (Phil. 1:27a), Paul cites Jesus, himself, Timothy, and Epaphroditus. However, despite those examples, the search for unity might be nullified if two key leaders of the church in Philippi, the women Euodia and Syntyche, did not heal their leadership rift.

Paul commends another Christian woman leader to the Romans—Phoebe. Her role seems critical to Paul's intentions in writing the letter to the Romans. Phoebe has exercised a leadership role in a local congregation near Corinth. Paul calls her a *diakonos*, the same term he reserves for himself and Apollos, as well as other male leaders in his mission—"servant" or "minister." Paul also refers to her as a "benefactor" or "patron" (*prostatis*) of many, including Paul, in the gospel mission. This probably means she has provided financial support for the mission. Thus Phoebe's role has been critical already in the Pauline mission. Therefore, she seems well suited to travel to Rome on Paul's behalf with this important letter that includes a request for unified support for Paul's mission to Spain. Phoebe had an important advance role to play in Paul's new venture, both to clarify any points of Pauline theology in the letter and to prepare the Roman Christians to support the Spanish mission. Thus Paul enthusiastically commended her leadership.

Paul commended leaders who followed, in some shape or form, many of the lessons he himself learned from the gospel mission. These lessons included that gospel leadership must entail singular attention to the welfare of gospel communities, especially those in the Pauline mission, but not exclusively. For example, Paul was very much concerned for the well-being of the Jerusalem church and organized a collection for them from his own largely Gentile churches. In every case, whether locally, in the mission, or beyond, service and hard work marked the good gospel leader.

Proclaiming Good News

Paul expected his leaders to proclaim good news to his communities. Titus can go to Corinth for the collection with "eagerness" (2 Cor. 8:16) because he has been there before, bringing about reconciliation between Paul and the Corinthians (2 Cor. 7:5–16). Phoebe not only provides monetary support to the Pauline mission, but as a leader in Cenchreae, she probably preached the gospel. Thus she was prepared to interpret Paul's theological teachings for the Roman churches. Euodia and Syntyche "struggled beside [Paul] in the work of the gospel," which implies proclaiming it in word and deed (Phil. 4:3). The commendations of Phoebe and Euodia and Syntyche also show that Paul, like Jesus, incorporated a diverse group of persons–socially, economically, and in terms of gender– into his leadership team as proclaimers of good news.

Thus Paul and his team productively shared a message in the middle years of the first century C.E. This message had a theological focus and an ultimate goal, both of which had implications for how the Pauline team would conduct its leadership. As noted in this study, Paul rarely, if at all, expounded on his theology systematically in the context of his letters. All of his letters, including what has been perceived as his most famously systematic, the letter to the Romans, were contingent documents based on a coherent theology, to paraphrase J. Christiaan Beker.[2] Paul was less concerned with expounding his core theological convictions than with addressing the immediate contextual crises or situations of his congregations. Thus, Paul was a "praxis theologian," less concerned with a clear, seminal declaration of his core theology than with ministering to churches in need with whatever theological truth would be most helpful at the moment. Such was the "theological leadership" that he gave his communities.

We do, of course, catch glimpses of Paul's core theology at critical junctures in his writings. Highlighting two of these should help us connect Paul's theology to his practice of leadership. First, at the conclusion of the biographical defense of his apostolic calling to the Gentiles of Galatia (Gal. 1:13–2:14), Paul indicates that the core of his theology entails Christ and the cross: "I have been crucified with Christ; and it is no longer I who live, but it is Christ who lives in me (Gal. 2:19b–20a). As in Philippians 2:5–11, Paul says that Christ has become a model for our life here on earth. Yet, this life includes something of the will to sacrifice as Christ did for the cause of the gospel, of bringing good news to those who need it most. A new life in Christ carries with it the call, especially to leaders, to sacrifice so that others might hear and live out that good news.

Another seminal passage in Paul adds to this sense of mission and leadership in his gospel theology. After achieving reconciliation with his Corinthian congregation, Paul proceeds to explain the gospel experience and the subsequent missionary impulse as a ministry of reconciliation: "In Christ God was reconciling the world to himself, not counting their trespasses against them, and entrusting the message of reconciliation to us. So we are ambassadors for Christ, since God is making his appeal through us (2 Cor. 5:19–20). Because God in Christ has restored right relations between us and our Creator, we, too, as "ambassadors for Christ," exercise, in our gospel leadership, the ministry of reconciliation, bringing divided parties into peace.

Throughout Paul's letters, bringing unity in the midst of the discord in many of his communities occupied and defined much of his leadership skills and practices. In Corinth, he had to heal division over leaders, between rich and poor, and ultimately about his own apostleship. In the assemblies of the Galatians, questions about his gospel and apostleship produced discord that Paul had to address both theologically and biographically. Even in Rome, with house churches that he did not establish, Paul sought to heal rifts between Gentile and Jewish constituents. Thus he wrote about the righteous justice of God that brings about personal justification with God, but also "peace" between divided peoples (Rom. 5:1–5).

Thus what stood at the heart of Paul's leadership activity, and that of his associates, was a firm belief in the gospel of Christ that calls one to accountability before God and asks one to engage in bringing others into the fold. Further, the implication of such a gospel for Paul was that peace and reconciliation should be pursued with one another, both within and outside the gospel community.

Lessons Learned from Paul's Leadership

Paul's leadership, then, teaches us a variety of factors with regard to religious leadership in general. First of all, like Paul, religious leaders today need to think through a careful strategy for carrying out their mission. Paul devised an urban ministry strategy, and it worked in terms of establishing key churches at critical junctions throughout the Roman Empire. We must think carefully if we are going to respond responsibly to crises that come our way, including what has happened to the world in the aftermath of September 11, 2001. In this and other crises, the rash judgments and actions of political and religious leaders will not serve us well.

Second, who will join us in the leadership task is an all-important question. Like Jesus, Paul surrounded himself with a band of associates, his "co-workers." When he commends these leaders, as well as emerging local leaders, to his congregations, he cites their track record, which for him must include hard work and sacrifice, *already*, on behalf of the gospel and of the gospel community. Their social status, and even gender–traditional qualifying criteria for commendation in imperial society–did not seem to matter as much to Paul as their proven sacrificial service to his congregations. What criteria do we expect of our leaders today? Paul did not expect any more than what he expected of himself. His singular concern for the growth and well-being of his gospel communities drove his ministry and leadership practices. We need religious leaders willing to take a stand and act on it with courage and integrity in today's day and age, especially at these moments of crisis that we now face. Issues of diversity, inclusion, and hearing from voices of women and men from all walks of life are part of that firm stance.

Third, we need firm conviction and a sense of mission from our leaders. Paul preached "Jesus Christ, and him crucified" (1 Cor. 2:2) and stood by that message in good times and bad times. However, the cross of Christ was not just an abstract teaching for Paul, but had practical implications. He expected himself and his leaders to live out their theology, and so gospel leadership included a willingness to sacrifice, even their own lives, for the cause of Christ and his people. The core message also included God's reconciling act on behalf of humanity in Christ. If that was the case, how much more should our leadership engage the ministry of reconciliation and bring healing to divided parties among us. Perhaps this is the greatest lesson from Paul's leadership for our own day. The gospel cannot be the gospel without the ministry of peace and reconciliation. We need more religious leaders who practice and promote the art of diplomacy and peacemaking rather than some kind of chauvinistic jingoism that divides rather than unites. Leadership in the Pauline mission included being "ambassadors for Christ," and in Christ God reconciled the world to its Creator. Therefore, a *sine qua non* of gospel leadership is reconciliation. How to achieve reconciliation between divided parties in our communities and our world, no matter how complicated that may seem, and it is, must lie at the heart of our theology, proclamation, and religious leadership activity in general.

Jesus, Paul, and Leadership for Our World Today

Thousands of innocent people lost their lives on September 11, 2001, as a result of criminal acts that call for police action, if not an all-out "war on terrorism." In addition to worldwide police action to bring to justice the perpetrators of this heinous act, the world needs strong, forthright, thoughtful, and compassionate leadership to ensure that something like this does not happen again. Religious leadership from all faiths and denominations must be counted among these leaders. What kind of response does the world need from our religious leadership?

The lessons from a New Testament study of the early Christian leaders Jesus and Paul may be helpful in this respect. Jesus showed a singular concern for the poor and oppressed in his context in light of an oppressive imperial hegemony. To keep those whom nobody else cares about in the forefront of our leadership thought and action must continue to be a major aspect of religious leadership, whether it is the poor and homeless in the South Bronx of New York City, or those in Afghanistan and Iraq in the aftermath of U.S. attacks on those countries after September 11, 2001.

Second, both Jesus and Paul refused to work alone. Given the complexity of what lies before us in the world forever changed after September 11, we dare not be lone rangers, especially those of us in religious leadership. To take right action in the complex matters that lie before us, dialogue, including dialogue between different races, classes, genders, and faiths, must be fostered. Religious leaders must show the way in such dialogue.

In line with team approaches to leadership is the need for careful thought and strategies. Paul, in particular, wisely used the resources of the Empire to carry out his mission, even if the mission carried a message that in some subtle and some not-so-subtle ways challenged the practices and ideologies of the Empire. All leaders, but religious leaders in particular, must plot together careful action that will promote peace, reconciliation, and "good news." Thus, not only is careful strategy needed but also a clear, just mission. Jesus taught his disciples "love to your enemy." Paul taught his churches that God, in Christ, was reconciling the world to Godself, and that, therefore, we need to be instruments of reconciliation. Religious leaders of today must also promote love and reconciliation if we are going to be true to the core values of all religious faith. Even the criminal actions of September 11, as horrific as they were, still call us for careful and just action. Bring in the "evildoers," as President Bush called us to do, but in the process let us not forget those values of justice and fair play that we as a nation espouse so loudly, especially when we are not the ones being attacked from outside.

Finally, religious leadership must remember to remain humble, especially in the jingoistic circumstances of a post-September 11 world where many cry out for revenge at all costs. When one of Jesus' disciples struck out at his accusers with a sword, Jesus healed the stricken enemy, and declared, "Put your sword back into its place; for all who take the sword will perish by the sword" (Mt. 26:52). He also went on to rebuke his accusers for their violence (Mt. 26:55). The message was clear—violence should not be our first reaction every time we are wronged. Hubris rather than sober thought could be behind our actions. Declaring an all-out "war on terrorism," rather than an appropriate, targeted police action, may have been an overreaction to the September 11 attacks, as difficult as it may be for many in our country, especially those who lost loved ones, to accept. My point is that religious leaders should weigh in and do so with humility and with a call for humility on all parts, reminding us all of our weaknesses and shortcomings and ultimate dependence on God. The apostle Paul put it this way:

> Therefore, to keep me from being too elated, a thorn was given me in the flesh, a messenger of Satan to torment me, to keep me from being too elated. Three times I appealed to the Lord about this, that it would leave me, but he said to me, "My grace is sufficient for you, for power is made perfect in weakness." So, I will boast all the more gladly of my weaknesses, so that the power of Christ may dwell in me. Therefore I am content with weaknesses, insults, hardships, persecutions, and calamities for the sake of Christ; for whenever I am weak, then I am strong. (2 Cor. 12:7–10)

True leaders refuse to hide in the face of calamity and weakness. They do not pursue calamity; they seek improvement in the midst of weakness. However, because illness and tragedy are often inevitable, the challenge lies in what we do with them when they come. If a greater cause motivates us, we seek to overcome the calamity and hardship; and we strengthen ourselves for the long haul in the midst of our weaknesses. Ultimately, we rely on God to help us through the crisis and show us the right way to respond. Without such dependence, we can fail miserably. After the crisis the September 11 attacks brought upon the world, as well as any other crises we face in this life, more than ever religious leaders are called upon to show the world how to rely on a higher power than ourselves—"for whenever I am weak, then I am strong." These are important lessons we learn from the leadership of Jesus and Paul.

The Rest of the New Testament

The legacy of Jesus and Paul with regard to the practice of religious leadership develops in a variety of ways in the various communities represented in the remaining writings of the New Testament. In the pastoral letters (1–2 Timothy and Titus), for example, a post-Pauline community determines that the best way to ensure its survival in the ongoing struggle with its imperial context will be to accommodate as best it can to its surroundings, especially in light of the death of its founders and the delay of the *parousia* of Christ. Thus, this community decides to "get organized" with a strong, strict hierarchical structure of official "bishops," "deacons," "elders," and "enrolled widows" (1 Tim. 3:1–13; 5:1–20). It will deal harshly with internal opponents, especially those who question the received tradition, the "sound doctrine" now handed down from one generation to the next as "the faith." Prior generations of Pauline churches, including those in Paul's time, practiced "faith" as Paul taught it, a dynamic relationship of trust between God and believers. Now "faith" became a body of beliefs to be accepted or rejected with little room for dialogue. Prior generations of Pauline believers, including Paul himself, also allowed for the engagement of women in leadership roles on behalf of the gospel mission. Now this post-Pauline community calls "women to learn in silence with full submission," for they should not "teach or...have authority over a man" (1 Tim. 2:11–12). The leadership practices of Jesus and Paul that allowed for a wide diversity of participation of the poor, the outcast, and women in leadership of the gospel mission seem to have been diluted for the sake of community survival for the long haul within its wider culture.[3]

The Johannine community, represented by the gospel of John and the letters of John, written toward the end of the first century C.E., also exhibited some discontinuity with the legacy of leadership one finds in Jesus and Paul. In particular, John's gospel depicts the opponents of Jesus, not so much as established leaders who have failed the community as a whole, but as "Jews" in general who have failed Christ's followers. The latter are depicted as "friends" and thus have special insider status. Even the love commandments are turned inwardly toward the community:

> "I give you a new commandment, that you love one another. Just as I have loved you, you also should love one another. By this everyone will know that you are my disciples, if you have love for one another." (John 13:34–35)

The late first-century conflict of this community with the synagogue has called for a rather defensive leadership, again, like the pastorals, to ensure its ongoing survival in light of its hostile environment.

In a later manifestation of the same community, depicted in the Johannine letters, the previous conflict with outside opponents has turned inward. Those believers in Christ who do not confess Christ the way leaders of this community expect them to have become "false prophets," "antichrists," and "deceivers." Thus the spirit of conflict and division set up in the gospel against "the Jews," outside nonbelievers, has now manifested itself in internal conflict over leaders and their doctrines, even though the gospel called for internal unity. Now, the "elder" of the community commended Gaius over Diotrephes, "who likes to put himself first, does not acknowledge our authority…[He is] spreading false charges against us. And not content with those charges, he refuses to welcome the friends" (3 John 9–10). Thus in the letters of John, "the figure who was, according to the Fourth Gospel, the abiding center of their life and unity, is here the focal point of dissension and division."[4] In both instances, the gospel and the letters, community leaders foment conflict, both with external forces and internal dissidents, whether over doctrine or practices, or both.[5]

In Petrine communities represented by the letters 2 Peter and Jude, such internal differences take on vituperative dimensions. Internal dissidents are called "false prophets" who bring in "destructive opinions," even denying "the Master who bought them," thus "bringing swift destructions on themselves" (2 Pet. 2:1; cf. Jude 8–13). In 1 Peter, written by a different author in a different region with different concerns, the language is softer. The author is concerned with fostering unity in the community even as it confronts outside opposition: "You are a chosen race, a royal priesthood, a holy nation, God's own people, in order that you may proclaim the mighty acts of him who called you out of darkness into his marvelous light" (1 Pet. 2:9). This stirring affirmation of the unity of the Christian community contrasts sharply with the internal conflict depicted in the Johannine letters and 2 Peter and Jude. Nonetheless, like the pastorals and John's gospel, 1 Peter has a clear outside opponent. This one is more evidently, as in Jesus and Paul, the Roman Empire, which has caused the dispersion of the readers of 1 Peter: "Peter, an apostle of Jesus Christ, To the exiles of the Dispersion in Pontus, Galatia, Cappadocia, Asia, and Bithynia" (1 Pet. 1:1). John Elliot has shown how the terms "exiles" in 1:1 and "aliens and exiles" in 2:11 probably refer to the actual imperial status of expatriate resident aliens for these Christian believers of 1 Peter.[6] For them, despite their lowly status in the Empire as dispersed peoples without a homeland, God has established in Christ, their "cornerstone" (2:4–8), a new "home," indeed a new "people."

Yet despite this affirmation, 1 Peter stands over against Jesus, who confronts the Empire with a message about justice for the poor in the "kingdom of God." Similarly, 1 Peter distances itself from Paul, who creates "assemblies" in major imperial cities that await the *parousia* of Christ to establish a new kingdom as the old one perishes. First Peter, in contrast, exhorts the suffering resident aliens of the Empire to be patient and obedient to that Empire and its leadership:

> Beloved, I urge you as aliens and exiles to abstain from the desires of the flesh that wage war against the soul. Conduct yourselves honorably among the Gentiles, so that, though they malign you as evildoers, they may see your honorable deeds and glorify God when he comes to judge.
>
> For the Lord's sake accept the authority of every human institution, whether of the emperor as supreme, or of governors, as sent by him to punish those who do wrong and to praise those who do right. For it is God's will that by doing right you should silence the ignorance of the foolish. As servants of God, live as free people, yet do not use your freedom as a pretext for evil. Honor everyone. Love the family of believers. Fear God. Honor the emperor. (1 Pet. 2:11–17)

Such exhortations promoted a wait-and-see attitude rather than a willingness to confront entrenched imperial power in the name of God, especially on behalf of those who suffer the most, even now as the faithful await God's ultimate victory in the eschaton. The latter—eschatological expectation—was certainly the vision the author of 1 Peter sought to promote, without necessarily, however, rocking the boat by current-day action for justice in spite of imperial domination. Jesus most certainly promoted the action for justice attitude, even if it cost him his life.

Of these various "sub-apostolic" communities, as Raymond Brown called them,[7] only the apocalyptic community of the last book of the New Testament, the book of Revelation, seems to have promulgated most vigorously the anti-imperial vision of Jesus. With its exalted view of the leadership of Christ, who will descend as the victorious Lamb of God to destroy the stronghold of Babylon—clearly symbolic of Rome and its Empire—this book minces no words, even with all its apocalyptic symbolism, that the Empire is the enemy of believers in Christ and that it will be destroyed. While a book of consolation for believers suffering imperial persecution at the end of the first century, this document follows in the tradition of Jesus and Paul, albeit in a very different way, to challenge the

Empire and promote a message of justice among believers of Christ and their leaders.[8]

This brief overview of the rest of the New Testament suggests that models and approaches to the leadership task in the Jesus movement in the decades following the ministry of its founder, Jesus of Nazareth, and of its most significant missionary, Paul the apostle, varied depending on the community, its needs, and the attitudes of its immediate leaders, theologians, and authors. The core values of justice, concern for the poor, and open access to leadership that identified the leadership of Jesus and Paul diminished in some quarters as the different communities sought to adjust to their specific situations. Some focused on other values such as correct teaching and personal morality so as not to draw too much attention to the Christian community's presence in a particular region. Others turned inward to deal with internal dissension and leadership structures. All continued to focus on Jesus but developed a variety of christological formulations to explain the meaning of Jesus for their own times and situations.

What will be our legacy for the practice of religious leadership today? Will the concerns of the poor and those without status continue to drive our leadership practices like they did for Jesus and Paul? Will we confront entrenched power like Jesus did and like the communities represented in the book of Revelation tried to do when such power practices injustice? One hopes that religious leaders will always promote peace and justice in the world, and not only when it is convenient, that we will not accommodate so much to our context in hopes of maintaining the status quo—as the authors of the pastorals and, to some extent, 1 Peter did—that we lose sight of the prophetic leadership exemplified by Jesus and Paul in dealing with the outside world. Nor should we fight so much among ourselves, as the Johannine communities and the communities represented in 2 Peter and Jude did at various points in their histories. And may we always have Christian leaders who promote peace and reconciliation with other faiths, not demonize them, as the author of John's gospel seems to have done when he called his community's opponents "the Jews," as if that entire community was to blame for the struggles of the Johannine community at that point in its history. We all know the sad legacy that such a leadership practice, labeling a whole people as one's enemies—whether Jews, Muslims, or Christians—has left throughout history. Religious leaders can and should do better than that.

Notes

Introduction

[1]See Eldin Villafañe, *The Liberating Spirit: Toward a Hispanic American Pentecostal Social Ethic* (Grand Rapids: Eerdmans, 1993), 89–102, for an outline of this history.

[2]Ibid., 107.

[3]See, for example, Robin Scroggs, "The Sociological Interpretation of the New Testament: The Present State of the Research," in *The Bible and Liberation: Political and Social Hermeneutics,* ed. Norman Gottwald (Maryknoll, N.Y.: Orbis Books, 1983), 337–56, for definitions of the method. Derek Tidball, *The Social Context of the New Testament: A Sociological Analysis* (Grand Rapids: Zondervan, 1984) provides an accessible, book-length introduction to the approach. For practical guidelines to social scientific methods, see John Elliott, *What Is Social-Scientific Criticism?* (Minneapolis: Fortress Press, 1993).

[4]Adolf Deissman, *Light from the Ancient Near East,* trans. Lionel Strachen (Grand Rapids: Baker Books, 1928, 1965), is a classic study of this question.

[5]E.A. Judge was an early proponent for a broad social class representation in the early church in his *The Social Pattern of Christian Groups in the First Century: Some Prolegomena to the Study of New Testament Ideas of Social Obligation* (London: Tyndale Press, 1960). See also Wayne Meeks, *First Urban Christians: The Social World of the Apostle Paul* (New Haven/London: Yale University Press, 1983), 51–73, who studies various names and other references in Paul's letters to show the wide range of social status levels in Pauline communities. For the argument that, given that the vast majority of people in Greco-Roman society were very poor, it is highly unlikely that any of the elite classes were present in Paul's congregations, see Justin Meggitt, *Paul, Poverty and Survival* (Edinburgh: T&T Clark, 1998), 97–154.

[6]See Gerd Theissen, *The Social Setting of Pauline Christianity: Essays on Paul,* ed. and trans. John H. Schütz (Philadelphia: Fortress Press, 1982), 69–119, for this assessment. I describe the conflict more fully later, in chapter 6 on the Corinthian correspondence.

[7]Max Weber, *Economy and Society: An Outline of Interpretive Sociology,* vol. 1, trans. and ed. Guenther Roth & Claus Wittich (New York: Bedminster Press, 1968), 215 (emphasis added).

[8]Chapters 2 and 3 will address leadership in the Jesus movement more fully. For this application of Weberian theory to the various wings of the New Testament church, including the Jesus movement, but especially Pauline and post-Pauline communities, see Bengt Holmberg, *Paul and Power: The Structure of Authority in the Primitive Church as Reflected in the Pauline Epistles* (Philadelphia: Fortress Press, 1980).

[9]Weber, *Economy and Society,* 215.

[10]Ibid., 215.

[11]On routinized charisma, see Weber, *Economy and Society,* 246–54; and a critical summary in Holmberg, *Paul and Power,* 161–65. On "dialectical authority," also see Holmberg, 198–201.

[12]To avoid Christian hegemony with the old designations A.D. (Year of Our Lord) and B.C. (Before Christ), I follow the practice of most scholars today and use C.E. (Common Era) and B.C.E. (Before the Common Era).

[13]See, for example, Ramsay MacMullen, *Roman Social Relations: 50 B.C. to A.D. 284* (New Haven/London: Yale University Press, 1974); Meeks, *First Urban Christians,* 9–50; Peter Garnsey and R. P. Saller, *The Roman Empire: Economy, Society & Culture* (London: SPCK, 1987); and Calvin Roetzel, *The World that Shaped the New Testament, Revised Edition* (Louisville/London: Westminster Press, 2002), 1–36.

[14]MacMullen, *Roman Social Relations,* 101.

[15]For this basic definition, plus an extensive study of Roman patronage from the era of the New Testament, see Richard Saller, *Personal Patronage under the Early Empire* (Cambridge: Cambridge University Press, 1982).

[16]Jerome Carcopino, *Daily Life in Ancient Rome: The People and the City at the Height of the Empire* (New Haven/New London: Yale University Press, 1940), 171.

[17]As suggested by Helen Doohan, *Leadership in Paul* (Wilmington, Del.: Michael Glazier, 1984), 17–18.

[18]Robert Greenleaf, *On Becoming a Servant-Leader,* ed. Don M. Frisk & Larry C. Spears (San Francisco: Jossey-Bass, 1996) 101.

213

[19]Doohan, *Leadership in Paul,* 24.

[20]Anthony T. Padovano, "Leadership and Authority," *N.C. World* 223 (1980): 224, as quoted in Doohan, *Leadership in Paul,* 25.

[21]Robert Bierstedt, "Authority," in *The Social Order,* ed. Bierstedt, 3d ed. (New York: McGraw-Hill, 1970), 298.

[22]Doohan, *Leadership in Paul,* 19.

[23]Ibid., 20.

[24]Robert K. Greenleaf, *Servant Leadership: A Journey into the Nature of Legitimate Power and Greatness* (New York/Mahwah: Paulist Press, 1977, 1991), 7.

[25]Ibid., 13.

[26]Margaret Wheatley, *Leadership and the New Science: Discovering Order in a Chaotic World* (San Francisco: Berrett-Koehler Publishers, 1999), 12.

[27]Ibid., 12.

[28]Ibid., 13.

[29]Ibid., 14.

[30]Peter Block, *Stewardship: Choosing Service over Self-Interest* (San Francisco: Berrett-Koehler, 1996).

[31]Doohan, *Leadership in Paul,* 20.

[32]Ibid., 21.

[33]Manning Marable, *Black Leadership* (New York: Columbia University Press, 1998), 23–97.

[34]Ibid., xiii.

[35]Ibid.

[36]Ibid., xv.

[37]These three aspects—call, style, and situation—reflect Helen Doohan's approach to the study of leadership in Paul. She identifies Paul's call to preach the gospel, his personal leadership style, and his situational approach to the exercise of leadership within his church communities. See *Leadership in Paul,* 23–29.

[38]An issue also raised by Doohan, *Leadership in Paul,* 22.

[39]A term utilized in Gerd Theissen, *Sociology of Early Palestinian Christianity,* trans. John Bowden (Philadelphia: Fortress Press, 1978), a study of this earliest, pre-gospels stage of the church.

[40]Raymond Brown, *The Churches the Apostles Left Behind* (New York: Paulist Press, 1984).

Chapter 1: The World of Jesus and Paul

[1]For a similar breakdown of these three phases see Ekkehard W. Stegemann and Wolfgang Stegemann, *The Jesus Movement: A Social History of Its First Century,* trans. O.C. Dean Jr. (Minneapolis: Fortress Press, 1999), 147.

[2]Gerd Theissen, *Sociology of Early Palestinian Christianity,* trans. John Bowden (Philadelphia: Fortress Press, 1978), 3–4. This statement about the relationship between the written gospels, the oral traditions about Jesus, and the historical Jesus represents a more moderate view than much of the more recent "third quest" for the historical Jesus. The latter appears in the work of such Jesus Seminar proponents as Robert Funk, John Dominic Crossan, and Marcus Borg.

[3]This history is detailed in most New Testament introduction books, but see Richard A. Horsley and John S. Hanson, *Bandits, Prophets and Messiahs: Popular Movements at the Time of Jesus* (Minneapolis, Chicago & New York: Winston Press, 1985), 8–46, for a helpful summary. Horsley and Hanson rely heavily on the accounts of a contemporary from the period, Josephus, who wrote a variety of works on the subject of Jewish history, including *Jewish Antiquities* and *Jewish War.* See also the more recent study by Calvin Roetzel, *The World that Shaped the New Testament,* rev. ed. (Louisville/London: Westminster Press, 2002), especially pp. 1–36.

[4]Horsley and Hanson, *Bandits,* xii.

[5]For a detailed study of the economic issues in ancient Palestine under Roman occupation see Stegemann and Stegemann, *Jesus Movement,* 7–52.

[6]Horsley and Hanson, *Bandits,* 53. For a detailed account of the socioeconomic conditions of the peasantry in Palestine, see pp. 52–63; see also Theissen, *Sociology,* 33–46.

[7]Stegemann and Stegemann, *Jesus Movement,* 49–51.

[8]Horsley and Hanson, *Bandits,* 55.

⁹See ibid., 61. Cf. Harold Recinos, *Who Comes in the Name of the Lord: Jesus at the Margins* (Nashville: Abingdon Press, 1997), 37–80, who describes the ruling class of the Jerusalem elite, both religious and political, as "established leadership" representing "mainline piety." Recinos compares their limitations to that of any society's social, political, and religious elite leadership that fails to exercise justice and mercy toward those whom Jesus called "the least of these" (Mt. 25:40).

¹⁰See Theissen, *Sociology*, 59.

¹¹As described in Horsley and Hanson, *Bandits*, 32.

¹²As argued in Jacob Neusner, *From Politics to Piety: The Emergence of Pharisaic Judaism* (Englewood Cliffs: Prentice-Hall, 1973). See also the detailed study of the social and religious status of the Pharisees in this period by Anthony Saldarini, *Pharisees, Scribes and Saducees in Palestinian Society: A Sociological Approach* (Wilmington, Del.: Michael Glazier, 1988). Roetzel, *World*, 38–60, has a good summary of the various social, religious, and political Jewish groups of first-century Palestine.

¹³Although, for an opposing viewpoint, see Saldarini, *Pharisees*, 128–33, who argues for some political involvement by Pharisees in the first century, especially during the time of Jesus.

¹⁴Horsley and Hanson, *Bandits*, 35.

¹⁵For a brief account of Pilate's reign, see Ibid., 38–39. The gospel depiction can be found in Mark 15:1–15 and parallels. For a comparison of the gospel texts with what might have been a more accurate historical picture, see Warren Carter, *Pontius Pilate: Portraits of a Roman Governor* (Collegeville, Minn.: Liturgical Press, 2003).

¹⁶As described in Theissen, *Sociology*, 71.

¹⁷Ibid., 71. Eventually, the Pharisaic party, because they distanced themselves from the center of power, survived the fall of Jerusalem in 70 to become the defining group for the post-war Judaism that becomes second-century C.E. "Rabbinic Judaism." See Neusner, *From Politics to Piety*, especially 143–59.

¹⁸See Horsley and Hanson, *Bandits*, 10–11; Stegemann and Stegemann, *Jesus Movement*, 47–52.

¹⁹For a description of various resistance groups during the early part of the first century, see Stegemann and Stegemann, *Jesus Movement*, 162–83.

²⁰For a description of the Essenes and their writings, see Roetzel, *World*, 49–57. For a comparison of Essenes to the Jesus movement, see Theissen, *Sociology*, 21–22, and Horsley and Hanson, *Bandits*, 23–26.

²¹Horsley and Hanson, *Bandits*, 41. See also Roetzel, *World*, 28–36.

²²Horsley and Hanson, *Bandits*, 42.

²³Ibid., 43. A variety of examples over the period of our study are cited in pages 34–43, including one notorious incident of repression carried out by Pontius Pilate and referred to even in the New Testament gospels (Lk. 13:1–3). See also Roetzel, *World*, 29–31.

²⁴Horsley and Hanson, *Bandits*, 48. See also Stegemann and Stegemann, *Jesus Movement*, 173–78.

²⁵Horsley and Hanson, *Bandits*, 70.

²⁶See ibid., 72–75 for other examples of social banditry. See also the chart on pp. 260–61 of that book, with names of all bandits, as well as royal pretenders, messiahs, and prophets. Eventually bandits like Eleazar joined the Zealot movement in the 60s C.E. that lead the Jewish Revolt; many also faced crucifixion for their rebellions. For fuller background, see Stegemann and Stegemann, *Jesus Movement*, 178–83.

²⁷Horsley and Hanson, *Bandits*, 76.

²⁸See the history and character of these movements in Horsley and Hanson, *Bandits*, 88–134, and Stegemann and Stegemann, *Jesus Movement*, 162–78.

²⁹For further details on these and other prophetic figures, see Horsley and Hanson, *Bandits*, 135–89, and Stegemann and Stegemann, *Jesus Movement*, 162–70. On the apocalyptic background of some of these groups and individuals, see Ibid., 144–48.

³⁰In particular, by Theissen, *Sociology*, especially 7–23.

³¹These are all designations assigned by Marcus J. Borg, *Jesus: A New Vision* (San Francisco: Harper & Row, 1987).

³²See, for example, John Dominic Crossan, *The Historical Jesus: The Life of a Mediterranean Peasant* (San Francisco: HarperCollins, 1991).

[33]Theissen, *Sociology,* 8.

[34]On the anti-institutional, anti-establishment aspect of charismatic movements and their leaders, including the Jesus movement, see Stegemann and Stegemann, *Jesus Movement,* 191–98.

[35]Theissen, *Sociology,* 13. This list of characteristics of the wandering charismatic leader of the early Christian movement is taken from Theissen's analysis in *Sociology,* 10–14.

[36]Theissen, *Sociology,* 15; see also Elizabeth Schüssler Fiorenza, *In Memory of Her: A Feminist Theological Reconstruction of Christian Origins* (New York: Crossroad, 1983), 110–30 for a discussion of eschatological expectations by Jewish renewal groups in the first century, including the Jesus movement.

[37]See the examples of jokes, nicknames, and insider stories one can find in the gospels according to Carl S. Dudley and Earle Hilgert, *New Testament Tensions and the Contemporary Church* (Philadelphia: Fortress Press, 1987), 24–26.

[38]This is a paraphrase of the words of Dudley and Hilgert, *New Testament Tensions,* 24.

[39]Theissen, *Sociology,* 17. See pp. 18–19 for the rules and expectations of such communities.

[40]This is a descriptive phrase used by Stegemann and Stegemann, *Jesus Movement,* 213–20, for the immediate followers of Jesus after his death, including the settled communities.

[41]Theissen, *Sociology,* 19–20.

[42]See Ibid., 20, for this understanding of the two binding and loosening texts in Matthew 16 and 18. See also J. Andrew Overman, *Church and Community in Crisis: The Gospel According to Matthew* (Valley Forge, Pa.: Trinity Press, 1996), 240–46, who discusses the interplay between the community and its leadership, as well as that of the leadership and authority represented in the person of Peter, whose role in Matthew's gospel "oscillates between representing the quintessential disciple and being a type or model of a community leader" (240).

[43]Overman, *Church and Community,* 242.

[44]Theissen, *Sociology,* 20.

[45]See Schüssler Fiorenza's discussion of the "discipleship of equals" in the earliest Jesus movement, in *In Memory of Her,* especially 140–54.

[46]See Richard Horsley, "General Introduction," in Horsley, ed., *Paul and Empire: Religion and Power in Roman Imperial Society* (Harrisburg, Pa.: Trinity Press, 1997), 1–8. For similar practices with other Roman and Pauline terms, see Dieter Georgi, "God Turned Upside Down. Romans: Missionary Theology and Roman Political Theology," in Horsley, *Paul and Empire,* 148–57.

[47]Horsley, "General Introduction," 8.

[48]This is a factor argued extensively by Wayne Meeks, *The First Urban Christians: The Social World of the Apostle Paul* (New Haven/London: Yale University Press, 1983), especially 9–50. This is not to say, however, that Hellenization and a measure of urbanization were not significant aspects of Jesus' world, including Galilee. See J. Andrew Overman, "Who Were the First Urban Christians? Urbanization in Galilee in the First Century," *Society of Biblical Literature Seminar Papers* 27 (1988): 160–68. Nonetheless, as a ministerial strategy, urban centers were crucial for the Pauline mission.

[49]Horsley, "General Introduction," 7–8.

Chapter 2: Leadership in the Synoptic Tradition

[1]On the nature of Q, see Leif E. Vaage, *Galilean Upstarts: Jesus' First Followers According to Q* (Valley Forge, Pa.: Trinity Press International, 1994), and Bruce Chilton and Jacob Neusner, *Types of Authority in Formative Christianity and Judaism* (London and New York: Routledge, 1999) 41–47.

[2]See, for example, John Dominic Crossan, *Jesus: A Revolutionary Biography* (San Francisco: Harper, 1994), ix-xiv, especially on the importance of the gospel of Thomas. For the role of the gospel of Peter in passion narratives, see Crossan, *Who Killed Jesus?* (San Francisco: Harper, 1995), 6–31. For a good overview of the "other gospels," see Bart Ehrman, *The New Testament: A Historical Introduction to the Early Christian Writings,* 3d ed. (Oxford/New York: Oxford University Press, 2000, 2004), 195–209. See also Ehrman, *The New Testament and Other Early Christian Writings: A Reader,* 2d ed. (Oxford/New York: Oxford University Press, 1998, 2004) for a helpful collection of both canonical and noncanonical gospels.

[3]Walter E. Pilgrim, *Uneasy Neighbors: Church and State in the New Testament* (Minneapolis: Fortress Press, 1999), 37.

[4]Ibid., 38, n. 2.

[5]In addition, my presentation in this and the next chapter will be based largely on my own analysis of the redactions by the synoptic gospel writers, using a gospel parallel, with just a few references to secondary sources.

[6]Josephus, *Antiquities,* 18.116–19, as translated by Richard A. Horsley and John S. Hanson in *Bandits, Prophets and Messiahs: Popular Movements at the Time of Jesus* (Minneapolis, Chicago, and New York: Winston Press, 1985,) 177.

[7]Horsley and Hanson, *Bandits,* 180.

[8]Not everyone agrees that John would have challenged Herod Antipas for the political instability created by his divorce and remarriage. Rather, the breaking of the Law with regard to marrying his living brother's ex-wife was what John had in view. See Joan Taylor, *The Immerser: John the Baptist within Second Temple Judaism* (Grand Rapids: Wm. B. Eerdmans, 1997), 235–42. Yet the fact remains that, according to Josephus, Antipas was attacked by King Aretas and suffered defeat. See Taylor, *The Immerser,* 239; and Josephus, *Jewish Antiquities* 18.109–115.

[9]On this political side of John's leadership, see Horsley and Hanson, *Bandits,* 180–81.

[10]Taylor, *The Immerser,* 233.

[11]See Horsley and Hanson, *Bandits,* 175–79. For a description of prophecy in Ancient Israel as well in the first century C.E., see *Bandits,* 135–75. See also Taylor, *The Immerser,* 223–34.

[12]Ekkehard W. Stegemann and Wolfgang Stegemann, *The Jesus Movement: A Social History of Its First Century,* trans. O.C. Dean Jr. (Minneapolis: Fortress Press, 1999), 196.

[13]See Jacob Neusner, *From Politics to Piety: The Emergence of Pharisaic Judaism* (Englewood Cliffs: Prentice-Hall, 1973), 67–80; and for a different view, see Anthony Saldarini, *Pharisees, Scribes and Saducees in Palestinian Society: A Sociological Approach* (Wilmington, Del.: Michael Glazier, 1988), 157–73, who posits more political engagement of the Pharisees in the first half of the first century C.E., and not just in the post-war era after the destruction of the Jerusalem temple. Thus the Pharisaic party's direct conflict with John and Jesus' challenge of established political as well as religious leadership could very well have been evident in Jesus' time. See also Taylor, *The Immerser,* 155–211, on "John and the Pharisees."

[14]Horsley and Hanson, *Bandits,* 179.

[15]For an extensive study of the relationship between John and Jesus, see Taylor, *The Immerser,* 261–316. I concentrate in what follows on what the gospel record of that relationship teaches us about aspects of gospel leadership.

[16]See J. Ramsey Michaels, *Servant and Son: Jesus in Gospel and Parable* (Philadelphia: Westminster, 1982), 25–41, who emphasizes the importance of the baptism of Jesus for the affirmation of his ministry. Michaels argues that Jesus actually received confirmation of the track he should take with his life and ministry upon hearing the baptismal voice say, in effect, "Yes, *you* are my Son in whom I am well pleased."

[17]Taylor, *The Immerser,* 209.

[18]Overman, *Church and Community,* 163.

[19]But see Overman, *Church and Community,* 162–65, who suggests that perhaps John was expecting more, including "religiopolitical" change in Israel with "an open challenge to Roman rule." Instead, Jesus offers a summary of Isaiah 61:1–2 ("The Spirit of Lord has anointed me to preach good news to the poor"), suggesting that "this is enough of an answer." However, would not such singular attention to the poor in and of itself present a challenge to established leadership, including Rome?

[20]As translated by David R. Cartlidge and David L. Duncan, *Documents for the Study of the Gospels* (Philadelphia: Fortress Press, 1980), 33.

[21]See John Dominic Crossan, *The Dark Interval: Towards a Theology of Story* (Allen, Texas: Argus, 1975), 90–92, for a discussion of the "tax collector" as, more likely, a "toll collector" for the government, a cheat, and, yet, still a disciple figure in the gospels.

[22]See, for example, Elisabeth Schüssler Fiorenza, *In Memory of Her: A Feminist Theological Reconstruction of Christian Origins* (New York: Crossroad, 1983), especially 105–59 on the Jesus movement; and Karen Torjesen, *When Women Were Priests: Women's Leadership in the Early Church & the Scandal of Their Subordination in the Rise of Christianity* (San Francisco: Harper, 1993), 4–46.

[23]See Schüssler Fiorenza, *In Memory of Her,* 137–38, and her comments on the Markan version of this story. She suggests the liberating impact of this story, not only on the woman to whom it may have happened, but also to the original readers of the gospel, including women and male disciples.

[24]See Schüssler Fiorenza, *In Memory of Her,* 139, who, citing Martin Hengel, observes how the grouping of these women in threes parallels "the special groups of three among the twelve (Peter, James, and John) and the leaders of the Jerusalem community (James, the brother of the Lord, Cephas, and John)." In this way the text subtly heightens their importance.

[25]For this designation, see Burton H. Throckmorton Jr., ed., *Gospel Parallels: A Comparison of the Synoptic Gospels,* 5th ed. (Nashville: Thomas Nelson, 1992), 111.

[26]John Koenig, "Hierarchy Transfigured: Perspectives on Leadership in the New Testament," *Word and World* 13, no. 1 (Winter, 1993): 29.

[27]Ibid., 30, citing John N. Collins, *Diakonia: Reinterpreting the Ancient Sources* (New York/Oxford: Oxford University, 1990), 245–63.

[28]Cf. Mk. 10:17; Mt. 19:16 (20); Lk. 18:18. Matthew refers to him as a "young man" and Luke, "a ruler."

[29]See John Dominic Crossan, *Jesus: A Revolutionary Biography* (San Francisco/New York: HarperCollins, 1994), 80–82, who describes the social dimensions of illness and disease in the ancient world. Jesus always sought to heal *illness,* the social stigma attached to disease, as well as eradicate the *disease,* its physicality.

[30]Ibid., 69.

[31]Ibid., 75–91.

[32]See Ibid., 88–91, for this suggestion.

[33]See Bruce J. Malina and Jerome H. Neyrey, "Honor and Shame in Luke-Acts: Pivotal Values of the Mediterranean World," in Jerome H. Neyrey, ed., *The Social World of Luke-Acts: Models for Interpretation* (Peabody, Mass.: Hendrickson, 1991), 32–34, for the importance of naming in order to acquire honor in the ancient world.

[34]Halvor Moxnes, "Patron-Client Relations and the New Community in Luke-Acts," in Neyrey, *Social World of Luke-Acts,* 255.

Chapter 3: Leadership in the Synoptic Tradition

[1]On Jesus' challenge to the "conventional wisdom" of his day, see Marcus Borg, *Jesus: A New Vision* (San Francisco/New York: HarperCollins, 1987), 97–124.

[2]Harold Recino's term in his *Who Comes in the Name of the Lord: Jesus at the Margins* (Nashville: Abingdon Press, 1997), 46–48. See also J. Andrew Overman, *Church and Community in Crisis: The Gospel According to Matthew* (Valley Forge, Pa.: Trinity Press, 1996), 99–103. Overman describes the Sermon as a whole as the "Constitution for Matthew's Church" (103–5).

[3]As suggested by Thomas Cahill, *Desire of the Everlasting Hills: The World Before and After Jesus* (New York: Anchor Books, 1999), 99–100.

[4]See Walter E. Pilgrim, *Uneasy Neighbors: Church and State in the New Testament* (Minneapolis: Fortress Press, 1999), 57–58 for an analysis of the three "passion predictions" Jesus makes in the triple tradition.

[5]See ibid., 58, who notes the significance of Luke mentioning the Roman involvement in this passion prediction, given his generally apologetic attitude toward Rome.

[6]Ibid.

[7]See Ekkehard W. Stegemann and Wolfgang Stegemann, *The Jesus Movement: A Social History of Its First Century,* trans. O.C. Dean Jr. (Minneapolis: Fortress Press, 1999), 119–21 for the history and practice of the temple tax. See also Pilgrim, *Uneasy Neighbors,* 78–80.

[8]Pilgrim, *Uneasy Neighbors,* 80.

[9]Ibid., 137.

[10]Ibid., 101.

[11]See Ibid., 103, for this understanding of the Greek term for "robbers" (*lestes*).

[12]Pilgrim proposes this analysis in ibid., 105–7.

[13]John Dominic Crossan, *Who Killed Jesus?* (San Francisco: Harper, 1995), 63.

[14]See Pilgrim, *Uneasy Neighbors,* 64–72 for a review of the options.

[15]See ibid. for a discussion of the "two kingdom" option (God first, then Caesar), as well as the "one kingdom" (God alone) option. Pilgrim also notes the gospel priority of God over Caesar, which therefore creates an ongoing tension for the faithful servant of God.

[16]For a review and analysis of recent debate on the eschatology of Jesus, see Dale C. Allison, *Jesus of Nazareth: Millenarian Prophet* (Minneapolis: Fortress Press, 1998), 95–171. For a different perspective than the one taken here, see Borg, *Jesus: A New Vision,* 8–17.

[17]See, for example, the discussion of patron-client relations in Luke-Acts by Halvor Moxnes, "Patron-Client Relations and the New Community in Luke-Acts," in Jerome H. Neyrey, ed., *The Social World of Luke-Acts: Models for Interpretation* (Peabody, Mass.: Hendrickson Publishers, 1991), 241–68, including an analysis of this text on pp. 260–61.

[18]Moxnes, "Patron-Client Relations," 261.

[19]Thus suggests I. Howard Marshall, *Commentary on Luke,* NIGNTC (Grand Rapids: Eerdmans, 1978), 824–25. See pp. 823–27 for a full discussion of alternative understandings of this text, including a shift in understanding on the part of Jesus on the use of swords, given the impending crisis and threat on their lives. More likely, the disciples misunderstood the metaphoric emphasis in Jesus' warning. "You will need to prepare for the impending crisis of opposition, but swords are not the obvious answer."

[20]Ibid., 823.

[21]For this understanding of "It is enough," see ibid., 827, who translates it, "That's enough."

[22]See Pilgrim, *Uneasy Neighbors,* 110–12 for a fuller discussion of Jesus' passion silence.

[23]Ibid., 112.

[24]See Crossan, *Who Killed Jesus?* (subtitled "Exposing the Roots of Anti-Semitism in the Gospel Story of the Death of Jesus") for the historical problem of the anti-Jewish statements in the gospels, especially those surrounding the death of Jesus (see especially pp. 31–38). The recent movie by Mel Gibson, *The Passion of the Christ,* revives some of these anti-Semitic feelings in its depiction of the actions of Jews against Jesus during his arrest, trial, and crucifixion.

[25]See Richard A. Horsley and John S. Hanson, *Bandits, Prophets and Messiahs: Popular Movements at the Time of Jesus* (Minneapolis, Chicago & New York: Winston Press, 1985), 38–39 for a discussion of Pilate as chronicled by Josephus and Philo.

[26]See Crossan's comments on this in *Who Killed Jesus?,* 111–12.

[27]As quoted by Crossan, *Who Killed Jesus?,* 147.

[28]See Warren Carter, *Pontius Pilate: Portraits of a Roman Governor* (Collegeville, Minn.: Liturgical Press, 2003), especially 35–54, for a thorough discussion of Pilate and what his actions as a provincial governor over a conquered territory were probably like historically, as well as in the overall picture in the four gospels.

[29]As does the noncanonical "Gospel of Peter"; see Crossan, *Who Killed Jesus?,* 93–100.

[30]As suggested by Marshall, *The Gospel of Luke,* 863; see also Sharon H. Ringe, *Luke,* Westminster Bible Companion (Louisville: Westminster John Knox Press, 1995).

[31]See the comments by Ringe, *Luke,* 275–76, on this point.

[32]On the textual analysis of Mark's ending in 16:8 (9–20) and how to "read" the shorter ending, see Donald H. Juel, *The Gospel of Mark,* Interpreting Biblical Texts (Nashville: Abingdon Press, 1999), 167–76.

[33]As argued in John Dominic Crossan, *Jesus: A Revolutionary Biography* (San Francisco: Harper, 1999), 123–58.

[34]Ringe, *Luke,* 281.

[35]Ibid.

[36]Mary Ann Tolbert, *Sowing the Gospel: Mark's World in Literary-Historical Perspective* (Minneapolis: Fortress Press, 1989), 295–96. See also Donald H. Juel, *Gospel of Mark,* Interpreting Biblical Texts (Nashville: Abingdon Press, 1999), 171–76.

Chapter 4: Windows into Pauline Leadership

[1]For example, see Bengt Holmberg, *Paul and Power: The Structure of Authority in the Primitive Church as Reflected in the Pauline Epistles* (Philadelphia: Fortress Press, 1978, 1980). See also John Schütz, *Paul and the Anatomy of Apostolic Authority* (London: Cambridge University Press, 1975). More recently, Andrew Clarke has focused on leadership in Paul with two major works: Andrew D. Clarke, *Secular and Christian Leadership in Corinth: A Socio-Historical & Exegetical Study of 1 Corinthians 1–6* (Leiden:: E.J. Brill, 1993) and *Serve the Community of the Church: Christians as Leaders and Ministers* (Grand Rapids: Wm. B. Eerdmans, 2000).

[2]Letters whose Pauline authorship is not questioned include Romans, 1–2 Corinthians, Galatians, Philippians, Philemon, and 1 Thessalonians. Many scholars doubt Paul's authorship of the other six (Colossians, Ephesians, 1–2 Timothy, Titus, 2 Thessalonians) for a variety of reasons.

[3]Wayne A. Meeks, *The First Urban Christians: The Social World of the Apostle Paul* (New Haven: Yale University Press, 1983), 9. However, see J. Andrew Overman, "Who Were the First Urban Christians? Urbanization in Galilee in the First Century." *SBLSP* 27 (1988): 160–68, for the suggestion that perhaps the Jesus movement was more urban than often assumed.

[4]Meeks, *First Urban Christians,* 9. On Paul's "tent-making" and its social implications, see Ronald F. Hock, *The Social Context of Paul's Ministry: Tentmaking and Apostleship* (Philadelphia: Fortress Press, 1980). On the importance of Tarsus in the Greco-Roman world and its possible influences on Paul's upbringing, see Calvin Roetzel, *Paul: The Man and the Myth* (Minneapolis: Fortress Press, 1999), 11–19.

[5]Roetzel, *Paul,* 12.

[6]For a helpful description of the cities in the Pauline mission, see Meeks, *First Urban Christians,* 40–50.

[7]On cities, roads, and the ancient economy, see Moses I. Finley, *The Ancient Economy,* 2d ed. (Berkeley and Los Angeles: University of California Press, 1985), especially 126–49.

[8]See Meeks, *First Urban Christians,* 75–84, for descriptions of these and other Greco-Roman groups and how they served as models for the formation of the Pauline Christian "group." For more specific information on the voluntary association, see Clarke, *Serve the Community,* 59–77.

[9]See John E. Stambaugh and David L. Balch, *The New Testament in Its Social Environment* (Philadelphia: Fortress Press, 1986), 124–26, for a description of the social "clubs" in the ancient city organized according to social class.

[10]See Meeks, *First Urban Christians,* 51–73, for this assessment.

[11]Clark addresses "leadership in the Roman colony and city," in *Serve the Community,* 35–58.

[12]For a study of Paul's relationship to the Jerusalem church *vis-à-vis* his status as an apostle, see Holmberg, *Paul and Power,* 15–56.

[13]See Stephen Barton, "Paul and the Cross: A Sociological Approach," *Theology* 85 (1982): 15–16.

[14]Ibid., 17.

[15]Ibid., 15.

[16]Although even in that letter Paul includes more individuals and even the whole church in his address, thus making his appeal to Philemon in a larger, community context. See Philemon 2.

[17]Although within the structure of a letter he might direct certain comments to certain groups within the church. For example, in Romans, one moment Paul addresses Jews in the churches, in another Gentiles (e.g., Rom. 2:17–29; 11:17–24). Also, in Galatians, at various times Paul addresses his Gentile believers, at other times his opponents, the "Judiazers." See the helpful chart of the various audiences and opponents Paul addresses and confronts in Galatians in Daniel Patte, *Paul's Faith and the Power of the Gospel: A Structural Introduction to the Pauline Letters* (Philadelphia: Fortress Press, 1983), 48.

[18]Roetzel, *Paul,* 72, citing Adolf Deissmann, *Light from the Ancient East,* trans. Lionel Strachan (New York: Doran, 1927), 234.

[19]See Stanley Stowers, *Letter Writing in Greco-Roman Antiquity* (Philadelphia: Westminster Press, 1986), who discusses the various literary types of ancient letters that are comparable to Paul. However, see also Roetzel, *Paul,* 73–76, who argues that Paul is too eclectic in his use of the letter form to be pinned down to either the everyday, ordinary papyri letters of Egypt (following Deissmann) or the more formal, literary letters of Greece and Rome (Stowers).

[20]So argues James W. Thompson, *Preaching Like Paul: Homiletical Wisdom for Today* (Louisville: Westminster Press, 2001), 27–60. However, this does not mean, I would argue, that Paul's "evangelistic preaching" was necessarily in a "public forum" like that depicted in the book of Acts. Rather, his "evangelistic preaching" to initially establish his *ekklēsiae* most likely began with members of the households to which he attached himself to earn a living in trade work. On Paul's "tentmaking" as a vehicle for his apostleship, see Hock, *The Social Context of Paul's Ministry.*

[21]Roetzel, *Paul,* 75–76.

[22]Ibid., 76.

[23]This is the argument presented in a well-known article by Robert Funk, "The Apostolic *Parousia*: Form and Significance," in *Christian History and Interpretation: Studies Presented to John Knox,* ed. William Farmer et al. (Cambridge: Cambridge University Press, 1967), 249–68.

²⁴See Roetzel, *Paul*, 76–81.

²⁵Argued at length in J. Christiaan Beker's seminal work, *Paul the Apostle: The Triumph of God in Life and Thought* (Philadelphia: Fortress Press, 1980).

²⁶Paraphrasing the title and intent of Paul Sampley's study, *Walking Between the Times: Paul's Moral Reasoning* (Minneapolis: Fortress Press, 1991).

²⁷See Robert Jewett, *The Thessalonian Correspondence: Pauline Rhetoric and Millenarian Piety* (Philadelphia: Fortress Press, 1986), 49–60, for the various theories on dating 1 Thessalonians, including the conclusion that the early 50s best fits the evidence.

²⁸Abraham Malherbe has discussed at length these passages of 1 Thessalonians with regard to how they show Paul's concern to not only show his concern for the Thessalonians, but to separate his missionary efforts from those of false "philosophers" in the ancient world. See Malherbe, *Paul and the Thessalonians: The Philosophic Tradition of Pastoral Care,* reprinted ed. (Mifflintown, Pa.: Sigler Press, 2000, original ed., 1987), esp. 46–60; and also his "'Gentle as a Nurse:' The Cynic Background to I Thess ii," *Novum Testamentum* 12 (1970): 203–17.

²⁹I will say more about this in chapter 6, but I follow Victor Furnish in his commentary, *II Corinthians,* Anchor Bible 32a (Garden City, New York: Doubleday, 1984), 429–33, with regard to the integrity of 2 Corinthians 1–9 and in seeing 2 Corinthians 10–13 as part of a subsequent letter.

³⁰See several articles on this topic in Karl P. Donfried, ed., *The Romans Debate*, rev. and exp. ed. (Peabody, Mass.: Hendrickson, 1991).

³¹One scholar states the issue this way: "Paul's argument responds to an incipient anti-Judaism, already rife among the Roman aristocracy and beginning to penetrate the Christian community as well." The return of Jews to Rome in the mid-50s after the Emperor Claudius's edict expulsing them a decade earlier may have precipitated further internal conflicts in the Christian house churches of Rome. See Neil Elliot, "Romans," *The New Oxford Annotated Bible,* 3d ed. (Oxford/New York: Oxford University Press, 2001), 242 [New Testament].

³²For this argument at length, see Elsa Tamez, *The Amnesty of Grace: Justification by Faith from a Latin American Perspective* (Nashville: Abingdon Press, 1993).

³³See Robert Jewett's argument along these lines in "Romans as an Ambassadorial Letter," *Interpretation* 36 (1982): 5–20.

³⁴Gordon Fee, *Paul's Letter to the Philippians*, NICNT (Grand Rapids: Wm. B. Eerdmans, 1995), 34–37, discusses the various options and opts for Rome for the Philippians imprisonment, thus implying a late date for the letter. See also Richard Cassidy, *Paul in Chains: Roman Imprisonment and the Letters of St. Paul* (New York: Crossroad, 2001), 68–84, 124–43, who also argues for a Roman imprisonment for both Philippians and Philemon.

³⁵For a rhetorical analysis of Philippians, see D.F. Watson, "A Rhetorical Analysis of Philippians and Its Implications for the Unity Question," *Novum Testamentum* 30 (1988): 57–88. The essay explains the meaning of deliberative rhetoric, its various components (*exordium, narratio, probatio, peroratio, adfectum,* and epistolary postscript), and how Paul follows these in his letter to the Philippians. For a commentary on Philippians based on this analysis, see Ben Witherington III, *Friendship and Finances in Philippi: The Letter of Paul to the Philippians* (Valley Forge, Pa.: Trinity Press, 1994).

³⁶Thus the unity of the letter is preserved against questions about its integrity. For a contrasting view, see Pheme Perkins, "Philippians: Theology for the Heavenly Politeuma" in *Pauline Theology, Volume I: Thessalonians, Philippians, Galatians, Philemon,* ed. Jouette M. Bassler (Minneapolis: Fortress Press, 1991), 89–14, who argues for three letter fragments in Philippians: a "consolation letter" (Phil. 1:1–3:1), a "polemical letter" (3:2–4:1), and a thanksgiving letter for a monetary gift (4:10–20). However, a rhetorical analysis holds together the various themes of unity and faith in the midst of opposition throughout the letter, with the concluding thanksgiving connected to Paul's "missionary report" from prison at the outset of the letter (1:3–26).

³⁷On the importance of Euodia and Syntyche for Paul's purposes in seeking unity in this church, see Elisabeth Schüssler Fiorenza, *In Memory of Her: A Feminist Theological Reconstruction of Christian Origins* (New York: Crossroad, 1983, 1990), 169–70.

³⁸See Cassidy, *Paul in Chains,* 169, who suggests that this text refers to opponents of Paul in Rome.

³⁹See James W. Thompson, *Preaching Like Paul: Homiletical Wisdom for Today* (Louisville: Westminster John Knox Press, 2001), 68–71, for a discussion of Paul's use of *pathos* (emotion), *ethos* (character), and *logos* (reason) in his rhetoric, including *ethos* and *pathos* in Phil. 1:12–26.

[40]In this case the letter has very clear rhetorical purposes, structure, and features.

[41]See John Knox, *Philemon among the Letters of Paul*, rev. ed. (New York: Abingdon Press, 1959).

[42]See Alan Callahan, *The Embassy of Onesimus: Paul's Letter to Philemon* (Valley Forge, Pa.: Trinity Press, 1996).

[43]We are not sure the exact location of Philemon's church community, although traditionally Colossae has been in view because of connected names and greetings (Philem. 23, Col. 4:7–17). See Luke Timothy Johnson, *The Writings of the New Testament*, rev. ed. (Minneapolis: Fortress Press, 1995), for the argument that Philemon was the "cover letter" for a packet of three letters to churches in the Lychan Valley, including Colossae (letter to Colossians), Ephesus (letter to Ephesians), and Laodicea and Hierapolis (cf. Col. 4:13,16). Questions about Paul's authorship of Colossians and Ephesians cast doubt on this theory, however.

[44]Note Margaret Mitchell's question about this text: "A mere commonplace, or a diplomatically framed hint to release him from slavery?" in "Philemon," *New Oxford Annotated Bible*, 3d ed. (Oxford/New York: Oxford University Press, 2001), 368 [New Testament].

[45]For an excellent discussion of how Paul, in the narrative structure of Philemon, argues for a new understanding of social roles and responsibilities in churches, see Norman Petersen, *Rediscovering Paul: Philemon and the Sociology of Paul's Narrative World* (Philadelphia: Fortress Press, 1985).

Chapter 5: Paul's Leaders

[1]E. Earle Ellis, "Paul and His Co-Workers," *New Testament Studies* 17 (1971): 438–52.

[2]Ibid., 437.

[3]Ibid.

[4]See the attention to this in ibid., 445–52.

[5]Bengt Holmberg, *Paul and Power: The Structure of Authority in the Primitive Church as Reflected in the Pauline Epistles* (Philadelphia: Fortress Press, 1978, 1980).

[6]Ibid., 58–67.

[7]See ibid., 67–70.

[8]For a discussion of these expectations and how Paul exhorted his churches to follow them, see ibid., 74–79.

[9]Ibid., 80.

[10]Wayne Meeks, *The First Urban Christians: The Social World of the Apostle Paul* (New Haven and London: Yale University Press, 1983), 131–36, which I follow in the description of Paul's leaders in this paragraph.

[11]On the function of letters as an exercise of power, see also Holmberg, *Paul and Power*, 80–86; Meeks, *First Urban Christians*, 113–27; and on financial issues, Holmberg, 86–93.

[12]Holmberg, *Paul and Power*, 80. On letters of introduction, also called "letters of mediation" and "letters of recommendation," see Stanley Stowers, *Letter Writing in Greco-Roman Antiquity* (Philadelphia: Westminster Press, 1986), 153–65.

[13]Richard Saller, *Personal Patronage under the Early Empire* (Cambridge: Cambridge University Press, 1982), 108.

[14]The work most often cited is Chan-Hie Kim, *Form and Structure of the Familiar Greek Letter of Recommendation*, SBL Dissertation Series 4 (Missoula, Mont.: Scholars Press, 1972). See also the author's dissertation, Efrain Agosto, "Paul's Use of Greco-Roman Conventions of Commendation," Boston University, 1996, and two essays on the subject: Agosto, "Patronage and Commendation: Imperial and Anti-Imperial" in *Paul & the Roman Imperial Order*, ed. Richard A. Horsley (Harrisburg, Pa.: Trinity Press International, 2004), 103–23; and "Paul & Commendation" in *Paul in the Greco-Roman World: a Hanbook*, ed. J. Paul Sampley (Harrisburg, Pa.: Trinity Press International, 2003), 101–33.

[15]Saller, *Personal Patronage*, 193.

[16]Cicero, *Ad Familiares* 12:2:3.

[17]Ibid.

[18]Saller, *Personal Patronage*, 108.

[19]Pliny, *Epistolae*, 10:26.

[20]See Kim, *Form and Structure*, 9–85, for a description of the various elements of an ancient commendation, especially those from the Greek papyri, which Kim studies most

closely. Clinton Keyes, "The Greek Letter of Introduction," *American Journal of Philology* 56 (1935): 28–44, studied the form across various commendation genre, including the literary letters of Cicero. Hannah Cotton looked more closely at the classic literary letters of commendation in her dissertation, "Letters of Recommendation: Cicero-Fronto (Oxford, 1977).

[21]I assume, with Victor Furnish among others, that 2 Corinthians is essentially two letters. Second Corinthians 1–9 is a description of Paul's reconciliation with the Corinthians, as mediated by his associate Titus. This letter includes a long description of the nature of Paul's "ministry of reconciliation" (2:14–6:13; 7:2–4) and a long request for Corinthian participation in the collection for Jerusalem, in light of their reconciliation with Paul (8:1–9:15). Second Corinthians 10–13 preserves a *subsequent* letter fragment after the renewal of hostilities between Paul and the Corinthians, perhaps as a result of confusion over the collection (cf. 11:7–11; 12:17–18). Second Corinthians 6:14–7:1 is most likely a fragment from another Corinthian letter. See Victor Paul Furnish, *2nd Corinthians,* Anchor Bible Commentary (Garden City, New York: Doubleday, 1984); cf. Ben Witherington III, *A Socio-Rhetorical Commentary on the Corinthian Correspondence,* who argues for the integrity of 2 Corinthians; and Hans Dieter Betz, *2 Corinthians 8 and 9,* Hermeneia (Philadelphia: Fortress Press, 1985), who sees five letters in 2 Corinthians (1–7, except for 6:14–7:1; 8; 9; and 10–13).

[22]See also 2 Cor. 6:3–10; 11:23–29; 1 Cor. 4:9–13, and the extensive study on Paul's hardship lists: John Fitzgerald, *Cracks in an Earthen Vessel: An Examination of the Catalogues of Hardships in the Corinthian Correspondence* (Atlanta: Scholars Press, 1988).

[23]Term employed by John H. Schütz, *Paul and the Anatomy of Apostolic Authority* (Cambridge: Cambridge University Press, 1975), 133; also cited by Meeks, *First Urban Christians,* 131.

[24]Meeks, *First Urban Christians,* 138.

[25]But see the broader reasons for refusal of aid as the refusal of Corinthians' elite patronage as argued in Peter Marshall, *Enmity in Corinth: Social Conventions in Paul's Relations with the Corinthians* (Tübingen: J.C.B. Mohr [Paul Siebeck], 1987), 218–58.

[26]Ibid., 274.

[27]Agosto, "Paul's Use," 144–49.

[28]As suggested by I. Howard Marshall, *1 and 2 Thessalonians,* New Century Bible Commentary (Grand Rapids: Wm. B. Eerdmans, 1983), 147.

[29]See Bo Reicke, "*proistēmi,*" in Gerhard Kittel and Gerhard Friedrich, eds., *Theological Dictionary of the New Testament* (hereafter TDNT), vol. 6, trans. Geoffrey W. Bromiley (Grand Rapids: Eerdmans, 1969), 700–703, for the range of meanings and frequency of use for this term.

[30]Ibid., 701.

[31]"*Noutheteō,*" in Walter Bauer, William F. Arndt, F. Wilbur Gingrich, and Frederick William Danker, eds., *A Greek-English Lexicon of the New Testament and other Early Christian Literature* (hereafter, BAGD), 3d ed. (Chicago: University of Chicago Press, 1999), 679.

[32]J. Behm, "*noutheteō,*" in TDNT 4:1019–22.

[33]The translation "because of their work" is by Ernest Best, *A Commentary on the First & Second Epistles to the Thessalonians,* rep. ed. (Peabody, Mass.: Hendrickson, 1988), 228.

[34]*Ad Familiares,* 1.4

[35]As suggested by Paul Ellingworth and Eugene Nida, *A Translator's Handbook on Paul's Letter to the Thessalonians* (Stuttgart: United Bible Societies, 1975), 118.

[36]Ibid.

[37]A pattern discerned by Robert Funk, "The Apostolic *Parousia* Form and Significance," in W.R. Farmer, et al., eds., *Christian History and Interpretation: Studies Presented to John Knox* (Cambridge: Cambridge University Press, 1967), 249–68.

[38]Kim, *Form and Structure,* 130.

[39]Gordon Fee, *The First Epistle to the Corinthians,* NICT (Grand Rapids: Wm. B. Eerdmans, 1987), 828–29.

[40]See Ibid., 829, n. 18, for these and other references.

[41]As suggested by, among others, Wayne Meeks, *First Urban Christians,* 51–73. See also Gerd Theissen, *Social Setting of Pauline Christianity: Essays on Paul,* ed. and trans. John H. Schütz (Philadelphia: Fortress Press, 1982), 83–99, and Holmberg, *Paul and Power,* 103–10. For a different perspective on the financial means of householders in Pauline churches, see Justin J. Meggitt, *Paul, Poverty and Survival* (Edinburgh: T&T Clark, 1998), 128–35.

[42]See BAGD, "*tassō*," 991.

[43]On this point, see Fee, *First Corinthians*, 830.

[44]For a discussion of "exemplification" in Paul, see J. Paul Sampley, *Walking Between the Times: Paul's Moral Reasoning* (Minneapolis: Fortress Press, 1991), 89–91. For its practice in 1 Corinthians, including with Stephanas, see Margaret Mitchell, *Paul and the Rhetoric of Reconciliation: An Exegetical Examination of the Language and Composition of 1 Corinthians* (Louisville: Westminster/John Knox Press, 1991), 42–60, 178–79.

[45]See Richard Horsley, *First Corinthians*, Abingdon New Testament Commentaries (Nashville: Abingdon Press, 2000), 225.

[46]But see Mitchell, *Paul and Reconciliation*, 178–79, who argues that Paul's rhetorical purposes in this commendation of Stephanas and household call for "obedience" to exemplary leaders in order to end discord in Corinth. Certainly, Paul commends Stephanas in order to exemplify the type of leadership he seeks and needs for unity in Corinth, but it is interesting that the criteria Paul invokes in this exemplification highlights service rather than status. For a perspective that also highlights the rhetoric and search for power and authority that lies behind Paul's language of imitation, see Elizabeth Castelli, *Imitating Paul: A Discourse of Power* (Louisville: Westminster/John Knox Press, 1991).

[47]However, see Meggitt, *Paul, Poverty and Survival*, 129–32, who suggests that owning a home and slaves need not always be the mark of high wealth and social status.

[48]See Margaret Mitchell, "New Testament Envoys in the Context of Greco-Roman Diplomatic and Epistolary Conventions: The Example of Timothy and Titus," *Journal of Biblical Literature*, 111 (1992): 641–62, for a complete list of envoy passages in Paul and an analysis of several that involve Timothy and Titus. See also Hans Dieter Betz, *2 Corinthians 8 and 9: A Commentary on Two Administrative Letters of the Apostle Paul* (Philadelphia: Fortress Press, 1985), which describes 2 Corinthians 8:16–23 as the "commendation of envoys."

[49]On this point, see also Sze-kar Wan, *Power in Weakness: The Second Letter of Paul to the Corinthians* (Harrisburg, Pa.: Trinity Press International, 2000), 5–10, which argues that 2 Corinthians 8 and 9 are letters of appeal for the collection appended to the letter of reconciliation in 2 Corinthians 1–2, and 7.

[50]Ibid., 115.

[51]See ibid., which refers to the Jerusalem collection as a "diaspora tribute."

[52]See J. Paul Sampley, *Pauline Partnership in Christ: Christian Community and Commitment in Light of Roman Law* (Philadelphia: Fortress Press, 1980) for helpful discussion on Paul's use of the term *koinonos*.

[53]Wan, *Power and Weakness*, 115, wonders why Paul not only does not identify this brother by name, but also why the churches aren't identified. Yet a logical assumption is that the same churches from which Paul is making the collection, namely churches he founded, are the same churches that appointed this brother and know his ministry well.

[54]*Apostoloi* and *doxa* are both in the nominative case and therefore agree with each other, and not with the "churches," which is in the genitive, or possessive case.

[55]From Robert Sherk, *Roman Documents from the Greek East* (Baltimore: Johns Hopkins Press, 1969), letter 34, lines 8–11, as cited by Betz, *2 Cor. 8 & 9*, 81.

[56]Ibid.

[57]Wan, *Power and Weakness*, 116–17.

[58]Ibid., 117.

[59]Carolyn Osiek, *Philippians, Philemon*, Abingdon New Testament Commentaries (Nashville: Abingdon Press, 2000), 76–77.

[60]Sampley, *Walking*, 65.

[61]Ibid.

[62]Pliny, *Epistles*, 10.87

[63]Osiek, *Philippians, Philemon*, 77.

[64]Peter T. O'Brien, *Commentary on Philippians*, NIGTC (Grand Rapids: Wm. B. Eerdmans, 1991), 331.

[65]However, see Osiek, *Philippians, Philemon*, 78–79, who suggests that *apostolos* carries more weight than just a "messenger." Rather, Epaphroditus became, with the blessing of the Philippians, an apostle—"one officially delegated by a church to proclaim the gospel in a missionary capacity." However, with his severe illness and general bad time as an apostle, he must now go back. This generous commendation reflects Paul's attempt to have the Philippians

receive Epaphroditus well despite his failure as an apostle. This is an intriguing interpretation that depends on an understanding of "apostle" as more wide-ranging than "the Jerusalem apostles and Paul, plus a very few others." See Meeks, *First Urban Christians,* 131-33.

[66]Osiek, *Philippians, Philemon,* 74.

[67]See ibid., 77-79.

[68]Ben Witherington III, *Friendship and Finances: The Letter of Paul to the Philippians* (Valley Forge, Pa.: Trinity Press International, 1994), 79.

[69]Ibid., 81.

[70]Osiek, *Philippians, Philemon,* 112.

[71]Witherington, *Friendship and Finances,* 109.

[72]As does Osiek, *Philippians, Philemon,* 109-15, and even more strongly Cynthia Briggs Kittredge, *Community and Authority: The Rhetoric of Obedience in the Pauline Tradition* (Harrisburg, Pa.: Trinity Press International, 1998), 91-94, 105-8.

[73]Kim, *Form and Structure,* 128.

[74]BAGD, "*synathleō,*" 964.

[75]Kittredge, *Community and Authority,* 91-92. Phronein, "to think, set one's mind on, be disposed to," appears in Phil. 1:7; 2:2, 5; 3:15,19; 4:2, 10.

[76]Osiek, *Philippians, Philemon,* 115.

[77]Ibid., with scriptural references.

[78]Most recently, opinions about the impact of this text on the whole of Philippians range from Witherington, *Friendship and Finances,* 104: "While it is probably saying too much to suggest that all of what has gone before was leading up to these verses...," to Kittredge, *Community and Authority,* who not only argues that "Euodia and Syntyche should be considered central to the rhetorical problem" in Philippians (93), but that their "disagreement" is with Paul, not each other (105-8).

[79]Osiek, *Philippians, Philemon,* 110-12. See also Witherington, *Friendship and Finances,* 30-33.

[80]Form adapted and translated by author from Kim, *Form and Structure,* 132.

[81]Margaret Y. MacDonald, "Reading Real Women through the Undisputed Letters of Paul," in *Women and Christian Origins,* ed. Ross Shephard Kraemer and Mary Rose D'Angelo, (New York/Oxford: Oxford University Press, 1999), 208.

[82]Ibid.

[83]Excerpted from James Walters, "'Phoebe' and 'Junia(s)'–Rom. 16:1-2, 7," in Carroll D. Osburn, *Essays on Women in Earliest Christianity,* vol. 1 (Joplin, Mo.: College Press, 1993), 173-74. For the full inscription see D. Pallas, et al., "Inscriptions liciennes trouvèes à Solômes près de Corinthe," *Bulletin de correspondance hellinque* 83 (1959): 505-6.

[84]Document cited by Robert Jewett, "Paul, Phoebe and the Spanish Mission," in Jacob Neusner, et al., *The Social World of Formative Christianity and Judaism: Essays in Honor of Howard Clark Kee* (Philadelphia: Fortress Press, 1988), 140, n. 62.

[85]See Walters, "'Phoebe' and 'Junia(s)'," 169-76, for his analysis of the Junia Theodora inscription and the conclusion that Phoebe's duties as a patron may have been "analogous to those of Junia Theodora."

[86]Meggitt, *Paul, Poverty and Survival,* 143-49.

[87]Ibid., 149.

[88]See Kim, *Form and Structure,* 65-68, for discussion and examples of commendation requests, including those that posit "general assistance"–an introduction, hospitality, help in some unstated "matter."

[89]Kim's term. See *Form and Structure,* 86-87, for examples of such clauses including "for he is worthy of consideration," "for he is a man of action," "for he is someone who would care about your interests," etc.

[90]Jewett, "Paul, Phoebe and the Spanish Mission," 142-61.

[91]Ibid., 154.

[92]Robert Jewett, "Romans as an Ambassadorial Letter," *Interpretation* 36 (1982): 5-20.

[93]MacDonald, "Reading Real Women," 209, citing Caroline Whelan, "Amica Pauli: The Role of Phoebe in the Early Church," *Journal for the Study of the New Testament* 49 (1993): 81.

[94]See MacDonald, "Reading Real Women," 208-9.

[95]See Jewett, "Paul, Phoebe and the Spanish Mission," 151.

[96]Meggitt, *Paul, Poverty and Survival,* 148.

[97]Ibid., 147–48, citing Saller, *Personal Patronage,* 1 and 10.

[98]Meggitt, *Paul, Poverty and Survival,* 148.

[99]See Kim, *Form and Structure,* 128.

[100]This basic narrative of the story of Paul's letter to Philemon is asserted, give or take a few details, by most commentators. Recent examples include Cain Hope Felder, "The Letter to Philemon," in *The New Interpreter's Bible: A Commentary in Twelve Volumes,* vol. 11 (Nashville: Abingdon Press, 2000), 833–905; Osiek, *Philippians, Philemon,* 133–46; and Sandra Hack Polaski, *Paul and the Discourse of Power* (Sheffield: Sheffield Academic Press, 1999), 57–59. See also Norman Petersen, *Rediscovering Paul: Philemon and the Sociology of Paul's Narrative World* (Philadelphia: Fortress Press, 1985). About the only major disagreement interpreters might have about the Philemon narrative is whether Paul called for the manumission of Onesimus or not. In addition, Allen Dwight Callahan, *Embassy of Onesimus: The Letter of Philemon* (Valley Forge, Pa.: Trinity Press International, 1997), has challenged the notion that Onesimus was a slave and Philemon his owner. Rather, Callahan argues, they were estranged brothers for whom Paul writes this letter of reconciliation.

[101]See Hope Felder, "Philemon," 883–84, for the range of possibilities. He opts for the more traditional view of Rome as the provenance. For a different assessment, see Osiek, *Philippians, Philemon,* 126 (and her longer argument on the Philippian imprisonment as well, 27–30).

[102]Polaski, *Paul and Power,* 57.

[103]Although see Callahan, *Embassy,* 31–32, who argues for a textual variant, *presbeutes,* "ambassador."

[104]So Osiek, *Philippians, Philemon,* 135.

[105]Callahan, *Embassy,* 24, translating *presbutes* as "ambassador" based on a textual variant.

[106]Polaski, *Paul and Power,* 62.

[107]Even though Paul probably did not write Colossians, Philemon could very well be a house church leader in that city, given the names connected to both letters (cf. Col. 4:7–17; Philem. 23). See Hope Felder, "Philemon," 884; Osiek, *Philippians, Philemon,* 126.

[108]As described by Sampley in *Pauline Partnership in Christ,* but see also Osiek, *Philippians, Philemon,* 22–23, who questions whether the legal contract of *koinonia, societas* in Latin, is the best explanation for the genre of Philippians. Yet here in Philemon it is not a matter of genre, but the nature of the relationship between Paul and Philemon.

[109]See Polaski, *Paul and the Discourse of Power,* 66, n. 56.

[110]See Osiek, *Philippians, Philemon,* 141.

[111]However, not all agree with the traditional designation of Philemon as the letter's primary recipient. See John Knox, *Philemon among the Letters of Paul* (Nashville: Abingdon Press, 1959), 62–70, who argues for Archippus, the last name mentioned in the greetings, as the primary recipient because Paul immediately mentions "the church [that meets] in your house" (Philem. 2) after his name. However, I agree with Carolyn Osiek, *Philippians, Philemon,* 133 (and most commentators), who posits, "It is more likely that the first person named is the addressee intended in the rest of the letter."

[112]Polaski, *Paul and the Discourse of Power,* 56.

[113]Thus, in terms of its rhetoric, the letter to Philemon is a "deliberative letter," i.e., a letter in which Paul persuades some future action from those to whom he writes. See George A. Kennedy, *New Testament through Rhetorical Criticism* (Chapel Hill: University of North Carolina Press, 1984).

[114]Polaski, *Paul and the Discourse of Power,* 60.

[115]Ibid., 65.

[116]Ibid.

[117]See Dale Martin, *Slavery as Salvation: The Metaphor of Slavery in Pauline Christianity* (New Haven/London: Yale University Press, 1990), especially 1–49, 86–116, for range of language and statuses in ancient slavery, including the "enslaved leader" metaphor that Martin argues Paul has in mind when he employs "slave of Christ" language.

[118]In the early second century, Ignatius of Antioch mentions Onesimus, the Bishop of Ephesus, probably not the same Onesimus of Paul's letter to Philemon written some fifty years earlier. Nonetheless, the possibility of a slave rising to a bishopric is intriguing. According to Martin, *Slavery as Salvation,* 1–49, it was not all that impossible for some slaves in Greco-Roman society to rise in status, at least on a limited basis. Perhaps the Pauline metaphor of "slave of

Christ" as a "leadership designation" (Martin, 51–60) became an actual reality for some Christian slaves, including Onesimus, in Paul's time.

[119]As detailed by Callahan in his commentary on this text in *Embassy of Onesimus,* 44–54.

[120]Callahan, *Embassy of Onesimus,* 56.

[121]Osiek, *Philippians, Philemon,* 140.

[122]Norman Petersen, *Rediscovering Paul: Philemon and the Sociology of Paul's Narrative World* (Philadelphia: Fortress Press, 1985), especially 89–109, 124–31, 151–70.

[123]Neil Elliot, *Liberating Paul: The Justice of God and the Politics of the Apostle* (Maryknoll, N.Y.: Orbis, 1994), 47.

[124]Petersen, *Rediscovering Paul,* 290.

[125]Elliot, *Liberating Paul,* 48.

[126]Ibid.

[127]Ibid.

[128]Again, see Martin, *Slavery as Salvation,* especially 86–116, for models of such transformation of slaves, particularly the "enslaved leader" motif, at least in the rhetoric of antiquity. Given Galatians 3:28 ("There is no longer Jew or Greek, there is no longer slave or free, there is no longer male and female; for all of you are one in Christ Jesus"), Paul wanted rhetoric to become practice in his assemblies.

[129]Meggitt, *Paul, Poverty and Survival,* 98–99. The evidence for Erastus as a "city-treasurer" (Rom. 16:23) may also be challenged (Meggitt, 135–41).

[130]Ibid., 153.

[131]Ibid., 129–32, quote from 132.

[132]See, for example, the discussion about the intimacy of the early Jesus movement in Carl Dudley and Earle Hilgert, *New Testament Tensions and Contemporary Issues* (Philadelphia: Fortress Press, 1987), 23–31.

Chapter 6: Problems in Leadership

[1]A good description of this diversity is provided by Craig Steven de Vos, *Church and Community Conflicts: The Relationships of the Thessalonian, Corinthian and Philippian Churches and Their Wider Civic Communities* (Atlanta: Scholars Press, 1999), 180–95. See also Ben Witherington III, *Conflict and Community in Corinth: A Socio-Rhetorical Commentary on 1 and 2 Corinthians* (Grand Rapids: Wm. B. Eerdmans, 1995), 5–19.

[2]See the description of these by Richard Horsley, *1 Corinthians* (Nashville: Abingdon Press, 1998), 27–28.

[3]For a description of "secular leadership" in Corinth, both political and economic, as well as the patronage system, see Andrew D. Clarke, *Secular and Christian Leadership in Corinth: A Socio-Historical & Exegetical Study of 1 Corinthians 1–6* (Leiden: E.J. Brill, 1993), 9–39. See also Richard Horsley, "1 Corinthians: A Case Study of Paul's Assembly as an Alternative Society," in *Paul and Empire: Religion and Power in Roman Imperial Society,* ed. Richard Horsley (Harrisburg, Pa.: Trinity Press International, 1997), 242–52, especially 242–43, which describes Roman imperial control over this patronage process in Corinth.

[4]For a reconstruction of the history of this letters exchange, see Witherington, *Conflict and Community,* 328–33. See also Calvin Roetzel, *The Letters of Paul: Conversations in Context,* 4th ed. (Louisville: Westminster John Knox Press, 1998).

[5]Victor Paul Furnish, *2 Corinthians,* Anchor Bible Commentary (Garden City, N.Y.: Doubleday, 1984) argues, convincingly in my estimation, that 2 Corinthians 10–13 was written subsequent to 2 Corinthians 1–9, especially because Paul refers to a collection visit by Titus and "the brother" in 2 Corinthians 12:18 (cf. 2 Cor. 8:16–24). Roetzel, *Paul and His Letters,* argues that 2 Corinthians 10–13 fits best as the letter of tears written before 2 Corinthians 1–9. For the integrity of all of 2 Corinthians, see Witherington, *Conflict and Community,* 328–39.

[6]L.L. Welborn, *Politics and Rhetoric in the Corinthian Epistles* (Macon, Ga.: Mercer University Press, 1997), 5.

[7]For a summary of many of these positions, see John C. Hurd, *The Origins of First Corinthians* (New York: Seabury, 1965), 80–117; Nils Dahl, "Paul and the Church at Corinth According to 1 Corinthians 1:10–4:21," in Dahl, *Studies in Paul: Theology for Early Christian Mission* (Minneapolis: Augsburg Press, 1977), 40–61.

[8]Gordon D. Fee, *The First Epistle to the Corinthians,* NICNT (Grand Rapids: Wm. B. Eerdmans, 1987), 56.

⁹Stephen Pogoloff, *Logos and Sophia: The Rhetorical Situation of 1 Corinthians* (Atlanta: Scholars Press, 1992), 7–34.

¹⁰Michael J. Gorman, *Cruciformity: Paul's Narrative Spirituality of the Cross* (Grand Rapids: Wm. B. Eerdmans, 2001), 4–5.

¹¹Ibid., 5.

¹²See Clarke, *Secular Leadership in Corinth*, 41–46; Gerd Theissen, *The Social Setting of Pauline Christianity: Essays on Corinth*, trans. John H. Schütz (Philadelphia: Fortress Press, 1982), 70–73; and Wayne Meeks, *The First Urban Christians: The Social World of the Apostle Paul* (New Haven/London: Yale University Press, 1983), 51–73. See also Pogoloff, *Logos and Sophia*, 158–62, for a discussion of the terms "sage," "scribe," and "debater" and their relationship to social status. For a critique of the general recent consensus, represented by Theissen and Meeks, among others, that 1 Corinthians 1:26 refers to actual high and low status individuals in the Pauline assemblies, see Justin Meggitt, *Paul, Poverty and Survival* (Edinburgh: T&T Clark, 1998), 100–106. See also Horsley, *1 Corinthians*, 31–33, for a discussion of these terms as related to "spiritual status."

¹³See his critique of the "new consensus" on social status in Pauline communities in Meggitt, *Paul, Poverty and Survival*, 97–154, in which Meggitt evaluates the various texts supporting this view.

¹⁴Meeks, *First Urban Christians*, 70.

¹⁵Ibid., 73.

¹⁶Clarke, *Secular Leadership in Corinth*, who discusses "evidence of leading figures in Corinth," 41–57, which therefore explains their "secular practices," 60–88, and "perceptions," 89–107, within the church. What I am suggesting, however, is that these Corinthian church leaders need not be "secular" leaders outside the church in order to practice "secular leadership" within the church.

¹⁷See Pogoloff's discussion of this point in *Logos and Sophia*, 101–2.

¹⁸See Pogoloff, *Logos and Sophia*, 108–19, for the connection between wisdom as exhibited by eloquent speech and the enhancement of social status in the Greco-Roman world. The phrase *hyperochēn logou hē sophias*–"lofty speech or wisdom" connotes this understanding of wisdom–"applied" wisdom, including by means of orality such that it demonstrates the speaker's high social status, rather than philosophical, speculative, religious, or mystical knowledge.

¹⁹Gorman, *Cruciformity*, 1, emphasis original, meaning that the focus of Paul's message about Jesus Christ was the cross.

²⁰Pogoloff, *Logos and Sophia*, 136, citing E.A. Judge, "Paul's Boasting in Relation to Contemporary Professional Practice," *Australian Biblical Review* 16 (1968): 37.

²¹Dio Chrysostom, *Discourses* 32.39, as cited in Pogoloff, *Logos and Sophia*, 136.

²²See Clarke, *Secular Leadership in Corinth*, 114–17, for this assessment and a summary of opposing arguments. See also Richard Horsley, "Rhetoric and Empire–and 1 Corinthians" in Horsley, *Paul and Politics: Ekklesia, Israel, Imperium, Interpretation* (Harrisburg, Pa.: Trinity Press International, 2000), 92 and 92, n. 57, for the political implications of Paul's language in this and related texts of 1 Corinthians.

²³Neil Elliott, *Liberating Paul: The Justice of God and the Politics of the Apostle* (Maryknoll, N.Y.: Orbis Press, 1994), 124.

²⁴Witherington, *Conflict and Community in Corinth*, 126.

²⁵Pogoloff, *Logos and Sophia*, 141.

²⁶Margaret Mitchell, *Paul and the Rhetoric of Reconciliation: An Exegetical Investigation of the Language and Composition of 1 Corinthians* (Louisville: Westminster/John Knox Press, 1991), 213.

²⁷Fee, *First Epistle to the Corinthians*, 149.

²⁸Witherington, *Conflict and Community in Corinth*, 135.

²⁹Clarke, *Secular Leadership in Corinth*, 118–19.

³⁰See Benjamin Fiore, "'Covert Allusion' in 1 Corinthians 1–4," *Catholic Biblical Quarterly* 47 (1985): 85–102; Clarke, *Secular Leadership in Corinth*, 122–24.

³¹See definitions, examples, and references in Fiore, "Covert Allusion," 89.

³²K.H. Rengstorf, "*hyperetes*," TDNT 7, 542. See also Clarke, *Secular Leadership in Corinth*, 121.

³³See Dale Martin, *Slavery as Salvation: The Metaphor of Slavery in Pauline Christianity* (New Haven: Yale University Press, 1990), 77–80, who discusses Paul's use of *oikonomia* in 1 Corinthians 9:17 ("I am entrusted with a commission [*oikonomian*]") as a declaration of the

servitude of his mission. See Pogoloff, *Logos and Sophia*, 214–17, for parallels to *oikonomos* (steward) in 1 Corinthians 4:1–2.

[34]Pogoloff, *Logos and Sophia*, 216.

[35]Martin, *Slavery as Salvation*, 34, citing Artemidorous, *The Interpretation of Dreams* (Oneiro critica), 1.74, trans. Robert J. White (Park Ridge, N.J.: Noyes Press, 1975), 55. Also cited in Pogoloff, *Logos and Sophia*, 217.

[36]Welborn, *Politics and Rhetoric*, 37.

[37]Welborn's phrase in ibid.

[38]Ibid.

[39]Ibid.

[40]Clarke, *Secular Leadership in Corinth*, 122.

[41]Pogoloff, *Logos and Sophia*, 221.

[42]Fiore, "Covert Allusion," 94–95.

[43]See Clarke, *Secular Leadership in Corinth*, 123, for this format, which I have translated from the Greek.

[44]Pogoloff, *Logos and Sophia*, 208, citing D. Sanger, "Die *dunatoi* in 1 Kor 1:26," *ZNW*, 285–91.

[45]Pogoloff, *Logos and Sophia*, 209.

[46]Ramsey MacMullen, *Roman Social Relations: 50 B.C. to A.D. 284* (New Haven: Yale University Press, 1966), 163, n. 52.

[47]Pogoloff, *Logos and Sophia*, 209, describing MacMullen's point.

[48]Ibid., 208, quoting Sanger, "Die *dunatoi* in 1 Kor 1:26."

[49]Actually, this is a "hardship list," of which Paul uses several throughout his correspondence with the Corinthians to contrast his leadership with that of internal and external Corinthian leadership. See John T. Fitzgerald, *Cracks in an Earthen Vessel* (Atlanta: Scholars Press, 1987).

[50]Martin, *Slavery as Salvation*, 123.

[51]Richard A. Horsley, *1 Corinthians* (Nashville: Abingdon Press, 1998), 72.

[52]Ibid.

[53]Fiore, "Covert Allusion," 99.

[54]Fee, *First Corinthians*, 184.

[55]Horsley, *1 Corinthians*, 73.

[56]Witherington, *Conflict and Community*, 147.

[57]As suggested by Mitchell, *Paul and the Rhetoric of Reconciliation*, 222–25.

[58]Pogoloff, *Logos and Sophia*, 222; see also Mitchell, *Paul and the Rhetoric of Reconciliation*, 91–95.

[59]Horsley, *1 Corinthians*, 73.

[60]Ibid.

[61]Witherington, *Conflict and Community*, 148.

[62]Horsley, *1 Corinthians*, 73.

[63]Mitchell, *Paul and the Rhetoric of Reconciliation*, 222.

[64]Fee, *First Corinthians*, 200. See 200, n. 24, for Jewish, Greek, and Roman condemnation of this or related practices. See also Clarke, *Secular Leadership in Corinth*, 77–80.

[65]John Kingman Chow, *Patronage and Power: A Study of Social Networks in Corinth* (Sheffield: Sheffield Academic Press, 1992), 130–41.

[66]Horsley, *1 Corinthians*, 82.

[67]de Vos, *Church and Community Conflicts*, 208.

[68]Marshall, *Paul and the Rhetoric of Reconciliation*, 116.

[69]De Vos, *Church and Community Conflicts*, 209. See also Clarke, *Secular Leadership in Corinth*, 60–68.

[70]Clarke, *Secular Leadership in Corinth*, 67.

[71]Fee, *First Corinthians*, 250, argues this based on Paul's specific reference to uniting with prostitutes (*pornes*) in 6:15–17. See also Mitchell, *Paul and the Rhetoric of Reconciliation*, 119–20, who states that "6:12–20 explicitly deals with intercourse with prostitutes."

[72]Dale Martin, *The Corinthian Body* (New Haven/London: Yale University Press, 1995), xvi–xvii.

[73]Ibid., xvii.

[74]Hans Conzelmann, *1 Corinthians: A Commentary on the First Epistle to the Corinthians*, trans. James W. Leitch (Philadelphia: Fortress Press, 1975), 113.

[75]Martin, *Corinthian Body,* 175.

[76]de Vos, *Church and Community Conflicts,* 206.

[77]See Bruce W. Winter, *After Paul Left Corinth: The Influence of Secular Ethics and Social Change* (Grand Rapids: Wm. B. Eerdmans, 2001), 88.

[78]*Exestin* is a form of the noun *exousia,* which refers to "the right to determine," and therefore, "authority," Fee, *First Corinthians,* 252.

[79]*Ordines* 62.3, as quoted by Winter, *After Paul Left,* 89.

[80]As pointed out by Conzelmann, *1 Corinthians,* 113.

[81]See Clarke, *Secular Leadership in Corinth,* 29–31, for a discussion of status symbols in the Greco-Roman world.

[82]As argued by Fee, *First Corinthians,* 195.

[83]Winter, *After Paul Left,* 89

[84]As suggested by Mitchell, *Paul and the Rhetoric of Reconciliation,* 121–25; Fee, *First Corinthians,* 250, n. 8; 274.

[85]See Theissen, *Social Setting,* 124–32.

[86]For the details of this argument, see Chow, *Patronage and Power,* 141–57.

[87]See Ronald Hock, *The Social Context of Pauline Ministry: Tentmaking and Apostleship* (Philadelphia: Fortress Press, 1980), for a discussion of the role of work in Paul's ministry. The problem of rejection because of Paul's stance on financial support from the Corinthians is stated more explicitly in 2 Corinthians 11.7: "Did I commit a sin by humbling myself so that you might be exalted, because I proclaimed God's good news to you free of charge?"

[88]See Theissen's essay on the Lord's supper passage in *Social Setting,* 121–46.

[89]Chow, *Patronage and Power,* 157.

[90]Theissen, *Social Setting,* 167–68.

[91]See Antoinette C. Wire, *The Corinthian Women Prophets: A Reconstruction through Paul's Rhetoric* (Philadelphia: Fortress Press, 1990), who in fact argues that the subtext for *all* of 1 Corinthians is Paul's problems with free, independent women and their leadership in the Corinthian community.

[92]However, see Elliott, *Liberating Paul,* 52–54, who among others, suggests that the "silencing of the women" in 1 Cor. 14:34–35 may be an interpolation, and therefore not written by Paul.

[93]On tongues as status indicator, see Dale B. Martin, "Tongues of Angels and Other Status Indicators," *Journal of the American Academy of Religion* 59 (1992): 547–89.

[94]See Wan, *Power in Weakness,* 30–56, although he specifies 2 Corinthians 1:1–2:13 and 7:5–16 in this way.

[95]See the reconstruction of the events surrounding the Jerusalem collection and Paul's efforts with the Corinthians in Dieter Georgi, *Remembering the Poor: The History of Paul's Collection for Jerusalem* (Nashville: Abingdon Press, 1992), 68–109.

[96]See "A Letter from the Romans to the Corinthians (1 Clement)" and the Introduction in *Early Christian Reader* with Introductions and Annotations by Steve Mason and Tom Robinson (Peabody, Mass.: Hendrickson Publishers, 2004), 690–716.

Conclusion

[1]See Efrain Agosto, "Religious Leadership in the Aftermath of September 11: Some Lessons from Jesus and Paul," in *September 11: Religious Perspectives on the Causes and Consequences,* ed. Ian Markham and Ibrahim M. Abu-Rabi' (Oxford: Oneworld, 2002), 164–88. I have incorporated some material from that essay in this concluding chapter, with permission from the editors.

[2]See J. Christiaan Beker, *Paul the Apostle: The Triumph of God in Life and Thought* (Philadelphia: Fortress Press, 1980), especially 11–36.

[3]For an overview of these themes in the pastoral letters, see David C. Verner, *The Household of God: The Social World of the Pastoral Epistles,* SBL Dissertation Series (Chico, Calif.: Scholars Press, 1983). For a discussion of the implications for ministry in and from the pastorals, see David L. Bartlett, *Ministry in the New Testament* (Minneapolis: Fortress Press, 1993), 150–84.

[4]Luke Timothy Johnson, *The Writings of the New Testament: An Interpretation,* Revised Edition (Minneapolis: Fortress Press, 1999), 561.

[5]For a historical reconstruction of the Johannine community that shows these various stages of external and internal conflict and the implications for the community's theology, see

Raymond Brown, *The Community of the Beloved Disciple: The Life, Loves and Hates of an Individual Church in New Testament Times* (New York: Paulist Press, 1979).

[6]John H. Elliott, *A Home for the Homeless: A Social Scientific Criticism of 1 Peter, Its Situation and Strategey* (Minneapolis: Fortress Press, 1990), especially 21–58.

[7]In Raymond Brown, *The Churches the Apostles Left Behind* (New York: Paulist Press, 1984).

[8]For more extensive discussion of the message of Revelation along these lines, see Catherine Gunsalus Gonzalez and Justo L. Gonzalez, *Revelation* (Louisville: Westminster John Knox Press, 1997).

Bibliography

Ancient Writers

Artemidorus. *The Interpretation of Dreams*. Oneiro critica 1.74. Translated by Robert J. White. Park Ridge, N.J.: Noyes Press, 1975.

Cicero. *Letters to His Friends (Epistolae Ad Familiares)*. Three Volumes. Translated by W. Glynn Williams. Loeb Classical Library. Cambridge: Harvard University Press, 1972.

Clement of Rome. "A Letter from the Romans to the Corinthians (1 Clement)," with an Introduction in *Early Christian Reader* with Introductions and Annotations by Steve Mason and Tom Robinson, 690–716. Peabody, Mass.: Hendrickson Publishers, 2004.

Dio Chrysostom. *Discourses*. Translated by J.W. Cohoon and H. Lamar Crosby. Loeb Classical Library. Cambridge: Harvard University Press, 1932–51.

Fronto. *Correspondence*. Translated by C.R. Haines. Two volumes. Loeb Classical Library. London & New York: Wm. Heinemann and G.P Putnam's Sons, 1920.

Gospel of Thomas. Translated by Thomas O. Lambdin. Reproduced in James M. Robinson, general editor. *The Nag Hammadi Library*, Rev. ed. San Francisco: Harper & Row, 1988.

Josephus. "Jewish Antiquities" in *The Works of Josephus*, Complete and Unabridged. Translated by William Whiston. Peabody, Mass.: Hendrickson Publishers, 1987.

Pliny the Younger. *Letters and Panegyricus*. 2 Volumes. Translated by Betty Radice. Loeb Classical Library. Cambridge: Harvard University Press, 1969.

Commentaries and Reference Works

Bauer, Walter, F. W. Danker, W. F. Arndt, and F. W. Gingrich. *A Greek-English Language Lexicon of the New Testament and Other Early Christian Literature,* 3d ed. Chicago: University of Chicago Press, 1999. [BAGD]

Best, Ernest. *A Commentary on the First & Second Epistles to the Thessalonians*. Reprint. Peabody, Mass.: Hendrickson, 1988.

Betz, Hans Dieter. *2 Corinthians 8 and 9: A Commentary on Two Administrative Letters of the Apostle Paul*. Hermeneia Commentary Series. Philadelphia: Fortress Press, 1985.

Bromiley, George, trans. and ed. *Theological Dictionary of the New Testament*. Grand Rapids: Wm. B. Eerdmans, 1964. [TDNT]

Conzelmann, Hans. *1 Corinthians: A Commentary on the First Epistle to the Corinthians*. Translated by James W. Leitch. Philadelphia: Fortress Press, 1975.

Ehrman, Bart. *The New Testament and Other Early Christian Writings: A Reader,* 2d ed. Oxford/New York: Oxford University Press, 1998, 2004.

Ellingworth, Paul, and Eugene Nida. *A Translator's Handbook on Paul's Letter to the Thessalonians.* Stuttgart: United Bible Societies, 1975.

Fee, Gordon D. *The First Epistle to the Corinthians.* NICNT. Grand Rapids: Wm. B. Eerdmans, 1987.

_____. *Paul's Letter to the Philippians.* NICNT. Grand Rapids: Wm. B. Eerdmans, 1995.

Felder, Cain Hope. "The Letter to Philemon." Vol. 11, *The New Interpreter's Bible: A Commentary in Twelve Volumes,* 833–905. Nashville: Abingdon Press, 2000.

Furnish, Victor Paul. *II Corinthians,* Anchor Bible 32a. Garden City, N. Y.: Doubleday, 1984.

Horsley, Richard. *First Corinthians.* Abingdon New Testament Commentaries. Nashville: Abingdon Press, 2000.

Marshall, I. Howard. *Commentary on Luke.* NIGTC. Grand Rapids: Wm. B. Eerdmans, 1978.

_____. *1 and 2 Thessalonians.* New Century Bible Commentary. Grand Rapids: Wm. B. Eerdmans, 1983.

The New Oxford Annotated Bible. 3d ed. Oxford/New York: Oxford University Press, 2001.

O'Brien, Peter T. *Commentary on Philippians.* NIGTC. Grand Rapids: Wm. B. Eerdmans, 1991.

Osiek, Carolyn. *Philippians, Philemon.* Abingdon New Testament Commentaries. Nashville: Abingdon Press, 2000.

Ringe, Sharon H. *Luke.* Westminster Bible Companion. Louisville: Westminster John Knox Press, 1995.

Sampley, J. Paul. "The First Letter to the Corinthians." Vol. 10, *The New Interpreter's Bible: A Commentary in Twelve Volumes,* 771–1003. Nashville: Abingdon Press, 2002.

Sherk, Robert. *Roman Documents from the Greek East.* Baltimore: John Hopkins Press, 1969.

Throckmorton, Burton H., Jr., ed. *Gospel Parallels: A Comparison of the Synoptic Gospels.* 5th ed. Nashville: Thomas Nelson, 1992.

Witherington, Ben, III. *Conflict and Community in Corinth: A Socio-Rhetorical Commentary on 1 and 2 Corinthians.* Grand Rapids: Wm. B. Eerdmans, 1995.

Articles and Monographs

Agosto, Efrain. "Patronage and Commendation: Imperial and Anti-Imperial." In *Paul and the Roman Imperial Order,* edited by Richard A. Horsley. Harrisburg, Pa.: Trinity Press International, 2004.

_____. "Paul and Commendation." In *Paul in the Greco-Roman World: A Handbook,* edited by J. Paul Sampley. Harrisburg, Pa.: Trinity Press International, 2003.

____. "Paul's Use of Greco-Roman Conventions of Commendation." Ph.D. Dissertation, Boston University, 1996.

____. "Religious Leadership in the Aftermath of September 11: Some Lessons from Jesus and Paul." In *September 11: Religious Perspectives on the Causes and Consequences,* edited by Ian Markham and Ibrahim M. Abu-Rabi', 164–88. Oxford: Oneworld, 2002.

Allison, Dale C. *Jesus of Nazareth: Millenarian Prophet.* Minneapolis: Fortress Press, 1998.

Bartlett, David L. *Ministry in the New Testament.* Minneapolis: Fortress Press, 1993.

Barton, Stephen. "Paul and the Cross: A Sociological Approach." *Theology* 85 (1982): 13–19.

J. Behm. "noutheteō." *TDNT,* Volume 4: 1019–22.

Beker, J. Christiaan. *Paul the Apostle: The Triumph of God in Life and Thought.* Philadelphia: Fortress Press, 1980.

BAGD. "*noutheteō*," 544.

____. "*synathleō*," 783.

____. "*tassō*," 805–6.

Bierstedt, Robert. "Authority." In Robert Bierstedt, *The Social Order,* 3d ed. New York: McGraw-Hill, 1970.

Block, Peter. *Stewardship: Choosing Service over Self-Interest.* San Francisco: Berrett-Koehler, 1996.

Borg, Marcus J. *Jesus: A New Vision.* San Francisco: Harper & Row, 1987.

Brown, Raymond. *The Churches the Apostles Left Behind.* New York: Paulist Press, 1984.

____. *The Community of the Beloved Disciple: The Life, Loves and Hates of an Individual Church in New Testament Times.* New York: Paulist Press, 1979.

Cahill, Thomas. *Desire of the Everlasting Hills: The World Before and After Jesus.* New York: Anchor Books, 1999.

Callahan, Alan. *The Embassy of Onesimus: Paul's Letter to Philemon.* Valley Forge: Trinity Press, 1996.

Carcopino, Jerome. *Daily Life in Ancient Rome: The People and the City at the Height of the Empire.* New Haven/New London: Yale University Press, 1940.

Carter, Warren. *Pontius Pilate: Portraits of a Roman Governor.* Collegeville, Minn.: Liturgical Press, 2003.

Cassidy, Richard. *Paul in Chains: Roman Imprisonment and the Letters of St. Paul.* New York: Crossroad, 2001.

Castelli, Elizabeth. *Imitating Paul: A Discourse of Power.* Lousville: Westminster/John Knox Press, 1991.

Chilton, Bruce, and Jacob Neusner. *Types of Authority in Formative Christianity and Judaism.* London/New York: Routledge, 1999.

Chow, John Kingman. *Patronage and Power: A Study of Social Networks in Corinth.* Sheffield: Sheffield Academic Press, 1992.

Clarke, Andrew D.. *Secular and Christian Leadership in Corinth: A Socio-Historical & Exegetical Study of 1 Corinthians 1–6.* Leiden: E.J. Brill, 1993.

_____. *Serve the Community of the Church: Christians as Leaders and Ministers.* Grand Rapids: Wm. B. Eerdmans, 2000.

Collins, John N.. *Diakonia: Reinterpreting the Ancient Sources.* New York/Oxford: Oxford University, 1990.

Cotton, Hannah. "Letters of Recommendation: Cicero-Fronto." Ph.D. Dissertation, Oxford University, 1977.

Crossan, John Dominic. *The Historical Jesus: The Life of a Mediterranean Peasant.* San Francisco: HarperSanFrancisco, 1991.

_____. *Jesus: A Revolutionary Biography.* San Francisco: HarperSanFrancisco, 1994.

_____. *Who Killed Jesus?* San Francisco: HarperSanFrancisco, 1995.

Dahl, Nils. "Paul and the Church at Corinth According to 1 Corinthians 1:10–4:21." In Dahl, *Studies in Paul: Theology for Early Christian Mission,* 40–61. Minneapolis: Augsburg Press, 1977.

Deissman, Adolf. *Light from the Ancient Near East.* Trans. Lionel Strachen. Grand Rapids: Baker Books, 1965.

De Vos, Craig Steven. *Church and Community Conflicts: The Relationships of the Thessalonian, Corinthian and Philippian Churches and Their Wider Civic Communities.* Atlanta: Scholars Press, 1999.

Donfried, Karl P., ed. *The Romans Debate.* Rev. and exp. ed. Peabody, Mass.: Hendrickson, 1991.

Doohan, Helen. *Leadership in Paul.* Wilmington, Del.: Michael Glazier, 1984.

Dudley, Carl S., and Earle Hilgert. *New Testament Tensions and the Contemporary Church.* Philadelphia: Fortress Press, 1987.

Ehrman, Bart. *The New Testament: A Historical Introduction to the Early Christian Writings.* 3d ed. Oxford/New York: Oxford University Press, 2000, 2004.

Elliot, Neil. *Liberating Paul: The Justice of God and the Politics of the Apostle.* Maryknoll, N.Y.: Orbis, 1994.

_____. "Romans." *The New Oxford Annotated Bible.* 3d ed. Oxford/New York: Oxford University Press, 2001. 242 [New Testament].

Elliott, John H.. *A Home for the Homeless: A Social Scientific Criticism of 1 Peter, Its Situation and Strategy.* Minneapolis: Fortress Press, 1990.

_____. *What Is Social-Scientific Criticism?* Minneapolis: Fortress Press, 1993.

Ellis, E. Earle. "Paul and His Co-Workers." *New Testament Studies* 17 (1971): 438–52.

Finley, Moses I. *The Ancient Economy.* 2d ed. Berkeley/Los Angeles: University of California Press, 1985.

Fiore, Benjamin. "'Covert Allusion' in 1 Corinthians 1–4." *Catholic Biblical Quarterly* 47 (1985): 85–102.

Fitzgerald, John. *Cracks in an Earthen Vessel: An Examination of the Catalogues of Hardships in the Corinthian Correspondence.* Atlanta: Scholars Press, 1988.

Funk, Robert. "The Apostolic *Parousia*: Form and Significance." In *Christian History and Interpretation: Studies Presented to John Knox,* edited by William Farmer, et al., 249–68. Cambridge: Cambridge University Press, 1967.

Garnsey, Peter, and R.P. Saller. *The Roman Empire: Economy, Society & Culture.* London: SPCK, 1987.

Georgi, Dieter. "God Turned Upside Down. Romans: Missionary Theology and Roman Political Theology." In *Paul and Empire: Religion and Power in Roman Imperial Society,* edited by Richard Horsley, 148–57. Harrisburg, Pa.: Trinity Press International, 1997.

_____. *Remembering the Poor: The History of Paul's Collection for Jerusalem.* Nashville: Abingdon Press, 1992.

Gorman, Michael J. *Cruciformity: Paul's Narrative Spirituality of the Cross.* Grand Rapids: Wm. B. Eerdmans, 2001.

Greenleaf, Robert K. *The Private Writings of Robert Greenleaf: On Becoming a Servant-Leader.* Compiled and edited by Don M. Frisk and Larry C. Spears. San Francisco: Jossey-Bass, 1996.

_____. *Servant Leadership: A Journey into the Nature of Legitimate Power and Greatness.* New York/Mahwah: Paulist Press, 1977, 1991.

Gunsalus González, Catherine, and Justo L. González. *Revelation.* Louisville: Westminster John Knox Press, 1997.

Hock, Ronald F.. *The Social Context of Paul's Ministry: Tentmaking and Apostleship.* Philadelphia: Fortress Press, 1980.

Holmberg, Bengt. *Paul and Power: The Structure of Authority in the Primitive Church as Reflected in the Pauline Epistles.* Philadelphia: Fortress Press, 1980.

Horsley, Richard. "1 Corinthians: A Case Study of Paul's Assembly as an Alternative Society." In *Paul and Empire: Religion and Power in Roman Imperial Society,* edited by Richard Horsley, 242–52. Harrisburg, Pa.: Trinity Press International, 1997.

_____. "General Introduction." In *Paul and Empire: Religion and Power in Roman Imperial Society,* edited by Richard Horsley, 1–8. Harrisburg, Pa.: Trinity Press, 1997.

_____. "Rhetoric and Empire–and 1 Corinthians." In *Paul and Politics: Ekklesia, Israel, Imperium, Interpretation,* edited by Richard Horsley, 72–102. Harrisburg, Pa.: Trinity Press International, 2000.

Horsley, Richard A., and John S. Hanson. *Bandits, Prophets and Messiahs: Popular Movements at the Time of Jesus.* Minneapolis, Chicago, & New York: Winston Press, 1985.

Hurd, John C. *The Origins of First Corinthians.* New York: Seabury, 1965.

Jewett, Robert. "Paul, Phoebe and the Spanish Mission." In *The Social World of Formative Christianity and Judaism: Essays in Honor of Howard Clark Kee,* edited by Jacob Neusner, et al., 142–61. Philadelphia: Fortress Press, 1988.

____."Romans as an Ambassadorial Letter," *Interpretation* 36 (1982): 5–20.

____. *The Thessalonian Correspondence: Pauline Rhetoric and Millenarian Piety.* Philadelphia: Fortress Press, 1986.

Johnson, Luke Timothy. *The Writings of the New Testament: An Interpretation.* Rev. ed. Minneapolis: Fortress Press, 1995, 1999.

Judge, E. A. "Paul's Boasting in Relation to Contemporary Professional Practice." *Australian Biblical Review* 16 (1968): 37–50.

____. *The Social Pattern of Christian Groups in the First Century: Some Prolegomena to the Study of New Testament Ideas of Social Obligation.* London: Tyndale Press, 1960.

Juel, Donald H.. *The Gospel of Mark.* Interpreting Biblical Texts. Nashville: Abingdon Press, 1999.

Kennedy, George A. *New Testament through Rhetorical Criticism.* Chapel Hill: University of North Carolina Press, 1984.

Keyes, Clinton. "The Greek Letter of Introduction," *American Journal of Philology* 56 (1935): 28–44.

Kim, Chan-Hie. *Form and Structure of the Familiar Greek Letter of Recommendation.* SBL Dissertation Series 4. Missoula, Mont.: Scholars Press, 1972.

Kittredge, Cynthia Briggs. *Community and Authority: The Rhetoric of Obedience in the Pauline Tradition.* Harrisburg, Pa.: Trinity Press International, 1998.

Knox, John. *Philemon among the Letters of Paul,* Rev. ed. New York: Abingdon Press, 1959.

Koenig, John. "Hierarchy Transfigured: Perspectives on Leadership in the New Testament." *Word and World.* Volume 13, no. 1 (Winter 1993): 26–33.

MacDonald, Margaret Y. "Reading Real Women through the Undisputed Letters of Paul." In *Women and Christian Origins,* edited by Ross Shephard Kraemer and Mary Rose D'Angelo, 199–220. New York/ Oxford: Oxford University Press, 1999.

MacMullen, Ramsay. *Roman Social Relations: 50 BC to AD 284.* New Haven/ London: Yale University Press, 1974.

Malherbe, Abraham. "'Gentle as a Nurse:' the Cynic Background to I Thess ii." *Novum Testamentum* 12 (1970): 203–17.

____. *Paul and the Thessalonians. The Philosophic Tradition of Pastoral Care.* Reprint. Mifflintown, Pa.: Sigler Press, 2000 (Original ed., 1987).

Malina, Bruce J. , and Jerome H. Neyrey. "Honor and Shame in Luke-Acts: Pivotal Values of the Mediterranean World." In *The Social World of Luke-Acts: Models for Interpretation,* edited by Jerome H. Neyrey, 25–65. Peabody, Mass.: Hendrickson Publishers, 1991.

Marable, Manning. *Black Leadership.* New York: Columbia University Press, 1998.

Marshall, Peter. *Enmity in Corinth: Social Conventions in Paul's Relations with the Corinthians.* Tübingen: J.C.B. Mohr [Paul Siebeck], 1987.

Martin, Dale. *The Corinthian Body*. New Haven/London: Yale University Press, 1995.

_____. *Slavery as Salvation: The Metaphor of Slavery in Pauline Christianity*. New Haven/London: Yale University Press, 1990.

_____. "Tongues of Angels and Other Status Indicators." *Journal of the American Academy of Religion* 59 (1992): 547–89.

Meeks, Wayne. *The First Urban Christians: The Social World of the Apostle Paul*. New Haven/London: Yale University Press, 1983.

Meggitt, Justin. *Paul, Poverty and Survival*. Edinburgh: T&T Clark, 1998.

Michaels, J. Ramsey. *Servant and Son: Jesus in Gospel and Parable*. Philadelphia: Westminster Press, 1982.

Mitchell, Margaret. "New Testament Envoys in the Context of Greco-Roman Diplomatic and Epistolary Conventions: The Example of Timothy and Titus." *Journal of Biblical Literature*. Volume 111 (1992): 641–62.

_____. *Paul and the Rhetoric of Reconciliation: An Exegetical Examination of the Language and Composition of 1 Corinthians*. Louisville: Westminster/ John Knox Press, 1991.

_____. "Philemon." *New Oxford Annotated Bible*. 3d ed. Oxford/New York: Oxford University Press, 2001. 368 [New Testament].

Moxnes, Halvor. "Patron-Client Relations and the New Community in Luke-Acts." In *The Social World of Luke-Acts: Models for Interpretation*, edited by Jerome H. Neyrey, 241–68. Peabody, Mass.: Hendrickson Publishers, 1991.

Neusner, Jacob. *From Politics to Piety: The Emergence of Pharisaic Judaism*. Englewood Cliffs, N.J.: Prentice-Hall, 1973.

Overman, J. Andrew. *Church and Community in Crisis: The Gospel According to Matthew*. Valley Forge, Pa.: Trinity Press, 1996.

_____. "Who Were the First Urban Christians? Urbanization in Galilee in the First Century." *Society of Biblical Literature Seminar Papers* 27 (1988): 160–68.

Padovano, Anthony T. "Leadership and Authority." *New Catholic World* 223 (Sept.-Oct. 1980): 222–24.

Pallas, D., et al. "Inscriptions liciennes trouvèes à Solômes près de Corinthe." *Bulletin de correspondance hellinque* 83 (1959): 505–6.

Patte, Daniel. *Paul's Faith and the Power of the Gospel: A Structural Introduction to the Pauline Letters*. Philadelphia: Fortress Press, 1983.

Perkins, Pheme. "Philippians: Theology for the Heavenly Politeuma." In *Pauline Theology, Volume I: Thessalonians, Philippians, Galatians, Philemon*, edited by Jouette M. Bassler, 89–104. Minneapolis: Fortress Press, 1991.

Petersen, Norman. *Rediscovering Paul: Philemon and the Sociology of Paul's Narrative World*. Philadelphia: Fortress Press, 1985.

Pilgrim, Walter E. *Uneasy Neighbors: Church and State in the New Testament*. Minneapolis: Fortress Press, 1999.

Pogoloff, Stephen. *Logos and Sophia: The Rhetorical Situation of 1 Corinthians.* Atlanta: Scholars Press, 1992.

Polaski, Sandra Hack. *Paul and the Discourse of Power.* Sheffield: Sheffield Academic Press, 1999.

Recinos, Harold. *Who Comes in the Name of the Lord: Jesus at the Margins.* Nashville: Abingdon Press, 1997.

Reicke, Bo. *"proistēmi." TDNT,* Vol. 6, 700–703.

Rengstorf, K. H.. *"hypēretēs." TDNT,* Vol. 8, 542.

Roetzel, Calvin. *The Letters of Paul: Conversations in Context.* 4th ed. Louisville: Westminster John Knox Press, 1998.

_____. *Paul: the Man and the Myth.* Minneapolis: Fortress Press, 1999.

_____. *The World that Shaped the New Testament.* Revised ed. Louisville/London: Westminster Press, 2002.

Saldarini, Anthony. *Pharisees, Scribes and Sadducees in Palestinian Society. A Sociological Approach.* Wilmington, Del.: Michael Glazier, 1988.

Saller, Richard. *Personal Patronage under the Early Empire.* Cambridge: Cambridge University Press, 1982.

Sampley, J. Paul. *Pauline Partnership in Christ: Christian Community and Commitment in Light of Roman Law.* Philadelphia: Fortress Press, 1980.

_____. *Walking Between the Times: Paul's Moral Reasoning.* Minneapolis: Fortress Press, 1991.

Schüssler Fiorenza, Elisabeth. *In Memory of Her: A Feminist Theological Reconstruction of Christian Origins.* New York: Crossroad, 1983.

Schütz, John. *Paul and the Anatomy of Apostolic Authority.* London: Cambridge University Press, 1975.

Scroggs, Robin. "The Sociological Interpretation of the New Testament: The Present State of the Research." In *The Bible and Liberation: Political and Social Hermeneutics,* edited by Norman Gottwald, 337–56. Maryknoll, N.Y.: Orbis Books, 1983.

Stambaugh, John E., and David L. Balch. *The New Testament in Its Social Environment.* Philadelphia: Fortress Press, 1986.

Stegemann, Ekkehard W., and Wolfgang Stegemann. *The Jesus Movement: A Social History of Its First Century.* Translated by O.C. Dean Jr. Minneapolis: Fortress Press, 1999.

Stowers, Stanley. *Letter Writing in Greco-Roman Antiquity.* Philadelphia: Westminster Press, 1986.

Tamez, Elsa. *The Amnesty of Grace: Justification by Faith from a Latin American Perspective.* Nashville: Abingdon Press, 1993.

Taylor, Joan. *The Immerser: John the Baptist within Second Temple Judaism.* Grand Rapids: Wm. B. Eerdmans, 1997.

Theissen, Gerd. *The Social Setting of Pauline Christianity: Essays on Paul.* Edited and translated by John H. Schütz. Philadelphia: Fortress Press, 1982.

_____. *Sociology of Early Palestinian Christianity.* Translated by John Bowden. Philadelphia: Fortress Press, 1978.

Thompson, James W. *Preaching Like Paul: Homiletical Wisdom for Today.* Louisville: Westminster Press, 2001.

Tidball, Derek. *The Social Context of the New Testament: A Sociological Analysis.* Grand Rapids: Zondervan, 1984.

Tolbert, Mary Ann. *Sowing the Gospel: Mark's World in Literary-Historical Perspective.* Minneapolis: Fortress Press, 1989.

Torjesen, Karen. *When Women Were Priests: Women's Leadership in the Early Church & the Scandal of Their Subordination in the Rise of Christianity.* San Francisco: Harper, 1993.

Vaage, Leif E.. *Galilean Upstarts: Jesus' First Followers According to Q.* Valley Forge: Trinity Press International, 1994.

Verner, David C. *The Household of God: The Social World of the Pastoral Epistles.* SBL Dissertation Series. Chico, Calif.: Scholars Press, 1983.

Villafañe, Eldin. *The Liberating Spirit: Toward a Hispanic American Pentecostal Social Ethic.* Grand Rapids: Wm. B. Eerdmans, 1993.

Walters, James. "'Phoebe' and 'Junia(s)'–Rom. 16:1–2, 7." In Vol. 1, *Essays on Women in Earliest Christianity,* edited by Carroll D. Osburn, 167–90. Joplin, Mo.: College Press, 1993.

Wan, Sze-kar. *Power in Weakness: The Second Letter of Paul to the Corinthians.* Harrisburg, Pa.: Trinity Press International, 2000.

Watson, D. F.. "A Rhetorical Analysis of Philippians and Its Implications for the Unity Question." *Novum Testamentum* 30 (1988): 57–88.

Weber, Max. *Economy & Society: An Outline of Interpretive Sociology.* Volume 1. Translated and edited by Guenther Roth and Claus Wittich. New York: Bedminster Press, 1968.

Welborn, L. L.. *Politics and Rhetoric in the Corinthian Epistles.* Macon, Ga.: Mercer University Press, 1997.

Wheatley, Margaret. *Leadership and the New Science: Discovering Order in a Chaotic World.* San Francisco: Berrett-Koehler Publishers, 1999.

Whelan, Caroline. "Amica Pauli: The Role of Phoebe in the Early Church." *Journal for the Study of the New Testament* 49 (1993): 67–85.

Winter, Bruce W. *After Paul Left Corinth: The Influence of Secular Ethics and Social Change.* Grand Rapids: Wm. B. Eerdmans, 2001.

Wire, Antoinette C. *The Corinthian Women Prophets: A Reconstruction through Paul's Rhetoric.* Philadelphia: Fortress Press, 1990.

Witherington, Ben, III. *Friendship and Finances in Phililppi: The Letter of Paul to the Philippians.* Valley Forge: Trinity Press, 1994.

Index of Subjects and Persons*

A

Acts, book of, 20, 121
African American leadership, 8
Alexander the Great, 99
Apollos, 122, 169, 175
apostles, apostleship: and service, servanthood , 177; and suffering , 103, 104, 105; Jerusalem apostles, 122; others, 138, 143; Paul's apostleship, 100–106, 113, 122; 176–80; 193–94
audience for Jesus' ministry, 38, 53–61; and "the little ones," 53–54; and the tax collectors, 55–56, 59–60; and those needing healing, 54–55
authority, 3–4 (Weber's "authority types"), 9, 22; charismatic, 3, 20 (Jesus), 195, 203 (Paul); the Corinthian elites, 189–90; for missionary purposes, 95; Paul's, 107, 140, 154, 180, 185; Philemon's, 158

B

Beker, J. Christiaan, 108–9, 112, 205
Betz, Hans Dieter, 138
Block, Peter, 7
Brown, Raymond, 12, 211

C

Callahan, Alan, 117, 157–58
Chow, John Kingman, 185, 190, 192
Cicero, 123–24
Cities of Paul, 23–24; 98, 99, 165–66 (Corinth)
Clarke, Andrew D., 171
collection for Jerusalem, 135–40, 194
commendation, see leadership: and commendation
Corinthians, first letter to the, 110–12, 166–93
Corinthians, second letter to the, 110–12, 167–68, 193–95
co-workers of Paul, 3, 10, 121–23, 132, 138, 142–43, 146–47, 155, 159, 206
Crossan, John Dominic, 55, 198
cross of Christ, crucifixion: 10, 90, 100, 205, 206–7; as model for leadership, 104–5, 182
cruciformity, 170, 180

D

Dead Sea Scrolls, 17
Deissmann, Adolf, 106
de Vos, Craig Steven, 188
disciples: 22, 35–53, 198–99; as apostles, 41; and their calling, 35–37; and commissioning, 39–44; and the cost of discipleship, 76; and their failures and shortcomings, 38, 44–53; and "greatness," 86–87; the high expectations of Jesus for, 52–53; and their mission, 36; and the nature of authentic discipleship, 42, 46; and opposition, 67; and tax collectors, 36; and women, 37, 93–94
dokimos, 137, 141, 161

E

ekklēsiae ("assemblies"), 24, 166–72, 176, 185, 186
Elliot, John H., 211
Ellis, E. Earle, 121–22, 142, 160
Epaphroditus, 115, 123, 138, 140–45, 155, 203–4
eschatological/endtime expectation and message: 21; and John the Baptist, 29; and the message of Jesus, 82–85; and Paul, 178, 179, 186; and the poor, 84–85
Essenes, 17
Euodia and Syntyche, 141, 145–47, 148, 155, 204, 205

F

Fee, Gordon, 181
Fiore, Benjamin, 177
Fronto, 123, 131

G

Galatians, letter to the, 112
Galilee, 18, 20

---

*Please note: Authors listed are those discussed in the main body of the book; for full listing of authors cited, see notes.

Index of Scriptures and Ancient Sources